SEX
In the
Cinema

SEX
In the
Cinema

The 'Pre-Code' Years
(1929–1934)

by Lou Sabini

BearManor Media

2017

Sex In the Cinema: The 'Pre-Code' Years (1929-1934)

For information, address:

BearManor Media
P. O. Box 71426
Albany, GA 31708

bearmanormedia.com

Typesetting and layout by John Teehan

Published in the USA by BearManor Media

ISBN—978-1-62933-107-2

Dedicated to

SUSAN K. SABINI

The one person who sat with me and viewed all of these films, providing me with insight and her own knowledge of movie history.

A loving wife and mother...

Table of Contents

The Films

ACKNOWLEDGMENTS

THERE ARE COUNTLESS INDIVIDUALS and organizations I would like to thank for making this book a reality. Through social media, I have become acquainted with so many talented people who have helped me with their postings on Facebook, not to mention my own classic film page called MY "REEL" LIFE. Thanking all the members (as of this writing, there are over 1,000) would be ludicrous, so for starters, I will give "honorable mention" to my new friends, who have posted some vital facts that have been incorporated into this book, namely Richard Adkins, one of my oldest pals, Richard W. Bann, Marie Behar, Ralph Celentano, Andy Dzamba, Hal Erickson, Karen Latham Everson, who is always there to lend an ear (or suggestion), Robert Fells, the late Leatrice Gilbert Fountain, John Giriat, Eric Grayson, David Lord Heath, Jeff Heise, Ron Hutchinson of the Vitaphone Project, Bill Knotts, Rick Lertzman, Annette D'Agostino Lloyd, Don J. Long, Scott and Jan MacGillivray, Steve Massa, Robert McKay, Gary McNerney, Gerry Orlando, Jenny Paxon of the Library of Congress, Nick Santa Maria, Rick Scheckman, Randy Skretvedt, my good pal, Stan Taffel, Frank Thompson, Mark Alan Viera, Melanie Wyler and Jordan Young.

Also, for making suggestions and helping me through this undertaking, I would like to thank my good friend, Bill Levy, who I met when I wrote *Behind the Scenes of They Were Expendable*. Also, to my very good pal of over forty years, Daniel S. Burke, who "kick-started" MY "REEL" LIFE on Facebook, which has grown in leaps and bounds since its inception in 2012. To my mentor, the late William K. Everson, a man who gave my life a definite direction and introduced me to the wonderful world of the "Pre-Code" era back in the early eighties, when he showed my wife, Sue and I, his prints of *Baby Face* and *Three on a Match*. After this initial experience, we couldn't get enough and Bill kept loaning us more and more 16mm prints from his vast archive. Also, I would like to thank Robert M. (Mike) Cline, who provided me with so many great prints back in the day along with John McElwee, who was always there when I needed help (he even helped me acquire prints of *Hard to Handle* and *Platinum Blonde*). My sincerest gratitude to my oldest (and dearest) friend, Jack Roth, who provided me with a rare 16mm print of *By Candlelight*.

Special thanks to my publisher, Ben Ohmart, who believed in this undertaking and one of my dearest friends, the late Carol Rugh, always there to give me assurance when after 35 years in sales, she convinced me to pursue my dream of becoming a writer of the history of motion pictures. To Aureo Brandao, who helped me to acquire some rare photographs (which are identified with "AB" following each caption) for this volume and to Richard Finegan, a man who is a wealth of information when it comes to classic cinema, who provided me with the bulk of the rare stills seen in this book from his vast collection (identified with "RF" following the caption). No words can express my sincere thanks for sharing these cinematic treasures. I am deeply indebted to Kim Krause, who went over the entire manuscript making various corrections and additions. Words cannot describe my deep appreciation. Also, I would like to thank film historian/author/scholar Richard Barrios for writing the foreword. I met Richard about ten years ago at Cinefest, a film festival for classic film buffs, which was held annually in Syracuse, New York. Richard was doing a presentation of vintage movie musicals, based on his superb book, *Song in the Dark*. I can't tell you how impressed I was with Richard's knowledge and I am honored to have him as my friend.

Lastly, I would like to thank the woman who has lived through all of life's happy times with me (and the darker ones, too), my wife of over forty-one years, Sue. Ever since we started dating in 1973, she has watched virtually thousands of movies with me, providing some excellent commentary and being not only the perfect wife, but a lady who has inspired me and made watching these movies an incredibly captivating experience.

– Lou Sabini
June 2016

FOREWORD

IT HAS BEEN SOME YEARS NOW, perhaps forty, that a seemingly odd hyphenated term—"Pre-Code"—has come to have a most particular connotation. As readers of this book may already know, the term refers most commonly to a very exact time in the history of a quite specific art form: American film. Beginning (most commonly) with 1930 and ending in 1934, both the United States and its motion pictures were subjected to a profound amount of stress on a bewildering number of levels. Much of this, of course, came from the onset of the Great Depression, for it was not long after the stock market crash that despair and deprivation came to be ever-present watchwords. By the dawn of 1932, all the hard realities had become clear: this was not a brief or ephemeral phenomenon, millions of people were suffering, and the country was in trouble. Not even the film industry, oblivious and privileged as it could sometimes be, was immune. Studios tottered on the brink of receivership and bankruptcy, attendance and grosses plummeted, budgets and salaries and employee rolls were all slashed.

There was, however, no way that the American film industry would go the way of the country's banks and simply shut down. If fewer people could afford to attend the movies, there were still many millions who continued to go, and in such a difficult time they had some very particular needs and tastes. Thus it was that mainstream American film of the early 1930s offered a remarkable type of entertainment: still escapist, naturally, still a diversion—but with a newly-acquired hard edge. Essentially, the films catered to their audiences' need to have their entertainment contain some sort of link with or reflection of the outside world. As a result, movies became more frank, in many ways, than they had ever been. A few key films were actually about the Depression and its effect; others were about other current harsh realities, most conspicuously crime and sex. All of it still had something of a patina, with stars and production trappings still in evidence, yet it gave Depression-numbed spectators the impression that detectable aspects of their own lives were being portrayed up on that big screen. A brutal gangster film such as *The Public Enemy* could be simultaneously an entertainment (no real-life hood had Jimmy Cagney's charisma), an indictment (these guys were, after all, scum), and a recollection of some real life incidents (just about everyone knew about the mob rule in cities such as Chicago). Similarly, a fallen-woman tale on the order of *Faithless* or *Safe in Hell* could be both titillation and sermon; yes, it was enjoyable, in a voyeuristic way, to see these gorgeous stars wallowing in the gutter, but their circumstances often occurred as a result of poverty and need. Those, rest assured, were things unfamiliar to virtually nobody.

Pre-Code cinema, then, embraced a certain frankness and candor that, clearly, America's audiences both wanted and needed. Evidently the studios' need was fulfilled as well. If the attendance figures for the era were far lower than those of the late-1920s, most of the definitive Pre-Code films were healthy profit-earners that helped to keep studios afloat in a precarious time. In at least one case, a major company, the one which produced Paramount films, was rescued from the brink of receivership by films that featured one of the Pre-Code era's essential figures. When Mae West joked about sex and enacted the role of erotic conqueror, much of the world gasped and then cheered. With *She Done Him Wrong* and *I'm No Angel*, West became a huge star and Paramount remained a going concern. If few of the other essential Pre-Code titles made the hit of those two, fewer of them were outright failures. In comparison with the dire condition of most of the rest of the nation, America's film industry was, by and large, doing rather well. At the very least, in its own fashion, it was managing to stay afloat.

Along with the redoubtable Ms. West, there was a significant contingent of actors whose work epitomized the Pre-Code era. The brash onscreen amorality of James Cagney was as irresistible as it was, most of the time, morally dubious. Constance Bennett, for her part, was better suited to sophisticated fare than to the roles that, in her early 1930s films, brought her major stardom: maidens who manage to find themselves seduced, abandoned, and pregnant. Helen Twelvetrees, now merely a dimly remembered figure, also specialized in primrose-path epics in which her skill in looking mournful could be exploited. Jean Harlow, only eighteen years old, skyrocketed to fame as an insincere hussy in Howard Hughes'

Hell's Angels when she uttered a definitive line of Pre-Code dialog to the gallant Ben Lyon: "Would you be shocked if I put on something more comfortable?" In most of her films over the next few years, her morals would remain as skimpy as her garments. Equally unclad, and perhaps the lingerie queen of the era, was Jeanette MacDonald, whose early musical vehicles were far more racy than her later operettas with Nelson Eddy. Joan Blondell was also undressing in most of her films, usually while spitting out wisecracks. Edmund Lowe and Warren William, for their parts, were commonly cast as suave seducers, victimizing the lovely likes of Loretta Young, whose Pre-Code persona was a conspicuously "loose" contrast to the morality of her later roles. Even Alice Faye, whose film career began just as the Pre-Code period was winding down, was a far and brassy cry from the musical sweetheart she would presently become; in her first films, audiences beheld her as a virtual dead ringer for Jean Harlow, platinum hair and all.

These actors, and many others, seemed eminently at home in on-screen situations that could veer at any time toward the seamy or lurid. If much of their material still seems "modern" or pertinent, some of it could get gratuitous, if not plain exploitive. In William Wellman's tough and entertaining *Night Nurse* (1931), a viewer can all but set a watch by the regularity with which Barbara Stanwyck and Joan Blondell remove their uniforms to show off the trim figures underneath. Another prominent entry in the bare-skin division is *Meet the Baron* (1933), a relentlessly trivial comedy with music released by MGM. Given that it was partly set at a girls' school, it took no further excuse to send a number of the most nubile (and naked) of the students into the showers for a production number called "Clean as a Whistle." (The cleanliness applied, naturally, to the young ladies in question, and decidedly not to the minds of those who devised the sequence.) Beyond such titillation, there could be some truly unnerving sadism, as in *Kongo* and *The Mask of Fu Manchu* (both 1932 products of MGM), in which some characters were subjected to especially baroque tortures. One of the defining Pre-Code titles, Cecil B. DeMille's *The Sign of the Cross*, went well over the distance in its depiction of the carnage of arena games during the reign of Nero. Spectators at modern screenings of *Sign's* uncut version have been heard to shriek in horror when an Amazon decapitates a pygmy onscreen; we can only imagine how it would have gone over early in 1933. A shock of a different sort comes in the early-1934 Fox musical *George White's Scandals*, when a cute little girl, aged about three, toddles out carrying a large fan and wearing little more than a diaper. Sure enough, she starts doing a lewd dance as she sings "Oh, You Nasty Man." Really! At such moments, the filmmakers were clearly doing something that we now call "pushing the envelope," baiting and sometimes defying the censors in order to make money while giving cash-poor crowds their money's worth, and then some. Taste, obviously, could be optional, and so could the objections of moral and religious spokespeople—which were key factors in ending the Pre-Code age in mid-1934. With the adoption of a strengthened Production Code, film changed virtually overnight. The whitewashing would, for the most part, remain for another thirty-plus years.

The films covered in this book, then, have some noticeable differences from the more familiar products of the so-called "Golden Age of Hollywood" that would soon ensue. Yet, it can be fairly asked, are they *necessarily* better? Does heightened honesty or candor always make for a superior result? The answers, here, are ambiguous. There can be no doubt that the sparkle of Ernst Lubitsch's jewel-like *Trouble in Paradise* would have been lessened after the coming of the enforced Production Code. Nor would George Cukor's masterly *Dinner at Eight* carry quite the impact that results from its depiction of low-rent doings in a high-society setting. These two are unquestioned classics, as are some others made around that same time, and there are others in the period that are less-remembered but equally effective. Still, we must remember that the traditional "Greatest Year" for movies is still cited as 1939, not 1933, and not simply because the industry fared better financially as the decade proceeded. The truth is that some post-Code films may actually have been improved by the threat of censorship. When being explicit was not an option, writers and directors could often come up with fascinating and valid ways to allude and imply without actively stating. Where, after all, would film noir be without its aura of vague yet unmistakable implication? Many intriguing things, clearly, could be effected in even a buttoned-up time, and when the Production Code was laid to rest in the later 1960s, millions of spectators learned that far greater explicitness would not always make for better-quality films.

The Pre-Code films, then, aren't always great, though many of them are better than good. They are, however, revelatory, especially for filmgoers who are unfamiliar with early-thirties cinema. Part of this has to do with how far they go, and also how contemporary and fresh they can seem. Naturally much of this comes with their comparative frankness, and some of it is because of their unfamiliarity. Few of them (with the unfortunate exception of Warners' *Convention City*) are truly "lost" films, but many of them remain, quite undeservedly, rather obscure. Many of them, at the very least, began to turn up on television in the late 1950s, doubtless startling some home viewers with their gamy content. (There were at least a few exceptions: MGM's *Red-Headed Woman* was judged too frank for TV, and Paramount's *Murder at the Vanities* was initially permitted to run, only to be pulled when it was discovered that it contained two extremely Pre-Code features: topless women and a song extolling the properties of marijuana.) Some of the biggest titles, alas, were familiar only in a more denatured form, since the rougher content of films like *King Kong* and *The Sign of the Cross* had been excised when the films were reissued in a more buttoned-up time.

Fortunately, with the advent of home video, cable television, and the internet, many Pre-Code films have become more available now than at any time since they were first released. With them comes a beguiling, if often somewhat shady, cornucopia of features that can only be termed *sui generis*: blunt language, ethnic stereotypes, exposed skin, violence, drug use, moral turpitude, unpunished crime, and much else. Some are more entertaining than others, some are racier or more honest, and they all benefit from a little context and interpretation. That is why the present book is as necessary as it is useful, informative and enjoyable. Lou Sabini is as familiar with Pre-Code films as anyone alive, yet his knowledge is not the only factor that makes him a natural guide to these wild and sometimes wooly entertainments. There is also his love of film and, most especially, his enthusiasm, which seems to know no bounds. He knows these movies, he enjoys them, he loves to discuss and share them—he is, in summary, the best friend a Pre-Code film could have. As you read about these films, you will be entertained, startled, and intrigued. Then, doubtless, you will feel compelled to go out and track down as many of these films as you can and watch them. Read the book, then see the movies. You'll be happy you did.

– Richard Barrios

INTRODUCTION TO PRE-CODE CINEMA

THE MAIN OBJECTIVE FOR WRITING this book is not a history of the 'Pre-Code era' of Hollywood (1929-1934), but a study of selected films themselves. In the past, there have been a number of excellent books written about this subject (i.e. *Sin in Soft Focus* by Mark Viera and *Pre-Code Hollywood* by Thomas Doherty), where the authors supplied historical data pertaining to the era itself and the institution of Hollywood's self-imposed Legion of Decency. I have carefully selected a good number of Pre-Code titles, some of which have been overlooked by other authors due to their unavailability, providing the reader with a complete cast and credits listing as well as a short synopsis and some background pertaining to the production of each title. Here, in each entry, I include research about the directors and the stars, as well as many of the supporting players. Also, I have attempted to extract some "behind-the-scenes" information about each of the titles and some of the reviews by major newspaper columnists of the time. True, there are many excellent titles that I have not included here. So, I do intend to write a volume II on this subject in the near future.

My interest in movies in general began when I was quite young, and like most children who grew up in the television age (the 1950s), I became mesmerized with classic comedies initially, which cropped up consistently on our old RCA console. Of course, comics like Laurel and Hardy, Abbott and Costello, and the Three Stooges became my means to pass the time when the weather didn't permit me to participate in any outdoor activities with my friends. After a while, I preferred to remain inside on beautiful days watching old classics like *Casablanca*, *Yankee Doodle Dandy* and *Mutiny on the Bounty* rather than hitting baseballs or practicing my dribbling.

Years later, in 1971, while I was attending School of Visual Arts in Manhattan, I became acquainted with noted film historian/archivist William K. Everson, whose film class became a source for screening extremely rare films from the Golden Age of Hollywood. Of course, this was long before anyone could just drop a video or DVD into a player and view their favorite film whenever they pleased. Besides, many of Professor Everson's films were so rare that they will probably never be available on any format other than 16mm. Professor Everson had an extensive private collection on film, and having a very modest assortment of titles in the same format, my desire to increase that number became an overwhelming passion which continues to this day! Admittedly, though, I have forgone collecting 16mm for the newer format of video projection recently. However, I still do screen many of the rarer titles on film.

My visits with Professor Everson at his apartment in Manhattan's Upper West Side became a sort of refuge for my wife and me. It was there that we had our first exposure to Pre-Code Hollywood when Bill threaded his RCA projector and screened us prints of *Three on a Match* and *Baby Face*, which are probably considered two of the best and most representative of that era. After that rather stimulating experience, we were both hooked and we couldn't get enough of these racy entries with their heavy doses of sex and violence carrying the proceedings. Naturally, having been aware of Hollywood films after 1934, where the subject matter was far less risqué but rather more family oriented, I was astonished by the realism and the frankness of these earlier works. After all, movies were always considered escapism for me and now I was witnessing real life stories, depicting fallen women who would denigrate themselves for a meal through prostitution or any other way for a fast buck, something movie heroines never dreamed of in the post-code era. Admittedly, one had to admire these dames for their "spunk", as they all seem to get what they want as long as there is a wealthy, willing, and virile male available, no matter what his marital status may be! Personally, I feel a sense of loss when I see how the code changed actresses such as Jean Harlow. Gone were the bulk of her sex appeal and sense of fun, replaced by conservative clothing and a newfound sense of morality.

Of course, there were to be other questionable subjects explored in these films, like infidelity, yellow journalism, white slavery, child abuse, drug addiction, murder, premarital sex, abortion, bootlegging, homosexuality, and so on. Many a time in these pictures, the fallen woman might reform at the film's conclusion, but usually never had to pay for her former misdeeds as she would a few short years later. Likewise, the city hoodlum would get away scot-free, as Clark Gable does after gunning down crooked newspaperman Richard Barthelmess in *The Finger Points* (1931). A good deal of the witty humor filled with double entendres that today's audience would so appreciate disappeared from post-code films. Fabulous lines like one delivered by Ronald Colman in *The Devil to Pay* (1930) after he's sold his bed at auction to an attractive young woman, "Sold. I've always wanted you to sleep in it", would no longer be permitted.

My ambition here was to include a good number of Pre-Code titles, merely to whet the appetite in the hope that the reader will wish to view as many as possible and more to come after gathering information about the director or star's background. I have tried to include as many genres as possible, ranging from gangster and crime films to dramas, comedies, musicals, social dramas, and murder mysteries. All of these movies have one thing in common...none of them would have passed the keen eye of the Breen Office for release after 1934. The film content would have been deemed "unacceptable to the morals of American youth."

The reason for this reform or censorship was the result of women's groups and the Catholic Church, who tried to incite a ban on any film which was labeled morally offensive. Hollywood, with their backs against the wall, decided to initiate their own set of rules rather than have outsiders set the standards! This resulted in a total overhauling in Hollywood. No longer could 'fallen women' be redeemed at the end of a picture. Now she would have to pay for her indiscretions by wholesale humiliation, or even worse, death! Now, the gangster, who was usually portrayed by Edward G. Robinson, Paul Muni, or James Cagney, had to end his life of crime by being "rubbed out" by a policeman's revolver. There was no glorification of the American hoodlum. As a result, after the code, Cagney and Robinson would be working on the side of law and order, fighting one-dimensional gang lords but using the same violent methods they had used before! Of course, this was perfectly accepted by the censors now that the stars were working for the law.

In the Pre-Code era, studios, especially Warner Brothers, would adapt their story lines from real life newspaper headlines. But now, with the introduction of this new censorship, they would often base their screenplays on literary classics such as *David Copperfield, A Tale of Two Cities* (both 1935), and *Pride and Prejudice* (1940). Movies that had been considered sophisticated bedroom farces like Ernst Lubitsch's *Trouble in Paradise* (1932) were now a thing of the past. No longer was sex considered a casual past time spurred on by a brief romance or one night fling. A new type of "adult" comedy was introduced called the Screwball Comedy, which was an attempt by the studios to bring back some of the sexual allure that had been present in the early thirties. Although these comedies are still a lot of fun today, they often lack sexual tension, which had been replaced by a series of knockabout pratfalls and constant banter in a wild battle of the sexes! Also, the American household was depicted as wholesome as the driven snow, with teenager Andy Hardy becoming the quintessential American teenager. Of course, theatregoers knew all along that no one family could be as perfect as Judge Hardy's brood, but they attempted to emulate them just the same.

Screening some of these post-code films today, many of them seem shallow while others lack real bite compared to their early thirties counterparts. I certainly hope that this book instills in the reader the desire to track down some of the titles I've included here, whether it's by purchasing it on DVD or merely spending an evening watching Turner Classic Movies. If that's the result, then I've succeeded.

The Younger Generation (1929)

A Columbia Picture. A Frank R. Capra Production. Produced by Jack Cohn. Directed by Frank Capra. Screenplay by Sonya Levien, based on the play "It Is to Laugh" by Fannie Hurst. Dialogue by Howard J. Green. Photographed by Ted Tetzlaff. Sound Cameraman: Ben Reynolds. Art Direction by Harrison Wiley. Edited by Arthur Roberts. Production Supervision by Joe Cooke. Technical Director: Edward Shulter. Assistant Director: Tinny Wright. Recorded by Western Electric with the Columbia Symphony Orchestra. Music Conductor: Constantine Bakaleinikoff. 88 min.

Cast: Jean Hersholt (Julius "Pa" Goldfish), Lina Basquette (Birdie Goldfish), Ricardo Cortez (Morris Goldfish), Rex Lease (Eddie Lesser), Rosa Rosanova (Tilda "Ma" Goldfish), Sid Crossley (Butler), Martha Franklin (Mrs. Lesser), Julanne Johnston (Irma Striker), Jack Raymond (Pinsky), Otto Fries (Grocer), Julia Swayne Gordon (Mrs. Striker).

DIRECTOR FRANK CAPRA'S name has definitely become closely associated with some of Hollywood's classic films. Titles like *It Happened One Night* (1934), *Lost Horizon* (1937), *Mr. Smith Goes to Washington* (1939), *Meet John Doe* (1941), and *It's a Wonderful Life* (1946) have become "American Treasures" which can be enjoyed by future generations, as long as prints are readily available to be studied and revered. There are, however, many of his earlier works that have been overlooked, not because they are inferior, but because of their unavailability throughout the years. Fortunately, Columbia Pictures has been working exhaustively to preserve many of the master's late silents and "Pre-Code" films, giving film students the added pleasure of seeing how this wonderful filmmaker was able to develop into one of the most prestigious directors of the century!

Capra was born in Palermo, Sicily, on May 18, 1897. His family emigrated to the U.S. in 1903 and eventually settled in California, where young Frank's father became an orange picker. After graduating from the

The Younger Generation (1929) Director Frank Capra's first talkie (actually, it was a part-talkie) with Lina Basquette as Birdie Goldfish and Rex Lease as her husband, Eddie Lesser. (AB)

California Institute of Technology in 1918 with a degree in chemical engineering, he enlisted in the army during the First World War. After the war, work was sparse in his particular field and he began drifting in and out of an assortment of occupations. Finally in 1922, Capra was working for a small independent film company and was talked into directing a twelve minute one-reeler called *Fultah Fisher's Boarding House*. After earning $75 for his first venture as a director, the enterprising youth began working in a film lab, where he printed, dried, and spliced the daily rushes, while studying different techniques and styles of various directors. Gaining confidence, Capra went on to the Hal Roach Studio where he became a gag writer for the famous "Our Gang Comedies." Unfortunately, Roach was not too pleased with Capra's gag writing, later claiming that he made the gang seem rather like an unruly bunch of hooligans, who were neither funny nor sympathetic.

Luckily, his career took a decided upswing, when Mack Sennett gave him the chance to write for his star comedian, Harry Langdon, whose meteoric rise to prominence was on the verge of surpassing that of Charlie Chaplin. When Langdon became disenchanted with Sennett and demanded more money than the producer could afford, he took Frank Capra with him over to First National, where they made three highly successful feature-length comedies.

Eventually, Capra was to find himself at Columbia Studios, a film factory of low-budget features. There, he would perfect his craft by churning out some rather light but highly entertaining silents like *That Certain Thing*, *So This is Love*, *The Matinee Idol*, *The Way of the Strong*, *Say It with Sables*, *The Power of the Press*, and *Submarine*, all of which were released in 1928 (an incredible output for anybody!).

The following year, with the coming of talkies, Capra was asked to direct the studio's first talking picture, entitled *The Younger Generation*. Since sound equipment was rather scarce, with few sound cameras to go around to the various studios, the movie was essentially a silent film with synchronized music and sound effects, sprinkled with a few scenes shot entirely in sound. Seen today, *The Younger Generation*, with its gripping story of a Jewish social climber (Ricardo Cortez) who turns his back on his heritage and his lower East Side origins, as well as his parents (beautifully enacted by Rosa Rosanova and especially Jean Hersholt), remains a compelling drama with a superbly fitting ending, with Cortez finally getting his well-deserved comeuppance. The film works superbly as a silent picture, but is handicapped by the rather stodgy use of sound in the lengthy talking sequences. Capra later told interviewers, "We couldn't rent a sound stage for a long duration of time, both because of the great demand and for economic reasons. So for *The Younger Generation* all the silent scenes were shot at one time and all the sound scenes at another time. Later they were intermixed. The script was not shot in continuity, and no decision was made about which scenes would be talking and which silent."

Applause (1929)

A Paramount Picture. Directed by Rouben Mamoulian. Produced by Jesse L. Lasky and Monta Bell. Screenplay by Garrett Fort. Based on the novel by Beth Brown. Photography by George Folsey. Edited by John Bassler. Sound Recording by Ernest F. Zatorsky. Songs: "What Wouldn't I Do for That Man?" by E. Y. Harburg and Jay Gorney; "Yaaka Hula Dickey Dula" by E. Ray Goetz, Joe Young and Pete Wendling; "Give Your Little Baby Lots of Loving" by Dolly Morse and Joe Burke; and "I've Got a Feelin' I'm Fallin'" by Billy Rose, Harry Link and "Fats" Waller. Also filmed as a silent. 78 min.

Cast: Helen Morgan (Kitty Darling), Joan Peers (April Darling), Fuller Melish, Jr. (Hitch Nelson), Henry Wadsworth (Tony), Jack Cameron (Joe King), Dorothy Cumming (Mother Superior), Jack Singer (Producer), Paul Barrett (Slim Lamont).

WITH THE ADVENT of talking pictures in the late 1920s, Hollywood producers were intent on getting a better grasp of this new medium. By the latter part of the decade silent movies had become more polished, and the expert craftsmanship was evident in almost every film from 1925 onwards. Sound, on the other hand, produced problematic results, with directors and sound technicians unaware as to how to film certain scenes and where to place the microphone in order to keep it concealed from the camera. Microphones were sometimes obscured behind props or hidden in floral arrangements on tables, with actors awkwardly bending over them, playing their lines into these props, thus resulting in a very static effect.

The tagline "All-Talking, All-Singing and All-Dancing" became familiar, due to the overwhelming need to hear as well as see stars of the day not only speaking their lines, but singing popular songs of the era in review-type musicals. However, this quickly became tiresome to audiences

Applause (1929) Publicity photo of Helen Morgan in Rouben Mamoulian's Applause. (RF)

of the early thirties, and musicals became as unwelcome as the landlady's weekly rent bill. One of the best early talkies to come out of 1929 was *Applause*, directed by Rouben Mamoulian, the Russian born Broadway stage director, whose unique style was evident in his most popular production, *Porgy and Bess*. Paramount Pictures, who had an east coast facility in Astoria, NY, was courting stage directors and stars to appear in films by convincing them they would not be interfering with their theatrical performances in the evenings since they would be filming during the day. Thus, Mamoulian was requested to direct this, his first motion picture. Studying the styles of the other directors of the day prior to embarking on this rather foreign new medium, he was hell-bent on making a movie which was both innovative and devoid of any clichés.

Today, *Applause* is regarded as a model of early sound cinema, which still seems amazing when one views the product from other Hollywood studios of the period, which had far better facilities and directors who knew the picture business inside and out. Despite the handicaps, Mamoulian's film remains an impressive array of beautifully photographed scenes, filmed in actual locations in and around the Big Apple. Camerawork is

Applause (1929) Helen Morgan (foreground) as stripper, Kitty Darling, in Applause. (AB)

fluid and there are many beautifully crafted shots using shadows along with excellent montage sequences, all recorded with two sound tracks overlapping simultaneously, a feat never attempted until that point. The story, which was based on a novel by Beth Brown, focuses on Kitty Darling (played by Helen Morgan), a washed-up burlesque stripper, whose daughter April (Joan Peers), has been in a Catholic convent since she was a little girl. April, of course, hasn't a clue how her mother has made a living all these years, but once the two are reunited, the daughter is exposed to the seedier side of her mother's sordid lifestyle. Kitty also has a live-in boyfriend, Hitch Nelson, played by Fuller Mellish, Jr., a lecherous scoundrel who has been using Kitty for a number of years by sponging off of her past successes. When Hitch meets the virginal April, he is taken in by her youthful naiveté and proceeds to make advances toward her. Luckily for April, she finds solace in the person of a young sailor named Tony (Henry Wadsworth), who is on leave from the navy, and the two eventually strike up a relationship—much to the consternation of Hitch, whose mental cruelty eventually drives Kitty over the edge!

Helen Morgan, who had been a huge success on Broadway, is excellent in her portrayal of the has-been aging burlesque queen, an accomplishment doubly incredible since she wasn't quite 29 at the time *Applause* was filmed. Miss Morgan's short-lived film career consisted of only ten movies, due to her rather difficult behavior on the sets as a result of her excessive drinking. It finally took its toll on her when she died in 1941 at the age of forty-one. Her greatest stage role would eventually become her most famous film role, as the downcast mulatto Julie in the 1936 version of *Showboat* for Universal (she also played the same role in the 1929 part-talkie, which starred Laura La Plante).

Stage star Fuller Mellish, Jr. had a promising career on Broadway and probably in motion pictures as well, but he died suddenly just one year after *Applause* was released. Joan Peers, who played April, remained on the stage after appearing in barely more than a handful of features for Radio Pictures. As for director Rouben Mamoulian, he became one of Paramount's biggest directors along with the likes of Cecil B. DeMille, Ernst Lubitsch, and Josef von Sternberg. Mamoulian's innovative camera angles and unique style kept him working in films successfully throughout the 1940s. Among his biggest hits were *City Streets* (1931), *Dr. Jekyll and Mr. Hyde* (1931), *Love Me Tonight* (1932), *Queen Christina* (1933), and *The Mark of Zorro* (1940), all considered bona-fide examples of classic cinema today.

The Big House (1930)

A Metro-Goldwyn-Mayer/Cosmopolitan Picture. Produced by Irving Thalberg. Directed by George Hill. Story by Frances Marion. Screenplay by Frances Marion, Joe Farnham, and Martin Flavin. Art Direction by Cedric Gibbons. Photography by Harold Wenstrom. Edited by Blanche Sewell. Sound by Douglas Shearer. Jute mill scenes filmed at the Pacific Woolen and Blanket Works, Long Beach. Also filmed in French, German, Italian and Spanish versions. 86 min.

Cast: Chester Morris (John Morgan), Wallace Beery (Butch Schmidt), Lewis Stone (Warden James Adams), Robert Montgomery (Kent Marlowe), Leila Hyams (Anne Marlowe), George F. Marion (Pop Riker), J. C. Nugent (Mr. Marlowe), Karl Dane (Olsen), DeWitt C. Jennings (Captain Wallace), Mathew Betz (Gopher), Claire McDowell (Mrs. Marlowe), Robert Emmett O'Connor (Sergeant Donlin), Tom Kennedy (Uncle Jed), Tom Wilson (Sandy, a guard), Eddie Foyer (Dopey), Roscoe Ates (Putnam), Fletcher Norton (Oliver), Adolph Seidel (Prison Barber), Leo Willis, Eddie Lambert and Michael Vavitch (Prisoners).

AFTER THE SUCCESSES of such gangster epics as *Little Caesar* (1930), *The Public Enemy* (1931), and *Scarface* (1932), audiences of the early 1930's were also treated to a new type of film that had become quite famous following the success of MGM's THE BIG HOUSE. The prison movie made it possible for filmgoers to observe the gangster's alternative plight if he managed to avoid cold-blooded death by the feds. Films like *The Criminal Code* (1931), *20,000 Years in Sing-Sing*, and *The Last Mile* (both 1932), proved so popular that a rash of similar "death row" vehicles resulted as the thirties dwindled on.

George Hill, director of *The Big House* (not to confused with the later director of *Butch Cassidy and the Sundance Kid* and *The Sting*), was rapidly becoming MGM's latest discovery of real note. His knack for "atten-

The Big House (1930) "Machine-Gun" Butch Schmidt (Wallace Beery), Kent Marlowe (Robert Montgomery) and John Morgan (Chester Morris) planning an escape. (RF)

tion to detail" was attained through an apprenticeship with the great D. W. Griffith, during which he acquired many of the old master's tricks. Hill, along with his wife, screenwriter Frances Marion, collaborated on many assignments with outstanding results. Their projects usually dealt with the seedier side of life, many of which have become minor classics in their own right. Unfortunately, George Hill had a career that was tragically short, dying at the age of thirty-nine, an apparent suicide, four years later.

Before production of *The Big House* began, the part of murderous Butch Schmidt was awarded to MGM's number one character actor, Lon Chaney. However, he was never able to take on the role, since after his sensational talkie debut in *The Unholy Three*, he was diagnosed with bronchial cancer and died a short time later. It was then that the studio hired an out of work actor named Wallace Beery to assume the part, after he'd been dropped by Paramount. Beery, a big, hulking, bear-like actor, whose nickname was 'Jumbo', was so adept at playing grotesque characters, but at the same time emitting a lovable persona as well. He proved perfect for the role. A former female impersonator and silent comic, Beery parlayed his early career playing villains and dumb but likable foils, often teaming with fellow comedian Raymond Hatton in films like *Behind the Front* (1926) and *Casey at the Bat* (1927). After his initial MGM venture, the gruff Beery found himself cast in many money-spinners for the burgeoning Culver City studio. In just another year, he was considered one of the top ten movie stars in Hollywood, and continued to be, almost consistently through the forties.

Co-starring with Beery in *The Big House* was actor Chester Morris, whose career was just beginning to take off after being cast in producer Roland West's vehicles *Alibi* (1929) and *The Bat Whispers* (1930). Morris' Dick Tracy-like features and intense style of acting usually resulted in his being cast (most effectively) in tough-guy roles. Unfortunately (for us, anyway), Morris was not a good judge in obtaining sure-fire vehicles for his particular talents, and after being awarded a lucrative non-exclusive contract with Metro, was loaned out to other studios in lesser films undeserving of his formidable dexterity. Eventually, he succumbed to the "B" movie units at different studios, occasionally appearing in a borderline "B" or nervous "A" with pleasing results. Two of his later 1939 releases do, however, stand out as being model "B" releases of that year, having surprised critics and audiences alike without the usual fanfare awarded a more "prestigious" picture. *Blind Alley* for Columbia and *Five Came Back* for RKO Radio were the two "sleepers" which eventually gave Morris the reputation as "King of the B's." By the early 1950s, after appearing in countless low budget pictures and thirteen Boston Blackie comedy mysteries (for which he's best remembered), his Hollywood career more or less dried up. As a result, the eventual venue, which seemed the most logical, was the New York stage, in which Chester's career obtained the boost it really needed. His last film appearance was in the 1970 release *The Great White Hope* with James Earl Jones. Of his long career, Chester Morris often considered his role in *The Big House* as his best, citing, "We all gave our roles the best that was in us, and the virility and truthfulness of the picture were more satisfying than anything I've ever done."

Also giving their best were newcomer Robert Montgomery and Lewis Stone, who are seen to good advantage as the new prisoner Kent and Warden Adams, respectively. After a false start in pictures, usually playing colorless romantic leads, as in Buster Keaton's *Free and Easy* (also 1930), Montgomery found it quite difficult to obtain meaty roles. Being cast in such a prestigious production as *The Big House* was quite the feather in his cap; but sadly, after this release it was back to playing 'boy next door' types, for the time being, anyway. It wasn't until 1937 that Montgomery's career really took off after he fought hard for the role of the psychopathic murderer in the Emlyn Williams film version of *Night Must Fall*. The other resident MGM contract player, Lewis Stone, had faded from his leading man roles of the silent era into character parts in the early talkies as wizened middle-aged men, such as the kindly Judge Hardy, in the long-running "Hardy Family" series.

The female interest in *The Big House* is the forgotten Leila Hyams, whose parents Johnny Hyams and Leila McIntyre were usually cast as rich couples in many drawing room comedies. Leila's film credits include *Red-Headed Woman* (also with Chester Morris), *Freaks*, *The Big Broadcast*, *Island of Lost Souls* (all 1932), and many more. Her role in *The Big House* was originally as the wife of Robert Montgomery, but after the initial preview, the censors rushed in and made MGM change her character to his sister. The Catholic Church found it appalling that she would become involved with Chester Morris while her husband was behind bars!

Critically and commercially, *The Big House* was an enormous success, and very few subsequent prison pictures have been able to hold a candlestick to it. Actor Wallace Beery was nominated in the Best Actor category (having lost to George Arliss in *Disraeli*), while the film itself was nominated for Best Picture (losing to Lewis Milestone's anti-war epic *All Quiet on the Western Front*). Screenwriter Frances Marion was awarded the Oscar for Best Writing and sound technician Douglas Shearer (Norma Shearer's brother) was the first recipient of the Best Sound Recording award.

As a side note, *The Big House* was one of the first films to be shot in French, Spanish, German and Italian, with different casts playing the various roles. For instance, the French version, which was entitled *Revolte dans la Prison*, starred newcomer Charles Boyer in the Chester Morris role. Even comedy producer Hal Roach decided to cash in on the film's success by casting his hit comedy team, Laurel and Hardy, in a direct spoof.

The Devil to Pay (1930)

United Artists Release for Samuel Goldwyn. Produced by Samuel Goldwyn. Directed by George Fitzmaurice. Screenplay by Frederick Lonsdale and Benjamin Glazer. Dialogue Director: Ivan Simpson. Photography by George S. Barnes and Gregg Toland. Musical Score by Alfred Newman. Art Direction by Richard Day. Assistant Director. H. Bruce Humberstone. Technical Advisors: Lady Maureen Stanley and Lt. Col. G. L. McDonell. Edited by Grant Whytock. 74 min.

Cast: Ronald Colman (Willie Hale), Loretta Young (Dorothy Hope), Florence Britton (Susan Hale), Frederick Kerr (Lord Leland Hale), David Torrence (Mr. Hope), Mary Forbes (Mrs. Hope), Paul Cavanagh (Grand Duke Paul), Crauford Kent (Arthur Hale), Myrna Loy (Mary Crayle), Ivan Simpson (Owner of Pet Shop), Forrester Harvey (Cabbie).

BY 1930, it was apparent to everyone in Hollywood that Ronald Colman had succeeded with ease through the transition of silents to sound. Producer Samuel Goldwyn, who was to have Colman under contract for another two and a half years, realized that he had struck pay dirt with his star. After commercial and critical successes like *Bulldog Drummond* (1929) and *Raffles* (1930), any doubts concerning Colman's British accent being a liability were totally eradicated.

Now was the time for Goldwyn to cast his top box-office draw in a sophisticated, drawing room comedy in which his winning personality would shine. This was to be found in the highly entertaining story *The Devil to Pay*, which, although relatively plotless, remains one of the best films of the early talkie era. Pacing, dialogue and fluid camerawork all mesh together perfectly when put into motion by director George Fitzmaurice. A master of highly successful forays into romantic comedies and dramas, he may be best remembered for Rudolph Valentino's *Son of The Sheik* (1926), *Night of Love* (1927), again with Ronald Colman and

The Devil to Pay (1930) Willie Hale (Ronald Colman) takes Dorothy Hope
(Loretta Young) on a date to the Derby. (RF)

his frequent silent screen co-star, Vilma Banky, and Garbo's *Mata Hari*
(1932). His expertise in the polished *The Devil to Pay* is so advanced technically that it seems that this film might have been a mid to late '30s release!

Sixteen year old Loretta Young seems somewhat immature to be cast
opposite thirty-nine year old Colman. However, Miss Young was not the
original choice as his leading lady. Constance Cummings was preferred,
possessing a more mature personality rather than the insecurities of a
minor. According to studio publicity stills, Miss Cummings did indeed
participate in filming, having left after a few days of shooting. Why she
left the production company is anybody's guess, for it does seem rather
sad that this gifted actress was eliminated from the final product. But to
be perfectly fair to Miss Young, she does come off as a poised, charming
youth, radiating innocence while exuding a confidence, something she
later confessed was through the tutoring of Mr. Colman himself! Myrna
Loy, taking time off from portraying avenging Orientals with wicked intent, is delightful as the 'other woman'. Her Mary Crayle seems perfect

(almost too perfect, in that one almost wishes that it was she who ended up with Colman for the final clinch). A charming eight reels nonetheless, it was greeted with positive accolades, with the *Herald Tribune* citing, "Six reels [sic] of Mr. Colman being charming, but since it happens that Mr. Colman can be charming without offense, ostentation or self-consciousness, and that Frederick Lonsdale (the screenwriter) is an expert at making something out of nothing, the result is a polished, tasteful and entirely likable screen comedy."

It's incredible to think that this highly successful bit of fluff wasn't nominated for any awards, for it seems much better than much of the product which was around at the time! As for Sam Goldwyn, he couldn't be more pleased, and again teamed this great combination of star and director, putting them into a steamy desert love story written by Ben Hecht, with only moderate results. That film, a forerunner to the classic Charles Boyer/Hedy Lamarr *Algiers* (1938) was entitled *The Unholy Garden*.

Stolen Heaven (1931)

Paramount Pictures. Directed by George Abbott. Based on a story by Dana Burnet. Adaptation by George Abbott. Written by George Hill. Photography by George J. Folsey. Edited by Emma Hill. Music by Leo Reisman. 72 min.

Cast: Nancy Carroll (Mary), Phillips Holmes (Joe), Louis Calhern (Steve), Edward Keane (Morgan), Joan Carr (Mrs. Woodbridge-Wood), G. Albert Smith (Harvey), Dagmar Oakland (Dorothea), Guy Kibbee (Police Commissioner), Joseph Crehan (Henry the Butler), Eddie Ryan (Child on Beach), Tom Carter (Traffic Controller), Buford Armitage (Mr. Cornell), Joan Kenyon (Mrs. Cornell), Carola Kip (Extra).

NOT SEEN IN DECADES, due to the fact that both stars, Nancy Carroll and Phillips Holmes, are all but forgotten today, *Stolen Heaven* is one of those films that starts off promisingly enough, but tends to drag until the plotline flows more evenly near its conclusion. Carroll, an actress who became a huge star after making the enormously successful *The Shopworn Angel* in 1929 opposite a young Gary Cooper, was being groomed to become the next Clara Bow, since Bow's career was spiraling downward. After making such early talkie hits as *Laughter* and *Follow Thru* (both 1930, and filmed in the early two-strip Technicolor process), she was re-teamed with her leading man, Phillips Holmes, in *The Devil's Holiday* (1930). Holmes, the son of stage and screen star, Taylor Holmes, was attending Princeton when director Frank Tuttle began shooting some location shots for his upcoming feature *Varsity* (1928) with Charles "Buddy" Rogers. Tuttle liked Holmes' boyish all-American good looks and put him into the picture. Apparently, the Paramount brass liked what they saw and put the twenty-one year old under contract. After he was signed, nobody knew what to do with him and he was forever being cast as whining weaklings, whose total dedication from his female leads seemed rather puzzling to audiences in the early thirties.

Stolen Heaven (1931) Former "lady of the night," Mary (Nancy Carroll) goes on a big spending spree with Joe (Phillips Holmes) on stolen money. (AB)

There were some good roles, though, for a short time. Holmes was suitably cast in Josef von Sternberg's *An American Tragedy* (1931) opposite Sylvia Sidney, where he plays an ambitious young man, torn between a rich society girl (Frances Dee) and a waif from the other side of the tracks (Miss Sidney). When he discovers that the latter is pregnant, he decides to drown her when he takes her out in a rowboat, in order to marry the rich girl. If all of this sounds familiar, it was remade twenty years later, under the title *A Place in the Sun*, by director George Stevens. This version was done much better because the audience becomes more involved with the characters, whereas the earlier version seems too dark and cold-hearted. Holmes' best film was probably Ernst Lubitsch's forgotten gem *Broken Lullaby* (released in England as *The Man I Killed*), where he was again teamed with the vivacious Miss Carroll.

Stolen Heaven, which was based on a play by Dana Burnet, who also wrote *The Shopworn Angel*, was directed by George Abbott, a successful Broadway stage director and scriptwriter. Signed to make eight pictures for Paramount, Abbott was assigned to shoot them at the Astoria Studio, where Nancy Carroll had already been shooting her previous film, *Laughter*. Very popular in its day, *Stolen Heaven* was one of those films that didn't enjoy a reissue due to its very downbeat subject matter, about a young thief who steals $20,000, befriends a "lady of the streets", and together they decide to go on one last spending spree incognito as husband and wife. They agree on a mutual pact that after the funds have been

"*You can't go now – I love you –––*"

1300-38

Stolen Heaven (1931) Mary (Nancy Carroll) and Joe (Phillips Holmes) living "in sin." (AB)

completely depleted, they will both commit suicide, a rather grim plot-line for Depression-era audiences. Luckily, the film plays rather well, with both stars getting through the proceedings quite nicely, and although the film wins audience approval overall, there are some rather poorly written scenes that tend to seem mawkish instead of compelling. The trade papers gave the movie the "thumbs-up" with *Variety* stating that *Stolen Heaven* was "pleasing entertainment all the way."

After appearing in some great 'Pre-Code' gems like *Wayward* (1932), *Hot Saturday* (1932), and *The Kiss Before the Mirror* (1933), Nancy Carroll's career began to fade. It's too bad, since she proved to be a very versatile actress, completely at ease doing both comedy and sensitive dramatic roles. By the late 1930s, she found herself in small supporting roles in films like *There Goes My Heart* (1938). People who have seen this film today are saddened to see that their once favorite leading lady had now been relegated to such an unimportant role that she is barely even noticed.

As for Phillips Holmes, his career declined simultaneously with Miss Carroll's. His last decent role was in the 1934 version of *Great Expectations*, where he was cast as Pip. It was just two years later that he was playing second-fiddle to the 'Our Gang' kids in their only feature-length production, *General Spanky*. During World War II, Mr. Holmes was killed in a mid-air crash aboard a Royal Canadian Air Force plane while flying over Ontario.

The Finger Points (1931)

A Warner Bros./First National Picture. Produced and Directed by John Francis Dillon. Story by W. R. Burnett and John Monk Saunders. Adaptation by Robert Lord. Photography by Ernest Haller. Edited by Le Roy Stone. Art Direction by Jack Okey. Costumes by Earl Luick and Edward Stevenson. Sound by Dolph Thomas. Music by David Mendoza. 88 min.

Cast: Richard Barthelmess (Breckenridge "Breck" Lee), Fay Wray (Marcia Collins), Regis Toomey (Charlie "Breezy" Russell), Robert Elliott (City Editor Frank Carter), Clark Gable (Louis J. Blanco), Oscar Apfel (Managing Editor Ellis Wheeler), Robert Gleckler (Larry Haynes), Mickey Bennett (Arthur, Office Boy), Lew Harvey (Henchman), Herman Krumpfel (Breck's Tailor), Frank Marlowe (Guard), J. Carrol Naish (Phone Voice), Bob Perry (Henchman).

ANOTHER ONE OF THOSE social dramas based on a true story, *The Finger Points* is a thinly veiled adaptation inspired by the real life gangland murder of *Chicago Tribune* reporter Jack Lingle, who was reportedly on Al Capone's payroll in 1930. Similar to the same year's other newspaper yarns, *Dance, Fools, Dance* and *Five Star Final*, but not quite as compelling, this film is hampered slightly by sluggish direction on the part of John Francis Dillon, a former director of silent comedies, whose career segued more successfully as the "flapper age" approached. Among his better films of the early thirties (he died in 1934) were *Millie* (1931) starring Helen Twelvetrees, and Clara Bow's next to last film, *Call Her Savage* (1932), which is considered one of the most outrageous "Pre-Code" movies ever made!

Top-billed silent screen star Richard Barthelmess is quite good in this early talkie as the honest, crusading reporter "Breck" Lee, who is eventually lured into the grasping claws of the underworld after being brutally beaten up by the mob because he has written a scathing article about them.

The Finger Points (1931) Although silent screen star Richard Barthelmess was the star, it was Clark Gable, cast as gangster Louis J. Bianco, who made an impression on audiences here. (AB)

Unable to pay for his resulting medical bills (his own newspaper won't even help him financially), he joins forces with the same gangsters who almost did him in. Of course, he gets himself entangled with corruption and violence, and finds that there is no turning back. Through the urgings of his girlfriend Marcia Collins (played by Fay Wray, an actress whose looks far outweighed her acting ability), he decides to double-cross his "elaborate meal ticket" and must face the consequences. The finale is quite shocking (for 1931 anyway) and the picture ends in true "Pre-Code" fashion.

The acting, for the most part, is carried diligently by Mr. Barthelmess, whose underplaying scores quite nicely, although I wish that they had dispensed with the southern accent. Always a huge box-office draw in the silent era, his boyish good looks in those early years brought him tremendous acclaim in pictures like *Broken Blossoms* (1919), *Way Down East* (1920), and most notably *Tol'able David* (1921). When talkies approached, he was offered a highly lucrative contract with Warner Bros./First National and continued making some excellent films, which were considered more thought provoking than the usual output that Hollywood was churning out in those Depression years. Among his best-remembered films during this period were the original *The Dawn Patrol* (1930), *Cabin in the Cotton*

(1932), *Heroes for Sale* (1933), and *Massacre* (1934). All were critically acclaimed, but as his contract began to expire, his movies failed to generate any excitement from theatregoers nationwide, who preferred more "escapist" entertainment. By 1935, he was making "programmers" for Paramount, having turned out one first-rate melodrama entitled *Four Hours to Kill* before retiring from the screen. He eventually made a "comeback" of sorts in 1939 when he was commissioned by Howard Hawks to co-star in the classic aviation picture *Only Angels Have Wings*, starring Cary Grant, Jean Arthur, and a young Rita Hayworth, appearing in her first 'important' screen role. Although Barthelmess is excellent in the film and he received rave reviews, he just wasn't happy playing character roles, and three years later retired from movies permanently. In 1942 he joined the Naval Reserve and later lived comfortably in Long Island for his remaining years.

The Finger Points suffers from an uneven screenplay, being based on a story by John Monk Saunders and W. R. Burnett, the latter having penned the gangster classic *Little Caesar* (1931) which made Edward G. Robinson an overnight success. Reviews at the time were rather tepid, and trade papers like *Variety* were no different, stating, "the lead characterization must have been a tough one for the writers. Even when the reporter goes bad, the script attempts to keep him clean, if not of hand at least of heart. This permits a sob-sister angle. Fay Wray interprets this assignment, constantly remonstrating with the lad to get out of the blood money class." Newcomer Clark Gable, playing gangster Louis Blanco, really gets a chance to shine in one of his earliest tough guy roles. It was only one year later that he would be the hottest new star under contract at MGM.

The Public Enemy (1931)

Warner Bros. Directed by William A. Wellman. Story by Kubec Glasmon and John Bright. Adaptation by Harvey Thew. Photography by Dev Jennings. Edited by Ed McCormick. Art Direction by Max Parker. Musical direction by David Mendoza. Costumes by Earl Luick. Make-up by Perc Westmore. Theme: "I'm Forever Blowing Bubbles". 84 min.

Cast: James Cagney (Tom Powers), Jean Harlow (Gwen Allen), Edward Woods (Matt Doyle), Joan Blondell (Mame), Beryl Mercer (Ma Powers), Donald Cook (Mike Powers), Mae Clarke (Kitty), Leslie Fenton (Samuel "Nails" Nathan), Robert Emmett O'Connor (Paddy Ryan), Murray Kinnell (Puddy Nose), Rita Flynn (Molly Doyle), Snitz Edwards (Hack), Ben Hendricks, Jr. (Bugs Moran), Frank Coghlan, Jr. (Tommy as a boy), Frankie Darro (Matt as a boy), Robert Emmett Homans (Officer Pat Burke), Dorothy Gee (Nails' Girl), Purnell Pratt (Officer Powers), Lee Phelps (Steve, Bartender), Mia Marvin (Jane), Clark Burroughs (Dutch), Adele Watson (Mrs. Doyle), Helen Parrish, Dorothy Gray, Nancie Price (Little Girls), Ben Hendricks III (Bugs as a boy), George Daly (Machine Gunner), Eddie Kane (Joe, Headwaiter), Charles Sullivan (Mug), Douglas Gerrard (Assistant Tailor), Sam McDaniel (Negro Headwaiter), William H. Strauss (Pawnbroker).

BY THE TIME *The Public Enemy* was released in May of 1931, Warner Bros. had already scored heavily with their earlier gangster saga *Little Caesar*, which made Edward G. Robinson an overnight star. Based on the story *Beer and Blood* by Kubec Glasmon and John Bright, this film proved to be the most potent crime film to date, until Howard Hughes' production of *Scarface* the following year. Originally slated for the lead role of Tom Powers was an up-and-coming actor named Edward Woods, while the part of his side-kick Matt was to be played by newcomer James Cagney, who already had about a half-dozen pictures to his credit in supporting parts.

The Public Enemy (1931) James Cagney became a major star as gangster Tom Powers (shown here with Jean Harlow as Gwen Allen). (RF)

After a few days' shooting, it became apparent to director William Wellman that Eddie Woods' acting was weak, especially when pitted up against the effervescent Mr. Cagney. As an experiment, Wellman had the two actors switch roles, verifying immediately that the spunky Irishman should be cast in the lead. Of course, this wasn't supported by those in the

Warners front office, who were afraid that the notorious gossip-columnist Louella Parsons might intercede, because her daughter was dating Eddie Woods. Luckily for us all, Wellman stood pat, making one of the most memorable gangster pictures of all time, brimming with many classic scenes that have become a part of Hollywood folklore. One of these, in which Cagney smashes a half of a grapefruit into the "kisser" of mistress Mae Clarke, was based on a real life incident in which actual mobster

The Public Enemy (1931) Studio portrait of James Cagney and Jean Harlow. (RF)

Hymie Weiss smeared an egg omelet into his girlfriend's face. Fortunately, for Miss Clarke, Bill Wellman thought an omelet would be too messy and substituted a grapefruit instead. He then took his actress aside and assured her that Cagney would fake it and not really hit her with the fruit, adding that the camera would stay on Cagney, and that afterwards they would insert a reaction of Mae's face in the aftermath. Wellman then took Jimmy aside and ordered him, "When the camera rolls, let her have it," which he did, totally startling Miss Clarke! The shocked expression on her face in the finished film is undoubtedly real.

One of the most dangerous scenes filmed in *The Public Enemy* had Cagney and Woods exiting an apartment, with the latter being gunned down by a rival mob before Cagney ducks down an alley. Briefly examining the aftermath, Jimmy peeks from around the corner of the building, only to be met by machine gun fire, which narrowly misses him, but shaves off an edge of the building in the process. If this sequence looks almost too realistic, it was! The scene was filmed with an expert marksman just out of camera range, firing real bullets, while the actor moved hastily out of the way in a split second! This became a standard practice for filming such scenes in the 1930s, proving what lengths actors would go to film a scene.

Also in the cast is Jean Harlow, who had just finished work on the World War I epic, *Hell's Angels* (1930), which also featured James Hall and Ben Lyon. For some strange reason, silent sex siren Louise Brooks was originally slated to play Harlow's role, but was dropped shortly after shooting began. Unfortunately, Miss Harlow was a newcomer, and her lack of training really shows in the finished product, in which she turns in one of her worst performances. Happily, she would find her niche in sexy comedy roles a year later in films like *Red Dust* and *Red-Headed Woman*.

For years *The Public Enemy* was seen at a disadvantage, since it had been code-cut. Much of the sex and violence had been sheared in order to get a seal of approval when the film was re-issued in 1953 on a double bill with *Little Caesar*. For the record, there is one complete 16mm version in existence, which belonged to film historian William K. Everson and is currently stored at the George Eastman House in Rochester, New York. Without certain scenes that were excised from the film, definite questions do indeed crop up. One of the most obvious is: "Who is responsible for Tom Power's demise after he single-handedly annihilates Schemer Burns' mob?" Although the re-released version leads viewers to believe the obvious, that Schemer Burns had Tom executed, the original cut implicates someone else. The key segment that was later cut shows Tom, too intoxicated to undress himself and reluctantly accepting help from Paddy Ryan's wife. In the truncated version, after tucking in her "Tommy Boy," she apparently walks out of the room, followed by a quick fade-out. The complete scene has her walking to the door of the bedroom, shutting off the lights, and heading back to the bed in which Tommy is trying to sleep. The scene darkens and only Cagney's voice is heard on the soundtrack complaining, "Hey, get away from me! You're Paddy Ryan's goil!" There are other clues, as well, that point to Tom Powers' assassin being none other than Paddy Ryan instead of Schemer Burns!

As for James Cagney, *The Public Enemy* is the movie that made him an overnight star, and we should be thankful that Warner Bros. finally restored the film to its complete length.

Smart Money (1931)

A Warner Bros. & Vitaphone Picture. Directed by Alfred E. Green. Screenplay by Kubec Glasmon and John Bright. Additional Dialogue by Lucien Hubbard and Joseph Jackson. Photography by Robert Kurrle. Edited by Jack Killifer. Musical Direction by Leo F. Forbstein. Makeup by Perc Westmore. 83 min.

Cast: Edward G. Robinson (Nick Venizelos), Evalyn Knapp (Irene Graham), James Cagney (Jack), Noel Francis (Marie), Morgan Wallace (District Attorney), Paul Porcasi (Mr. Amenoppopolus), Maurice Black (Greek Barber), Margaret Livingston (D.A.'s Girl), Clark Burroughs (Schultz), Billy House (Salesman), Edwin Argus (Two-Time Phil), Ralf Harolde (Sleepy Sam), Boris Karloff (Sport Williams), Mae Madison (Small Town Girl), Walter Percival (Dealer Barnes), John Larkin (Snake Eyes), Polly Walters (Lola), Ben Taggart (Hickory Short), Gladys Lloyd (Cigar Stand Clerk), Eulalie Jensen (Matron), Charles Lane (Desk Clerk), Edward Hearn (Reporter), Eddie Kane (Tom, a Customer), Clinton Rosemond (George, the Porter), Charles O'Malley (Machine Gunner), Gus Leonard (Joe, Barber Customer), Wallace MacDonald (Cigar Stand Clerk), John George (Dwarf on Train), Harry Semels (Gambler), Charlotte Merriam (Girl at Gaming Table).

BY THE END OF 1930, gangster pictures accounted for an estimated eleven percent of the Hollywood studios output. Exactly a year later, that figure rose to an incredible twenty percent. The reason for this was the overwhelming box-office response to films like *Little Caesar* (1931) and *The Public Enemy* (1931). Both were hard-hitting prohibition-era gangster dramas, which made stars of newcomers Edward G. Robinson and James Cagney. Realizing that they had a hit on their hands, but not realizing to what extent, Warner Bros. decided to cast Cagney in another crime drama in support of Eddie Robinson, while *The Public Enemy* was being

Smart Money (1931) Big time gambler, Nick Venizelos (Edward G. Robinson) has a "thing" for the ladies. Here, he makes a pass at manicurist, Lola (Polly Walters). (AB)

edited and readied for preview. Most historians claimed that the two new "bad boys of Hollywood" were to costar in a new venture entitled *Smart Money*. But, in actuality, Robinson's costar was Evelyn Knapp, while Cagney had a meaty supporting role as E.G.'s cohort in crime. By the time the movie was re-released years later, new title cards were designed with Cagney receiving equal billing with Robinson.

Following hot on the heels of the success, which awarded *The Public Enemy* its deserved reputation, *Smart Money*, although an interesting film, doesn't live in any way up to the standards of Cagney's first starring vehicle. It seems a shame that the two stars were never to appear in another movie together. One can only imagine the excitement of a Robinson/Cagney teaming, with the two as rival bootleggers trying to claim each other's territory. While Robinson receives the lion's share of footage as barber NickVenizelos, whose penchant for gambling and women eventually result in his downfall, Cagney plays his eager to learn protégé, Jack. Although it is never spelled out in the film's photoplay, Jack's interests are in gambling and Nick! Obviously, there are no homosexual references in the film. However, it is easy to read between the lines, which makes this effort way ahead of its time.

Another point of interest is the casting of Boris Karloff as a gambler, who makes his short appearance at the beginning of the picture. This was only months before he was cast as Frankenstein's monster in the 1931 James Whale classic. Also on hand is actress Gladys Lloyd, who plays the cigar-stand clerk after Nick is trimmed by professional gambler "Sleepy Sam." Gladys just happened to be Mrs. Edward G. Robinson and appeared in small parts in a few of her husband's films, most notably *Five Star Final* that same year.

Mordaunt Hall of *The New York Times* wrote, "it is fast moving and fairly interesting...Mr. Robinson gets all that is humanly possible out of the part of Nick the Barber, who, aside from his penchant for gambling, also has a weakness for blondes, canaries, and meticulously polished fingernails ...(He) leaves no stone unturned to attract the spectator's attention." He went on to write "James Cagney, who figured as the officious gangster in *The Public Enemy*, is to be seen in this current contribution ever ready with his short-arm jab. His role is of minor importance, for the boastful barber is the limelight in most scenes."

While *Smart Money* did well financially, it also cemented the career of James Cagney from then on. His next vehicle, *Blonde Crazy* gave him star billing opposite Joan Blondell, and with that film's success, he remained a major box-office draw until his retirement in 1961.

A Free Soul (1931)

A Free Soul (1931) A Metro-Goldwyn-Mayer Picture. Directed by Clarence Brown. Based on the book and magazine serial by Adela Rogers St. John and the play dramatized by Willard Mack. Adapted by John Meehan. Art Direction by Cedric Gibbons. Photography by William Daniels. Edited by Hugh Wynn. Sound by Anstruther MacDonald and Douglas Shearer. 91 min.

Cast: Norma Shearer (Jan Ashe), Lionel Barrymore (Steve Ashe), Clark Gable (Ace Wilfong), Leslie Howard (Dwight Winthrop), James Gleason (Eddie), Lucy Beaumont (Grandmother Ashe), Claire Whitney (Aunt Helen), Frank Sheridan (Prosecuting Attorney), E. Alyn Warren (Bottomley, Ace's Chinese Boy), George Irving (Johnson, Defense Attorney), Edward Brophy (Slouch), William Stacy (Dick), James Donlin (Reporter), Sam McDaniel (Valet), Lee Phelps (Court Clerk), Roscoe Ates (Men's Room Patron), Larry Steers (Casino Proprietor), Henry Hall (Detective), Francis Ford (Skid Row Drunk), Bess Flowers (Birthday Party Guest).

BASED ON A MAGAZINE SERIAL entitled *A Free Soul* by Adela Rogers St. Johns, the story was soon published as a book in 1924 before it became a Broadway play in 1928. Directed by a young George Cukor, who would later direct such movie classics as *Little Women* (1933), *Holiday* (1938), *The Philadelphia Story* (1940), and *Gaslight* (1944), the stage adaptation starred Kay Johnson and Lester Lonergan in the Norma Shearer and Lionel Barrymore roles respectively. Melvyn Douglas was cast as the gangster 'Ace' Wilfong, the role that Clark Gable portrayed in the screen version, where he furthered his reputation as a preeminent tough guy. Gable, at the time, was generating considerable interest in these early gangster roles, where he rubs out reporter gone crooked Richard Bathelmess in *The Finger Points*, starves two small children in order to

A Free Soul (1931) Advertisement for *A Free Soul* starring Norma Shearer.

gain an inheritance in *Night Nurse* and murders Joan Crawford's brother in *Dance, Fools, Dance* (all 1931). In one short year, he would be at the top of the heap when he was cast opposite Jean Harlow in Victor Fleming's *Red Dust*, where he was finally put into a romantic lead.

Although MGM's reigning queen Norma Shearer received top billing in *A Free Soul*, Lionel Barrymore and Clark Gable stole the picture out from under her. Barrymore would win the Academy Award as Best Actor for his work as the alcoholic lawyer/father of Norma Shearer, whose efforts to cure him of his addiction are doomed to failure. Gable, on the other hand, displays an animalistic sex-appeal quality in his scenes opposite Miss Shearer. As a matter of fact, Gable was taken aback at how arduously Norma would play her role during their lovemaking scenes, with Clark musing, "She would get so passionate with me that I used to wonder if she was getting enough at home." But as soon as the cameras stopped rolling she would shut down immediately. Another thing that shocked Gable during filming of *A Free Soul* was Norma's wardrobe, which still shocks viewers today. Gable, who commented on the sheerness of her white, clinging satin gown quipped to one of his friends, "Damn, the dame doesn't wear any underwear in her scenes." Miss Shearer, of course, was happily married to the studio's production head Irving Thalberg, and would remain MGM's top star until his passing in 1936 in films like *The Divorcee* (1930), *Private Lives* (1931), *The Barretts of Wimpole Street* (1934), and many others. Obviously, receiving all of the plum female roles for the studio didn't make Miss Shearer very popular with the other actresses at MGM, especially Joan Crawford, who barked, "At least I don't sleep with the boss!"

A Free Soul (1931) Clark Gable as mob boss, Ace Wilfong and Norma Shearer as "free-thinking" Jan Ashe, moments before she lies on the divan and invites him to "Put 'em around me."

A Free Soul (1931) Director Clarence Brown (left) goes over some details with his stars, Leslie Howard, Clark Gable and Norma Shearer.

When *A Free Soul* was initially previewed by the Hays Office, they objected to the scene where Miss Shearer is lying on a divan in a provocative pose with a 'come hither' glance and orders Clark Gable to "C'mon. Put 'em around me." Also, her aforementioned wardrobe was the subject of an article in Photoplay Magazine, where they noted, "Her clothes are breathtaking in their daring. But you couldn't get away with them in your drawing room."

Fourteen years later, Paramount Pictures released a powerful film about the effects of alcoholism called *The Lost Weekend*, which was directed by Billy Wilder and starred Ray Milland. The film won Academy Awards for the director and its star and also was awarded the Best Picture of the Year. Wilder had always claimed that this was the first time the subject matter had ever been addressed (I guess he never saw *A Free Soul* or *A Tree Grows in Brooklyn*, which was released nine months prior). Up until the mid-forties, alcoholism was treated in a comedic vein and comic drunks like Jack Norton and Arthur Housman were injected into movies for comic relief. *A Free Soul* was probably one of the first movies that dealt with this social problem seriously. *A Free Soul* presents a very honest depiction of how the disease of alcoholism affects the lives of the alcoholic, his family, and everyone with whom he comes into contact, and can be a source of knowledge, understanding, and comfort to millions suffering from the same thing today.

Confessions of a Co-ed (1931)

Paramount-Publix Pictures. Directed by David Burton and Dudley Murphy. Photography by Lee Garmes. Art Direction by Hans Dreier. Music by John Leipold. 75 min.

Cast: Phillips Holmes (Dan Carter), Sylvia Sidney (Patricia Harper), Norman Foster (Hal Evans), Claudia Dell (Peggy), Florence Britton (Adelaide), Martha Sleeper (Lucille), Dorothy Libaire (Mildred Stevens), Marguerite Warner (Sally), George Irving (College President), Winter Hall (Dean Winslow), Eulalie Jensen (Dean Marbridge), Bruce Coleman (Mark), Bing Crosby and the Rhythm Boys (Bing Crosby, Al Rinker, Harry Barris), John Breeden (Student), Bruce Cabot (College Student at Dance), Claire Dodd (Co-ed in Chapel), Dickie Moore (Patricia's Son), Joseph North (Butler), Imboden Parrish (Student).

AS THE 1920'S APPROACHED, a new movie craze had hit theatre screens, creating a wave of interest in college life. Films like the Charles Ray vehicle, *Two Minutes to Go* (1921), and *The Plastic Age* (1925) starring Clara Bow, proved to be popular film fare in the wake of the grim realities of the First World War. Harold Lloyd and Buster Keaton even gave their slant on college life in *The Freshman* (1925) and *College* (1927) respectively. All of these pictures gave us a rather romanticized account of a world which was so alien to most American youths that the idea of achieving a higher education was a thing that only the wealthy could hope for. Also, Hollywood's account of college consisted mainly of sporting events, wild parties, or wooing the school's campus queen, never once mentioning the real objective of a higher education. However, as the roaring twenties came to a grinding halt due to the onslaught of the Great Depression, the idea of living on a school campus became a far-fetched dream to the working class. As a result, films depicting life behind the ivy-covered walls in a frat house or dormitory were now beginning to con-

Confessions of a Co-ed (1931) College student Patricia Harper (Sylvia Sidney) loves Dan Carter (Phillips Holmes), so why does she marry Hal Evans (Norman Foster)? (AB)

centrate more on the harsh realities that could befall many naïve teenagers once they set out on their own. Topics like pre-marital sex, pregnancy and excessive drinking were now the plot elements of early thirties films like *Age of Consent* and *This Reckless Age* (both 1932), which brought up various questions about the obstacles one would have to endure while acquiring a higher education. One of the lesser-known titles depicting college life was *Confessions of a Co-ed*, which was the second starring vehicle for twenty year old Sylvia Sidney, who had made quite an impression in her prior picture, Rouben Mamoulian's *City Streets* (1931) opposite Gary Cooper.

Perhaps because the film was presumably based on a diary by an anonymous college student (there are no screenplay credits), it is very episodic, a common symptom of early talkies. The lack of pace in the plot may be due to the fact that two directors were credited, which had become a curse to most foredoomed motion pictures. Years later, Miss Sidney emphatically stated to me that this was one of her worst films, and she hadn't seen it since its original release and had no desire to see it again! The male leads (there are two to form the typical love triangle) are Phillips Holmes and Norman Foster, who are not the most captivating of leading men, leading the viewer to surmise that the pickings for male companionship are indeed sparse at this university—which looks suspiciously like Berkeley! The expert cinematography is provided by Lee Garmes, whose superb lighting gives the film an added technical gloss. Eagle-eyed film fanatics will spot early appearances by Bruce Cabot, Claire Dodd, and a very young Bing Crosby (one of the Rhythm Boys) before he ventured out on his own. Hal Roach fans will be thrilled to see pre-'Our Gang' star Dickie Moore as Miss Sidney's offspring, as well as Martha Sleeper, who was so delightful in her appearances with Max Davidson and in Charley Chase two-reelers, where she displayed superb comic timing. Unfortunately, here and in subsequent roles in the mid-thirties, she was sadly wasted.

While *Confessions of a Co-ed* really doesn't quite come off, it's truly a product of its time, where viewers can witness first-hand the trials and tribulations of college students from a bygone era at a safe distance. Reviews of the film were generally cool, with *The New York Times* stating "it is no wonder the author (of the story) should prefer to remain anonymous." However, the film did moderate business in lieu of the popularity of this type of film, and Paramount felt that Miss Sidney and Phillips Holmes were a good box-office team, so they recast them together in *An American Tragedy* later that year, based on the story by Theodore Dreiser and remade twenty years later by George Stevens under the title *A Place in the Sun* with Montgomery Clift and Elizabeth Taylor.

Night Nurse (1931)

Warner Bros. Directed by William A. Wellman. Screenplay by Oliver H. P. Garrett, based on the novel by Dora Macy. Dialogue by Oliver H. P. Garrett and Charles Kenyon. Photography by Chick McGill. Edited by Ed McDermott. Running Time: 72 min.

Cast: Barbara Stanwyck (Lora Hart), Ben Lyon (Mortie), Joan Blondell (Maloney), Clark Gable (Nick), Charles Winninger (Dr. Bell), Vera Lewis (Miss Dillon, Head Nurse), Blanche Frederici (Mrs. Maxwell), Charlotte Merriam (Mrs. Ritchey), Edward Nugent (Egan, Intern), Ralf Harolde (Dr. Milton Ranger), Walter McGrail (Mac), Allan Lane (Intern), Marcia Mae Jones (Nannie), Bob Perry (Bootlegger), Polly Walters (Party Guest).

NOTED DIRECTOR WILLIAM WELLMAN began his film career as an actor in the 1919 Douglas Fairbanks vehicle *Knickerbocker Buckaroo*, but found, to his dismay, that acting could be a terrifying experience, so he decided to tackle the production end of the movie industry. In three short years he graduated from property man to assistant director, gradually progressing from 'B' westerns to one of his most famous assignments, *Wings*, in 1927, which won the first Academy Award as best picture. Based on his own personal accounts of World War I, "Wild Bill" (as he was later nicknamed because of his violent temper), was able to film some of the most harrowing air sequences that remain impressive even today! His reputation as a first-rate director remained with him throughout his career, during which he turned out such diverse classics as *The Public Enemy* (1931), which put James Cagney's name on the map, *Star Witness* (1931) and *Wild Boys of the Road* (1933, two excellent social dramas), *Call of the Wild* (1935), notable as being the first teaming of Clark Gable and (ahem!) Loretta Young, the original *A Star is Born* (1937, itself a remake of *What Price Hollywood?*), actioners like *Beau Geste* (1939), *The Light That Failed* (1939), and *The Ox-Bow Incident* (1943). But in the early days of sound, he impressed critics and the general public with a fast-paced little Warner Bros. release entitled *Night Nurse*, a hospital drama, which was later imitated but never equaled by the other studios. What resulted were films like *Men in White* (1934, one of the last of the Pre-Codes with abortion being the main theme), *Private Worlds* (1935), *Vigil in the Night* (1940), *A Child is Born* (1940), and *Internes Can't Take Money* (1937, the first Dr. Kildare starring Joel McCrea in the title role, was so successful that it prompted MGM to purchase the property and follow up with their long-running series starring Lew Ayres).

The cast in *Night Nurse* is most interesting in that it features Barbara Stanwyck in one of her early 'nice girl' roles and teams her with the ever delightful Joan Blondell, both playing off one another marvelously! Ben Lyon, who scored rather heavily in the previous year's *Hell's Angels*, directed by Howard Hughes, plays his part with tongue firmly in cheek. But the most fascinating cast member, who eventually became world renowned as Rhett Butler, has one of his earliest roles as Nick the villainous chauffeur, a man of no morals, who starves little girls and slaps heroines around at the drop of a hat.

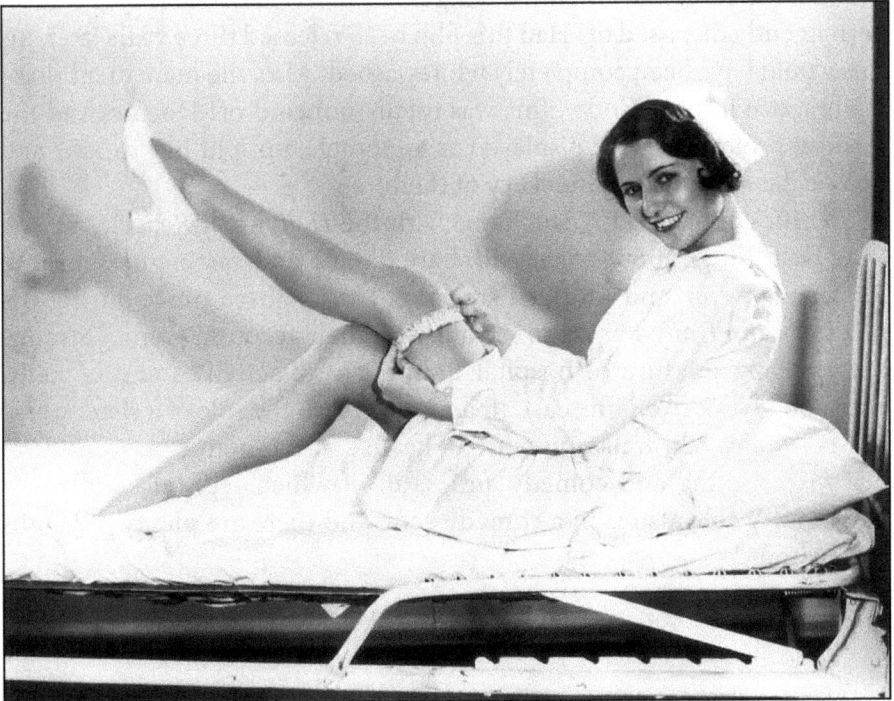

Night Nurse (1931) Barbara Stanwyck as Nurse Lora Hart in a delightful publicity pose.

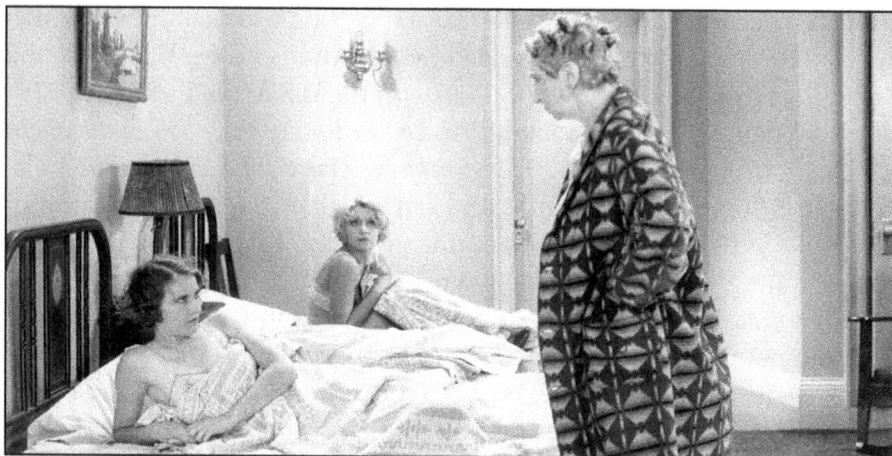

Night Nurse (1931) Lora Hart (Barbara Stanwyck) and her roommate Maloney (Joan Blondell) are caught by Miss Dillon (Vera Lewis) sneaking into their dorm room after staying out past curfew.

Of particular interest are the pre-Hays Office elements inherent in *Night Nurse*. Ben Lyons' bootlegger character is not only glorified, but in the final reel he gets away with having the villain (Clark Gable in this case) permanently disposed of! Had this film been released three years later, his role would have been completely whitewashed. Also, the mere mention of malpractice in post-Code films was totally unheard of! Doctors and the medical profession were displayed as honorable, upright institutions and no one dared to make a mockery of them!

Critics applauded *Night Nurse* with the *Hollywood Reporter* saying "The best things about *Night Nurse* are its title and cast names plus the Misses Stanwyck and Blondell stripping two or three times during the picture." *Film Daily* was more serious with their account, citing, "Strange but amusing mixture of hospital drama, crook activities and comedy, with good work from fine cast...Joan Blondell, in the role of a sister nurse to Miss Stanwyck, walks off with a big slice of the honors as a result of her wisecracking and comedy antics, all of which register solidly. Lyon's bootleg role also is in a comedy vein, and there are plenty of laughs throughout."

Five Star Final (1931)

A First National & Vitaphone Production. Produced by Hal B. Wallis. Directed by Mervyn LeRoy. Screenplay by Robert Lord. Based on the play by Louis Weitzenkorn. Additional Dialogue by Byron Morgan. Photography by Sol Polito. Art Direction by Jack Okey. Vitaphone Orchestra conducted by Leo Forbstein. Edited by Frank Ware. Assistant Director: G. Hollingshead. Gowns by Earl Luick. 89 min.

Cast: Edward G. Robinson (Joseph Randall), H.B. Warner (Michael Townsend), Marian Marsh (Jenny Townsend), Anthony Bushell (Phillip Weeks), George E. Stone (Ziggie Feinstein), Frances Starr (Nancy 'Voorhees' Townsend), Ona Munson (Kitty Carmody), Aline MacMahon (Miss Taylor), Boris Karloff (T. Vernon Isapod), Polly Walters (Telephone Operator), Robert Elliott (Brannegan), Gladys Lloyd (Miss Edwards), Evelyn Hall (Mrs. Weeks), David Torrence (Mr. Weeks), Harold Waldridge (Arthur Goldberg), Oscar Apfel (Bernard Hinchecliffe), Purnell Pratt (Robert French), William Burress (Bartender), James Donlan (Reporter), Frank Darien (Schwartz, Assistant Undertaker).

BY 1931 IT WAS APPARENT that the talkies were here to stay. Only two silent films were released that year: Chaplin's *City Lights*, and the Robert Flaherty/F. W. Murnau collaboration *Tabu*. After a shaky start, the new medium was able to overcome the rather primitive strictures of concealing the microphone while utilizing fluid camera motion. Also, many of the silent film stars proved unusable due to their lack of stage and voice training. In haste, Hollywood ventured to the New York stage to acquire new names who could overcome these obstacles. Names like Paul Muni, Spencer Tracy, James Cagney, and others were to become superstars almost overnight with their new "delivery" of machine gun-like dialogue.

One of these stage stars, who achieved immediate stardom due to his performance in *Little Caesar*, was Edward G. Robinson. A thorough

Five Star Final (1931) Gladys Lloyd a.k.a. Mrs. Edward G. Robinson is cast as Miss Edwards, secretary to newspaper owner, Hinchecliffe (Oscar Apfel). Miss Lloyd appeared in other films starring her husband, such as Smart Money, The Hatchet Man and Two Seconds. (RF)

professional, whose pronounced delivery has become a favorite of T.V. impressionists, Robinson had earned a vast following regardless of his short stature (5' 5") and his bulldog features. Always attempting to veer away from the gangster roles, which made him famous, he has completely verified the fact that he was a most gifted performer. Just two films after *Little Caesar*, Robinson was awarded the lead in *Five Star Final*, an excellent play by Louis Weitzenkorn, and the rights to which First National had purchased following its final run.

Although the film still bears some of the stodginess, evident in many early talkies (such as bad or stiff performances by the second leads), it is Robinson's film all the way. The pungent verbal exchange in the closing sequence, wherein Randall (Robinson) lashes out at his superiors, is beautifully written. Just listening to this scene is justification enough to prove how our screenwriters of today have fallen to a new low with every other word being some four-letter expletive!

If nothing else to recommend it, *Five Star Final* was a product of its day, a social indictment against "yellow journalism", much like *The Front*

Page (1931), *Blessed Event* (1932), and *Hi Nellie!* (1934), but with much heavier social undertones. As was mentioned before, the acting supplied by the second leads is, by today's standards, laughable. However, there are some good performances by newcomers Aline MacMahon and Boris Karloff. MacMahon, in her first film role, is excellent as Robinson's lovestruck secretary Miss Taylor, while Karloff proves what a first-rate character actor he could have been had it not been for his typecasting in horror films. His portrayal of the slimy reporter who had been kicked out of divinity school because he was once involved in some sort of sex scandal, remains one of Karloff's best pre-*Frankenstein* roles. George E. Stone, Ona Munson, and Oscar Apfel all deserve a passing nod of approval for their performances also. As a further note, the role of Miss Edwards is played by Gladys Lloyd, who was Mrs. Edward G. Robinson!

When *Five Star Final* was released, it received a tremendous reception. Mordant Hall of *The New York Times* relayed, "it is a picture which in the matter of production and acting takes its place beside the film of *Front Page*...With a big cigar in the corner of his mouth most of the time, Edward G. Robinson as Randall, the editor of the New York Gazette, makes the most of every line." So popular was this film critically and financially that the Academy of Motion Pictures Arts and Sciences nominated it for Best Picture of 1931-32. However, the much larger scaled *Grand Hotel* received that honor.

Years later, Edward G. Robinson would reflect, "I loved Randall because he wasn't a gangster. I suspect he was conceived as an Anglo-Saxon. To look at me nobody would believe it, but I enjoyed doing him. He made sense, and thus I'm able to say that *Five Star Final* is one of my favorite films."

Apparently it must have been one of Warner Bros./First National's favorites too, for it was remade as a Humphrey Bogart vehicle entitled *Two Against the World* in 1936. A passable little "B" entry, it changed the setting from a newspaper office to a radio station.

Palmy Days (1931)

United Artists Release. A Samuel Goldwyn Production. Directed by A. Edward Sutherland. Screenplay by David Freedman, Morrie Ryskind, Keene Thompson, and Eddie Cantor. Photography by Gregg Toland. Edited by Sherman Todd. Dances and Ensembles by Busby Berkeley. Art Direction by Richard Day and Willy Pogany. Costumes by Alice O'Neill. Sound by Vinton Vernon. Music and Lyrics by Benny Davis and Eddie Cantor. Musical Direction by Alfred Newman. 77 min.

Cast: Eddie Cantor (Eddie Simpson), Charlotte Greenwood (Helen Martin), Barbara Weeks (Joan Clark), Spencer Charters (Mr. Clark), Paul Page (Steve), Charles Middleton (Yolando), George Raft and Harry Woods (Yolando's Henchmen), Sam Lufkin (Detective), Eddie Dillon (Cop), Arthur Hoyt (Bit), Georgia Coleman, Ruth Eddings, Betty Grable, Olive Hatch, Betty Stockton, Loretta Andrews, Edna Callaghan, Nadine Dore, Virginia Grey, Amo Ingraham, Jean Lenivich, Betty Lorraine, Neva Lynn, Nancy Nash, Fay Pierre, Nita Pike, Betty Slocum, Hyca Slocum, Dorothy White, Toby Wing, and Hazel Witter.

SAUCER-EYED COMEDIAN EDDIE CANTOR (1892–1964) was one of the true legends of show business, appearing in almost every facet of the entertainment industry, from stage and radio to movies and television. His remarkable success as an entertainer dates back to his days as a singing waiter in Florence Ziegfeld's "Follies" on New York's Broadway stage, which culminated with a Hollywood contract. Unfortunately his first two films, *Kid Boots* (1926) and *Special Delivery* (1927), were silents and never quite captured the Cantor magic. Luckily, talkies arrived soon after, with Eddie landing a one-picture deal with producer Samuel Goldwyn for the lavish comedy musical based on Cantor's recent stage success, *Whoopee!* (1930). Filmed in the early two-strip Technicolor process, the film, although rather primitive in nature, was a tremendous hit and

Palmy Days (1931) Meek Eddie Simpson (Eddie Cantor) is being romanced by fitness expert Helen Martin (Charlotte Greenwood). (RF)

Goldwyn immediately put Eddie under contract. The releases that followed not only capitalized on Eddie Cantor's unique brand of comedic song and dance, but also featured some outstanding "all talking and all singing" production numbers from the up-and-coming genius choreographer, Busby Berkeley.

His very next movie, *Palmy Days*, made two years before the tightening of the production code, is a risqué little comedy set in a super art-deco bakery, where all the employees are scantily-clad young lovelies who wait on (and flirt) with their customers in the cafeteria. These young chorines, billed as "The Goldwyn Girls", were sort of an answer to Mack Sennett's "Famous Bathing Beauties", with many of the alumni to become future stars, like Betty Grable (seen here), Lucille Ball, Virginia Bruce, and Paulette Goddard. Also on hand is high-stepping comedienne Charlotte Greenwood, cast as a physical culturalist whose main duty is keeping the female employees in top condition, exercising to the catchy tune "Bend Down, Sister", with all the young ladies bending down toward the camera in medium-shot, exposing rather ample cleavage! Of course, Eddie gets to sing two excellent songs: "There's Nothing Too Good for My Baby" in blackface (in doing this, he was paying homage to black entertainers from that era) and "Yes, Yes!"

The comedy, in general, is quite funny, with Eddie, who can make even the oldest joke seem fresh, displaying his expert timing, as well as

Palmy Days (1931) Failing to arouse the inner passions of Eddie Simpson (Eddie Cantor), Helen Martin (Charlotte Greenwood) resorts to imitating Marlene Dietrich singing Falling in Love Again.

Palmy Days (1931) The Goldwyn Girls performing the unforgettable Bend Down, Sister number. (RF)

his boundless energy. Director Edward Sutherland, a veteran of silent comedies and talkies, was a good choice for *Palmy Days*. His credits date back to the twenties, when he was assistant director for Charles Chaplin's *A Woman of Paris* in 1923. Later, he joined W. C. Fields and guided the irascible comedian through a few good vehicles including *International House* (1933) and *Poppy* (1936). He even turned out one for Laurel and Hardy (*The Flying Deuces*), as well as Abbott and Costello's screen debut, *One Night in the Tropics* (1940).

Two supporting players in *Palmy Days* who are put to good use playing the villains are future star George Raft and supporting player Charles Middleton. Raft, cast here as a strong-arm, was only a year away from capturing the public's attention as the coin-flipping Gino Renaldo in the Howard Hughes/Howard Hawks classic gangster prohibition-era saga *Scarface*. Charles Middleton, who appeared in more films than one could count, achieved his greatest success for his portrayal of Ming the Merciless in the very famous *Flash Gordon* serials of the late 1930s!

The Tip-off (1931)

An RKO-Pathe Picture. Produced by Charles R. Rogers. Directed by Albert Rogell. Associate Producer: Harry Joe Brown. Screenplay by Earl Baldwin. Based on an original story by George Kibbe Turner. Dialogue Direction by Ralph Murphy. Photography by Edward Snyder. Art Direction by Carroll Clark. Edited by Charles Craft. Sound by Charles O'Loughlin and T. Carman. Musical Direction by Arthur Lange. Costumes by Gwen Wakeling. Assistant Director: E. J. Babille. 75 min.

Cast: Eddie Quillan (Tommy), Robert Armstrong (Kayo McClure), Ginger Rogers (Baby Face), Joan Peers (Edna), Ralf Harolde (Nick Vatelli), Charles Sellon (Pop Jackson), Mike Donlin (Swanky), Ernie Adams (Slug), Jack Herrick (Joe), Cupid Ainsworth (Miss Waddums), Frank Darien (Edna's Uncle), Luis Alberni (Roadhouse Manager), Ivan Linow (Kayo's Sparring Partner), Dorothy Granger (Hatcheck Girl), John Quillan, Tommy Jordan, Edna Moreno, and Swanky Jones (Bit Parts).

RARELY SEEN TODAY, and interesting only as a curio for Ginger Rogers fans, who can get an early glimpse of her extraordinary talent at displaying a comedic tough gal, *The Tip-Off* is nothing more than harmless film fare. This was Miss Rogers' sixth appearance in a feature length picture after being cast in four shorts for Paramount Pictures, following a long-term contract with RKO-Pathe. It was there that she acquired superstardom when she was teamed opposite Fred Astaire in *Flying Down to Rio* in 1933. Third billed in *The Tip-Off*, she virtually holds her own, even though she is cast opposite such veteran scene-stealers as Eddie Quillan and Robert Armstrong.

Quillan, an ex-vaudevillian on stage with his family since the age of seven, was the twenties and thirties' facsimile of youth and energy. Possessing an expressive face with prominent eyeballs and an ever-present smile, he was usually cast as the typical boy-next-door, always winning

The Tip-Off (1931) Tommy Jordan (Eddie Quillan) dances with Edna Moreno (Joan Peers), the girlfriend of mobster, Nick Vatelli. (AB)

the heroine at the close of every film he appeared in. Beginning in Hollywood under the aegis of the legendary Mack Sennett, Quillan was to grind out a considerable number of short subjects, such as *A Love Sundae*, *Her Actor Friend* (both 1926), *The Plumber's Daughter*, *College Kiddo*, and *Love in a Police Station* (all 1927), before branching into features at the close of the silent era. Later, when his type of character became passé, he was to become a leading character actor, appearing in many major motion pictures. Some of his most memorable performances were as the ill-fated mutineer Ellison in Frank Lloyd's *Mutiny on the Bounty* (1935) and wife deserter Connie Rivers in John Ford's *The Grapes of Wrath* (1940). He also became a familiar face on television in the sixties and seventies, appearing in shows like "Little House on the Prairie" and "Baretta."

Another busy character actor who is featured in *The Tip-Off* is Robert Armstrong, the man who made Carl Denham a household name in the horror classic *King Kong* (1933). Armstrong, whose ambitions rose above his means as an actor, studied law at the University of Washington before entering vaudeville, when he couldn't find jobs as a lawyer. Beginning in films in 1927, Armstrong was soon to become one of Hollywood's busiest character actors, playing leads, second leads, good-bad guys, comic sidekicks, and just about anything a script would call for. Some of his better roles can be found in *The Most Dangerous Game* (1932), *Son of Kong*

The Tip-Off (1931) Radio repairman Tommy Jordan (Eddie Quillan) gets more than he bargained for when he winds up hiding under the bed in Baby Face's (Ginger Rogers) boudoir just as her boyfriend, prizefighter "Kayo" McClure is about to enter the room. (AB)

(1933), and *G-Men* (1935). After working in almost every type of film, including low-budget second features and serials, Armstrong also found himself a reliable character actor in the television medium. He retired in the early 1960s and passed away in 1973 at the age of eighty-three.

The Tip-Off was directed by Albert Rogell, a specialist in second features and programmers, who enjoyed a relatively successful career, while never joining the ranks of the big-time directors. It's too bad, for in this film, he does a commendable job of adapting this clever little gangster spoof by Earl Baldwin into a fast-paced, although not entirely credible mixture of low-comedy and excitement. Released in the U.K. under the rather bland title of *Looking for Trouble*, its working title in the U.S. was first *Eddie Cuts In*, then changed to *The Lady Killer*, before settling on *The Tip-Off*. Critics pointed out Ginger Rogers' rather saucy character with praise, and stated that her repartee with the dim-witted Robert Armstrong was extremely funny.

The Unholy Garden (1931)

United Artists Corporation. Produced by Samuel Goldwyn. Directed by George Fitzmaurice. Screenplay by Ben Hecht and Charles MacArthur. Photography by George S. Barnes. Music by Alfred Newman. Art Direction by Richard Day and Willy Pogany. Edited by Grant Whytock. Sound by Frank Grenzback. 74 min.

Cast: Ronald Colman (Barrington Hunt), Fay Wray (Camille de Jonghe), Estelle Taylor (Hon. Mrs. Elize Mowbry), Warren Hymer (Smiley Corbin), Tully Marshall (Baron Louis de Jonghe), Lawrence Grant (Dr. Shayne), Ullrich Haupt (Colonel von Axt), Kit Guard (Kid Twist), Henry Armetta (Nick-the-Goose), Lucille LaVerne Mme. Lucie Villars), Mischa Auer (Prince Nicolai Poliakoff), Henry Kolker (Police Inspector), Charles H. Mailes (Alfred de Jonghe), Morgan Wallace (Captain Kruger), Arnold Korff (Louis Lautrac), Nadja (Native Dancer), Wilhelm von Brincken and A. E. Anson (Bit Parts).

A DEFINITE PREDECESSOR to *Algiers* released seven years later, *The Unholy Garden* is a film that should have been much better than it actually was. Despite a top named star, a good director, and one of the best writing teams in the industry, the film is nothing more than a rather tepid exercise in romance and foreign intrigue. It does, however, hold an audience's interest with its sardonic touches of black humor, delivered perfectly by one of the biggest stars of the early thirties, Ronald Colman, whose Pre-Code films produced by Samuel Goldwyn were all huge moneymakers at the box office.

Unfortunately, *The Unholy Garden* was considered a "bread and butter" picture for its producer and star, and was sandwiched between two of Colman's biggest successes, *The Devil to Pay* (1930) and *Arrowsmith* (1931). The haste in which the production was put together sadly shows in that it was hampered by bad production values, and a script which was,

56

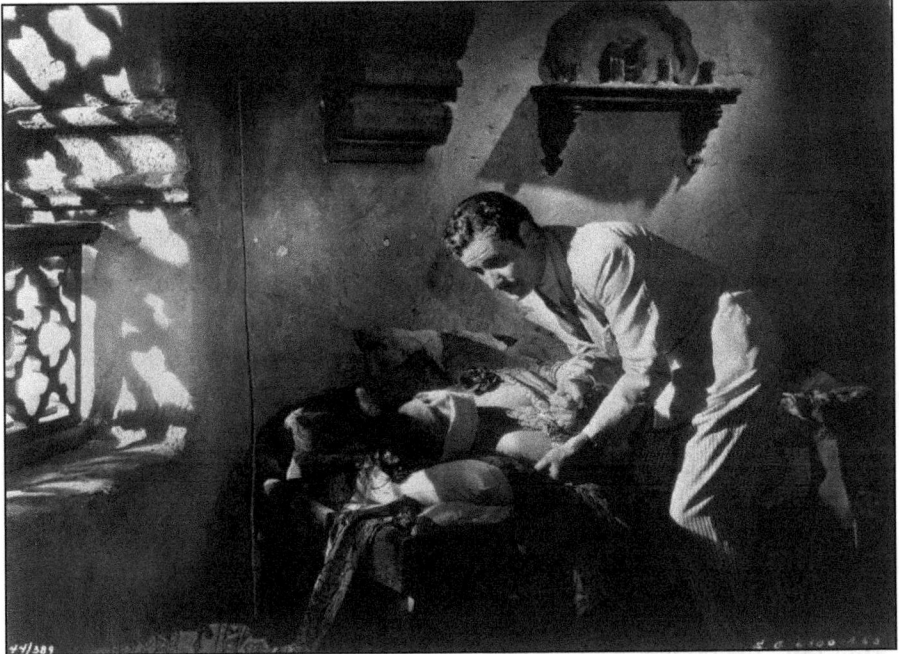

The Unholy Garden (1931) Wanted criminal, Barrington Hunt (Ronald Colman) binds and gags Eliza Mowbray (Estelle Taylor) with the intention of stealing her car to escape. (RF)]

in screenwriter Ben Hecht's words, "dictated in one evening." Many feel that Hecht and Charles MacArthur relegated the assignment to subordinates because they were still working under tremendous pressure trying to finish their script for the Howard Hawks/Howard Hughes production of *Scarface* with Paul Muni. When producer Sam Goldwyn read the finished screenplay, he was horrified, but was unable to call for rewrites because the picture was already in production. In spite of expressing total displeasure with the script, Ronald Colman would continue to act totally professionally on the set, arriving fully prepared and devoid of any animosity. Playing a gentleman thief was right up Colman's alley, in that he had already portrayed some rather charming reprobates in *Raffles* (1930) and other similar ventures. Luckily, Colman turns in a rather effortless, light-hearted acting job, and outshines his rather wooden female lead Fay Wray, reminding the viewer of how bad an actress she really was at this stage in her career!

However, there are some high points throughout. Actress Estelle Taylor (the wife of boxing champ, Jack Dempsey) plays a vamp named Elise, turning in a rather fiery performance in which she attempts to seduce con man Barrington Hunt, as a means to a share in his proposed riches. Of course, Elise is rejected (big time), with Hunt's affection veering toward the direction of innocent Camille (Fay Wray).

The director of *The Unholy Garden* was George Fitzmaurice, who was working with his star for the eighth and last time in his career. Born in Paris in 1895, Fitzmaurice began as a painter-turned-set designer and steadily graduated to screenwriting as early as 1908. In 1914, he tried his hand at directing and churned out some rather commercially successful entries like *Son of the Sheik* (1926), with Rudolph Valentino, *Mata Hari* (1932), with Greta Garbo, and *Suzy* (1935), with Jean Harlow and Cary Grant. Although he had a flair for comedy, most of his films were considered romantic dramas.

When *The Unholy Garden* premiered at the Rialto Theatre in New York City on October 28, 1931, it did manage to garner some positive response, with one reviewer claiming that it was a "thoroughly enjoyable packet of fun and excitement." Sadly, many didn't agree positively and the film died a rather slow death. As for Ronald Colman, he decided to "wait out" his obligatory contract for two more years with the Goldwyn Company until he could take the "free agent" route, which would lead, creatively, to his biggest pictures, such as *A Tale of Two Cities* (1935), *Lost Horizon*, and *The Prisoner of Zenda* (both 1937).

Platinum Blonde (1931)

A Columbia Picture. Produced and Directed by Frank R. Capra. Executive Producer: Harry Cohn. Story by Harry E. Chandler and Douglas W. Churchill. Dialogue by Robert Riskin. Screenplay by Jo Swerling. Continuity by Dorothy Howell. Photography by Joseph Walker. Art Direction by Stephen Gooson. Edited by Gene Milford. Sound by Edward Bernds. Technical Director: Edward Shulter. Assistant Director: C. C. Coleman. 90 min.

Cast: Loretta Young (Gallagher), Robert Williams (Stew Smith), Jean Harlow (Ann Schuyler), Halliwell Hobbes (Smythe, the butler), Reginald Owen (Dexter Grayson), Edmund Breese (Conroy, the editor), Donald Dillaway (Michael Schuyler), Walter Catlett (Bingy Baker), Claude Allister (Dawson, the valet), Louise Closser Hale (Mrs. Schuyler), Bill Elliot (Dinner Guest), Harry Semels (waiter), Olaf Hytten (Radcliffe), Tom London, Hal Price, Frank Holliday, Eddy Chandler, Charles Jordan (Reporters), Richard Cramer (Speakeasy Proprietor), Wilson Benge (Butler).

WHILE MOST PEOPLE only remember the classic films of Frank Capra like *Mr. Deeds Goes to Town* (1936), *Mr. Smith Goes to Washington* (1939), and *It's a Wonderful Life* (1946), few can recall his earlier films prior to his first big box-office and critical success *It Happened One Night* (1934). Although definitely not as ambitious as his late thirties entries, these Pre-Code ventures mustn't go unnoticed. Films like *The Miracle Woman* (1931), *American Madness* (1932), and especially *Platinum Blonde* still hold up incredibly well today. The secret behind the film's success not only must go to the expert touch of Frank Capra, but also the superb screenplay by Jo Swerling and the snappy dialogue by Capra's soon-to-be favorite screenwriter, Robert Riskin. Loretta Young, who was on loan from Warner Bros., is her usual lovely self, cast here as the lovelorn reporter Gallagher, whose infatuation with fellow newspaper reporter Stew Smith

Platinum Blonde (1931) Rival newspaperman, Bingy (Walter Catlett) takes one "on the chin" from Stew Smith (Robert Williams) as the butler (Halliwell Hobbes) breaks his fall. (RF)

is shattered by his marriage to a platinum blonde, played rather woodenly by newcomer Jean Harlow.

According to Capra, Harlow, who up to this time had never been considered much of an actress (he had the darndest time teaching her to pronounce "library" correctly), was always willing to learn her craft, reporting to the set early to go over the day's script and basically to observe the more seasoned actors. Capra also recalled that she wasn't very popular with Loretta Young, who felt that Harlow was given too much publicity as Hollywood's new sex symbol (she was already appearing on many magazine covers), causing resentment from the other actors. Even though Harlow would not achieve superstardom for another year, Platinum Blonde Clubs sprang up in over one hundred cities, and women not only began bleaching their hair, but copied Jean's make-up, clothing, and speech as well!

The male lead for *Platinum Blonde*, Robert Williams, was a relative newcomer to pictures. A sort of cross between Lee Tracy and Lynne Overman, this was Williams' first starring role, having appeared in only three films prior to this in supporting categories. When viewed today, audiences are completed captivated by Robert Williams' performance, which prompts the question, "Whatever became of...?" Sadly, *Platinum Blonde* was the last film in the very short career of this unjustly forgotten actor, who died shortly after the film's release on November 3, 1931, following surgery after a burst appendix. Frank Capra often spoke highly of his "new discovery," further stating that, "he could have been as big (or bigger) than Gable, Bogart, or Cagney!"

The film did brisk business for Columbia Pictures, giving Harry Cohn's little poverty-row studio an added boost toward achieving major status in a matter of a few years! Richard Watts of the *New York Herald Tribune* cited, "it is a colorful, fast and snappy story for the most part which awaits you at the Strand, and it is well acted by Robert Williams in the hero's role... Miss Harlow, as the society girl, is competent but not much more, while Loretta Young seems better than usual as the newspaper girl."

Blonde Crazy (1931)

Warner Bros. and Vitaphone Pictures. Directed by Roy Del Ruth. Screenplay by Kubec Glasmon and John Bright. Based on an original story by Kubec Glasmon and John Bright. Photography by Sid Hickox. Edited by Ralph Dawson. Musical Direction by Leo F. Forbstein. Make-up by Perc Westmore. Songs: "When Your Lover Has Gone" by E. A. Swan. "I Can't Write the Words" by Gerald Marks and Buddy Fields. "Ain't That the Way It Goes?" by Roy Turk and Fred Ahlert. "I'm Just a Fool in Love With You" by Sidney Mitchell, Archie Gottler and George W. Meyer. 79 min.

Cast: James Cagney (Bert Harris), Joan Blondell (Ann Roberts), Louis Calhern ('Dapper Dan' Barker), Noel Francis (Helen Wilson), Guy Kibbee (A. Rupert Johnson, Jr.), Raymond Milland (Joe Reynolds), Polly Walters (Peggy), Charles Levison/Lane (Four Eyes, Desk Clerk), William Burress (Colonel Bellock), Peter Erkelenz (Dutch), Maude Eburne (Mrs. Snyder), Walter Percival (Lee), Nat Pendleton (Hank), Russell Hopton (Jerry), Richard Cramer (Cabbie), Wade Boteler (Detective), Ray Cooke, Edward Morgan (Bellhops), Phil Sleman (Conman).

AFTER JAMES CAGNEY'S star-making performance in Warner Bros.' *The Public Enemy*, he was assured of subsequent starring vehicles. His next film, *Smart Money* (1931), was yet another gangster-era saga in which he was teamed with the multi-talented Edward G. Robinson (their only film together), who, like Cagney, was already being typecast as the quintessential tough guy. In order not to be associated with only gangster roles, Cagney fought the "higher-ups" for more diversified parts. As a result, Cagney wound up being cast in several highly entertaining "programmers", such as *Blonde Crazy*, which exploited his vast talents considerably.

    Blonde Crazy, which was released as *Larceny Lane* in Britain, reteamed Jim with his old pal Joan Blondell for already the fourth time! Luckily, the casting department at Warner Bros. recognized the perfect

Blonde Crazy (1931) James Cagney as conman Bert Harris checks out the "goods." (AB)

chemistry between them. As a film, *Blonde Crazy* is a routine melodrama, mixed with comedy and an assortment of wisecracks, handled superbly by its two stars. Like most of Cagney's films between 1931 and 1933, it was made on a meager budget, efficiently produced with absolutely no wasted moments. Its scenarists, Kubec Glasmon and John Bright, are the same duo who wrote the screenplay for *The Public Enemy*, the film responsible for Cagney's meteoric rise to stardom.

Blonde Crazy's director was Roy Del Ruth, a specialist in atmospheric dramas and rough and tumble comedies. A graduate of the Mack Sennett "School of Comedy," his forte was zippy dialogue delivered with rapid-fire assurance, a movie-making formula which Cagney would render to its fullest. Technically, his films never quite rose to "brilliant" due to their low budgets (a distinction among most Warner Bros. productions at the time). However, the scripts, with their snappy dialogue and fast moving action, were attributes evidenced throughout his early "talkie" career. Films like *Bureau of Missing Persons*, *Blessed Event*, *Beauty and the Boss* (all 1932), and *Employees' Entrance*, *The Little Giant* and *Lady Killer* (all 1933), are breathlessly paced, thoroughly enjoyable "programmers" which

Blonde Crazy (1931) Bert Harris (James Cagney) bursts into the bathroom of
Anne Roberts (Joan Blondell). (AB)

seem, despite their age, to improve with the passing years. Unfortunately,
Del Ruth's later films didn't fare as well. Some of his later productions (*The
West Point Story* and *On Moonlight Bay*) are ambitious indeed, but lack
the excellent writing and pacing of his earlier works.

The supporting cast for *Blonde Crazy* is excellent, with Louis Calhern playing his "Dapper Dan" Barker character to the hilt. Ray Milland,
with this being his seventh American screen appearance, plays his typical
"other man" role earnestly (so earnestly in fact that it took studio executives years to cast him in anything but).

Time Magazine wrote: "A chipper, hardboiled, amusing essay on pet-
ty thievery. In his first starring performance [actually it was his second],
James Cagney has a role in which he is more mischievous than wicked.
He makes rascality seem both easy and attractive as he did in *The Public
Enemy* and *Smart Money.*"

Dr. Jekyll and Mr. Hyde (1931)

A Paramount Picture. Directed by Rouben Mamoulian. Based on the Robert Louis Stevenson story. Adaptation and Dialogue by Samuel Hoffenstein and Percy Heath. Assistant Director: Bob Lee. Art Direction by Hans Dreier. Costume Designs by Travis Banton. Photography by Karl Struss. Edited by William Shea. Sound by Martin Paggi. 98 min. Reissued at 82 min.

Cast: Fredric March (Dr. Henry Jekyll/Edward Hyde), Miriam Hopkins (Ivy Pearson) Rose Hobart (Muriel Carew), Holmes Herbert (Dr. Lanyon), Halliwell Hobbs (Brig. General Sir Danvers Carew), Edgar Norton (Poole, Jekyll's Butler), Arnold Lucy (Utterson), Colonel MacDonald (Hobson, Carew's Butler), Tempe Pigott (Mrs. Hawkins), Eric Wilton (Briggs, Lanyon's Butler), Douglas Walton (Student), John Rogers (Waiter), Murdock MacQuarrie (Doctor), Major Sam Harris (Dance Extra). Robert Louis Stevenson, a nephew of the author, also has a bit role.

ROBERT LOUIS STEVENSON'S 1885 CLASSIC has been transferred to the screen no less than a dozen times, most notably in 1920 with John Barrymore, in 1941 with Spencer Tracy, and of course this 1931 version with Fredric March as the good doctor whose experiments lead to his eventual downfall. March, an extremely disciplined and versatile performer, proves nothing less than brilliant in his portrayal of the sympathetic and sexually frustrated Dr. Henry Jekyll and his simian-like alter ego Mr. Hyde. Not only did his considerable skills earn him an Oscar for Best Actor (tying with Wallace Beery for *The Champ*), but some critics have declared it as one of the best performances of the decade!

Miriam Hopkins, whose Ivy Pearson is also a standout, is incredible as the prostitute who is abused, beaten, and repeatedly raped by the disgustingly repulsive Hyde. That this is one of her best performances is indeed an understatement. This, which was only her fourth, though important role, was an ultimate avenue to better ones. In less than a year, she was cast in a varied assortment of films, tapping her unfulfilled skills in comedies like Ernst Lubitsch's *Trouble in Paradise* (1932) and *Design for Living* (and the film which aroused the wrath of the Hays Office almost single-handedly, *The Story of Temple Drake*, both 1933).

Stylistically directed by the great Rouben Mamoulian whose first two films, *Applause* (1929) and *City Streets* (1931) were still earning him the plaudits of his contemporaries, this classic still remains the best of all, not only for its content, but for the masterful photography of Karl Struss, whose fluid camera movement and the use of extremely slow optical wipes (giving a paralleled account of two different scenes simultaneously) prove effective. As for March's transformation segments from the kindly Dr. Jekyll to the despicable Mr. Hyde, this was accomplished by applying makeup, which was sensitive to the bright klieg lights and when heated would change from pancake white to an ashen shade.

Dr. Jekyll and Mr. Hyde (1931) A simian-like creature, Edward Hyde (Fredric March) lurks about, terrorizing all of London. (RF)

Rarely seen except in recent years, MGM had shelved the Mamoulian version after purchasing the property from Paramount Pictures for a 1941 remake starring Spencer Tracy. Unfortunately, this 1940's version received a bad rap, especially from Spencer Tracy himself, who claimed that it was his all time worst performance. This is absurd. Viewing it for reappraisal, it does hold up extremely well today, and it remains a credit to Tracy's acting ability that he was able to handle the transformation scenes with a minimum of makeup and still come off quite menacing! It's also further puzzling to note that after Spencer Tracy attended the premier of his version of *Dr. Jekyll and Mr. Hyde*, he phoned his friend Fredric March and reportedly told him that he had just done him a big favor.

Most extant 35mm and 16mm prints of the Mamoulian version of the Stevenson classic are from a late 1930s reissue, drastically trimmed due to the rigid terms of the production code. Despite its truncated length, it has not lost any of its impact when one views the 82 minute reissue. Luckily, for film purists, the complete 98 minute version has been restored and is available on DVD through Warner Bros.

Taxi! (1932)

A Warner Bros. and Vitaphone Picture. Directed by Roy Del Ruth. Screenplay by Kubec Glasmon and John Bright. Based on the play *The Blind Spot* by Kenyon Nicholson. Photography by James Van Trees. Art Direction by Esdras Hartley. Edited by James Gibbons. Musical Direction by Leo F. Forbstein. Make-up by Perc Westmore. 70 min.

Cast: James Cagney (Matt Nolan), Loretta Young (Sue Reilly), George E. Stone (Skeets), Guy Kibbee (Pop Reilly), David Landau (Buck Gerard), Ray Cooke (Danny Nolan), Leila Bennett (Ruby), Dorothy Burgess (Marie Costa), Matt McHugh (Joe Silva), George MacFarlane (Father Nulty), Polly Walters (Polly), Nat Pendleton (Truck Driver), Berton Churchill (Mr. West), George Raft (William Kenny), Hector V. Sarno (Monument Salesman), Aggie Herring (Cleaning Lady), Lee Phelps (Onlooker), Harry Tenbrook (Cabbie), Robert Emmett O'Connor (Cop), Eddie Fetherston and Russ Powell (Dance Judges), Ben Taggart (Cop), and the Cotton Club Orchestra.

JAMES CAGNEY'S FOURTH STARRING VEHICLE following *The Public Enemy*, *Smart Money* and *Blonde Crazy* (all 1931) was *Taxi!* The film had gone through two working titles: *The Blind Spot*, which was the name of the play it was based upon, and then *Taxi, Please!*, before the studio settled on *Taxi!* The excellent script gave Jim a deeper, more emotional depth to his acting, instead of just playing a tough hoodlum. Here, cast as cabbie Matt Nolan, he was even given the chance to do a complete scene in Yiddish, which he had learned growing up listening to his Jewish friends while playing in the streets of Manhattan. The short sequence begins when a man approaches Cagney's taxi and asks, "Du farhtayst Ellis Island?" (Do you understand Ellis Island?) Cagney carries on a complete conversation with the man, while a bewildered cop listens in. The dialogue continues with "Vie vilst du gayn?" (Where do you want to go?)

Taxi! (1932) Matt Nolan (James Cagney) and his buddy "Skeets" (George E. Stone) are skeptical about the "peace" among rival taxicab companies. (RF)

Later, the man, impressed that Cagney speaks his tongue, asks, "Vu den— a Yiddisher yung?" (Of course—a Jewish youth?") Jim responds "Vu den, a shaygetz?" (What else, a Gentile?) By now, the cop is completely puzzled and walks over to Jim's cab and says, "Nolan, what part of Ireland did your folks come from?" and Jim responds with a twinkle in his eye "Delancey Street, denk you!"

For his leading lady, he was cast opposite beautiful, eighteen-year-old Loretta Young, a replacement for Dorothy Mackaill, then Nancy Carroll, and still later, Joan Blondell! Like Cagney, Miss Young's career was also on the rise, and she was already a veteran of motion pictures since she was fourteen, having appeared with the likes of Lon Chaney in *Laugh, Clown, Laugh* (1928), Ronald Colman in *The Devil to Pay* (1930), Jean Harlow in *Platinum Blonde* (1931), among others. Now, she was part of the Warner Bros./First National star roster, where she would become an important leading lady in many of the studio's best 'Pre-Code' entries, including *Big Business Girl* (1931), *They Call it Sin* (1932), and *Employees' Entrance* (1933). Later, she would leave Warners with producer Darryl F. Zanuck when he formed his new production company, 20th Century

Pictures, where she was given carte blanche, since she was one of the only female stars under contract to the new studio.

Since *Taxi!* was a movie about taxi warfare among competing companies, there would obviously be some driving involved by some of the stars. Studio head Jack Warner found, to his bitter disappointment, that his leading man never drove a car in his life, leaving Cagney to scramble for much-needed driving lessons from his wife, as well as family friend, Joan Blondell. After a few weeks, Jim was managing to operate the controls of the taxicab assuredly, and the scenes were filmed without any accidents, although Cagney would shy away from driving most of his life, leaving that responsibility to his spouse.

One thing that James Cagney always denied throughout his life was that he ever uttered the famous line, "You dirty rat" in any movie. Throughout the years, many impressionists and mimics on television and the nightclub circuits have always misquoted him. In *Taxi!*, he comes the closest to uttering it as he is about to empty his .45 caliber into the villain of the picture. "Come out and take it, you dirty, yellow-bellied rat, or I'll give it to you through the door!" is the actual line. A similar fate occurred with the 1942 classic *Casablanca*, where Humphrey Bogart orders Dooley Wilson (Sam) to "Play it!" not "Play it again, Sam."

Critics were totally appreciative of *Taxi!*, and *Time* magazine exclaimed, "If you have seen *The Public Enemy*, *Smart Money*, or *Blonde Crazy*, you have some idea of what to expect of *Taxi!* Authors Kubec Glasmon and John Bright are camera-minded writers and their stories, which usually deal in an offhand way with violent happenings, have speed, vigor and assurance. Fortunately for all concerned, James Cagney attracted Hollywood's attention at about the same time as authors Bright and Glasmon. When he appears in one of their inventions the result is often brilliantly successful...*Taxi!* is a sordid but amusing observation on minor endeavors." Another thing to look for in the picture is an early glimpse of future tough guy star, George Raft, as a dance contest contestant who gets into a scuffle with Jim. Also, the sequence where Jim and Loretta go to the movies with George E. Stone and Leila Bennett on a double date, Stone points out a film that is being exhibited in the front of the theatre called *The Mad Genius* with John Barrymore, to which Miss Bennett responds that she prefers Joe E. Brown. Of course both Barrymore and Brown were Warners contract players, and here they not only promote one of their own products, but the foursome goes inside to view *Side Show,* (a Warners release) which starred Evelyn Knapp and Donald Cook!

This Reckless Age (1932)

A Paramount Picture. Directed by Frank Tuttle. Based on the play *The Goose Hangs High* by Lewis Beach. Screenplay by Joseph Mankiewicz. Adaptation by Frank Tuttle. Photography by Henry Sharp. Music by John Leipold. Sound Recording by Frank Goodwin. 76 min.

Cast: Charles "Buddy" Rogers (Bradley Ingals), Richard Bennett (Donald Ingals), Peggy Shannon (Mary Burke), Charles Ruggles (Goliath Whitney), Frances Dee (Lois Ingals), Frances Starr (Eunice Ingals), Maude Eburne (Rhoda), Allen Vincent ('Pig' Van Dyke), Mary Carlisle (Cassandra Phelps), David Landau (Matthew Daggett), Reginald Barlow (Lester Bell), George C. Pearce (John Burke), Grady Sutton ('Stepladder' Schultz), Harry Templeton (Monk Turner), Berton Churchill (Bank President), Leonard Carey (Braithwaite).

SIMILAR TO THE 1937 DRAMA *Make Way For Tomorrow* in concept, although certainly not taken as seriously, *This Reckless Age* is one of those pleasant experiences that benefits from solid direction and fine acting from its assorted cast members, including Richard Bennett and Frances Starr as the unappreciated elderly parents of two thoughtless college children. Bennett, a former matinee idol of the stage and father of daughters Constance, Barbara, and Joan by his second wife Adrienne Morrison, is seen at his best as the father who sacrifices everything in order that his children have whatever they desire in the midst of the worst days of the Depression. The children, Charles "Buddy" Rogers and Frances Dee, however are so wrapped up in their own free-spirited lives that they come off as being selfish and unfeeling for the two put-upon parents, whose lives have become so lonely that all they have is each other when their children desert them on Christmas Eve and go out partying all night. Of course, when the father becomes involved in a scandal, it's up to the irresponsible offspring to save the day.

Based on the Lewis Beach play *The Goose Hangs High*, *This Reckless Age* had been adapted into a silent movie once before in 1925 by the Famous Players/Lasky Corporation as a vehicle for Constance Bennett, Myrtle Stedman, George Irving, and Edward Peil, Sr., and directed by James Cruze of *The Covered Wagon* fame. Sadly, the silent version is not available for reevaluation and the remake has not been shown in decades, not since MCA held the television rights up until the 1970s when it was bought out by Universal. Even then, the film received scant distribution and was barely seen even on a late night broadcast.

Director Frank Tuttle, who took up acting and directing while in college, worked as an assistant editor for *Vanity Fair* before he began writing screenplays for Paramount Pictures in the 1920s. It was soon afterward that he turned to directing many minor, but extremely entertaining films throughout the thirties and forties, most notably *This Is the Night*, which was Cary Grant's first appearance in a feature picture, *The Big Broadcast* (both 1932), *Roman Scandals* (1933), *The Glass Key* (1935), as well as the superb film noir which introduced Alan Ladd to movie audiences, *This Gun For Hire* (1942).

Intended as a "B" picture, since most of the cast were no longer big-name stars and its running time was a mere seventy-six minutes, *This Reckless Age* did occasionally play on the top half of the double bill in some areas where Buddy Rogers' name was still a box-office draw. Rogers, whose film career skyrocketed after he was cast in the Oscar-winning World War I drama *Wings* in 1927, the first year of the Academy of Motion Pictures Arts and Sciences, became a familiar face throughout the late twenties. His boyish, good looks benefited him greatly, resulting in some excellent roles, especially when Mary Pickford cast him opposite her as her love interest in one of her top later vehicles, *My Best Girl* (1927). According to Rogers in later years, he had immediately found himself smitten with his co-star, who was eleven years older than he. In 1936, when Miss Pickford and Douglas Fairbanks—considered the most perfectly matched married couple in the world—divorced, Rogers and Pickford began dating, later married and remained a devoted couple until Pickford's death in 1979.

Frances Dee, who plays the mischievously impish Lois Ingals, began her Hollywood career as an extra in 1929 and within a year found herself cast opposite Maurice Chevalier in *Playboy of Paris*. Soon, she was on a roll, where she was usually cast as nice girls next door in films like *An American Tragedy* (1931) and *The Night of June 13* (1932). Better parts

This Reckless Age (1932) Goliath Whitney (Charles Ruggles, second from right) accidentally sprays himself with insect repellent while Donald Ingals (Richard Bennett), his wife, Eunice (Frances Starr), cook Rhoda (Maude Eburne) and their daughter, Lois (Frances Dee) are amused. (RF)

followed, like *Little Women* (1933), *The Gay Deception* (1935), where she ventured successfully into romantic comedy, and *If I Were King* (1938), where she was cast opposite Ronald Colman, who played the part of French poet Francois Villon to perfection. One of her most offbeat roles came in the outrageous 1933 crime drama, *Blood Money*, where she portrayed a spoiled rich nymphomaniac opposite George Bancroft. A year earlier, she had married actor Joel McCrea and later she preferred to stay home and raise their three sons rather than pursue her acting career on a full-time basis. That marriage would last until McCrea's death in 1990.

Panama Flo (1932)

RKO-Pathe Pictures. A Charles R. Rogers Production. Associate Producer: Harry Joe Brown. Directed by Ralph Murphy. Story and Screenplay by Garrett Ford. Photography by Arthur C. Miller. Edited by Edward Shroeder. Art Direction by Carroll Clark. Music by Harold Lewis. Costume Design by Gwenn Wakeling. Sound by Buddy Myers. Musical Direction by Arthur Lange. 73 min.

Cast: Helen Twelvetrees (Flo), Robert Armstrong (Babe), Charles Bickford (McTeague), Marjorie Peterson (Pearl), Maude Eburne (Sadie), Paul Hurst (Al), Reina Velez (Chacra), Hans Joby (Pilot), Ernie Adams (Jake/ Speakeasy Doorman), Willie Fung (Bartender), Harry Tenbrook (Bartender), Fred Warren (Piano Player).

TO MODERN AUDIENCES the name Helen Twelvetrees bears no real significance, totally forgotten by all except for the few who have been lucky enough to see her pictures. Helen was to RKO-Pathe what Sylvia Sidney was to Paramount, the sad-eyed ingénue who could produce more tears in the course of a movie's running time than the Johnstown flood! Unfortunately, Ms. Twelvetrees' popularity lasted a mere three years, not due to any lack of talent on her part, but because the studio cast her in some good, yet never outstanding roles. None of her films ever attained classic status (no fault of her own) but had she acquired better scripts with first-rate directors and higher budgets, today we would be celebrating this wonderful actress' acting skills rather than allowing her memory to descend into oblivion.

Panama Flo, although a totally 'forgotten film,' is an atypical entry in her filmography, with Helen cast as Flo, a woman of questionable morals who works as a dancer in a clip joint (another term for a house of 'ill repute') run by Sadie (Maude Eburne), a grotesque characterization which would become a specialty of hers in films like *The Bat Whispers* (1930) and *Ladies They Talk About* (1933). When Sadie informs her "girls" that she can no longer pay them their "salaries," she offers them her place to "trim some rich suckers." With nowhere to go, Flo meets up with McTeague (Charles Bickford), a hard-fighting, hard-drinking oilman, who soon becomes one of Flo's victims. Catching on to her device when she tries to "slip him a Mickey," McTeague forces her to go to South America with him while he works his oil fields and become his housekeeper (a.k.a. sex slave). Sound like a perfect scenario for a steamy "Pre-Code" drama? You can bet on it!

Ralph Murphy, dialogue director on another Helen Twelvetrees film, *Young Bride* (1932), directed *Panama Flo*. Born in Rockville, Connecticut in 1895, Murphy is equally forgotten. He started his career as a stage actor of moderate success before entering films in the early twenties, first as a dialogue coach and then as a screenwriter. Having graduated to the position of director, his films were generally low-budget "B" pictures or "programmers". Some more interesting efforts throughout his career included *Golden Harvest* (1933), *Private Scandal* (1934), *Men Without Names* (1935), and the much later *The Town Went Wild* (1944).

Released on January 29, 1932 during the height of the Great Depression, *Panama Flo*, whose working title was *The Second Shot*, received less

Panama Flo (1932) Prostitute Flo (Helen Twelvetrees) attempts to slip McTeague (Charles Bickford) a "Mickey" and pick his pockets.

than favorable reviews from critics, and like most RKO-Pathe releases, failed miserably at the box-office. Through the years, however, it has gained a respectable reputation among students of the "Pre-Code" era. One reviewer, Andre Sennewald of *The New York Times*, gave a rather negative, although interesting, account of the film by stating that "the story offers all the coherence and realism of a hasheesh dream, and it managed to confound a startled audience last night right down to the fade-out." And it certainly does exactly that with its surprise twist at the film's conclusion.

Seven years later, RKO Pictures would present this property before the censorship board with the intention of remaking it by changing some of the plot and disinfecting the story line. The result was a sad affair with Lucille Ball and Allan Lane playing the Helen Twelvetrees and Charles Bickford roles, respectively, under the title *Panama Lady*.

Union Depot (1932)

A First National-Vitaphone Picture. Directed by Alfred E. Green. Based on a play by Joe Laurie, Jr., Gene Fowler, and Douglas Durkin. Screenplay by Kenyon Nicholson and Walter DeLeon. Dialogue by Kubec Glasmon and John Bright. Photography by Sol Polito. Edited by Jack Killifer. Art Direction by Jack Okey. Costume Design by Earl Luick. Music by Leo F. Forbstein. 65 min.

Cast: Douglas Fairbanks, Jr. (Chick Miller), Joan Blondell (Ruth Collins), Guy Kibbee (Scrap Iron Scratch), Alan Hale (The Baron), David Landau (Kendall), George Rosener (Dr. Bernardi), Earle Foxe (Jim Parker), Frank McHugh (The Drunk), Adrienne Dore (Sadie), Hooper Atchley (Station Agent), Irving Bacon (Depot Hotel Waiter), Lillian Bond (Actress on Train), Nat Carr (Magazine Counter Clerk), George Chandler (Panhandler), Spencer Charters (Police Officer Bert Brady), Dorothy Christy (Society Woman), Frank Coghlan, Jr. (Ragged Street Urchin), Charles Coleman (Reverend Harvey Pike), Frank Darien (Doctor), Mary Doran (Daisy), Lester Dorr (Sailor), Maude Eburne (Passenger at Information Desk), George Ernest (Eight-Year Old Boy), Willie Fung (Chinese Man), Harrison Greene (Eight-Year Old Boy's Father), Ethel Griffies (Cross Woman at Magazine Stand), Ruth Hall (Welfare Worker's Charge), Otto Hoffman (Station Agent), Robert Emmett Homans (Policeman in Paddy Wagon), Gladden James (Taxi Driver), Eulalie Jensen (Dress Shop Proprietress), Lucille La Verne (Lady with Pipe), Charles Lane (Luggage Checkroom Clerk), John Larkin (Porter), George MacFarlane (Train Caller), Mae Madison (Waitress), Sam McDaniel (Red Cap Train Porter), Claire McDowell (Little Boy's Mother), Walter McGrail (Pickpocket), Dickie Moore (Little Boy), Toshia Mori (Chinese Woman), Franklin Parker (Station Agent), Jack Raymond (Photographer), Cyril Ring (Track 4 Ticket Taker), Jason Robards, Sr. (Station Agent), Virginia Sale (Woman on Platform), Ray Turner (Men's Room Attendant), Polly Walters (Mabel), Huey White (Sailor).

A NEAT, LITTLE COMPACT "programmer", similar in structure to *Grand Hotel*, which was released a mere three months later; *Union Depot* is a fast-paced effort without a minute of screen time wasted. Made during the "Pre-Code" era at Warner Bros., its plot point centers around various characters, all of whom have "skeletons in their closets." Included are Douglas Fairbanks, Jr., a petty thief and pickpocket; Joan Blondell, an

Union Depot (1932) Con man Chick Miller (Douglas Fairbanks, Jr.) hooks up with "hooker" Ruth Collins (Joan Blondell). (AB)

ex-chorus girl, about to turn to "walking the streets" to earn the cost of a meal; Alan Hale, a counterfeiter; Guy Kibbee, a guy "down on his luck", in cahoots with Fairbanks; Frank McHugh, a hopeless drunk; and George Rosener, a crazed sex-fiend who has designs on Joan Blondell! All of their stories are explored in a tight 65 minutes, told in "real time", a device used much later in classic films like *The Set-Up* (1949) and *High Noon* (1952).

Based on an unproduced play by Joe Laurie, Jr., Gene Fowler, and Douglas Durkin, the budget-conscious Warner Bros. bought the movie rights for a song. Apparently, it was just the type of property that Warners enjoyed making; real-life stories that came blasting from the newspaper headlines, and this film was no exception!

Resident director, Alfred Green, whose film credits include other excellent Pre-Code dramas, such as *Smart Money* (1931), *It's Tough to Be Famous* (1932), and the notoriously raunchy *Baby Face* (1933), again utilizes his sure-fire, no-nonsense directorial ability to keep *Union Depot* running smoothly and efficiently. The two leads, Fairbanks and Blondell, are so engaging together that one is rather perplexed that neither of them reached the heights of super stardom.

It's amazing to think that a film like *Union Depot* could never have been made in Hollywood three years later, due to subjects like sex perversion, pre-marital sex and infidelity. One thing the censors insisted upon was that the rather amply-endowed Miss Blondell make sure her breasts be completely covered throughout the film. The reason being that in every Blondell film up to that point she had been involved in scenes where she undressed down to her rather flimsy undergarments, and it was beginning to cause quite a stir throughout the Catholic Church. What did get past the code was the fact that she tries to sell herself for $64, a rather hefty sum for 1932 and something that would have been eliminated later on. Another rather questionable bit of business, which would have been deleted a few years later, was the aspect of Blondell's character being hired to read risqué stories to Dr. Bernardi, whose character is depicted as a sex fiend!

While *Union Depot* initially did rather brisk business at the box-office, interest in it waned when MGM released their star-studded extravaganza *Grand Hotel* in April, using the same format of various characters' lives being intercut in a common locality. Due to the success of *Grand Hotel*, this device was used in many movies to come, such as *Skyscraper Souls* (1932), *China Seas* and *Four Hours to Kill* (both 1935), *Stagecoach* (1939), and many others with varying results. Unfortunately, *Union De-*

pot couldn't have been released at a worse time, for had it been exhibited a year or so earlier, it might have generated far more attention, due to its groundbreaking premise.

Nevertheless, the film did receive good reviews, with Mordant Hall of *The New York Times* describing the film as "raw" and "ingenious", and comparing Douglas Fairbanks to James Cagney, who had made a sensational splash in the movie industry in William Wellman's *The Public Enemy* the year before. He went on to say, "In its hectic action this film recalls *Grand Hotel*."

Note: Around the same time that *Union Depot* was released (January 1932), Warner Bros./First National was experimenting with a new format for displaying the screen credits. The movie would begin with one title card heralding the two leads, the title, and the director credit and then go directly into the movie. At the film's conclusion, 'The End' title would appear, followed by a cast list and the rest of the technical staff. This practice was short-lived but was used in other films such as *Safe in Hell* (1931) and *Taxi!* (1932) before the practice was abandoned.

The Greeks Had a Word for Them (1932)

United Artists/Samuel Goldwyn Release. Produced by Samuel Goldwyn. Directed by Lowell Sherman. Screenplay by Sidney Howard, from a play by Zoe Akins. Photography by George Barnes. Original Music by Alfred Newman. Edited by Stuart Heisler. Sound by Frank Maher. Gowns by Chanel. Reissue Title: *Three Broadway Girls*. 79 min.

Cast: Joan Blondell (Schatzi), Ina Claire (Jean Lawrence), Madge Evans (Polaire), Lowell Sherman (Boris Feldman), David Manners (Dey Emery), Sidney Bracy (The Waiter), Louise Beavers (Maid), Wilson Benge (Butler), Ward Bond (Cab Driver), Charles Coleman (Host), Albert Conti (Prospective Suitor), Betty Grable (Hat Check Girl), Creighton Hale (Servant), Barbara Weeks (Beauty Parlor Employee), Arthur Housman (Drunk), Sam Lufkin (Bartender).

"**THROUGHOUT THE AGES,** half of the women of the world have been working women - - -And the rest of the women have been working men," read the opening titles to this wonderfully racy and ribald comedy about three gold-digging gals who are out to land "sugar daddies." The first one, Joan Blondell (Schatzi) is a worldly, but good-natured individual, whose character acts as a counter-balance to Madge Evans' Polaire, the most innocent of the three, and Ina Claire (Jean), whose one ambition in life is to land a rich millionaire, even if it means double-crossing her two best friends.

The expert direction by Lowell Sherman, who plays the pompously conceited pianist Boris Feldman, is superb, giving him a rare opportunity to shine against scene-stealers Blondell and Claire. Sherman, who was born into a show business family, became an important stage actor in the early years of the 20th century before venturing out to Hollywood and co-starring in dozens of pictures, usually portraying lecherous heels and other assorted bedroom villains. By the early 1930s he grew tired of

81

The Greeks Had a Word for Them (1932) Three gold diggers "on the make"—Ina Claire as Jean Lawrence, Joan Blondell as Schatzi Sutro and Madge Evans as Polaire Quinn. (RF)

acting and graduated to film directing, without completely abandoning his successful career as an actor. Some of his more important works as a director included *What Price Hollywood?* (1932), the very first version of the oft-told Hollywood rags to riches saga *A Star is Born*. Sherman also directed Mae West in her first starring role, as 'Diamond Lil' in *She Done Him Wrong* (1932), and Katharine Hepburn in an excellent starring vehicle for her entitled *Morning Glory* (1933). Sadly, Lowell Sherman died the following year while he was directing the filming of the first three-strip Technicolor feature *Becky Sharp* (1935). Rouben Mamoulian finished the picture and received full director credit.

The Greeks Had a Word for Them was such a huge success that it spawned many imitations, such as the *Gold Digger* series at Warner Bros., and 20th Century Fox's later hits *Moon Over Miami* (1941) and *How to Marry a Millionaire* (1953). The publicity department at United Artists coined the outrageous tagline, "Here's to our men—Long may they give," to promote the picture, which received the plaudits of audiences and

The Greeks Had a Word for Them (1932) The three girls stick together, no matter what…even if it means Jean's (Ina Claire) wedding is broken up by her pals Polaire (Madge Evans) and Schatzi (Joan Blondell). (RF)

critics alike. Variety called it a "Grand rowdy comedy…a revel in femme clothes and a picture calculated to fascinate women. Backwater clienteles questionable."

The sassy screenplay by Sidney Howard, who would later be given the arduous task of writing a worthwhile adaptation for *Gone with the Wind*, proved without a doubt that he deserved his reputation as one of Hollywood's most respected screenwriters. Mr. Howard's life ended tragically in an automobile accident while he was finishing his treatment for Margaret Mitchell's classic civil war novel. Despite having numerous writers on that overwhelming project (including the producer David O. Selznick himself), Sidney Howard received sole screen credit.

Tarzan the Ape Man (1932)

A Metro-Goldwyn-Mayer Picture. Produced by Irving Thalberg. Directed by W. S. Van Dyke. Screenplay by Cyril Hume and Ivor Novello. Based on the character created by Edgar Rice Burroughs. Photography by Harold Rosson and Clyde DeVinna. Edited by Ben Lewis and Tom Held. Art Direction by Cedric Gibbons. Sound by Douglas Shearer. 99 min.

Cast: Johnny Weissmuller (Tarzan), Neil Hamilton (Harry Holt), Maureen O'Sullivan (Jane Parker), C. Aubrey Smith (James Parker), Doris Lloyd (Mrs. Cutten), Forrester Harvey (Beamish), Ivory Williams (Riano).

WHEN EDGAR RICE BURROUGHS first sold the rights to his story *Tarzan of the Apes* to *All-Story Magazine* in 1912 for a mere $700, little did he realize the future earnings potential of his fictional jungle hero. Two years later, his story was published in book form, which proved to be an overwhelming success. Hollywood, knowing a good thing when they "read" it, paid Burroughs for the rights to film a screen version, which was eventually released on January 27, 1918, entitled *Tarzan of the Apes*, and cast brawny Elmo Lincoln donning the loin cloths.

In 1931, Metro-Goldwyn-Mayer was about to unveil their newest release entitled *Trader Horn*, which starred Harry Carey, Edwina Booth, and Duncan Renaldo. Filmed entirely in Africa (a rarity in those days), the studio found that they had an exorbitant surplus of unused footage of native tribes, wild animals, and various safaris. MGM's boy wonder Irving Thalberg thought of utilizing the old African footage by putting it into a new Tarzan picture. Paying Burroughs a handsome figure, Metro secured exclusive film rights for this and any subsequent ventures. Woodbridge (Woody) S. Van Dyke, who had directed *Trader Horn*, was the obvious choice as director of this new Tarzan picture, which promised to be "the biggest, most colossal jungle epic to date." Out of the many hopefuls who were considered for the role of the jungle lord, Van Dyke chose former

Tarzan the Ape Man (1932) James Parker (C. Aubrey Smith), his daughter Jane (Maureen O'Sullivan) and Harry Holt (Neil Hamilton) are about to be plunged into a pit, which houses a giant gorilla and a tribe of native dwarfs. (RF)

Tarzan the Ape Man (1932) Jane Parker (Maureen O'Sullivan) proves that she can handle a rifle with precision. (RF)

Olympic swimmer Johnny Weissmuller over Charles Bickford, who he considered "too old", Johnny Mack Brown ("not tall enough"), Clark Gable ("he has no body"), and Joel McCrea ("never heard of him").

Weissmuller was discovered by scriptwriter Cyril Hume when he was swimming in the hotel pool where they were both staying. After inviting the six-foot-three-inch athlete to meet director Van Dyke, the two men immediately insisted that Weissmuller strip to his shorts. Without even so much as a screen test, Weissmuller was hired on the spot!

For the part of Jane Parker, Van Dyke selected a beautiful young twenty-year-old from Ireland named Maureen O'Sullivan, whose delicate beauty and effortless charm were a direct contrast to the grunts and groans of Mr. Burroughs' "ape man." Here was a perfect teaming of two completely different personalities, and the top brass at MGM knew that they had produced a winner at the box-office! When *Tarzan the Ape Man* was released in March of 1932, it bore little resemblance to the original novel, which told of Tarzan's origin in England. However, some of his

Tarzan the Ape Man (1932) In a deleted scene, hunter James Parker (C. Aubrey Smith) and his daughter Jane (Maureen O'Sullivan) are greeted by a curious group of natives (Elvira and Jenny Lee Snow, both of whom were featured as "Zip" and "Pip" in Tod Browning's *Freaks*). (RF)

Tarzan the Ape Man (1932) W. S. "Woody" Van Dyke directing Maureen O'Sullivan and Johnny Weissmuller. (RF)

background is fleetingly mentioned seven years later in the fourth entry of the series, *Tarzan Finds a Son!* (1939).

Coming in at just under a million dollars, *Tarzan the Ape Man* was voted as one of the top ten moneymakers of 1932, ranking alongside other blockbusters like *Mata Hari*, *Grand Hotel*, *Arrowsmith*, and *Dr. Jekyll and Mr. Hyde*. So pleased with their newest success, MGM promised to deliver additional Tarzan pictures. Therefore, they secured Johnny Weissmuller's services by offering him a contract, which stated that he was limited to only playing the part of Tarzan! The following 1930s entries, *Tarzan and His Mate* (1934), *Tarzan Escapes* (1936), and *Tarzan Finds a Son!* (1939) were all considered prestigious "A" pictures. But, by the 1940s, the Tarzan films weren't drawing as much as they used to, and with MGM beginning to lose interest in the series, the property was eventually sold lock, stock, and barrel to RKO's "B" production unit, run by producer Sol Lesser.

Critically, *Tarzan the Ape Man* received rave reviews, with cynical British critic Francis Birrell of the London magazine *The New Statesman and Nation* writing, "For an hour and three quarters (a long stretch for a film) the eye is continually delighted, the nerves unceasingly harassed. Armies of elephants, torrents of monkeys, prides of lions sweep across the screen…Tarzan has a hundred percent entertainment value, and gains enormously over such pictures as *Trader Horn* by never pretending to provide accurate information. It is just a terrific piece of gusto in the romantic manner."

The Miracle Man (1932)

Paramount Pictures. Directed by Norman Z. McLeod. Screenplay by Waldemar Young and Samuel Hoffenstein based on a play by Frank L. Packard, George M. Cohan and Robert Hobart Davis. Photographed by David Abel. Original Music by W. Franke Harling. 85 min.

Cast: Sylvia Sidney (Helen Smith), John Madison (Chester Morris), Hobart Bosworth (The Patriarch), Virginia Bruce (Margaret Thornton), Ned Sparks (Harry Evans), John Wray (The Frog), Boris Karloff (Nikko), Robert Coogan (Bobbie), Frank Darien (Hiram Hughes), Lloyd Hughes (Thornton), Lew Kelly (Parker), Florine McKinney (Betty), Irving Pichel (Henry Holmes), Jackie Searl (Little Boy).

RARELY SEEN AND ALMOST FORGOTTEN today, this remake of the 1919 Lon Chaney classic has been unjustly overlooked for over eight decades. If nothing else, it is a very good blueprint of what the earlier version must have been like, considering it is a lost film, with one key sequence still extant. Directed by George Loane Tucker and making stars of future silent greats like Betty Compson, Thomas Meighan, and Lon Chaney, it reaped praises from film critics and the public alike. The story concerns a gang of thieves who accidentally discover a faith healer in a rural town who has been gaining some notoriety. Thinking that he is just a "phony" like them, they decide to use this "miracle man" to their advantage by getting suckers to donate funds for the building of a place of worship devoted to healing the poor unfortunates. Before long, the crooks find, to their amazement, that the patriarch's faith-healing abilities really do work. Of course, rather than defying this god-like individual, the thieves, one-by-one, reform, leading them to the righteous path through religion.

The 1932 remake of *The Miracle Man* was also quite successful, since it starred Paramount's top female star at the time, Sylvia Sidney, and Chester Morris, who was being loaned out from MGM. This was a differ-

The Miracle Man (1932) Con man John Madison (Chester Morris, left) splits his "take" among his compatriots, Helen Smith (Sylvia Sidney) and Nikko (Boris Karloff).

ent role entirely for Miss Sidney, who had always been cast as the fallen heroine, and usually exposed to the horrors of the depression and its grim realities. Here she plays pickpocket Helen Smith, who, along with her crooked boyfriend John Madison (Morris) and two other colleagues, the Frog and Harry Evans, is part of a moderately successful fleecing racket, until they flee to a hick town to elude the police hot on their trail.

Many years later Miss Sidney would dismiss *The Miracle Man* as one of her worst pictures, claiming that the movie was outdated (by 1932 standards) and poorly acted. It's too bad she felt that way, because, seen today (if lucky) it is most enjoyable and usually gets a favorable response from present-day audiences. Its rarity is without question, since it has never been released on videotape or DVD and is totally overlooked in other film books as well!

Director Norman Z. McLeod, a former gag writer and specialist in silent comedies for Al Christie Comedies, was an odd choice for *The Miracle Man*. His many credits included two excellent Marx Brothers vehicles, *Monkey Business* (1931) and *Horse Feathers* (1932), as well as the

W. C. Fields classic *It's a Gift* (1934). A few years later he directed four excellent screwball comedies for Hal Roach entitled *Topper* (1937) and its superb sequel *Topper Takes a Trip* (1939), as well as *Merrily We Live* and *There Goes My Heart* (both 1938). Despite these comedic credentials, he does a top-notch job of making *The Miracle Man*, a film that needs to be examined today for its excellent direction of the cast, managing to avoid the pitfall of making the film too syrupy.

Another point of interest is the appearance of Boris Karloff, cast in the small role of the slimy villain Nikko. At this point in his career Karloff had just finished making the classic horror film *Frankenstein* and immediately after that film wrapped, he went to work on *The Miracle Man*. However, when *Frankenstein* was released on December 4, 1931, Karloff would soon become a household name and would thereafter be forever associated with horror roles!

Young Bride (1932)

RKO-Pathe Pictures. Produced by David O. Selznick. Directed by William A. Seiter. Based on the play *Love Starved* by Hugh Stanislaus Stange. Screenplay by Garrett Fort. Dialogue by Ralph Murphy and Jane Durfin. Photography by Arthur C. Miller. Edited by Joseph Kane. Art Direction by Carroll Clark. Sound by John E. Tribby. Music by Max Steiner. 76 min.

Cast: Helen Twelvetrees (Allie Smith Riggs), Eric Linden (Charlie Riggs), Arline Judge (Maisie), Roscoe Ates (Mike), Polly Walters (Daisy), Blanche Friderici (Miss Margaret Gordon), Cliff Edwards (Pete), Allen Fox (Skeets), Edwin Maxwell (The Doctor), Walter Percival (Master of Ceremonies), Phyllis Crane (The Taxi Dancer), Edmund Breese (C.B. Chadwick), Harry Stubbs (Mr. Perlman), Nora Cecil (Landlady), Ray Cooke (Pool Player), Jim Farley (Policeman), Frank Mills (Dance Hall Bartender), Joe Sauers/Sawyer (Library Patron).

WHILE THE NAME HELEN TWELVETREES doesn't mean a thing to most contemporary audiences, for a brief period in the early thirties, she was a very popular leading lady in a handful of "Pre-Code" soap operas. Born Helen Marie Jurgens in Brooklyn, New York, on Christmas Day of 1908, Helen always possessed a yen for acting. Working as a top model for magazines, she enrolled at the American Academy of Dramatic Arts, where she met Clark Twelvetrees, a fellow student. Within months, the two married and moved to New York, where they began "pounding the pavements" looking for acting assignments. Helen did land the role of Sondra in a production of *An American Tragedy* in Chicago, and after acting in a few flops, was nevertheless discovered by a talent scout from the Fox Film Corporation, bringing her to Hollywood. Unfortunately, her films at Fox were very lackluster affairs, her marriage was beginning to crumble, and the two eventually divorced. It was in 1930 that she was signed by Pathe, where her career suddenly began to blossom with a rip-off of the *Frankie and Johnny* saga entitled *Her Man*. Her biggest successes under the Pathe/RKO banner were films where she usually played "fallen woman" or victimized "nice girls", whose fates seemed to be manipulated by lecherous men with one thing on their minds.

Millie (1931) was her biggest hit to date, with Helen turning in one of her best performances as a single mother who kills her daughter's seducer. This was considered a first-rate "soaper" with critics hailing Ms. Twelvetrees' performance where she had the opportunity to metamorphose from a young innocent to a woman in her forties. The *Los Angeles Times* called the film "A real gem. Helen Twelvetrees is a better actress than Ruth Chatterton." Helen's rather soulful eyes became her trademark and, as a result, she was cast in some other interesting films like *Bad Company* (1931), a gritty gangster drama, *Panama Flo, State's Attorney*, and *Is my Face Red?* (all 1932).

One of her least remembered films of 1932 was *Young Bride*, an effort very similar in context to the 1928 King Vidor silent classic, *The Crowd*, which it resembles but doesn't imitate. Again, it's the story of a newly married couple and the obstacles they must endure living in a New York apartment during the height of the Great Depression. In *The Crowd*, the husband is a likable soul, although he lacks the drive to be a success, and from this the story develops. In *Young Bride*, the husband (Eric Linden) is a loud-mouthed braggart, constantly telling his wife and friends about some of the "big deals" he is about to land, which are nothing more than mere fabrications. Obviously, his character is not endearing, and if the "happy ending" seems rather jolting, it's obvious the screenwriters had written themselves into a corner. It's really pointless to even compare *Young Bride* with *The Crowd* because King Vidor's film is far superior and is still regarded as one of the best films of the twenties, while William Seiter's film is totally forgotten. Nevertheless, it remains an interesting photoplay, with Helen Twelvetrees and Eric Linden (one of the better juvenile leads in films at the time) giving solid performances. Unfortunately, Helen's career began to falter due to losing roles to some "up-and-coming" actresses like Constance Bennett and Katharine Hepburn. One part that was considered for Helen was the lead in *What Price Hollywood?* (1932), which was the first version of *A Star is Born*, a role that would have solidified her reputation in the movie industry. Much to Ms. Twelvetrees' chagrin, the lead went to Constance Bennett instead and, as a result, Miss Bennett became the Queen of the RKO lot...for the time being, anyway.

Young Bride (1932) Newly married Charlie Riggs (Eric Linden, center) loses all of his money to Pete (Cliff Edwards) and "Skeets" (Allen Fox). (RF)

William Seiter, a director whose talent for recreating an era with total precision, but never sacrificing his sense of sophistication and style, keeps *Young Bride*'s narrative running at a good clip. His films are usually very economical (although there were exceptions) in budget, yet they all seem to possess a knack for good taste. Ginger Rogers had always mentioned him in interviews, even though his films have been generally ignored today. But when one is exposed to some of his delightful romantic comedies such as *Hot Saturday* (1932), *Professional Sweetheart* (1933), *Rafter Romance* (1933), *In Person* (1935), and *If You Could only Cook* (1935), one can't help wanting more. He even worked with some of the biggest comedians successfully in films like *Diplomaniacs* (1933), with Wheeler and Woolsey, *Sons of the Desert* (1933), with Laurel and Hardy, and *Room Service* (1938), with the Marx Brothers. Many Laurel and Hardy aficionados claim that William Seiter was the team's best director. It's too bad that he only made this one film with them.

Grand Hotel (1932)

MGM. Directed by Edmund Goulding. From the play *Menschen im Hotel* by Vicki Baum. American version by William A. Drake. Art Direction by Cedric Gibbons. Gowns by Adrian. Assistant Director: Charles Dorian. Photography by William Daniels. Edited by Blanche Sewell. Music by Dr. William Axt. Sound by Douglas Shearer. 113 min.

Cast: Greta Garbo (Grusinskaya), John Barrymore (Baron Felix von Geigern), Joan Crawford (Flaemmchen), Wallace Beery (Preysing), Lionel Barrymore (Otto Kringelein), Lewis Stone (Dr. Otterschlag), Jean Hersholt (Senf), Robert McWade (Meierheim), Purnell B. Pratt (Zinnowitz), Ferdinand Gottschalk (Pimenov), Rafaela Ottiano (Suzette), Morgan Wallace (Chauffeur), Tully Marshall (Gerstenkorn), Frank Conroy (Rohna), Murray Kinnell (Schweimann), Edwin Maxwell (Dr. Waitz), Mary Carlisle (Honeymooner), John Davidson (Hotel Manager), Sam McDaniel (Bartender), Rolfe Sedan (Clerk), Herbert Evans (Clerk), Lee Phelps (Extra in Lobby).

THE 1930 GERMAN PLAY, *MENSCHEN IM HOTEL* by Vicki Baum had a successful run on Broadway, running 257 performances before MGM bought the film rights. The play, which starred Eugenie Leontovich, Siegfried Rumann, Hortense Alden, Henry Hull, and Sam Jaffe, caught the attention of producer Irving Thalberg. Thalberg's intention was to find a suitable property in which to cast a sizeable amount of big-named performers in a multi-starred motion picture. For the parts of the lovestruck leads, Thalberg cast Greta Garbo as the ballerina Grusinskaya and John Gilbert as Baron von Geigern. Unfortunately, Gilbert's drawing power was waning, so the studio opted for John Barrymore to play the part. This came as a major blow to Garbo, who had wanted Gilbert all along, and felt that Barrymore was nothing more than a stuck-up ham. All of her doubts were soon forgotten after working with Barrymore a few days. He never once tried to upstage her in any way. So to show her appreciation, she asked the director and set designers if they could rearrange the settee so that in the love scenes his famous left side profile would be shown to its full advantage.

Realizing that there would be many difficult egos to comply with on the set of *Grand Hotel*, Thalberg hired the services of director Edmund Goulding. Nicknamed the "Lion Tamer" on the MGM lot, he was known

Grand Hotel (1932) Tragedy strikes when Director General Preysing (Wallace Beery) murders the "Baron" (John Barrymore). Joan Crawford as stenographer Flaemmchen is aghast at the sight. (RF)

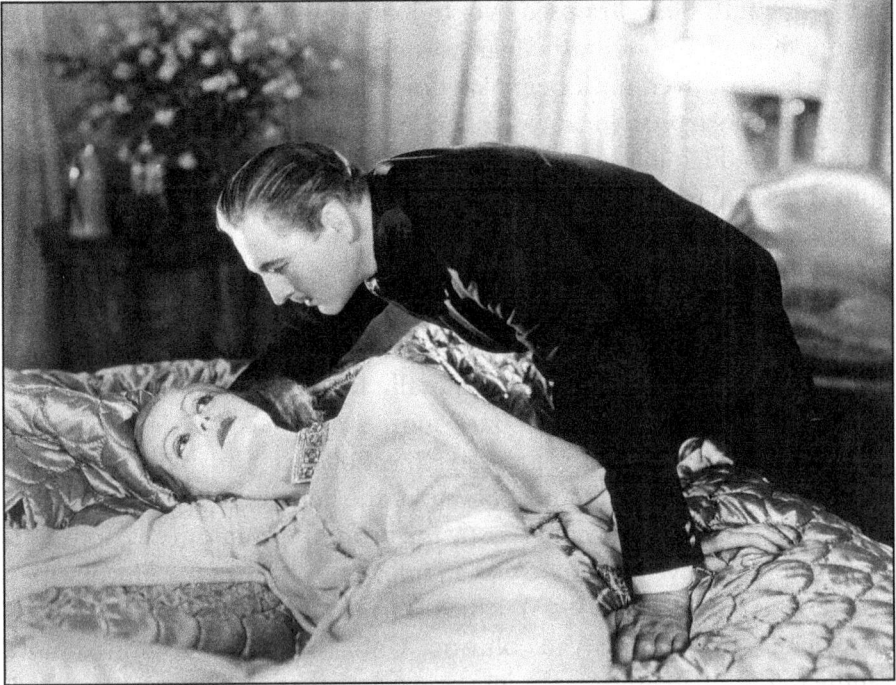

Grand Hotel (1932) The "Baron" (John Barrymore) sneaks into ballerina Grusinskaya's (Greta Garbo) boudoir intending to rob her, but is sidetracked with other more important matters. (RF)

for settling arguments with the most difficult of actors. And difficult they were…Joan Crawford felt that Garbo was getting the sexiest scenes in the picture, while Garbo was afraid that the ambitious Crawford would steal the whole show from her. Wallace Beery, on the other hand, would purposely ad-lib to throw the actors off from finding their cue. An ornery, no-nonsense kind of guy, Beery didn't like actors who held up production in any way. As a matter of fact, he would grumble if a shot had to be done over again.

On one occasion, Beery was waiting for Joan Crawford to step onto the set to resume shooting. With director, cameramen, and technicians ready to begin, Beery walked over to Crawford and asked why she was holding up production. Sitting on the sidelines equipped with a portable Victrola, Crawford told the impatient actor that she liked to listen to classical music before shooting a scene, to "get her in the proper mood," and suggested that maybe he should try listening to something soothing, causing Wally to walk away muttering to himself. The next morning, the rather uncouth Beery traipsed over to Joan, smilingly informing her that he took her advice seriously. Joan was elated that perhaps she had won the burly actor over, until Beery sat down next to her, telling her that he had a special surprise in store for her. With that, he put his fingers to his mouth, let out a loud whistle, and suddenly, a brass band came marching onto the set playing "Marching Through Georgia", prompting Crawford to walk off the set in a rage!

While many critics agree that *Grand Hotel* is an excellent film, they also feel that it contains what is probably Garbo's worst performance in that she was sadly miscast as a ballerina. With all the solid talent crammed into one motion picture, it was eventually Joan Crawford who turned in the best acting job, with Lionel Barrymore a close second. Coming in at a cost of $700,000, the picture grossed $2,594,000 after its initial first run, a staggering amount in the midst of one of the depression's worst years. As a matter of fact, MGM would reissue the property from time to time, netting even more revenue. There was an inferior remake of the film, entitled *Weekend at the Waldorf* (1945), which starred Ginger Rogers, Walter Pidgeon, Lana Turner, and Van Johnson. Unfortunately, it couldn't hold a candle to the Academy Award-winning original of 1932!

Love is a Racket! (1932)

First National Pictures. Directed by William A. Wellman. Based on a novel by Rian James. Adaptation by Courtney Terrett. Photography by Sidney Hickox. Edited by William Holmes. Art Direction by Jack Okey. Music by Leo F. Forbstein. 72 min.

Cast: Douglas Fairbanks, Jr. (Jimmy Russell), Ann Dvorak (Sally Condon), Frances Dee (Mary Wodehouse), Lee Tracy (Stanley Fiske), Lyle Talbot (Edward Griswold Snow), Warren Hymer (Bernie Olds), Andre Luguet (Max Boncour), Cecil Cunningham (Aunt Hattie Cunningham), Terrence Ray (Seeley), George Beranger (Manager of Elizabeth Morgan's), Gino Corrado (Sardi's Waiter), George Ernest (Newsboy), Harrison Greene (City Editor), Eddie Kane (Sardi's Captain of Waiters), John Larkin (Tod, Elevator Operator), John Marston (George Curley), Matt McHugh (Stoney Davis), Edward McWade (Messenger), Charles R. Moore (Sam, Elevator Operator), Henry Oth (Police Sergeant in Eddie's Apartment), Bob Perry (Bernie's Henchman), Marjorie Peterson (Hat Check Girl), Aloha Porter (Girl), Polly Walters (Switchboard Operator), Lillian Worth (Girl).

DIRECTED BY WILLIAM WELLMAN, *Love is a Racket!* is regarded as one of his lesser efforts, due to its short running time and rather meager budget. While "Wild Bill" Wellman (as most of his colleagues called him) was known as a director of action films like *Wings* (the first recipient of the Best Picture Academy Award of 1927), *Beau Geste* (1939), and *The High and the Mighty* (1954), he was quite successful in making screwball comedies like *Nothing Sacred* (1937), one of the best of that particular genre, not to mention bona fide classics like *The Public Enemy* (1931), *A Star is Born* (1937), *The Ox-Bow Incident* (1943), and *The Story of G.I. Joe* (1945). His tenure at Warner Bros. Studios in the early thirties brought us some excellent films as well, all very worthwhile entries in his impressive

Love is a Racket! (1932) Newspaper columnist Jimmy Russell (Douglas Fairbanks, Jr.) sets his sights for actress Mary Wodehouse (Frances Dee), who uses him to retrieve some blackmailing letters from a noted racketeer. (AB)

filmography; *Other Men's Women, Night Nurse, The Star Witness* and *Safe in Hell* (all 1931), *Frisco Jenny* (1932), *Heroes for Sale* and *Wild Boys of the Road* (both 1933), all showing us what a gutsy director he was, tackling such subjects as prostitution, drug abuse, medical malpractice, infidelity, and other forbidden topics that the soon-to-be imposed Hays Office would object to.

Based on a novel by Brooklyn newspaperman Rian James, *Love is a Racket!* (released in Britain as *Such Things Happen*) is a breezy, unpretentious little vehicle that was typical film fare in the early portion of the decade and followed hot on the heels of Lewis Milestone's *The Front Page* (1931), a landmark film about the newspaper game, enhanced with rapid-fire dialogue delivered by two masters, Adolphe Menjou and Pat O'Brien. This film became the yardstick against which all other journalistic endeavors were measured. Other excellent entries followed, with *The Finger Points* and *Five Star Final* (both 1931) being prime examples. In *Love is a Racket!*, Warner Bros.' contract player Douglas Fairbanks, Jr. gives a

Love is a Racket! (1932) Stanley Fiske (Lee Tracy) and Jimmy Russell (Douglas Fairbanks, Jr.) seem to have an overnight guest at their flat, Sally Condon (Ann Dvorak). (AB)

crackling performance cast as a Walter Winchell-type journalist named Jimmy Russell, whose weekly column for *The New York Globe*, "*Up and Down Broadway*", gets him in more trouble than he bargains for. Jimmy's downfall is his infatuation with an up-and-coming society girl (Frances Dee), who uses him whenever she sees fit. At the same time, Jimmy's female colleague, Sally Condon (underrated Ann Dvorak), is smitten with him, but of course, he hasn't a clue. Gangsters, politicians, blackmail, and eventually murder ensue in this engaging entry, which winds up with a murderer who goes unpunished at the film's conclusion. *The New York Times* called the film "a hustling comedy of life among the Broadway chroniclers", and if the film does contain one flaw it's the fact that it might move a little too briskly and doesn't allow the viewer time to digest everything before it goes on with its narrative. Nevertheless, *Love is a Racket!* (released June 18, 1932) is a most enjoyable way to spend a little over an hour, and it almost seems like it was a launching pad for two of William Wellman's later newspaper classics, *Nothing Sacred* (1937) and *Roxie Hart* (1942). A little less than three months later Warner Bros./First National released another scathing newspaper yarn, with Lee Tracy, who plays Doug Jr.'s pal Stanley Fiske in LIAR, portraying yet another variation on Walter Winchell, so well, in fact, that this kind of part would become a "Lee Tracy" signature role for the rest of his career. The film was *Blessed Event* and it's considered one of the best 'Pre-Code' films ever!

Red-Headed Woman (1932)

A Metro-Goldwyn-Mayer Picture. Produced by Paul Bern. Associate Producer: Al Lewin. Directed by Jack Conway. From the book by Katherine Brush. Screenplay by Anita Loos. Photography by Harold Rosson. Edited by Blanche Sewell. Costumes by Adrian. 81 min.

Cast: Jean Harlow (Lil Andrews), Chester Morris (Bill Legendre), Lewis Stone (William Legendre, Sr.), Leila Hyams (Irene Legendre), Una Merkel (Sally), Henry Stephenson (Gaersate), May Robson (Aunt Jane), Charles Boyer (Albert the Chauffeur), Harvey Clark (Uncle Fred), William Pawley (Bootlegger).

BORN HARLEAN CARPENTER on March 3, 1911, Jean Harlow started in pictures doing extra work at Paramount before eventually appearing in two-reel comedies for producer Hal Roach. Although being used as nothing more than a fashionable comedic 'prop,' she appeared in such titles as *The Unkissed Man* (1928), *Why is a Plumber?* (1929), *Thundering Toupees* (1929), and, most notably, in the silent Laurel and Hardy classic, *Double Whoopee* (1929). Soon afterwards, producer Howard Hughes signed her up to co-star in his World War I aviation drama, *Hell's Angels* (1930). By now, stardom was just a stone's throw away when Louis B. Mayer signed Jean to a contract at MGM, which began with the release of *The Secret Six* (1931) with Wallace Beery, Johnny Mack Brown, and a newcomer named Clark Gable. Other titles for which Harlow is best remembered during her early years at the studio are *The Beast of the City* (1932), *Red Dust* (1932) with Clark Gable, Mary Astor, and Gene Raymond, the classic *Dinner at Eight* (1933) with an all-star cast including Marie Dressler, John and Lionel Barrymore, Wallace Beery, Lee Tracy, Edmund Lowe, and Billie Burke, and *Bombshell* (1933), a scathing satire on 1930's Hollywood.

But, for pure unadulterated fun, *Red-Headed Woman* casts Harlow as a gold-digger who uses all of her sensual charms to get what she wants,

Red-Headed Woman (1932) Director Jack Conway (seated in chair) directs a scene with Jean Harlow and Chester Morris.

namely, her rich married boss, Chester Morris, or anyone else who has more to offer! Due to the objectionable subject matter so evident in the film, *Red-Headed Woman* was banned in England! The spicy dialogue was written by Anita (*Gentlemen Prefer Blondes*) Loos, while the superb direction was credited to Jack Conway, who, after working as assistant to the great D. W. Griffith, made a name for himself, directing such classics as *Viva Villa!* (1934), *A Tale of Two Cities* (1935), *Libeled Lady* (1936), *Boom Town* (1940), and scores of others.

The male lead in *Red-Headed Woman* was the under-rated Chester Morris, who began his film career in 1929, having been nominated for an Academy Award for his performance in his first starring role, *Alibi*. Like Harlow, Chester was put under a non-exclusive contract to MGM, appearing in two-fisted dramas, such as *The Big House* (1930) opposite Wallace Beery and Robert Montgomery, *Public Hero No. 1* (1935), *Three Godfathers* (1936, an excellent effort compared to the 1948 John Ford/John Wayne remake), and *Thunder Afloat* (1939). Unfortunately, Morris' career

Red-Headed Woman (1932) Chester Morris as Bill Lengendre can't resist the temptations of Lil Andrews (Jean Harlow).

began to slip, and by the late thirties, he found himself in lower-budgeted pictures, occasionally landing a plum role in quality "B" films, such as 1939's *Blind Alley*, one of the first movies to deal with psychiatry. In this, Morris plays a ruthless killer who has just escaped from prison, having taken refuge at the home of noted psychiatrist Ralph Bellamy. Bellamy learns through Morris' gun moll (played by Ann Dvorak) that Morris suffers from Salvador Dali-like nightmares. A battle of the minds ensues, with Bellamy trying to unravel the meaning of Morris' nightmares, and at the same time trying to capture him. As always, Morris gives a gutsy performance, sprinkled with a certifiable intensity that almost ignites the screen! By 1941, he was typecast as thief-turned-detective, *Boston Blackie*, in thirteen low-budget crime thrillers at Columbia. Although some were poorly scripted, these films proved very popular with war-torn audiences of the forties, due to Chester's winning personality and ability to make inferior dialogue sound better than it really was. He died in 1970 from an overdose of barbiturates, shortly after completing *The Great White Hope* with James Earl Jones.

One other actor in *Red-Headed Woman* deserving a nod of approval for his work is Charles Boyer (in a very early role), who plays Albert the chauffeur, the man who can give Lil what her rich "sugar daddies" could not!

Red-Headed Woman garnered rave reviews (much to the chagrin of studio-head Louis B. Mayer, who prided himself on making films the whole family could enjoy), with the *New York Daily News* heralding, "Red hot cinema! The Capitol's current offering is lurid and laugh-enticing in the bigger and better box-office manner. And the ex-platinum Jean Harlow now sparkles as a titian siren, her emoting improved immeasurably along with the change in the shade of her tresses. Svelte, slender and seductive, Harlow gives a splendid performance, making the picture more a character study of a woman who trades on her physical charms than a narrative romance."

Unfortunately for Harlow fans, Jean passed away on June 7, 1937 from uremia. Through her superstardom she left behind a wealth of films, and paved the way for other sex-symbols like Marilyn Monroe and Jane Mansfield to carry on the legacy of the platinum blonde.

Freaks (1932)

MGM. Directed by Tod Browning. Based on *Spurs* by Tod Robbins, which appeared in Munsey's Magazine February 1923. Screenplay by Willis Goldbeck and Leon Gordon. Dialogue by Edgar Allan Woolf and Al Boasberg. Photography by Merritt B. Gerstad. Edited by Basil Wrangell. Sound by Gavin Burns. 64 min.

Cast: Wallace Ford (Phroso), Leila Hyams (Venus), Olga Baclanova (Cleopatra), Roscoe Ates (Roscoe), Henry Victor (Hercules), Harry Earles (Hans), Daisy Earles (Frieda), Murray Kinnell (Sideshow Barker), Rose Dione (Madame Tetrallini), Daisy and Violet Hilton (Siamese Twins), Edward Brophy and Matt McHugh (Rollo Brothers), Olga Roderick (Bearded Lady), Johnny Eck (Boy with Half a Torso), Randian (Hindu Living Torso), Schlitzie, Elvira and Jennie Lee Snow (White Pin Heads), Pete Robinson (Living Skeleton), Koo Koo (Bird Girl), Josephine-Joseph (Half-Woman Half-Man), Martha Morris (Armless Wonder), Frances O'Connor (Turtle Girl), Angelo Rossito (Midget), Zip and Pip (Specialties), Elizabeth Green (Specialty), Albert Conti (Land Owner), Michael Visaroff (Jean, the Caretaker), Ernie S. Adams (Sideshow Patron), Louise Beavers (Maid).

TOD BROWNING HAD EARNED (and deservedly so) his reputation as a fine director of horror films through a string of silent classics starring Lon Chaney, such as *The Unholy Three* (1923), *Road to Mandalay* (1926), and *London After Midnight* (1927). In 1931, he was loaned to Universal Pictures to direct yet another horror vehicle, based on Bram Stoker's *Dracula*, which was also to star Mr. Chaney. Weakened from the cancer that would soon claim his life, Chaney had to reluctantly bow out from what would have been another important role. Producer Carl Laemmle Jr. had seen Hungarian-born Bela Lugosi on the stage performing his interpretation of the "blood-thirsty" count and hastily recruited him. Of

Freaks (1932) The Rollo Brothers (Edward Brophy and Matt McHugh) mock Josephine/ Joseph, the half-woman half-man sideshow attraction. (RF)

course, the rest was history, with Lugosi giving the performance of a lifetime, and Browning being hailed as the new "King of Horror."

The following year, Browning was summoned by Irving Thalberg, the boy wonder of MGM, to make a film that would "out-horror *Frankenstein*," a recent release and box-office champion from Universal. Relying on memories of his early years when he was working with a sideshow, Browning decided to make a film about people with physical abnormalities entitled *Freaks*. The movie was based on a story by Tod Robbins called *Spurs*. The director searched the circuses, sideshows, and freak shows of the world and enlisted real midgets, dwarfs, legless and armless people, as well as Siamese twins, human skeletons, and other disfigured unfortunates to star in his new project.

When the film was actually released, it was the subject of much controversy, with the public and critics alike finding the proceedings too grotesque for human consumption. Reportedly, at a San Diego preview, a woman ran screaming hysterically up the aisle of the theatre during a

Freaks (1932) Hans (Harry Earles) is smitten with trapeze artist, Cleopatra (Olga Baclanova). Little does he know what's in store for him. (RF)

performance, which caused MGM boss, Louis B. Mayer, to have the film drastically edited and eventually shelved before the film could possibly have broken even. It was banned in England, and remained literally unseen for over thirty years until an independent company re-released the property to play at revival houses and college campuses, where it has attained a certain cult status.

Although not technically a horror film (until its final ten minutes), this much-maligned motion picture tells of the human emotions and inner feelings of a community of deformed monstrosities who have been shunned by humanity and how they cope with their unpleasant plights. The real "freaks" in the picture are actually the "normal" individuals who constantly poke fun at and harass the sideshow population. After the initial shock of being exposed to the poor creatures, we, the audience become wrapped up in their little world, and feel embarrassed by the cruelty of their so-called "normal" co-workers. Of course, *Freaks* is definitely not a film for everyone, since many are still repulsed by what they are witnessing on screen. It has only been fairly recently that the film has received classic status. It holds up exceedingly well today, confirming the assertion that this was one of Browning's crowning achievements.

As a filmmaker, Browning wasn't a totally accomplished director, relying more on horrific content than on style. His sound films are more often than not quite static, and it's sad to say that after only four more films, Tod Browning retired from the screen in 1939. He did, however, make two more very successful films before his retirement, which would be rated among his best: *Mark of the Vampire* (1935), a remake of the earlier *London After Midnight*, which reunited him with his Dracula star Bela Lugosi, and the superb *The Devil Doll* (1936) with Lionel Barrymore.

Horse Feathers (1932)

Paramount Pictures. Produced by Herman J. Mankiewicz. Directed by Norman Z. McLeod. Screenplay by Bert Kalmar, Harry Ruby, S. J. Perelman, Will B. Johnstone and Arthur Sheekman (uncredited). Photography by Ray June. Original Music by John Leipold. Sound by Gene Merritt. Music and Lyrics by Bert Kalmar and Harry Ruby. Make-up by Robert Schiffer. 68 min.

Cast: Groucho Marx (Professor Quincy Adams Wagstaff), Harpo Marx (Pinky), Chico Marx (Baravelli), Zeppo Marx (Frank Wagstaff), Thelma Todd (Connie Bailey), David Landau (Jennings), Bobby Barber (Speakeasy Patron), Reginald Barlow (Retiring College President), Vince Barnett (Speakeasy Patron), Sheila Bromley (Wagstaff's Secretary), E.H. Calvert (Professor in Wagstaff's Study), Edgar Dearing (Bartender), Robert Greig (Biology Professor), Theresa Harris (Laura), Edward LeSaint (Professor in Wagstaff's Study), Florine McKinney (Peggy Carrington), Nat Pendleton (MacHardie), James Pierce (Ed Mullen), Frank Rice (Doorman at Speakeasy), Syd Saylor (Speakeasy Patron at Slot Machine), Arthur Sheekman (Typing Sportswriter), Ben Taggart (Policeman), Phil Tead (Football Broadcaster).

MOST PEOPLE CONSIDER the Marx Brothers' 1935 MGM release *A Night at the Opera* as their comedy masterpiece, while others say *Horse Feathers* (1932) or *Duck Soup* (1933) deserve that designation. I can readily ascertain that *A Night at the Opera* did much to resuscitate their career after a two-year hiatus from movies following the release of their Paramount Picture, *Duck Soup*, which didn't do very well critically or financially. While the film has much going for it with many hilarious classic routines (particularly the highly acclaimed stateroom scene), its biggest drawback is the intrusive romantic subplot between Kitty Carlisle and Allan Jones, which slows down the pace for Marx purists who had come

111

to expect something similar to their earlier film's frenetic style. Out of the five pictures they made for Paramount prior to their induction at MGM, the final three are truly outstanding, with the four brothers wreaking havoc on anybody or anything that happens to get in their way. Their first two

Horse Feathers (1932) Professor Quincy Adams Wagstaff (Groucho Marx) tries passing the time with the "college widow," Connie Bailey (Thelma Todd). (RF)

Horse Feathers (1932) Thelma Todd appearing in her second (and last) film with the Marx Brothers. The first one was Monkey Business (1931). (RF)

efforts, *The Cocoanuts* (1929) and *Animal Crackers* (1930), which were based on Broadway shows, are considered a bit too stagy, although the second film, *Animal Crackers*, happens to be a particular favorite of many Marx enthusiasts. *The Cocoanuts*, which came a year earlier, is an early talkie and seems very creaky and claustrophobic.

The next three, *Monkey Business*, *Horse Feathers* and *Duck Soup* are all pure, 100% proof Marx Brothers fare, with not a wasted moment in any of them. As for plot, I doubt whether I could give the details since story lines were so miniscule in these offerings. Also, the films are so fast-paced, with Groucho's unforgettable insults, as well as Chico's mutilation of the English language, and Harpo's totally "other-world" behavior, it left audiences surrendering in unabashed hysterics!

Written by a team of extremely talented writers including Bert Kalmar, S. J. Perelman, and Harry Ruby, *Horse Feathers* is one of those films which once again, throws all logic to the winds with Groucho playing the head of Huxley College (now who would have put him in that position in the first place?). His many "one-liners", including the one in the opening sequence where he is looking for his son before giving a welcoming speech to the student body, are classic. As he peruses the auditorium, hoping to locate his errant son, he asks a young co-ed, "Young lady, would you please get off my son's lap so I can watch the son rise?" This is one of those quips which must have raised the ire of the Hays Office. Another favorite has leading lady Thelma Todd commenting to Grouch that he's "full of whimsy", to which he responds, "Can you notice it from over there? I always get that way after I eat radishes." As usual, Chico and Harpo are on hand and their zany antics include them trying to sneak into a speakeasy, driving a traffic cop to distraction, disrupting a biology class, and kidnapping a couple of college football players with hilarious results. As for the fourth brother, Zeppo, he is given the rather thankless job of being the straight man in the midst of all of this insanity. There are two excellent songs here, too, with Groucho warbling "I'm Against It" to the student body, and the Four Marx Brothers singing various verses to a catchy ditty called "Everyone Says I Love You" in their own unique style, with lyrics written to fit their personalities (Harpo performs his rendition on the harp).

Also on hand, is beautiful Thelma Todd, who had scored magnificently in her scenes with Groucho in their previous venture *Monkey Business*. Here, she plays the campus "widow" who is attempting to steal the football signals so Huxley College will lose their championship game. The melee that ensues in her apartment is one of the many highlights, along with Chico's rendition of "Collegiate" on the piano (what else?), with Thelma (who is trying to suppress her laughter) cuddling next to him, and constantly "goosing" him (we weren't supposed to notice) while he's playing, practically ruining the take!

Norman McLeod, who was given the almost impossible task of keeping the four brothers in line, was a specialist in comedy, beginning as a gag writer for the 'Christie Comedies' before collaborating with William Wellman as assistant director on the fabled World War I aviation classic, *Wings* in 1927. This led to his becoming a full-fledged director in some superb screwball comedies, most notably *Topper* (1937), its sequel *Topper Takes a Trip* (1939), and the equally delightful *Merrily We Live* (1938), all produced by Hal Roach.

In its brief 68 minute running time, *Horse Feathers* is a film that, along with *Duck Soup*, shows the Marx Brothers at their frenetic best! While some might complain about the film's lack of logic or plot, it all becomes immaterial when it comes to the real Marx Brothers style. Critic Philip Scheuer said it best when he stated that "the current Marx comedy is the funniest talkie since the last Marx comedy, and the record it establishes is not likely to be disturbed until the next Marx comedy comes along. As for any comparison, I was too busy having a good time to make any."

The Age of Consent (1932)

Radio Pictures. Produced by David O. Selznick. Associate Producer: Pandro S. Berman. Directed by Gregory LaCava. Based on the play *Cross Roads* by Martin Flavin. Screenplay by Sarah Y. Mason, Francis M. Cockrell, and H. N. Swanson (uncredited). Photography by J. Roy Hunt. Edited by Jack Kitchin. Art Direction by Carroll Clark. Sound by Denzil A. Cutler. Music by Max Steiner. 63 min.

Cast: Dorothy Wilson (Betty Cameron), Arline Judge (Dora Swale), Richard Cromwell (Michael Harvey), Eric Linden (Duke Galloway), John Halliday (Prof. David Matthews), Aileen Pringle (Barbara), Reginald Barlow (Mr. Swale), Frederick Burton (Assistant District Attorney Gifford), Betty Grable (Student at Dormitory), Howard C. Hickman (Doctor), Buddy Messinger (Junior), Mildred Shay (Student at Dormitory), Grady Sutton (Student at Dormitory).

IN THE 1920S going to college was considered a luxury, and many teenagers who had yearned for a higher level of education were sadly disappointed, as their parents just couldn't afford it. This became even more evident when the Great Depression faced us and these same teens had to go to work in order to make ends meet and help support their families. Of course, Hollywood certainly didn't help the situation, showing college as a romantic place where a cute co-ed can match up with the college's football captain or local campus hero; and an ordinary young man can win over the affections of the campus queen. Films like *The Plastic Age* (1925), which starred Donald Keith and the up-and-coming "It Girl" Clara Bow, was typical of this era, with similar movies that followed utilizing the same formula. Even comedians like Harold Lloyd and Buster Keaton graced the ivy halls of various fictitious universities, where they eventually won the campus cutie—and single-handedly—the championship football game (not to mention besting the college bully at fisticuffs for a rousing finale!) Universal

The Age of Consent (1932) College student Mike Harvey (Richard Cromwell) is taken aback at how "forward" Betty Cameron (Dorothy Wilson) is.

Pictures even had a popular two-reel series called *The Collegians*, which ran from the late silent era to the early talkies. In 1930, director George Stevens launched a moderately successful series of two-reelers for Hal Roach and dubbed them *The Boy Friends*. That series, which starred future stuntman Dave Sharpe, along with Gertie Messinger, Grady Sutton, and ex-*Our Gang* stars Mickey Daniels and Mary Kornman, proved successful until director Stevens left the Roach lot to move onto greener pastures.

By the early thirties, films about college life had changed drastically, concentrating more on the sexual mores of the students than on athletics. Pre-marital sex became the prime focus in films like *Confessions of a Co-ed* (1931) and *The Age of Consent*. The latter, based on the Martin Flavin play *Cross Roads*, was considered quite daring in its day, earning the ire of the Catholic Church, who had been appalled at the thought of promiscuous co-eds indulging in premarital sex, not even thinking about the possibility of marriage! Newcomer Dorothy Wilson, making her film debut here, had been a secretary to director Gregory LaCava before he gave the photogenic actress a screen test and awarded her the lead in his upcoming picture. Other young stars, like wooden Richard Cromwell, pert Arline Judge as the college womanizer who later turns noble, and Eric Linden, were added to the cast. Although some of the acting seems a bit mawkish at times (after all, this IS an early talkie), the two female leads seem to come off best, with Eric Linden's performance not far behind.

It seems very curious that Richard Cromwell had the best film career out of the four leads, appearing in such films as *Emma* and *The Strange of Molly Louvain* (both 1932), *The Lives of a Bengal Lancer* (1935), and *Young Mr. Lincoln* (1939). In virtually all of his performances he comes off as rather whiny and weak. Eric Linden, on the other hand, seemed to have a firmer grasp regarding his acting skills and understanding his screen roles. His character always comes off as endearingly boisterous, without being unlikable, in films like *Young Bride*, starring the unjustly forgotten Helen Twelvtrees, and as James Cagney's younger brother in *The Crowd Roars* (both 1932). Bridgeport, Connecticut-born Arline Judge enjoyed a rather lengthy career in movies, albeit in lesser vehicles. Raised in a Catholic convent, this vivacious vixen became more renowned for her eight marriages and numerous sex scandals than for her movies. Dorothy Wilson, on the other hand, was prominent in many "B" westerns of the thirties, as well as giving a pleasing performance in one of Harold Lloyd's best talkies, *The Milky Way* (1936), directed by Leo McCarey. In 1937, Miss Wilson abandoned her movie career and married screenwriter Lewis Foster—who who would later win an Oscar for penning the original story for *Mr. Smith Goes to Washington* (1939). Their marriage lasted until Foster's death in 1974. Miss Wilson died in 1998 at the age of eighty-eight.

Love Me Tonight (1932)

Paramount Pictures. Produced and Directed by Rouben Mamoulian. Story by Leopold Marchand and Paul Arment. Screenplay by Samuel Hoffenstein, Waldemar Young and George Marion, Jr. Photography by Victor Milner. Songs by Richard Rodgers and Lorenz Hart: "The Song of Paree", "How Are You?", "Isn't It Romantic?", "Lover, Mimi", "Poor Apache", "Love Me Tonight", "A Woman Needs Something Like That", "The Son of a Gun Is Nothing But a Tailor". 89 min.

Cast: Maurice Chevalier (Maurice Courtelin), Jeanette MacDonald (Princess Jeanette), Charles Ruggles (Vicomte Gilbert de Vareze), Charles Butterworth (Count de Savignac), Myrna Loy (Countess Valentine), C. Aubrey Smith (The Duke), Elizabeth Patterson (First Aunt), Ethel Griffies (Second Aunt), Blanche Frederici (Third Aunt), Major Sam Harris (Bridge Player), Joseph Cawthorn (The Doctor), Robert Greig (Major-Domo, Flamond), Ethel Wales (Madame Dutoit, Dressmaker), Marion "Peanuts" Byron (Bakery Girl), Mary Doran (Madame Dupont), Bert Roach (Emile), Cecil Cunningham (Laundress), Tyler Brooke (Composer), Edgar Norton (Valet), Herbert Mundin (Groom), Rita Owin (Chambermaid), Clarence Wilson (Shirtmaker), Gordon Westcott (Collector), George Davis (Pierre Dupont), Rolfe Sedan (Taxi Driver), Tony Merlo (Hat Maker), William H. Turner (Boot Maker), George "Gabby" Hayes (Grocer), Tom Ricketts (Bit), Mel Kalish (Chef).

PROBABLY NO OTHER FILMMAKER had achieved more success in the early talkie era than Rouben Mamoulian. It was he who utilized advanced methods of fluid camera movement and the simultaneous wipe, in which an optical wipe is held at mid-point to show two scenes at the same time. Other innovations were outstanding tracking shots and rhythmic dialogue, evident in his classic musical *Love Me Tonight*. "One of the best musicals ever made," wrote film historian Leonard Maltin in his best-

Love Me Tonight (1932) Man-hungry Countess Valentine (Myrna Loy) distracts Maurice (Maurice Chevalier) from paying attention to Princess Jeanette (Jeanette MacDonald). (RF)

selling "T.V. Movies," a rather controversial statement indeed when this early talkie is pitted up against classics like *42nd Street* (1933) and *Singin' In the Rain* (1952). When viewed today, one can readily agree with Maltin's statement, even though this, the best of the Maurice Chevalier-Jeanette MacDonald musicals, has not received proper exposure in recent years, until now. Everything works perfectly in this operetta, in which all of the Rodgers and Hart themes seem to be put into motion. Never in the whole movie does the narrative stop suddenly for a musical interlude. The music is incorporated at random, never bothering to pause the action, showing favorably how far the musical had come since the early arrival of sound.

In *Love Me Tonight*, Mamoulian's style resembles the same airy flavor of Ernst Lubitsch. That he improves upon the Lubitsch formula is no small undertaking indeed, for throughout the 1920s to the early 1940s Lubitsch was considered one of the greatest directors in the history of cinema. He had successfully directed Chevalier and MacDonald in their first pairing entitled *The Love Parade* (1929), with delightful results, and outdid himself with the wittily risqué *One Hour With You* (1932). The matter of why he was not chosen to direct *Love Me Tonight* remains a mystery, for it turned out to be unquestionably the best vehicle starring this delightful team. It has always seemed rather puzzling that today's audiences remember the team of Nelson Eddy and Jeanette MacDonald, but overlook her work with Chevalier. The truth of the matter is that MacDonald's work with Chevalier is considered her best work, in which she exudes a sensuality lacking in her later films with Eddy. Sadly, they only made one more vehicle together, *The Merry Widow* (1934), again directed by Lubitsch, released by MGM, and displaying the same carefree and breezy style of their earlier efforts at Paramount.

Sadly, current prints of *Love Me Tonight* run only eighty-nine minutes instead of the complete ninety-six minutes. When Paramount reissued it in the late 1930s, they had to cut some scenes deemed objectionable under the watchful eyes of the Hays Office. According to co-star Myrna Loy, looking extremely seductive in this, her short rendition of *Mimi* had to be taken out due to the scantiness of her lingerie. She added that it really wasn't the sheerness of the garment, but the baring of her navel that had raised the censors' eyebrows. Even still, this marvelous essay in music, drawing room comedy, and romance is as delightful today as it was then, with audiences leaving the film humming "Isn't it Romantic?" (later used in countless Paramount films), "Mimi", or the title tune.

The Night of June 13 (1932)

The Night of June 13 (1932) Paramount Pictures. Directed by Stephen Roberts. Based on the story *Suburbs* by Vera Caspary. Screenplay by Agnes Brand Leahy and Brian Marlow. Photography by Harry Fischbeck. Original Music by John Leipold. 80 min.

Cast: Clive Brook (John Curry), Lila Lee (Trudie Morrow), Frances Dee (Ginger Blake), Adrianne Allen (Elna Curry), Gene Raymond (Herbert Morrow), Helen Jerome Eddy (Martha Blake), Charles Ruggles (Philo Strawn), Mary Boland (Mazie Strawn), Charley Grapewin ('Grandpop' Jeptha Strawn), Helen Ware (Mrs. Morrow), Billy Butts (Junior Strawn), Richard Carle (Otto), Wallis Clark (Defense Attorney), Otto Fries (Bailiff), Arthur Hohl (Prosecuting Attorney), Edward LeSaint (Mr. Morrow).

A FILM THAT HAS ALL BUT VANISHED off the face of the earth (due to the negligent policies of Universal, who presently own the rights to the film), *The Night of June 13* is a delightful surprise for those fortunate enough to see it. Directed by the all-but-forgotten but always interesting Stephen Roberts, whose later Pre-Code offering, *The Story of Temple Drake* (1933), created such a stir with the Hays Office that it almost single-handedly brought the more stringent set of rules which formed Hollywood's Legion of Decency in July of 1934. Considered more of a stylist whose particular brand of filmmaking was innovative (for the time anyway), his other pictures, such as *Romance in Manhattan* and *Star of Midnight* (both 1935) remain less interesting, while his *One Sunday Afternoon* (1933) and *The Ex-Mrs. Bradford* (1936) are definitely first rate.

The Night of June 13 is an excellent account of a reputed murder in suburbia, recounting the tale of four neighboring families and how their lives are affected when the husband in one of the households is accused of murdering his wife. Intelligently told and riveting, the film holds up extremely well today, with the original story by Vera Caspary, who would

The Night of June 13 (1932) Mrs. Lizzie Morrow (Helen Ware) has caught her drunken son, Herbert (Gene Raymond) with nightgown-clad Ginger Blake (Frances Dee). (RF)

later write the excellent film noir classic *Laura* (1944). Director Stephen Roberts uses many old tricks most effectively, like cross-cutting (a device dating back to D. W. Griffith) to keep the proceedings moving at a good pace in order to film each characters' recollections in a matter of about one minute! Also, the use of lap dissolves, especially in the courtroom scenes, prove effectively done when each character gives testimony to the prosecutor and the defense attorneys, with their accounts of what happened the night of the "murder" being reenacted for the audience as well.

The cast, most of which are forgotten today, turn out excellent performances, with distinguished British leading man Clive Brook bringing much sympathy to his character as the ever-loving husband who is accused of murdering his psychotic wife, played by Adrienne Allen. Relative newcomers Frances Dee (who married actor Joel McCrea a year later) and Gene Raymond (who would become the husband of singing star Jeanette MacDonald) are both impressive, the latter veering away from his usual all-American boy roles. While never a star of the first rank, Mr. Raymond did make some good pictures, such as *Red Dust* (1932), *Zoo in Budapest*, and *Flying Down to Rio* (both 1933). But his best part came in MGM's 1934 tearjerker *Sadie McKee*, where he played the philandering husband of Joan Crawford, whose blind devotion to him causes much unhappiness and heartbreak, until the final reel of the film, when she is reunited with old flame Franchot Tone (Crawford's real life husband).

While *The Night of June 13* is far from being a classic (how could it be, since it's been out of circulation so long), it must be advised that it is one of those missing gems that should be rediscovered and preserved for the benefit of future generations of filmgoers. The respected trade newspaper *Variety* noted at the time that the film was "absorbingly worked out with fascinating character studies and a touch of satire."

Blonde Venus (1932)

A Paramount Picture. Directed by Josef von Sternberg. Screenplay by Jules Furthman and S. K. Lauren. Photography by Bert Glennon. Art Direction by Wiard Ihnen. Musical Score by Oscar Potoker. Costumes by Travis Banton. Based on a story by Josef von Sternberg. Songs: "Hot Voodoo" and "You Little So and So" by Sam Coslow and Ralph Rainger. "I Couldn't Be Annoyed" by Leo Robin and Dick Whiting. 91 min.

Cast: Marlene Dietrich (Helen Faraday), Herbert Marshall (Edward Faraday), Cary Grant (Nick Townsend), Dickie Moore (Johnny Faraday), Gene Morgan (Ben Smith), Rita La Roy ("Taxi Belle" Hooper), Robert Emmett O'Connor (Dan O'Connor), Sidney Tolar (Detective Wilson), Francis Sayles (Charlie Blaine), Morgan Wallace (Dr. Pierce), Evelyn Preer (Viola), Robert Graves (La Farge), Lloyd Whitlock (Baltimore Manager), Cecil Cunningham (Norfolk Woman Manager), Emile Chautard (Chautard), James Kilgannon (Janitor), Sterling Holloway (Joe/Student), Charles Morton (Bob/Student), Ferdinand Schuman-Heink (Henry/Student), Harry Schultz (Otto), Harold Berquist (Big Fellow), Dewey Robinson (Greek Restaurant Proprietor), Clifford Dempsey (Night Court Judge), Bessie Lyle (Grace), Mildred Washington (Viola), Hattie McDaniel (Negro Girl), Gertrude Short (Receptionist), Brady Kline (New Orleans Cop).

IT'S EASY TO SEE WHY Paramount's Josef von Sternberg/Marlene Dietrich pictures of the early thirties fared so well at the box office. Beautiful, sexy, and alluring, Dietrich was the studio's answer to MGM's Garbo, their major female attraction of the late silent era and well into the talkies.

Dietrich started out in films in Germany, playing a minor role as a servant girl in *Der Kleine Napolean* (The Little Napolean) in 1923, and after fifteen more movies, she finally landed the role that made her internationally famous, as Lola-Lola in von Sternberg's *Der Blaue Engel* (The Blue

Blonde Venus (1932) Sultry Marlene Dietrich as Helen Jones a.k.a Helen Faraday in a very sexy pose. (AB)

Blonde Venus (1932) Cora (Hattie McDaniel) and Helen Faraday (Marlene Dietrich) are being watched by a private detective. (AB)

Angel) in 1930. Shortly after, von Sternberg brought his protégé to Hollywood, where she landed a long-term contract with Paramount. Their first American collaboration as director and star was *Morocco* (1930) with Gary Cooper, a major hit that cemented Dietrich's new reputation as a sex goddess. Capitalizing on this recent success, more Dietrich/von Sternberg films were forthcoming, until their partnership ended with the mediocre *The Devil is a Woman* in 1935.

Their 1932 release, *Blonde Venus*, was one of their best in the group. Written by scenarists Jules Furthman and S. K. Lauren, it tells the highly

Blonde Venus (1932) Very provocative poster art of Marlene Dietrich. (AB)

Blonde Venus (1932) Marlene Dietrich in the "Hot Voodoo" number.

improbable story of a woman who must sacrifice herself to save her terminally ill husband (Herbert Marshall). The expert cinematography by Bert Glennon is worth noting in that he employs soft lighting in the earlier scenes of the picture, yet as the Dietrich character slowly falls into the clutches of degradation, the lighting (as well as her make-up) takes on a much harsher look. Also, throughout the film, Glennon makes use of stark, vivid shadows surrounding the brightly lit faces of the actors, to denote a sense of despair evident in many depression-era movies of the time.

Twenty-eight year old Cary Grant, appearing in his fifth film, is slightly awkward at first, but does redeem himself in the final moments of *Blonde Venus*. Wasted in many of his early Paramount films in the early thirties, Grant would ultimately find his niche in romantic screwball comedies five years later with the Hal Roach classic *Topper* and Leo McCarey's *The Awful Truth*. He would reach another level of comedic height in 1938 opposite Katharine Hepburn in Howard Hawks' *Bringing Up Baby*.

Reviews at the time for *Blonde Venus* were decidedly mixed, with Mordant Hall of *The New York Times* admitting that the film was "an excellent example of von Sternberg's preoccupation with style and method", while Forsythe Hardy of the Cinema Quarterly stated that "this latest film of von Sternberg's has a more brilliantly polished surface than any other that America has sent us this year."

When this notorious Pre-Code picture was reissued after the Legion of Decency took hold on Hollywood, the first sequence of *Blonde Venus*, which featured Marlene swimming in the raw, was cut from some prints.

Hell's Highway (1932)

An RKO Picture. Produced by David O. Selznick. Directed by Rowland Brown. Screenplay by Rowland Brown, Samuel Ornitz, and Robert Trasker. Photography by Edward Cronjager. Edited by William Hamilton. Art Direction by Carroll Clark. Sound by John E. Tribby. Music by Max Steiner. Assistant Director: James H. Anderson. 62 min.

Cast: Richard Dix (Frank "Duke" Ellis), Tom Brown (Johnny Ellis), Rochelle Hudson (Mary Ellen), C. Henry Gordon (Blacksnake Skinner), Oscar Apfel (William Billings), Stanley Fields (F.E. Whiteside), John Arledge (Joe Carter), Warner Richmond (Pop-Eye Jackson), Charles Middleton (Matthew), Louise Carter (Mrs. Ellis), Sandy Roth (Blind Maxie), Clarence Muse (Rascal), Fuzzy Knight (Society Red), Eddie Hart (Turkey Neck), Robert Homans (Sheriff), John Lester Johnson (Blubber Mouth), Jed Kiley (Romeo Schultz), Bob Perry (Spike), Harry Smith (Buzzard), Bert Starkey (Hype).

AFTER THE INITIAL SUCCESS of MGM's classic prison drama *The Big House* (1930), movie studios of the early thirties decided to do follow-up versions of social reform prison dramas. Always on the lookout for controversial material, RKO producer David O. Selznick fulfilled his desire to film an indictment against the chain-gang system of the south. Released two months before the Warner Bros. classic *I am a Fugitive from a Chain Gang* on September 23rd, this film lacks the strength of the later film, but does give a convincing account of the brutal treatment of convict laborers on such penal colonies. Richard Dix, an all but forgotten actor today, with steely eyes and overwhelming stage presence, is cast as hard nosed convict "Duke" Ellis, whose plans for a prison escape go awry when his younger brother (Tom Brown) is newly incarcerated into the same camp. What the younger Ellis is subjected to in the film's brief sixty-two minutes' running time, makes for a most disturbing experience.

The opening prologue title of *Hell's Highway* sets the tone for the rest of the film: "Dedicated to the early end of the conditions portrayed here—which though a throwback to the Middle Ages actually exist today." The titles then segue into a montage of newspaper clippings, such as "Prison Guards Accused of Murder as Tortured Youth Dies in Sweat

Hell's Highway (1932) Poster art. (AB)

Box," while a chorus of black convicts warble hymns (there is no musical score throughout the whole picture). That same gang of black prisoners is symbolically used as a Greek chorus, commenting on the brutality with work tunes and offhanded wisecracks ("Yes, suh, boss—mules cost $40 a head and convicts don't cost nothing").

Besides the two male leads, the audience is introduced to the other inmates as well. One of them, who fashions himself quite the ladies man, decorates his bunk with pictures of Bette Davis and Greta Garbo, claiming to know them both. Another inmate, who was sent up for having three wives, is a Bible-quoting polygamist who spouts religious scripture. At one point he denounces Duke by stating, "It takes a lot of nerve to rob a bank," at which point Duke replies, "It takes a lot of backbone to keep three wives happy." "Yea, brother!"

Director Rowland Brown, whose other directorial credits were rather limited, was a highly respected screenwriter in the 1930s. His hardboiled writings usually were of the gangster genre; among his more famous were *State's Attorney* (1932), *The Devil is a Sissy* (1936), *Angels with Dirty Faces* (1938), and *Johnny Apollo* (1940). Here, in *Hell's Highway*, he uses some rather innovative film techniques in a montage sequence, employing still illustrations sketched in charcoal by a black convict to render a murder and a funeral. Brown not only focuses on the brutality in the chain gangs, but touches on such issues as racism and homosexuality as well. Unfortunately, the climax of this powerful drama doesn't fare as well, with its ending bringing forth hope as well as a need for social reform. In the film's original ending, preview audiences gasped when "Duke," who has finally had enough of this torture, decides to "take it on the lam" one last time, knowing full well that the guards will definitely kill him this time. When audiences balked at this rather unsettling finale, RKO relented and decided to let the hero survive. Nevertheless, critics were unanimous, praising the direction and the acting by all participants, with one citing, "Starkly realistic, explosive dram of a Southern prison camp...Brown's direction is responsible for one of the most gripping scenes in any film, when a deaf mute escapee fails to hear the command to surrender and is shot in the back..."

The Big Broadcast (1932)

Paramount Pictures. Directed by Frank Tuttle. Screenplay by George Marion, Jr. From the play "Wild Waves" by William Ford Manley. Photography by George J. Folsey. Original Music by Harold Arlen and John Leipold. Music and Lyrics by Ralph Rainger and Leo Robin. 80 min.

Cast: Bing Crosby (Himself), Stuart Erwin (Leslie McWhinney), Leila Hyams (Anita Rogers), Sharon Lynn (Mona), George Burns (Himself), Gracie Allen (Herself), George Barbier (Clapsaddle), Ralph Robertson (Announcer), Alex Melesh (Animal Man), Spec O'Donnell (Office Boy), Anna Chandler (Mrs. Cohen), Thomas Carrigan (Officer), Donald Mills (Himself), Harry Mills (Himself), Herbert Mills (Himself), John Mills (Himself), Donald Novis (Himself), Irving Bacon (Prisoner), Connee Boswell (Herself), Martha Boswell (Herself), Cab Calloway (Himself), Leonid Kinskey (Ivan), Eddie Lang (Himself), Vincent Lopez (Himself), Edgar Norton (Secretary to T.F. Bellows), Dewey Robinson (Basso), Kate Smith (Herself), Arthur Tracy (Himself).

BY 1932, after a brief decline at the box office, musicals were back in vogue. This was due in large part to the films of Busby Berkeley and musical comedies like *The Big Broadcast*. When "talkies" arrived almost exclusively in 1929, it seemed that every film was a musical, with the framework being nothing more than all-star revues with many of Hollywood's top stars awkwardly attempting to sing and dance. Among these dismal entries were MGM's *The Hollywood Revue of 1929*, as well as Warner Bros.' *Show of Shows* and *Paramount on Parade*. Of course, there were exceptions, with highly successful operettas, successfully combining a romantic love story with musical interludes. Films like Ernst Lubitsch's *The Love Parade* (1929, which was the first teaming of Maurice Chevalier and Jeanette MacDonald) and *The Rogue Song* (1930), with Lawrence Tibbett, were just about the only breath of life the Hollywood musical still had.

The Big Broadcast (1932) Bing Crosby (playing himself) is getting lots of attention from Anita Rogers (Leila Hyams), much to the chagrin of her boyfriend, hayseed Leslie McWhinney (Stuart Erwin). (AB)

As a matter of fact, to attract moviegoers, theatres began to post "not a musical" on the marquee if the title might have even hinted at being one.

The Big Broadcast was the very first film to employ radio personalities, a rather novel idea in 1932, since radio was competing with the film industry as America's number one form of entertainment. One of radio's hottest properties was Bing Crosby, who would go on record as holding the longest career at Paramount of anyone. Crosby, who was one of the Rhythm Boys, appeared in Universal's Technicolor extravaganza *King of Jazz* (1930), which showcased Paul Whiteman and his band. Following this, Crosby signed on with Mack Sennett and starred in six rather engaging shorts while continuing to fulfill his radio and record commitments. This led to Bing's first starring role in *The Big Broadcast*, where he would sing "Please" (it later became his signature song), as well as two other smash hits, "Here Lies Love" and "Where the Blue of the Night".

The delightful comedy team of George Burns and Gracie Allen, also graduates of the Mack Sennett "school of comedy," make their first appearance in a feature-length picture here. Their particular brand of humor, although very popular throughout the 1930s, was never deemed strong enough to warrant building a complete film around. However, Burns

The Big Broadcast (1932) Poor Bing! Women galore!

and Allen continued to provide excellent support in features for years to come. It wasn't until the 1950s, when Burns and Allen were awarded the opportunity to be the starring attraction, only on television, in a series that proved so popular it still is in syndication today.

The director, Frank Tuttle, had previously been a publicity writer and editor for "Vanity Fair." He entered films in 1922, writing screenplays exclusively for Paramount, and later advanced to the position of director. Some of his films like *This is the Night* (1932), *Roman Scandals* (1933) with Eddie Cantor, and *College Holiday* (1936), are light examples of his breezy and dependable expertise as a filmmaker. Later, he would go on to tackle more ambitious projects like *This Gun for Hire* (1942), a superb film noir entry, which made major stars of Alan Ladd and Veronica Lake (teamed together for the first time), and another well-done crime drama, *Lucky Jordan* (1942), again with Ladd.

On its reissue, *The Big Broadcast* was tampered with by local censors in various states. The cocaine-related Cab Calloway number, "Where is Minnie?" (a follow-up to Calloway's famous "Minnie the Moocher") was cut, as well as the scene where Bing Crosby and Stu Erwin attempt suicide after being jilted by their respective girlfriends.

The Phantom of Crestwood (1932)

RKO Radio Pictures Release. Executive Producer: Merian C. Cooper. Produced by David O. Selznick. Directed by J. Walter Ruben. Screenplay by Bartlett Cormack and J. Walter Ruben from an original story by J. Walter Ruben. Photography by Henry W. Gerrard. Music by Max Steiner. Art Direction by Carroll Clark. 77 min.

Cast: Ricardo Cortez (Gary Curtis), Karen Morley (Jenny Wren), Anita Louise (Esther Wren), Pauline Frederick (Faith Andes), H. B. Warner (Priam Andes), Mary Duncan (Dorothy Mears), Sam Hardy (Pete Harris), Tom Douglas (The Boy), Richard "Skeets" Gallagher (Eddie Mack), Aileen Pringle (Mrs. Walcott), Ivan F. Simpson (Mr. Vayne), George E. Stone (The Cat), Robert McWade (Herbert Walcott), Hilda Vaughn (Carter), Gavin Gordon (Will Jones), Matty Kemp (Frank Andes), Eddie Sturges (Bright Eyes), Robert Elliott (Tall Man).

BY THE MID-1920S, Hollywood was in the midst of a financial crisis prompted by the invention of the radio. The American public was finding it just as entertaining to sit by a warm fire in the comfort of their homes, listening to their favorite soap opera, pulp western, or crooner rather than going out on the town to one of the movie houses. In order to recoup their losses, the studio chiefs had to dream up ideas to lure the American public from their comfortable domiciles, away from the cursed radio.

The advent of sound proved to be just what the public needed...the ability to see and hear their favorite stars. Unfortunately, many movie personalities tested unfavorably before the dreaded microphone and, as a result, were dropped from their current contracts, only to be relegated to obscure roles. For many this proved tragic indeed, with several dying shortly after following bouts with alcohol or drugs. In haste, Hollywood combed the New York theatre circuit, obtaining the services of stage actors who would soon become superstars, like Paul Muni, Edward G. Robinson, James Cagney, Joan Blondell, Spencer Tracy, and many others.

In 1932, RKO Radio Pictures hit upon a novel idea, and with the cooperation of the NBC Radio Network, devised a plan which would bring in numerous financial rewards for both concerns. In August of 1932, NBC began a six-week murder-thriller serial entitled *The Phantom of Crestwood*, written by Bartlett Cormack and J. Walter Reuben. As the melodrama unfolded, radio listeners were engulfed in a mysterious web of murder and foul play, all leading to the inevitable question, "Who killed Jenny Wren?" Following the conclusion of chapter six, NBC announced that the radio public should submit their own ending, identifying who they think the culprit would be, with various prizes being sent out to the winner (or winners). The studio also informed listeners that RKO Radio Pictures would release the whole story in a feature-length photoplay, with the "secret solution" to the murder fully resolved! Although the film held no real surprises for Depression-era audiences, it did make a $100,000 profit, a tidy sum indeed considering that RKO was suffering one of its worst movie seasons in one of the bleakest years of the period.

For the lead roles, the studio borrowed actress Karen Morley from MGM in the role of the insufferable Jenny Wren, with Ricardo Cortez cast as one of the unlikely suspects, a gangster with a rather likable streak. The man chosen to direct this moody melodrama was none other than J. Walter Reuben, who was also one of the writers. Surprisingly, he turns in a

The Phantom of Crestwood (1932) Faith Andes (Pauline Frederick) leads unsuspecting Esther Wren (Anita Louise) through the underground caverns of the Andes Estate.

fine job, giving considerably good characterizations to the long list of red-herrings involved in the plot. His success in this picture led to another rather offbeat filmic chore, and another foray into the macabre, *Trouble for Two* (1936), starring Robert Montgomery and Rosalind Russell, based on Robert Louis Stevenson's story, *The Suicide Club.*

Recently *The Phantom of Crestwood*, once thought to be a lost film, has been restored in its entirety, including the prologue, which was supposedly filmed at the NBC Radio Network, telling audiences the origin of the production. Seen today, the film is rather predictable, with no real surprises. However, the superb camera work with the characters falling in and out of the shadows of an old castle still continues to delight mystery fans today!

According to film historian Hal Erickson, "The precedent for this (movie) was *The Trial of Vivienne Ware* (1932), which began as a New York radio serial in 1931 (featuring genuine jurists in the acting roles), was "syndicated" by way of shipping the script out to other stations and other actors, then converted into a novel—and a movie. However, it did not withhold the ending until the film came out. The ending of the radio version of *The Phantom of Crestwood* (that is, the one that won the contest) was not the same as the one in the movie. *The Phantom of Crestwood*'s prologue was cut from the C&C TV print in 1956, but restored for later cable showings. The most famous product of this radio-movie synergetic experience was Fox's *Chandu the Magician*, the script of which was an abridged version of the radio series' first sixty-eight episodes."

The Old Dark House (1932)

A Universal Pictures Release. Produced by Carl Laemmle, Jr. Directed by James Whale. Screenplay by Benn W. Levy, J. B. Priestley, and R.C. Sheriff based on the novel "Benighted" by J.B. Priestly. Photography by Arthur Edeson. Edited by Clarence Kolster. Art Direction by Charles D. Hall. Sound by William Hedgcock. Make-up by Jack Pierce. Assistant Director: Joseph A. McDonough. Music by David Broekman and Heinz Roemheld. 71 min.

Cast: Boris Karloff (Morgan), Melvyn Douglas (Roger Penderel), Charles Laughton (Sir William Porterhouse), Lillian Bond (Gladys DuCane), Ernest Thesiger (Horace Femm), Raymond Massey (Philip Waverton), Eva Moore (Rebecca Femm), Gloria Stuart (Margaret Waverton), Elspeth Dudgeon (Sir Roderick Femm), Brember Wills (Saul Femm).

JAMES WHALE IS GENERALLY REMEMBERED as the director of some of Universal's best horror films of the 1930s. But what some don't realize is that this prolific filmmaker only turned out four from this genre throughout his entire career! Beginning as a stage actor in England, he migrated to the U.S., where he was put to work on the Howard Hughes spectacular *Hell's Angels* (1930), the film that made Jean Harlow a star. Following this, he was invited to direct a film version of his London stage play *Journey's End*, which would have been a greater success had it not been for the concurrent release of another war melodrama, *All Quiet on the Western Front*. It was then that Carl Laemmle Jr. of Universal Pictures signed him to a contract, rewarding Whale with such "prestige pictures" as *Waterloo Bridge* (1931) with Mae Clarke and Douglass Montgomery, *Frankenstein* (1931), *The Invisible Man* (1933) with Claude Rains, the exceptional *By Candlelight* (1933) with Elissa Landi and Paul Lucas, *The Bride of Frankenstein* (1935), *Remember Last Night* (1935), a murder mystery which has improved through the years due to the current acceptance of black comedy, and the 1936 version of *Show Boat*.

After his overwhelming hit *Frankenstein*, which made Boris Karloff a household name, Whale was given another vehicle for him. Although Karloff is sadly wasted in this classic horror film, *The Old Dark House* is nevertheless a superb example of the creepy murder mystery thrillers of the silent era. As a matter of fact, this film was definitely influenced by Paul Leni's silent classic *The Cat and the Canary* (1927) with Laura LaPlante and Creighton Hale. Not only are the sets almost identical in certain scenes (both films having Charles D. Hall as set designer), but the camera angles are basically the same.

The cast of *The Old Dark House* is also quite impressive, with Melvyn Douglas cast as the romantic lead opposite Lillian Bond, and Raymond Massey (in his first film role) and Gloria Stuart cast as stranded motorists who must spend a night in the spooky old mansion. Charles Laughton was originally brought to America to co-star with Tallulah Bankhead in Paramount's *The Devil and the Deep*, however, due to unforeseen delays, Laughton had some free time on his hands and was cast in this, his first American film. The icing on the cake is the casting of Whale's chum from

The Old Dark House (1932) Margaret Waverton (Gloria Stuart) is being annoyed by Rebecca Femm (Eva Moore). (RF)

The Old Dark House (1932) Philip Waverton (Raymond Massey), Sir William Porterhouse (Charles Laughton) and Margaret Waverton (Gloria Stuart) are all wondering about the strange "goings-on" that are occurring in Horace Femm's (Ernest Thesiger) home. (RF)

the English stage, Ernest Thesiger, who is excellent as Horace Femm, head of a most unusual household. His deliberate enunciation and his bravura performance make *The Old Dark House* a treasure to behold! (For more on Thesiger, one only has to screen his performance in *The Bride of Frankenstein* as Dr. Pretorius three years later.) Another favorite is Eva Moore's casting as the "slightly deaf" Rebecca Femm, screeching her lines "No beds! You can't have beds!" to the weary travelers as they wonder where they will be put up for the night.

One of two bizarre roles was given to the small-statured British actor Brember Wills, who plays the crazed maniac Saul Femm, the so-called "skeleton" in the Femm household. With the other odd bit of casting, James Whale had a laugh on his cast and crew, as well as the audience, when the senior member of the Femm clan, the aged Sir Roderick, was played by one John Dudgeon. Never letting anyone in on his little gag, Whale introduced a little old woman named Elspeth Dudgeon to his crew after the picture had wrapped, telling them that this sweet old lady had actually played Sir Roderick! With the expert make-up applications by Jack Pierce, it came as a total surprise to everyone!

Critics again lauded James Whale for even outdoing his *Frankenstein*, with William Boehnel of the *New York World-Telegram* exclaiming, "When shockers are inherently sound as this one there is cause for considerable cheering, for this is the type of story that movies can do superlatively well". Thank heavens we can still enjoy this horror classic today, for there was a time when all prints of *The Old Dark House* were thought to be lost. Even the original negative had badly decomposed beyond saving. So for many years, film enthusiasts had to be content with publicity stills and glowing reviews. Fortunately in 1968, a somewhat shrunken 35mm positive was found in the Universal vaults and a safety negative was immediately struck for future generations to enjoy. After viewing this treasure, lines like "Have a potato" and "It's only gin…only gin, you know…I like gin" stay with the viewer, among the many other classic quotes from this timeless thriller!

Three on a Match (1932)

A First National Picture. Directed by Mervyn LeRoy. Screenplay by Lucien Hubbard. Dialogue by Kubec Glasmon and John Bright. Based on a story by Kubec Glasmon and John Bright. Photography by Sol Polito. Edited by Ray Curtis. Art Direction by Robert Haas. Orchestral Arrangements by Ray Heindorf. Musical Direction by Leo F. Forbstein. 64 min.

Cast: Joan Blondell (Mary Keaton), Warren William (Henry Kirkwood), Ann Dvorak (Vivien Revere), Bette Davis (Ruth Westcott), Lyle Talbot (Mike Loftus), Humphrey Bogart (The Mug), Edward Arnold (The Boss), Ann Shirley (Vivien, as a Child), Virginia Davis (Mary, as a Child), Betty Carrs (Ruth, as a Child), Buster Phelps (Junior), Patricia Ellis (Linda), Sheila Terry (Naomi), Grant Mitchell (Principal of School), Glenda Farrell (Inmate), Frankie Darro (Bobby), Clara Blandick (Mrs. Keaton), Hale Hamilton (Defense Attorney), Dick Brandon (Horace), Junior Johnson (Max), Sidney Miller (Schoolmate), Allen Jenkins (Henchman), Jack La Rue (Henchman), Herman Bing (Orchestra Leader).

ONE OF THE MOST SHOCKING "pre-Hays Code" releases of 1932, *Three on a Match* deals with such taboo subject matters as infidelity, drug abuse, and a dash of child abuse thrown in for good measure. Naturally, civic groups, and especially the Catholic Church, were appalled by such amoral behavior as depicted in this and other films that were being ground out by the major studios in the early thirties. As a result, these same crusaders of decency attempted to propose a ban on certain films containing themes about "fallen women," feeling they would harm the morals of American youth. Gangster movies, especially, were the rage of the movie-going nation, and all too often the cheap hoodlum was depicted as a Prohibition-era hero who would get away scot-free at the film's conclusion.

Three on a Match (1932) Kidnapping thugs Harve (Humphrey Bogart), Dick (Allen Jenkins) and two other henchmen (Jack La Rue and Stanley Price) threaten drug-addicted Vivian Revere (Ann Dvorak). (AB)

To appease these righteous organizations, and before there was imminent government intervention, Hollywood decided to institute their own set of censorship rules. As a result, they selected Will H. Hays, a former U.S. Postmaster General dating back to President Harding's administration, to oversee all of Hollywood's output. This originally took place in 1922, following numerous Hollywood scandals (i.e. the Fatty Arbuckle scandal and the William Desmond Taylor murder). But, as the 1920s moved on, the "code" was generally ignored and almost ridiculed by filmmakers. By 1933, after a number of films dealing with prostitution, suicide, white slavery, etc. were released, there was another public outcry stating that these films were demoralizing in their depictions of women. So, in 1934, Will Hays elected Joseph Breen as director of the Code Administration, with Breen stating "that no picture shall be produced which will lower the standards of those who see it. Hence the sympathy of the audience should never be thrown to the side of crime, wrongdoing, evil, or sin." After forming a rigid set of rules that had to be adhered to, Hollywood's output was totally whitewashed, with all of their productions staying within the boundaries of "wholesome entertainment."

Not so with *Three on a Match*, released before the code was instituted. Viewing it today for nostalgic purposes, one can readily see some of the up-and-coming "superstars" (and I'm not using that term loosely) like Humphrey Bogart and Bette Davis. This was Bogie's tenth film in two years, having attained really nothing more than supporting roles in a string of films at Fox and two for Warners. It wasn't until four years later that he would gain success, in a part reprised from his stage appearance as Duke Mantee in the screen version of Robert Sherwood's *The Petrified Forest*. Naturally, the brothers Warner signed him to a contract, but, to his dismay, he was cast mainly in secondary gangster roles opposite Edward G. Robinson or James Cagney. It wasn't until 1941 that Bogart accepted plum leads in two film noir classics: *High Sierra* and *The Maltese Falcon*, which had originally been offered to George Raft, who immediately turned them down!

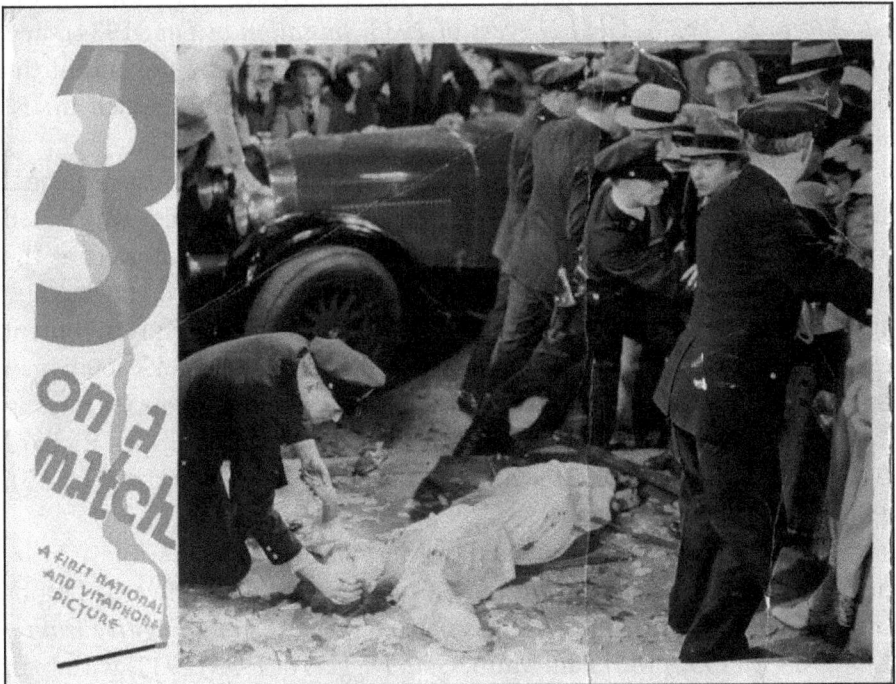

Three on a Match (1932) Vivian Revere (Ann Dvorak) leaps to her death to attract the police in order to save the life of her little boy. (AB)

Likewise, Bette Davis was being totally wasted in small, unimportant ingénue roles, until in 1934, she pleaded with studio executives to be loaned out to star in RKO's *Of Human Bondage*. Impressed by her performance, Warners realized that they had a truly gifted performer in their midst, and a year later, cast her in her first Oscar winner entitled *Dangerous*.

As for the rest of the cast, Joan Blondell came to Hollywood after a long stint on Broadway with fellow thespian, James Cagney. They ultimately were cast together in the screen version of *Penny Arcade*, which was re-christened *Sinner's Holiday* (1930). Both Cagney and Blondell, whose work had been perfected in many "Pre-Code" movies, clicked with the public instantly, exchanging rapid-fire verbal jibes at one another and delighting Depression-era audiences everywhere.

Warren William began his career in silent films, using his real name Warren Krech. When talkies took over, he then changed his name to William and ultimately was enlisted by Warner Bros. as a sort of John Barrymore replacement. With his tall frame, good looks, and cultured voice, William enjoyed a most lucrative career in the early thirties, appearing in not only *Three on a Match*, but also *Skyscraper Souls* (1932), *Employees' Entrance* (1933), *Gold Diggers of 1933*, *Imitation of Life* (1934), and *Cleopatra* (1934), cast as Julius Caesar. Unfortunately, by the end of the decade, his popularity began to fade and he soon found himself in "B" movies or secondary leads in bigger-budgeted films.

Acting honors for *Three on a Match* go to one of the most neglected actresses of all time: Ann Dvorak, who plays Vivien Revere. Ann started as an extra at Metro-Goldwyn-Mayer and later achieved notoriety as the kid sister of Paul Muni's Tony Camonte in the 1932 Howard Hawks classic, *Scarface* (a film whose violence and hints of incest are pretty potent even by today's standards). Like Warren William, Ms. Dvorak's star began to dim and she also was wasted in "B" pictures after some meaty roles in *The Strange Love of Molly Louvain* (1932), *Massacre* (1934), with Richard Barthelmess, *G-Men* (1935), with James Cagney, and *Dr. Socrates* (1935), again with Paul Muni.

Three on a Match was directed by Mervyn LeRoy, who, while at Warners, turned out such classics as *Little Caesar* (1930) with Edward G. Robinson, Glenda Farrell, and Douglas Fairbanks, Jr., *I Am a Fugitive from a Chain Gang* (1932) with Paul Muni, *Gold Diggers of 1933* (1933) with Joan Blondell and Warren William, and *Anthony Adverse* (1936) with Fredric March, as well as the powerful social drama *They Won't Forget* (1937) with

Claude Rains and Gloria Dickson. Giving up his directorial chores for the time being, LeRoy produced many fine films at MGM after being lured to that studio by Louis B. Mayer, filling the void following Irving Thalberg's death. By 1940, the hankering to direct returned to the producer, and MGM, eager to oblige, put him to work on such box-office hits as *Waterloo Bridge* (1940) with Vivien Leigh and Robert Taylor, *Random Harvest* (1942) with Ronald Colman and Greer Garson, *Madame Currie* (1943) with Greer Garson and Walter Pidgeon, and *Thirty Seconds Over Tokyo* (1944) with Spencer Tracy and Van Johnson.

Red Dust (1932)

A Metro-Goldwyn-Mayer Picture. Directed by Victor Fleming. Based on the play by Wilson Collison. Screenplay by John Lee Mahin. Photography by Harold Rosson. Edited by Blanche Sewell. Art Direction by Cedric Gibbons. Sound by Douglas Shearer. 83 min.

Cast: Jean Harlow (Vantine), Clark Gable (Dennis Carson), Gene Raymond (Gary Willis), Mary Astor (Barbara Willis), Donald Crisp (Guidon), Tully Marshall (McQuarg), Forrester Harvey (Limey), Willie Fung (Hoy).

BY 1932, Jean Harlow and Clark Gable's screen careers were accelerating rapidly. So rapidly, in fact, that Metro-Goldwyn-Mayer would subsequently co-star them in a racy, steamy love triangle drama set in the jungles of an Indonesian rubber plantation entitled *Red Dust*. This first teaming (they had previously appeared together in *The Secret Six*, but not as a team) was the most successful of the five films they co-starred in.

MGM purchased the film rights in 1927, but was worried that the property, a play by Wilson Collison, was considered too hot to be translated into a movie. After all, the two female leads were a prostitute and an adulteress, and the male lead was a double-dealing snake. Originally intended as a vehicle for Greta Garbo, it was then considered for either Norma Shearer or Joan Crawford. Production chief Irving Thalberg had other ideas as to the casting of Vantine, the hooker with a heart of gold. After realizing the enormous success of Harlow's previous performance as a female of questionable morals in *Red-Headed Woman* (1932), he thought that Jean could bring a funny slant to the picture while being sexy at the same time. Thalberg was also set on casting fading silent film heartthrob John Gilbert, who would lend a sense of refined dignity as the plantation foreman, Dennis Carson. Unfortunately for Gilbert, studio head Louis B. Mayer despised him and nixed that plan, suggesting Gable instead.

Red Dust (1932) Dennis Carson (Clark Gable, right) wonders how Hoy (Willie Fung) got the "shiner," while McQuarg (Tully Marshall) tends to more important matters. (RF)

When production began, the stars were subjected to a tortuous workload. A miniature rain forest with foreman's cabin was built on Soundstage Six, with the studio arc lights constantly blaring at full steam, turning the set into a nightmarish hell, with the heat levels hitting well into the nineties. When the actors and technicians complained to director Victor Fleming, he casually reminded them that they were supposed to be in the jungle, and that everybody sweats in the jungle.

The filming went smoothly enough until, on the morning of Labor Day, Jean Harlow's husband, MGM executive Paul Bern, was found dead from a gunshot wound to the head. Rumors ran rampant through the scandal sheets, stating that Bern and Harlow never consummated their marriage. Other reports claimed that Bern was either homosexual or impotent. Whatever the reason, Harlow was in a state of shock, which forced the production of *Red Dust* to be shut down indefinitely. After one week, Harlow called Irving Thalberg and told him that she couldn't stand sitting around the house day in and day out, claiming that going back to work might lift her spirits. When she returned to the set, Fleming was shocked

Red Dust (1932) Dennis Carson (Clark Gable) administers First Aid to one of his workers while Barbara Willis (Mary Astor) wishes that he would tend to her. (RF)

to see an exhausted and saddened Harlow reporting to the set. He decided to shoot long shots only for the next few days until she looked more rested. However, on day two, she was ready to do retakes on the famous "bathing scene," in which Vantine takes a bath in the raw in a rain barrel, much to the consternation of Gable. Always the little vixen, Harlow, who was indeed topless, stood up during one of the takes and shouted playfully, "Something for the boys in the lab!"

When the film was previewed in October of 1932 it was very well received. However, the studio heads were concerned about the inevitable censorship restrictions that would greet the film. Since this was a Pre-Code release, there is a much more open frankness involving sex and adultery, not evident in films two years later, when the new censorship board, with much stricter (albeit ridiculous) rules would be in effect. Coming in at a cost of $408,000, the film made a huge profit of $399,000. Not bad considering that this was at the height of the Great Depression. Released on November 4, 1932, the film garnered excellent reviews universally. *Time* magazine stated, "Given *Red Dust*'s brazen moral values,

Gable and Harlow have full play for their curiously similar sort of good-natured toughness. The best lines go to Harlow. She bathes hilariously in a rain barrel, reads Gable a bedtime story about a chipmunk and a rabbit. Her effortless vulgarity, humor, and slovenliness make as noteworthy a characterization in the genre as the late Jeanne Eagle's *Sadie Thompson.*"

Red Dust was later remade by MGM two more times. The first one was entitled *Congo Maisie* (1940), a programmer starring Ann Sothern and John Carroll, and was part of the popular Maisie series, which ran from 1939 to 1947. The second was called *Mogambo* (1953), a Technicolor extravaganza directed by John Ford and recasting Clark Gable in the lead. Despite a bigger budget and MGM superstars Ava Gardner and Grace Kelly, the film, although quite good in parts, was not nearly as entertaining as *Red Dust*.

Call Her Savage (1932)

Fox Film Corporation. Produced by Sam E. Rork. Directed by John Francis Dillon. Screenplay by Edwin Burke. Based on the novel by Tiffany Thayer. Photography by Lee Garmes. Art Direction by Max Parker. Assistant Director: Jack Boland. 88 min.

Cast: Clara Bow (Nasa "Dynamite" Springer), Monroe Owsley (Lawrence Crosby), Gilbert Roland (Moonglow), Thelma Todd (Sunny DeLan), Estelle Taylor (Ruth Springer), Willard Robertson (Peter Springer), Weldon Heyburn (Ronasa), Anthony Jowitt (Jay Randall), Fred Koehler, Sr. (Silas Young), Margaret Livingston (Molly), Dorothy Peterson (Mrs. Young), Carl Stockdale (Mort), Arthur Hoyt (Attorney), Hale Hamilton (Cyrus Randall), Katherine Perry (Maid), John Elliott (Hank), Mischa Auer (Agitator in Restaurant), Mary Gordon (Tenement Lady), Bert Roach and Walter Long (Johns).

ALTHOUGH REVIVALS OF THE FILMS of Clara Bow are few and far between, it must be remembered that during the jazz age, she was one of its most popular attractions. Born on August 25, 1905 in Brooklyn, New York, Clara was sent to Hollywood at the age of sixteen after winning a beauty contest. Starting in bit parts, she soon elevated to meaty supporting roles, and, through the auspices of producer B. P. Schulberg, landed a contract with Paramount Pictures. Once settled there, her fun-loving, liberated attitude (on and off the screen) was well suited to the mores of the roaring twenties. With a starring role in Elinor Gynt's story *It* in 1927, Clara was now a full-fledged star, winning the nickname the "It Girl" after the movie. Soon, this tag was used to describe many other stars, who possessed that something extra, a quality which makes one stand out in a crowd.

Soon, after other box office attractions like *Wings* (1927) and *Red Hair* (1928), Clara found, to her dismay, that the arrival of talkies was to be a great threat, not only to her career, but to many other silent screen veterans. Unfortunately, her early talkies contain a combination of poor scripts and lackluster performances, a detriment which would eventually hamper her career. Also plagued with ill health and numerous scandals, her reputation was in question, resulting in the Catholic Church (who would later cast a stronghold on Hollywood) denouncing her current movie output. In 1931, she married ex-cowboy star Rex Bell, who would later become lieutenant governor of Nevada. Never one to be out of the limelight for long, she attempted to take another crack at Hollywood, signing with the Fox Film Corporation, who immediately cast her in the potent 'Pre-Code' vehicle *Call Her Savage*, which was based on Tiffany Thayer's steamy novel. Unquestionably one of the era's most outrageous movies, this film offers a varied assortment of interesting highlights, including sequences taking place in a gay bar in Greenwich Village, a romp with a Great Dane, and other questionable episodes.

The director, John Francis Dillon, does a remarkable job trying to keep the overly contrived plot believable, for there is enough material in

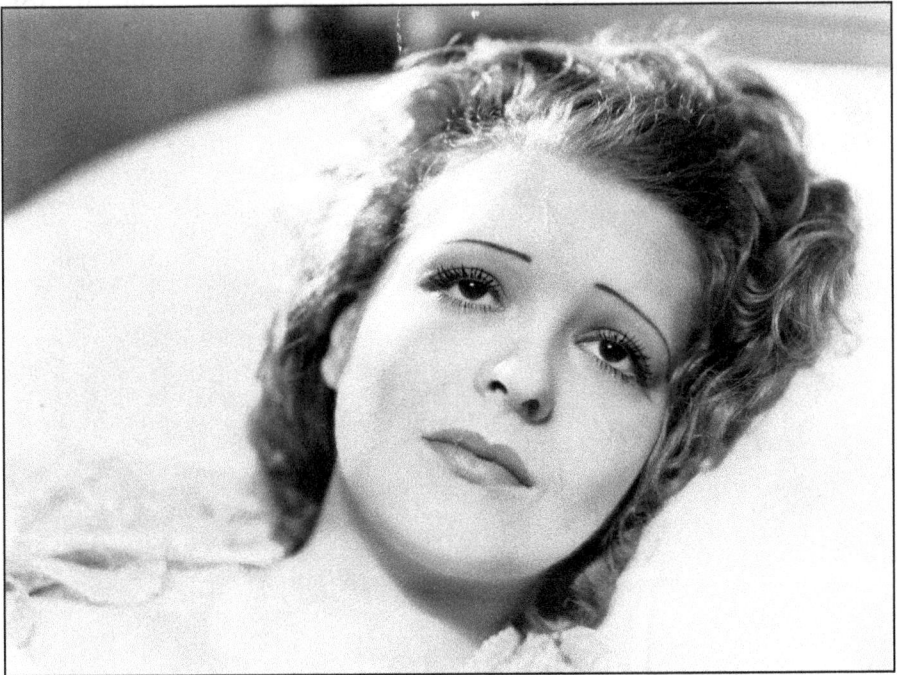

Call Her Savage (1932) Clara Bow plays rebellious Nasa Springer, whose life goes through many phases, from schoolgirl, to unwed mother, to prostitute in a matter of a few reels of film. (RF)

Call Her Savage for three movies! Nevertheless, Miss Bow turns in a fine performance, even though we are not supposed to recognize the Brooklyn twang in her speech. Also, there must have been much commotion with the temperamental star, because throughout the film she was drinking heavily and overeating, which explains her tremendous weight gain in some scenes. But, as fate would allow, after one more film entitled *Hoopla* (another good endeavor, which didn't attract any attention), Miss Bow retired from the screen.

According to some sources, she was later considered for the part of Belle Fawcett in 20th Century Fox's spectacular *In Old Chicago* five years later. This was to be a vehicle for Clark Gable and Jean Harlow, whom MGM was to loan to Fox in exchange for the services of Shirley Temple, originally set to star in *The Wizard of Oz*. But, as fate would have it, Miss Harlow's untimely death would curtail all plans, and ultimately Fox executives decided on their resident heartthrob Tyrone Power for the lead. When Clara Bow was eventually summoned to the studio for a screen test, the powers that be were astonished to see that the former "It" girl was exceedingly overweight. As a result, the vivacious Alice Faye landed the role instead! Whether this story is true or not, it seems a shame that this energetic, "modern" young lady's movies are so forgotten today.

The Kid from Spain (1932)

United Artists Release. Produced by Samuel Goldwyn. Directed by Leo McCarey. Dances by Busby Berkeley. Story and Screenplay by William Anthony McGuire, Bert Kalmar and Harry Ruby. Photography by Gregg Toland. Edited by Stuart Heisler. Sound by Vinton Vernon. Songs by Bert Kalmar and Harry Ruby: "Look What You've Done", "In the Moonlight", and "What a Perfect Combination" by Bert Kalmar, Harry Ruby and Harry Akst. 96 min.

Cast: Eddie Cantor (Eddie Williams), Lyda Roberti (Rosalie), Robert Young (Ricardo), Ruth Hall (Anita Gomez), John Miljan (Pancho), Noah Beery (Alonza Gomez), J. Carrol Naish (Pedro), Robert Emmett O'Connor (Crawford), Stanley Fields (Jose), Paul Porcasi (Gonzales, Border Guard), Julian Rivero (Dalmores), Theresa Maxwell (Martha Oliver), Walter Walker (The Dean), Ben Hendricks, Jr. (Red), Sidney Franklin (The American Matador), Betty Grable, Paulette Goddard and Toby Wing (The Goldwyn Girls), Edgar Connor (Negro Bull Handler), Leo Willis (Robber), Harry Gribbon (Traffic Cop), Eddie Foster (Patron), Harry C. Bradley (Man on Line).

A GRADUATE OF THE BURLESQUE and vaudeville circuits from 1910 to 1916, Eddie Cantor first hit his stride in the Broadway production of *The Midnight Frolics* (1916), where he did a comedic song and dance act. Famed showman Florenz Ziegfeld soon brought Eddie into his *Ziegfeld Follies*, where he joined the likes of such future legends as Fanny Brice, Will Rogers, and W. C. Fields. By the late 1920s, he was the toast of Broadway, starring in such hits as *Kid Boots* (1926) and *Whoopee* (1930), which would later that year become his ticket to Hollywood, signing a long-term contract with Samuel Goldwyn. Realizing the enormous popularity of *Whoopee* and its star, Goldwyn quickly made a screen version of the stage play, also employing the unique talents of legendary cho-

155

reographer Busby Berkeley, whose amazing displays of young ladies in perfect symmetry enhanced by crane shots created an incredibly surreal kaleidoscopic effect. Before long, Berkeley was one of the most sought after dance directors in Hollywood, eliciting a style revered and copied by many other choreographers as well.

Following the instant success of *Whoopee*, Goldwyn followed through with another Eddie Cantor/Busby Berkeley collaboration entitled *Palmy Days* (1931) which was a slight improvement over their first venture, due to less static camerawork and a more cohesive plot line. By 1932, Goldwyn assigned Leo McCarey to direct *The Kid from Spain*, which remains one of the best Eddie Cantor vehicles, combining the expert skills of its star, dance director, as well as the inimitable Lyda Roberti as Cantor's sex hungry love interest. Director McCarey was a graduate of the Hal Roach Studio, where as supervising director (and sometime director) of the now famous Laurel and Hardy short subjects, he was able to learn the fine craft

The Kid From Spain (1932) Eddie Williams a.k.a Don Sebastian II (Eddie Cantor) is being told by Rosalie (Lyda Roberti) where she keeps her clothes. (RF)

of making classic comedies. While at Roach, he also directed almost all of the Charley Chase and Max Davidson silents, which withstand the test of time even today! After his tenure at Roach, McCarey worked with the best comedians in Hollywood, like the Marx Brothers (*Duck Soup*), Mae West (*Belle of the Nineties*), W. C. Fields (*Six of a Kind*) and Harold Lloyd (*The Milky Way*). With a proven track record like that, he finally found himself in the elite company of Irene Dunne and Cary Grant, where he won his first Academy Award directing the classic screwball comedy *The Awful Truth* in 1937. From there, his career quickly accelerated with future releases like *Love Affair* (1939), *Going My Way* (1944), *The Bells of St. Mary's* (1945), *My Son John* (1952), and *An Affair to Remember* (1958), which was a remake of his own earlier and much better *Love Affair*.

When *The Kid from Spain* was released, it received great reviews, supported by incredible box-office receipts, making the film one of the top grossers of 1932. Its Pre-Code dialogue between Eddie and his nymphomaniac love interest Lyda Roberti is one of the highlights, as well

The Kid From Spain (1932) Another titillating still from the same scene with Rosalie (Lyda Roberti) and Eddie Williams (Eddie Cantor). (RF)

The Kid From Spain (1932) The Goldwyn Girls. Among the more famous ones are Betty Grable, Paulette Goddard and Toby Wing. (RF)

The Kid From Spain (1932) Dorm monitor, Miss Martha Oliver (Theresa Maxwell Conover) admonishes Eddie Williams for being caught in the girl's dormitory…in one of their beds! (RF)

as the snappy numbers "Look What You've Done" and "What a Perfect Combination" by Bert Kalmar and Harry Ruby. One can't forget to mention the eye-popping Busby Berkeley numbers, enhanced by the scantily clad Goldwyn Girls, who include newcomers Betty Grable, Paulette Goddard, and Toby Wing. The film's only detriment is the romantic subplot between bland Robert Young and Ruth Hall, who seem very ill at ease with their uninteresting material. Thankfully, we aren't away from Eddie and Lyda long enough for boredom to set in. Totally forgotten, though unjustly, because her career was shortened by her untimely death in 1938, Lyda Roberti only appeared in eleven features and several shorts, but her mere presence was a guarantee to enliven many a film during the early 1930s. According to comedienne Patsy Kelly, who had been teamed with her briefly in a handful of shorts, Miss Roberti bent over to tie a shoelace when she was stricken with a massive heart attack at age thirty-one.

While some audiences of today might frown upon the inevitable "black-face" number evident in almost all of the Eddie Cantor films, one must remember that ethnic and racial humor was a staple on vaudeville stages from the late 1800s well into the 1930s. Entertainers like Al Jolson and Eddie Cantor weren't performing these numbers to ridicule or embarrass African-Americans, but rather to pay homage to their unique style of song and dance. It would be a shame to store films like *The Kid from Spain* in a film vault from now on because some narrow-minded individual found something offensive in it. It should be remembered that these movies are mini-time capsules and reflect the time and mores of a bygone generation.

I Am a Fugitive from a Chain Gang (1932)

Warner Bros. Directed by Mervyn LeRoy. Based on a story by Robert E. Burns, *I Am a Fugitive from a Georgia Chain Gang*. Screenplay, Howard J. Green and Brown Holmes. Art Director, Jack Okey. Photography, Sol Polito. Film Editor, William Holmes. Gowns, Orry-Kelly. Technical Advisors, S. H. Sullivan and Jack Miller. Cut from existing prints: Spencer Charters (C. K. Hobb), Roscoe Karns (Steve), William Janney (Sheriff's Son), Harry Holman (Sheriff of Monroe). Actors replaced during production: Oscar Apfel by Edward Le Saint, C. Henry Gordon by Douglass Dumbrille, John Marston by Willard Robertson, Russell Simpson by Erville Alderson, Sam Baker by Everett Brown, Dewey Robinson by Walter Long, Edward Arnold by Wallis Clark, Morgan Wallace by Robert McWade. 93 min.

Cast: Paul Muni (James Allen), Glenda Farrell (Marie Woods), Helen Vinson (Helen), Preston Foster (Pete), Allen Jenkins (Barney Sikes), Edward Ellis (Bomber Wells), John Wray (Nordine), Hale Hamilton (Reverend Robert Clinton Allen), Harry Woods (Guard), David Landau (Warden), Edward J. McNamara (Second Warden), Robert McWade (Ramsey), Willard Robertson (Prison Commissioner), Noel Francis (Linda), Louise Carter (Mrs. Allen), Berton Churchill (The Judge), Sheila Terry (Allen's Secretary), Sally Blane (Alice), James Bell (Red), Edward LeSaint (Chairman of Chamber of Commerce), Douglass Dumbrille (District Attorney), Robert Warwick (Fuller), Charles Middleton (Train Conductor), Reginald Barlow (Parker), Jack La Rue (Ackerman), Charles Sellon (Owner of Hot Dog Stand), Erville Alderson (Chief of Police), George Pat Collins (Wilson), William Pawley (Doggy), Lew Kelly (Mike, Proprietor of Diner), Everett Brown (Sebastian T. Yale), William LeMaire (Texan), George Cooper (Vaudevillian), Wallis Clark (Lawyer), Walter Long (Blacksmith), Frederick Burton (Georgia Prison Official), Irving Bacon (Barber, Bill), Lee Shumway, J. Frank Glendon (Arresting Officers), Dennis O'Keefe (Dance Extra).

BASED ON A BOOK about the author's own experiences, *I Am a Fugitive From a Georgia Chain Gang* by Robert Burns, this classic social drama depicts the harsh treatment the inmates suffer in a southern penal system.

The film's director, Mervyn LeRoy, became interested in adapting the book into a movie in 1931 when he begged Warner Bros. studio head Jack Warner to purchase the rights to the novel from its author. As it turned out, Burns, who was still a fugitive from justice after his last escape, was living peacefully in New Jersey, a state which had no extradition agreements with Georgia. For added authenticity, producer Hal Wallis had Burns smuggled incognito to Hollywood to lend further insight into the project as 'special' technical advisor. Naturally, Burns was rather reluctant to make the long trek since he was at risk of being arrested for a third time! After many promises and assurances that his identity would be kept a secret, Burns made the trip to Burbank and proved an invaluable asset to the production, especially to Paul Muni. Muni, an actor of great depth, managed to bring an added dimension to his role by studying the author's movements, walk, mannerisms etc. explaining, "I don't want to imitate you, I want to *be* you!"

The cinematography by Sol Polito proved extremely effective, with its dark shadows and dimly lit sets ideally enhancing the bleak brutalities with which these poor souls were victimized. As for the film's director, Mervyn LeRoy, he was one of Warners' premier directors, sharing the spotlight with the great Michael Curtiz. LeRoy's vast filmography includes such diverse classics as *Five Star Final* (1931) with Edward G. Robinson (another crackling depression-era social drama about yellow journalism), *Gold Diggers of 1933* (1933), *Waterloo Bridge* (1940), and *Random Harvest* (1942).

With *Chain Gang*, LeRoy guided Muni perfectly through the film, right up to the final curtain line where girlfriend Helen Vinson pleadingly questions the now desperate fugitive James Allen (Muni), "How do you live?" "I steal!" is the swift reply, with the shadowed visage of Allen suddenly disappearing as the screen turns black, while footsteps are heard running on the soundtrack. In actuality, this last segment of the movie was a faux pas. A fuse blew during shooting causing all the lights to go out at that very moment, after which they replaced the fuse and filmed the scene as planned. At the next morning's rushes, the director and producer decided that the 'ruined' take proved more effective than the one originally conceived.

I Am a Fugitive From a Chain Gang (1932) James Allen (Paul Muni) is about to receive a lashing from a prison guard (Harry Woods) for speaking his mind. (RF)

When *Chain Gang* was released in November of 1932, it did moderate business but eventually gained a solid reputation with the critics, who rallied for public awareness against the Georgia state penal code. Letters were written, laws were passed and eventually conditions softened, prompting studio head Jack Warner and Mervyn Le Rody to travel south for a road show engagement. Before embarking, however, both men were receiving anonymous letters and telephone calls threatening their lives if they made the journey. Naturally all agreements were canceled!

All concerned were justly proud of the film, especially Paul Muni, who garnered his first Oscar nomination as best actor. It wasn't until 1936 that his *The Story of Louis Pasteur* won him such accolades. Although *I Am a Fugitive from a Chain Gang* was nominated for best picture, it lost out to Fox's less remembered *Cavalcade* (1933).

As originally intended, the movie was to bear the book's title, but studio officials decided to eliminate the name Georgia because they did not want to offend anyone from that state. Curiously, the film has been reissued under the title *I Am a Fugitive* for television distribution. Luckily, the original titles have been reinstated and audiences can now view the film exactly how it was released in the late fall of 1932.

I Am a Fugitive From a Chain Gang helped to improve conditions in our penal system and also opened the eyes of law enforcers by showing the brutal and harsh treatment inflicted on the inmates of a southern chain gang. Other films, released around the same time, like *Hell's Highway* (also 1932) were instrumental in bringing about more social reform. Even if Paul Muni's character James Allen had been guilty of the crime of which he was accused, the treatment while on the chain gang is overly harsh and extremely unpleasant. This is a film that holds up extremely well today, when watchdog groups of all types are continually on the lookout for social injustice.

The Mask of Fu Manchu (1932)

A Metro-Goldwyn-Mayer Picture. Produced by Hunt Stromberg. Directed by Charles Brabin and Charles Vidor (uncredited). Screenplay by Irene Kuhn, Edgar Allan Woolf and John Willard. Based on the novel *The Mask of Fu Manchu* by Sax Rohmer. Photography by Tony Gaudio. Art Direction by Cedric Gibbons. Edited by Ben Lewis. Makeup by Cecil Holland. Sound by Douglas Shearer. Special Effects by Kenneth Strickfaden. Makeup by Cecil Holland. 68 min.

Cast: Boris Karloff (Dr. Fu Manchu), Lewis Stone (Sir Denis Nayland Smith), Karen Morley (Sheila Barton), Myrna Loy (Fah Lo See), Charles Starrett (Terry Granville), Jean Hersholt (Prof. Von Berg), Lawrence Grant (Sir Lionel Barton), David Torrence (McLeod), E. Alyn Warren (Goy Lo Sung), Ferdinand Gottschalk (British Museum Official), C. Montague Shaw (British Museum Official), Willie Fung (Ship's Steward).

BY 1932, BORIS KARLOFF'S CAREER had skyrocketed due to his superlative performance as the monster in James Whale's production of *Frankenstein* (1931) for Universal. Usually cast as oily villains in films like *The Criminal Code, Smart Money, Five Star Final*, and *The Yellow Ticket* (all 1931), he soon found himself typecast in horror films, causing something of a sensation with the public and the press, and thereby resuscitating that genre. While he was contractually obligated to Universal Pictures, he was loaned to MGM to star in the title role of *The Mask of Fu Manchu*, that studio's only foray into comic strip melodrama, played fully to the hilt with tongue firmly in cheek!

Based on Sax Rohner's popular book *The Mystery of Fu Manchu*, published in America as *The Insidious Dr. Fu Manchu* in 1913, it was an immediate hit, inducing the author to write fourteen more books about the celebrated master villain. When MGM purchased the movie rights producer Hunt Stromberg wanted his film to emphasize elements of sadistic sexual

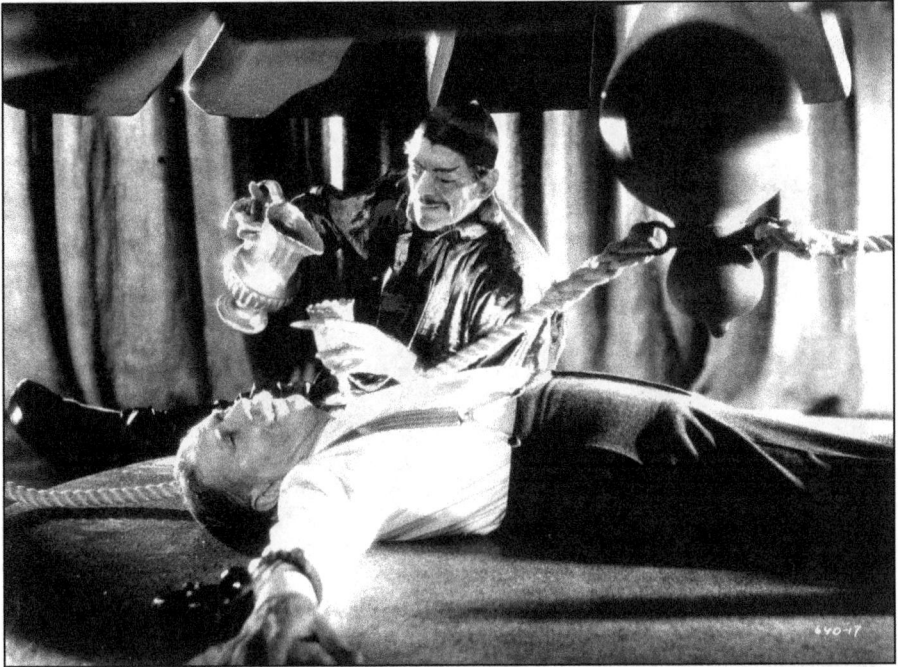

The Mask of Fu Manchu (1932) Sir Lionel Barton (Lawrence Grant) is about to be subjected to the "torture of the bells" by Dr. Fu Manchu (Boris Karloff). (RF)

behavior, something not typical in the Pre-Code style of the early 1930s. Here, Fu Manchu's lair is adorned in futuristic marble furnishings complete with torture chambers, exotic reptiles, drug-laden elixirs, not to mention Fu's sex-starved daughter, portrayed by Myrna Loy, who seems to take relish in her role as Fah Lo See.

Originally, director Charles Vidor began work on *The Mask of Fu Manchu*, but after seeing two weeks' worth of rushes MGM executives were appalled at the horrific content of the film. They hastily fired Vidor and turned over the directorial chores to Charles Brabin, whose constant rewritings of the script and numerous retakes soon became the scorn of producer Hunt Stromberg. Before long the whole affair went way over budget, with Brabin's uncertainty evident throughout the entire production. One of his many changes occurred while shooting a scene in which Sir Nayland Smith (Lewis Stone) is strapped to a torture device having steel spikes protruding from a flat surface on either end designed to close in on the unfortunate victim. Brabin felt that a more portly victim such as Professor Von Berg (Jean Hersholt) would be far more effective if he was

The Mask of Fu Manchu (1932) Fu Manchu's nymphomaniac daughter, Fah Lo See (Myrna Loy) has Terry Granville (Charles Starrett) temporarily under her power. (RF)

the person being impaled! The production took two-and-a-half months to film and went way over budget, at a final cost of $325,000.

The film did moderate business at the box-office, but today, with its strong emphasis on sex, sadism, and miscegenation, it has become a cult classic, particularly in colleges and theatrical midnight revivals. Audiences in 1932 were repulsed by some of the dialogue, which was eventually cut for a 1972 reissue when politically-correct interest groups vehemently objected to some of the more racist lines. For instance, Fu Manchu orders his followers to "Rain down on the white race and burn them!" Finally, when he presents his new offering, Sir Lionel Barton's daughter Sheila (Karen Morley), he asks his congregation, "Would you all have maidens such as this for your wives?" The crowd roars with glee…"Then conquer and breed! Kill the white man and take his women!"

The New York Times wasn't impressed with *Mask* and they snidely criticized the film, stating "And still the cinema goes busily about its task of terrorizing children. The latest of the bugaboo symposiums arrived at the Capitol yesterday under the fairly recent title *The Mask of Fu Manchu*. Its properties include Boris Karloff, one well-equipped dungeon, several hundred Chinamen, and the proper machinery for persuading a large cast…"

The Penguin Pool Murder (1932)

An RKO Radio Picture. Produced by David O. Selznick. Associate Producer: Kenneth MacGowan. Directed by George Archainbaud. Screenplay by Willis Goldbeck. Based on the novel by Stuart Palmer and the story by Lowell Brentano. Photography by Henry Gerrard. Edited by Jack Kitchin. Music by Max Steiner. British Title: *The Penguin Pool Mystery*. 70 min.

Cast: Edna Mae Oliver (Hildegarde Martha Withers), James Gleason (Inspector Oscar Piper), Mae Clarke (Gwen Parker), Robert Armstrong (Barry Costello), Donald Cook (Philip Seymour), Clarence H. Wilson (Bertrand B. Hemingway), Edgar Kennedy (Donohue), Mary Mason (Secretary), Rochelle Hudson (Telephone Operator), Guy Usher (Gerald Parker), James Donlon (Fink), Joe Hermano (Chicago Lew), William Le Maire (MacDonald), Gustav von Seyffertitz (Max), Sidney Miller (Isadore Horowitz), Jesse Scott (Abraham), Edith Fellows (Little Girl).

AFTER THE RECENT SUCCESSES of Charlie Chan's *The Black Camel* (1931) and the original *The Maltese Falcon* (1931) starring Ricardo Cortez and Bebe Daniels, many of the major studios were hopping on the bandwagon searching for stories featuring similar super sleuths. RKO, hoping to acquire a sure-fire property, purchased the rights to a story by Stuart Palmer entitled *The Penguin Pool Murder*, which featured a stuffy, middle-aged schoolmarm named Hildegarde Withers, who also has a penchant for solving murders with her inspector friend, Oscar Piper. In an inspired bit of casting, Miss Withers was played by the ever-delightful Edna Mae Oliver (it's always a treat hearing her introducing herself to the inspector in this first entry), while Inspector Piper was gloriously portrayed by the cigar-chewing gruff, yet lovable James Gleason.

As a film, *The Penguin Pool Murder* starts off promisingly enough, but as is always the case with these RKO programmers, the pacing is slightly off. What remains the saving grace to this and other entries in the series are the personalities of the two stars and the supporting cast of assorted suspects like Mae Clarke, Edgar Kennedy, Robert Armstrong, and Clarence Wilson. George Archainbaud was never more than a utility director, always doing nothing more than a capable job. He dabbled in virtually every film genre imaginable before confining himself almost exclusively to westerns.

As for the Hildegarde Withers/Inspector Piper series, it was more than a year before a follow-up was released, with *Murder on the Blackboard* proving almost as good as its predecessor. However, the third entry in the series, *Murder on a Honeymoon* (1935), is considered the best, resulting from a new director of action films in Lloyd Corrigan, and beautiful location filming at Catalina Island. By 1936, Edna Mae Oliver left the series to go on to greener pastures (and first-rate character roles over at MGM), and Helen Broderick was cast to fill in. The result: *Murder on a Bridle Path* rates as the worst in the series, proving to be a surefire cure for

The Penguin Pool Murder (1932) Attorney Barry Costello (Robert Armstrong) holds evidence that might point the "finger" at Hildegarde Withers (Edna May Oliver) as a possible suspect. (RF)

insomnia, with audiences hoping that their theatre experience would be salvaged by the "Mickey Mouse" or "Silly Symphony" that had preceded the feature!

Refusing to be "out for the count," RKO then signed on comedienne Zasu Pitts to tackle the role of the harried schoolteacher. This proved to be a happy solution, even though Miss Pitts played the part totally differently from her two forerunners. Her engaging comedic expressions and fluttery mannerisms were welcome indeed. The first of these, *The Plot Thickens* (1936), is almost as good as the first two entries. However, the next venture, *Forty Naughty Girls* (1937), suffers from bad direction, a stale framework, and a plot, which is more heavy-handed, highlighted by too much forced comedy. By this time, RKO had lost interest in this promising series and gave up the ghost. This seems a shame, for four out of the seven entries still remain most enjoyable.

As for the two stars, Edna Mae Oliver went on to bigger things in lavish, big-budgeted vehicles, such as *David Copperfield* (1935), *A Tale of Two Cities* (1935), *Pride and Prejudice* (1940), and *Drums Along the Mohawk* (1939). Never married, she died in 1942 at the age of 59. James Gleason, on the other hand, was one of the most sought-after character actors in Hollywood. After trying his hand as a screenwriter, he found his niche as wisecracking cops, city editors, and other hard-boiled types, being found to his best advantage in films like *The Ex-Mrs. Bradford* (1936), *Meet John Doe* (1941), and especially, *Here Comes Mr. Jordan* (1941). After much work in films and television, he died in 1959 at the age of 73.

Central Park (1932)

First National Pictures. Produced by Darryl F. Zanuck. Directed by John G. Adolfi. Screenplay by Ward Morehouse and Earl Baldwin. Photography by Sid Hickox. Edited by Herbert Levy. Art Direction by Arthur Gruenberger. Costumes by Orry-Kelly. Music by Ray Heindorf. Conducted by Leo F. Forbstein. 57 min.

Cast: Joan Blondell (Dot), Wallace Ford (Rick), Guy Kibbee (Policeman Charlie Cabot), Henry B. Walthall (Eby), John Wray (Robert Smiley), Harold Huber (Nick Sarno), Henry Armetta (Tony, Hot Dog Vender), Irving Bacon (Oscar), William Bailey (Gangster Eddie), Wilson Benge (Waiter at Benefit), Wade Boteler (Barney Goodman), A.S. "Pop" Byron (Policeman), Jack Carlyle (Man), Spencer Charters (Policeman Sergeant Riley), Davison Clark (Policeman Eddie), G. Pat Collins (Gangster Spud), William B. Davidson (Police Lieutenant), Patricia Ellis (Vivian), Holmes Herbert (Benefit Emcee), Harry Holman (Police Captain), DeWitt Jennings (Police Desk Sergeant Monahan), Edward LeSaint (Police Commissioner), Larry McGrath (Gangster Smitty), Bud Flanagan/Dennis O'Keefe (Casino Diner), Ted Oliver (Policeman Joe, the Jailer), William Pawley (Gangster Hymie), Rolfe Sedan (Casino Patron), Charles Sellom (Luke, the Lion Keeper), Harry Seymour (Gangster Posing as Guard), Lee Shumway (Al, Police Lieutenant), Larry Steers (Headwaiter), Ben Taggart (Policeman Mike), Ray Turner (Kitchen Help), Morgan Wallace (District Attorney), Lucille Ward (Police Matron).

MADE DURING DARRYL F. ZANUCK'S tenure at Warner Bros./ First National, *Central Park* was another efficiently made, low budget "B" entry, which was released later in the year following the success of *Union Depot*. Similar in construction, with its numerous subplots linking various characters whose individual storylines hold the audience's attention throughout the very brief running time (57 minutes), it was shot in a mere twenty-three days on a tight budget of only $202,500. This format

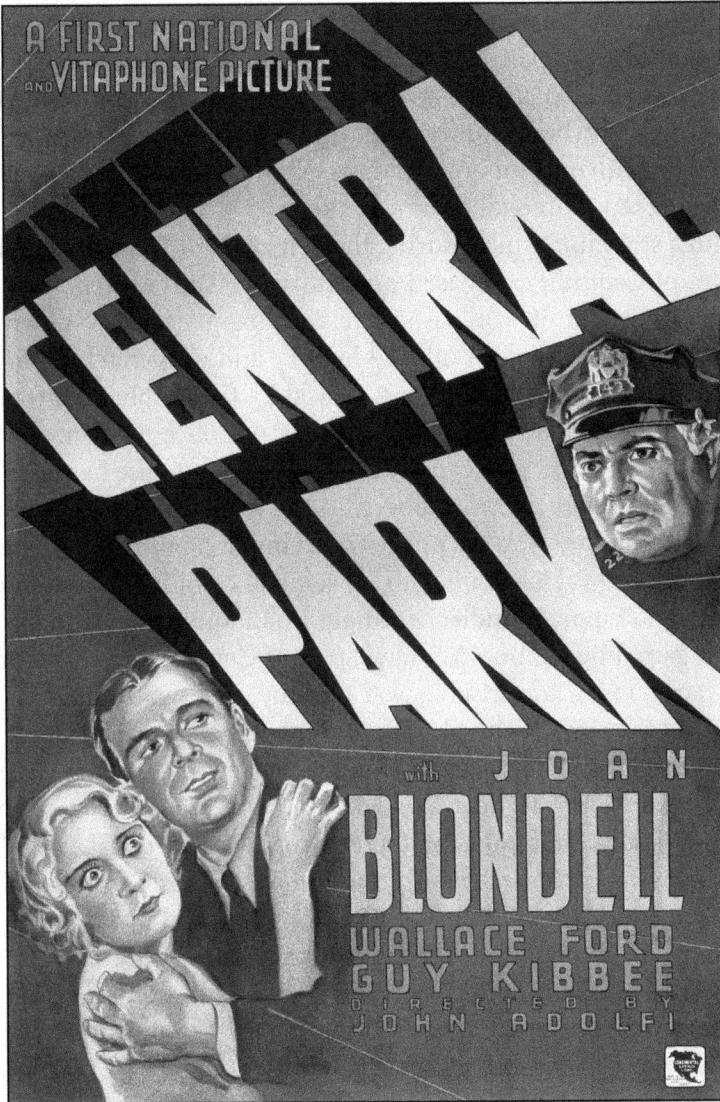

Central Park (1932) Poster art with Joan Blondell and Douglas Fairbanks, Jr. (AB)

of multiple subplots being incorporated into one photoplay would be expanded and improved upon when MGM released their all-star classic *Grand Hotel* that same year.

Director John Adolfi, after entering movies as an actor, began direct-ing in the mid teens, with varying degrees of success. His films were gen-erally low budget ventures, and he was known for working fast and very efficiently, usually turning in a picture under budget. He sent a second unit production company to Manhattan to film shots of the real Central Park to be used later as rear projection while the actors never left the confines of the Burbank studio. Today, the obviousness of this technique seems so primitive to modern audiences, but back in 1932, theatre patrons were taken in hook, line, and sinker.

With a story line typical during the height of the Depression, the main plot point of *Central Park* (based on a story by Ward Morehouse) centers around Dot, an out of work usherette who happens upon "down on his luck" Rick (Wallace Ford). Both are hungry and desperately in need of a job. Rick meets a good natured cop, played by Guy Kibbee, who tells him about a temporary job washing motorcycles at police headquarters, while Dot comes upon some "undercover cops" who want to use her as an unwitting accomplice in an armed robbery. In the meantime, there is a psychopath loose in the park who the police are trying to capture, thus making this a thoroughly enjoyable romp, with all semblance of logic thrown out the window. Contemporary audiences might find it quite interesting in knowing that a gambling casino was indeed part of Central Park at the time and it was a haven for rich tourists as well as many underworld figures.

During the time of the filming of *Central Park*, Joan Blondell had to be one of the busiest actresses in Hollywood, turning out ten feature pictures that year! She had been brought to the west coast two years prior after making quite an impression on the Broadway stage in the play "Penny Arcade." Another actor in that production was James Cagney, and shortly after, the two were swept up by Warner Bros. and put under contract where they reprised their roles under the rechristened title *Sinner's Holiday* (1930). Audiences loved the chemistry between these two and it wasn't long before Blondell and Cagney were re-teamed in films like *The Public Enemy*, *Blonde Crazy* (both 1931), *The Crowd Roars* (1932), *Footlight Parade* (1933), and *He Was Her Man* (1934). In all of these films, Ms. Blondell excelled brilliantly at playing sassy, working girls with a heart of gold.

Fast paced, with not a wasted frame of footage, Mordaunt Hall of *The New York Times* called *Central Park* "a racy melodrama" and commended the studio for putting together a compact little picture. There were two songs written for the picture: "Central Park" (which was played over the opening titles) and "Young Love", both written by Cliff Hess, as well as a recycled orchestration of "I'm Makin' Hay in the Moonlight" written by Jesse Greer and Tot Seymour, which was sung previously by Dick Powell in *Blessed Event* earlier that year.

The Half-Naked Truth (1932)

RKO Radio Pictures. Produced by David O. Selznick. Directed by Gregory La Cava. Associate Producer: Pandro S. Berman. Screenplay by Bartlett McCormack, Corey Ford, and Gregory La Cava. Based on a story by Ben Markson and H. N. Swanson, from the book *Phantom Fame* by David Freedman. Photography by Bert Glennon. Edited by C. K. Kimball. Music by Max Steiner. Sound by John E. Tribby. Edited by Charles L. Kimball. 75 min.

Cast: Lupe Velez (Teresita), Lee Tracy (Jimmy Bates), Eugene Pallette (Achilles), Frank Morgan (Merle Farrell), Robert McKenzie (Col. Munday), Shirley Chambers (Gladys), Charles Dow Clark (Sheriff), James Donlon (Press Agent), Mary Mason (Farrell's Secretary), Franklin Pangborn (Hotel Manager), Thomas Jackson (Marshall), Theresa Harris (Emily), Frank Austin (Carnival Patron), Bess Flowers (Secretary), Milton Kibbee (Carnival Patron), Brooks Benedict (Reporter).

A FILM WHICH DEFINITELY FALLS into the "forgotten" category, *The Half-Naked Truth* is a sheer delight from beginning to end. The pace is fast and furious under director Gregory La Cava's astute guidance, as he crams so many unforgettable vignettes into a breathless seventy-five minutes! Of course La Cava would go on to direct some excellent classics such as *Gabriel Over the White House* (1933), *My Man Godfrey* (1936), and *Stage Door* (1937). Star Lee Tracy delivers one of his best performances as a carnival barker turned press agent, who uses every possible means to achieve success, regardless of who gets in his way. Although this rather unlikable character seems repulsive and overbearing, it worked for Tracy, who was typecast in this kind of role thereafter. Usually cast as an obnoxious con man, newspaper reporter, or publicity agent, his tough exterior would ultimately reveal a genuinely human nature. One can only recall his Walter Winchell-like journalist in *Blessed Event* (a part turned down

The Half-Naked Truth (1932) Fast-talking publicity agent, Jimmy Bates (Lee Tracy) with his "hot tamale" protégé, Teresita (Lupe Velez).

by James Cagney), or his fast-talking publicity man in *Bombshell*, who writes studio gossip (all false of course) about a movie sex queen (played superbly by Jean Harlow in an almost autobiographical role).

The rest of the cast provides terrific support, especially Lupe Velez, as the hot-tempered "tamale" Teresita, who is unbeatable and a perfect foil for the ill-mannered Tracy. Frank Morgan as the Florenz Ziegfeld-like Merle Farrell is at home in his role as the bumbling theatrical impresario. And lastly, always a nod of approval for comedy veteran Eugene Pallette, wise-cracking endlessly, as Achilles, the escape artist. Director La Cava used Pallette extensively in further amusing ventures, notably as Carole Lombard's frustrated father in the screwball comedy classic, *My Man Godfrey* (1936).

Although music director Max Steiner receives screen credit (he is even seen conducting the orchestra briefly) for the score of *The Half-Naked Truth*, he really had little to do—only the title sections and two small bits within the film. However, one can readily see why he was one of Hollywood's finest musicians. "The Carpenter Song" (performed by Steiner and his orchestra and written by Edward Eliscu) is a cute ditty sung by Velez, and later in the film he exhibits his versatility by putting different sounds or noises to music, a device which critics raved about later that year in the musical classic *Love Me Tonight*. When sound pictures became the new art form in the early 1930's, producers wanted to get as far from silent pictures as they possibly could. Whereas silent movies were always shown with musical accompaniment, filmmakers felt that music would interfere with the dialogue, and, after all, in every day life music is only incidental (i.e. a person turning on a radio, playing a stereo or Victrola, etc.). Whatever the case, background music later became the norm in motion pictures, thanks to great artists like Steiner, Alfred Newman, Franz Waxman, and others.

Incidentally, this was one of the first films produced by David O. Selznick, under his new contract with RKO. There he would end his two-year tenure with another classic, *King Kong*, before moving over to Metro Goldwyn-Mayer, and ultimately forming his own independent studio, which would release quality productions thereafter.

Cynara (1932)

A United Artists Release. Produced by Samuel Goldwyn. Directed by King Vidor. Screenplay by Lynn Starling, Frances Marion (from the play by H. M. Harwood and Robert Gore Browne and the novel *An Imperfect Lover* by Robert Gore Browne). Photography by Ray June. Musical Score by Alfred Newman. Art Direction by Richard Day. Edited by Hugh Bennett. Running Time: 80 min. New York Premiere: December 25, 1932. Reissued in 1945 as *I Was Faithful.*

Cast: Ronald Colman (James Warlock), Kay Francis (Clemency Warlock), Phyllis Barry (Doris Lea), Henry Stephenson (John Tring), Viva Tattersall (Milly Miles), Florine McKinney (Gorla), Clarissa Selwin (Onslow), Paul Porcasi (Joseph), George Kirby (Mr. Boots), Donald Stewart (Henry), Wilson Benge (Merton), C. Montague Shaw (Constable), Charlie Hall (Court Spectator), Halliwell Hobbes (Coroner).

AN UNJUSTLY FORGOTTEN FILM, certainly deserving of reevaluation, *Cynara* presents actor Ronald Colman in the unlikely role of an adulterer. Straying away from the customary handsome hero from the 1930s, producer Sam Goldwyn attempted a vast change in the Colman persona. As a result, audiences stayed away in droves, not wishing to see their favorite matinee idol in a part so alien to him. However, critics at the time were generally pleased with his performance. The Los Angeles Times praised the film, calling it "One of the most distinguished features of this or any other year...presented here recently to no great popular acclaim...a fine, serious and absorbing study...with Ronald Colman at his very best...a microscopic study of psychology and emotion with characters well-nigh perfectly drawn and situations that rise to rare reality and touch deep poignancy."

Viewing *Cynara* today, one feels that the film was slightly ahead of its time, with its contemporary views on infidelity. As always, Colman gives

Cynara (1932) London barrister Jim Warlock (Ronald Colman) is engaged in an illicit affair with commoner Doris Lea (Phyllis Barry). (AB)

a bravura performance as the guilt-ridden barrister, who must live his life feeling responsible for his mistress' suicide. Kay Francis, an actress of limited thespian abilities, is given little screen time until the final reels in which she is superbly directed by the more than capable hands of Vidor.

Incidentally, Phyllis Barry, who plays Doris Lea, was soon relegated to minor roles in "B" pictures and short subjects. This is a shame, for her performance in *Cynara* seems both sincere and sympathetic.

Technically, as with other Goldwyn productions, the producer utilized the efforts of many talented individuals, such as director King Vidor, whose countless screen credits included *The Big Parade* (1925), *The Crowd* (1928), *Hallelujah!* (1929), *The Champ* (1931), and *Our Daily Bread* (1934), all classics which dealt with human relationships. The musical score (which in itself was a rarity in Pre-Code cinema) was written by none other than Alfred Newman, whose notable contributions included *Dodsworth* (1936), *The Hurricane* (1937), and two of his most famous achievements, *Gunga Din* and *Wuthering Heights* (both 1939).

Frisco Jenny (1932)

A Warner Bros./First National Picture. Production Supervision by Raymond Griffith. Directed by William A. Wellman. Screenplay by Wilson Mizner and Robert Lord. Based on a story by Gerald Beaumont, Lillie Hayward and John Francis Larkin. Photography by Sid Hickox. Edited by James Morley. Art Direction by Robert Haas. Costumes by Orry-Kelly. 70 min.

Cast: Ruth Chatterton (Jenny Sandoval), Louis Calhern (Steve Dutton), Donald Cook (Dan Reynolds), James Murray (Dan McAllister), Helen Jerome Eddy (Amah), Hallam Cooley (Willie Gleason), Pat O'Malley (O'Houlihan), Robert Warwick (Kelly), Harold Huber (Weaver), Frank McGlynn, Sr. ("Good Book" Charlie), J. Carrol Naish (Ed Harris), Noel Francis (Rose), Robert Emmett O'Connor (Jim Sandoval), Sam Godfrey (Kilmer), Franklin Parker (Martel), Willard Robertson (Police Captain), Edwin Maxwell (Tom Ford), Nella Walker (Mrs. Reynolds), Berton Churchill (Judge Thomas B. Reynolds), Buster Phelps (Dan as a child), Dorothy Granger (Dance Hall Girl), William Wellman (Reporter).

A REWORKING OF THE SAME basic plotline as the oft-filmed *Madame X*, *Frisco Jenny* stars the near forgotten Ruth Chatterton, who, in the early thirties, along with Kay Francis, was Warner Bros.' top female star. Born in New York City on Christmas Eve 1893, Miss Chatterton made her stage debut at twelve years old, reached the Broadway stage at eighteen, and was a bona-fide star at twenty in her triumphant role in *Daddy Long Legs*. Her screen debut came in 1928 when she was cast opposite Emil Jannings in *Sins of the Fathers*, after which she was Oscar-nominated for her roles in the first version of *Madame X* (1929) as well as *Sarah and Son* (1930). Her brief tenure with Warner Bros. was probably the most prolific period in her short movie career. There she turned out some excellent Pre-Code melodramas as well as light romantic farce such as *The Rich are*

Frisco Jenny (1932) Ruth Chatterton stars as Jenny Sandoval, notorious "madame" of the Barbary Coast. (AB)

Always with Us (1932), *Lilly Turner*, and *Female* (both 1933). Although these films exhibited her natural flair for comedy and drama and were well received, they remain forgotten by audiences today.

Her last American film, William Wyler's classic *Dodsworth* (1936), probably contains her best remembered performance as Fran Dodsworth, the middle-aged, self-centered wife, whose denial of approaching her twilight years causes much havoc between her and her industrialist husband, played to perfection by veteran Walter Huston. After making two more films in England, *The Rat* and *The Royal Divorce* (both 1938), she returned to the Broadway stage as actor and director before turning to writing in the 1950s. Always the liberated woman, she owned and operated her own plane and flew cross-country on numerous occasions.

According to Miss Chatterton, *Frisco Jenny* was her favorite of all her films, probably because the role of Jenny Sandoval goes through numerous changes in the movie's relatively short running time, proving how versatile an actress she really was! A no-nonsense performer who wouldn't allow any bullying from her directors, her relationship with director William "Wild Bill" Wellman began with the two of them not agreeing with her conception of how the role of Jenny Sandoval should be played. After heated arguments and frequent out-and-out displays of temper for the first three days of filming, they both decided on a truce after Mr. Wellman was informed that Miss Chatterton was dating one of his best pals, actor George Brent, whom she married soon after. Wellman, who'd been known in the industry as one of its greatest filmmakers, was a curious choice as the director of *Frisco Jenny*, in that it was considered a soap opera, which would appeal to female audiences. His forte was in a more rugged setting, in gangster films like *The Public Enemy* (1931), action pictures like *Beau Geste* (1939), socially significant westerns such as *The Ox-Bow Incident* (1943), and many other classics covering three decades! His early films are mere reflections of a turbulent youth in which he joined the French Foreign Legion during World War I and later becoming a fighter pilot after America became engaged in the conflict. After the war and three near fatal crashes, he barnstormed as a stunt flyer before a chance meeting with Douglas Fairbanks changed the course of his career. Beginning in films as an actor in 1919, he later found that he was more interested in what took place behind the camera instead of in front of one. His first big picture was the classic aviation World War I melodrama *Wings* (1927), which won the first ever Academy Award for Best Picture. Many of his subsequent films turned out to be bona-fide classics as well, a result of his "no nonsense" brand of directing that actually sometimes included engaging in fisticuffs with some of his leading male stars. He could be rather tough with his female leads as well; however, it has been said that he tamed many a temperamental starlet by throwing temper tantrums on the set.

No Man of Her Own (1932)

Paramount Pictures. Produced by Albert Lewis. Directed by Wesley Ruggles. Original Story by Benjamin Glazer and Edmund Goulding. Screenplay by Milton Herbert Gropper and Maurine Dallas Watkins. Photography by Leo Tover. Music by W. Franke Harling. Costumes by Travis Banton. 85 min.

Cast: Clark Gable (Babe Stewart), Carole Lombard (Connie Randall), Dorothy Mackaill (Kay Everly), Grant Mitchell (Vane), George Barbier (Mr. Randall), Elizaberth Patterson (Mrs. Randall), J. Farrell MacDonald ('Dickie' Collins), Tommy Conlin (Willie Randall), Walter Walker (Mr. Morton), Paul Ellis (Vargas), Lillian Harmer (Mattie), Jerry Tucker (Boy in Library), Frank McGlynn Sr. (Minister), Charley Grapewin (Clerk), Clinton Rosemond (Porter), Oscar Smith (Porter), Wallis Clark (Thomas Laidlaw), Ferdinand Munier (Antique Dealer).

RIDING HIGH ON THE HEELS of success following the overwhelming response from the public and the press for his performance in *Red Dust*, Clark Gable was now the hottest new attraction at Metro-Goldwyn-Mayer. Every studio in Hollywood wanted part of the action, and Paramount Pictures was no exception. On a loan-out agreement with MGM, Paramount was able to attain his services when they cast him in a minor, but very charming comedy entitled *No Man of Her Own*. Based on a book by Val Lewton (the same man who later was responsible for a wonderful series of nine "B" horror films at RKO) entitled *No Bed of Her Own*, the movie has the distinction of being the only picture co-starring Carole Lombard and Clark Gable. They had both appeared in a silent movie entitled *The Johnstown Flood*, but only in bit roles, a few years earlier.

By the time *No Man of Her Own* was in production, both Lombard and Gable were embarking on careers that would supercede just about any other actors in Hollywood. Lombard, who began her career working

No Man of Her Own (1932) Babe Stewart (Clark Gable) tells his chums, Vargas (Paul Ellis) and Charlie Vane (Grant Mitchell) to "beat it," while he attends to Kay Everly (Dorothy Mackaill). (RF)

in Buck Jones westerns and the Mack Sennett school of silent comedy as one of the Sennett Girls, co-starred in numerous two-reelers opposite such comic veterans as Andy Clyde, Billy Bevan, Mack Swain and Chester Conklin. After a while, she returned to feature pictures, where she made mainly routine films like *Fast and Loose* (1930), *Man of the World* and *Ladies' Man* (both 1931), two of these opposite her future husband, William Powell, whose career was also on the rise. Carole's knack for knockabout comedy was really put to the test when she was cast in the Howard Hawks classic screwball comedy *Twentieth Century* (1934), where she wowed audiences, making her the preeminent screwball heroine of the thirties. Gable, on the other hand, was gaining considerable attention playing tough gangsters opposite such big name leading ladies as Barbara Stanwyck, Norma Shearer, and Joan Crawford. But, by 1932, he was cast opposite blonde bombshell Jean Harlow, in a role originally intended for fading silent leading man John Gilbert. The film, *Red Dust*, made Gable a veritable stir in the movie industry, and it wasn't long before both stars were MGM's hottest new love team.

Although *No Man of Her Own* didn't do much to further either Gable or Lombard's careers, it was a rather pleasant love story about a gambler who is reformed by his new bride. The *Motion Picture Herald* exclaimed that it had "lots of prolonged howls of laughter and loads of action that presents Gable at his present best, sophisticated comedy. Luscious Carole

No Man of Her Own (1932) Babe Stewart (Clark Gable) hooks up with small-town librarian, Connie Randall (Carole Lombard). Watch those hands, Babe! (RF)

Lombard is appropriately the object of his tomfoolery and frustrations. Both are magnificent in this modern day fairy story of love and games that gaily flits across the screen too quickly, leaving the audience in want of more. Plan on it for a light, carefree evening's enjoyment."

Much of the film's success can be credited to the expert direction of Wesley Ruggles (brother of character comedian Charles Ruggles), who guides his actors in and out of every situation with great ease. A veteran of silent comedies dating back to the Keystone days, he was one of the Keystone Kops and also worked in some of Charlie Chaplin's classic shorts. A director whose career was quite successful in the early thirties with films like *Cimarron* (1931) and *I'm No Angel* (1933), his career generally petered out by the latter part of the decade. His good-natured style of directing must have kept the production of *No Man of Her Own* running smoothly, because both Gable and Lombard got along quite well on the set. A mat-

No Man of Her Own (1932) Babe Stewart (Clark Gable) tries impressing Connie Randall's (Carole Lombard) family (Tommy Conlon, Elizabeth Patterson and George Barbier) by showing up during the Sunday services. (RF)

ter which has become part of Hollywood folklore was Miss Lombard's rather salty language, which kept the cast and crew equally amused as well as shocked (her favorite retort for irritating directors or producers was "Kiss my ass!"). Aside from this, there was not a single person in Hollywood who ever said a negative thing about Lombard, whose good sense of humor and overall frankness was much beloved by all of her associates. It's no wonder that a few short years later Gable and Lombard would marry after a rather lengthy courtship. According to friends, she was a perfect companion for Gable, making his hobbies of hunting and fishing her hobbies as well! Sadly, their harmonious marital bliss was curtailed when Miss Lombard went on a War Bond-selling tour in the Midwest in January of 1942. Returning to California after a successful tour, she was killed in a plane crash, leaving a nation of fans shocked at the tragic news. President Roosevelt sent his condolences to a grief-stricken Clark Gable in a telegram, which stated, "She brought great joy to all who knew her and to millions who knew her only as a great artist. She gave unselfishly of time and talent to serve her government in peace and war. She loved her country. She is and always will be a star, one we shall never forget nor cease to be grateful to."

Cavalcade (1933)

Fox Film Corporation. Produced by Winfield Sheehan. Directed by Frank Lloyd. Based on the play by Noel Coward. Adaptation and Dialogue by Reginald Berkeley. Continuity by Sonya Levien. Art Direction by William Darling. Ladies' Costumes by Earl Luick. Men's Costumes by A. McDonald. Art Direction by William Cameron Menzies. Technical Advisor: Lance Baxter. Dialogue Direction by George Hadden. Unit Manager: Charles Woolstenhulme. Assistant Director: William Tummel. Photography by Ernest Palmer. Edited by Margaret Clancy. Sound by Joseph E. Aiken. Dances by Sammy Lee. Song: "Twentieth Century Blues" by Noel Coward. 109 min.

Cast: Clive Brook (Robert Marryot), Diana Wynyard (Jane Marryot), Ursula Jeans (Fanny Bridges), Herbert Mundin (Alfred Bridges), Una O'Connor (Ellen Bridges), Merle Tottenham (Annie), Irene Browne (Margaret Harris), Beryl Mercer (Cook), Frank Lawton (Joe Marryot), John Warburton (Edward Marryot), Margaret Lindsay (Edith Harris), Tempe Pigott (Mrs. Snapper), Billy Bevan (George Grainger), Desmond Roberts (Ronnie James), Frank Atkinson (Uncle Dick), Ann Shaw (Mirabelle), Adele Crane (Ada), Will Stanton (Tommy Jolly), Stuart Hall (Lieutenant Edgar), Mary Forbes (Duchess of Churt), C. Montague Shaw (Major Domo), Lionel Belmore (Uncle George), Dick Henderson, Jr. (Edward, Age 12), Douglas Scott (Joey, Age 8), Sheila MacGill (Edith, Age 10), Bonita Granville (Fanny, Ages 7 – 12), Howard Davies (Agitator), David Torrence (Man at Disarmament Conference), Lawrence Grant (Man at Microphone), Winter Hall (Minister), Claude King (Officer), Pat Somerset (Ringsider), Douglas Walton (Soldier Friend), Tom Ricketts (Waiter), Betty Grable (Girl on Couch), Harry Allen, John Rogers (Buskers), Brandon Hurst (Gilbert & Sullivan Actor).

DURING THE 1930S AND THE 1940S, Hollywood churned out countless bona-fide classic films, many of which achieved Academy Awards in various categories. Many film historians and film critics gener-

Cavalcade (1933) Best Picture Academy Award winner of 1932-33 starring
Diana Wynyard and Clive Brook as Jane and Robert Marryott. (RF)

ally agree that this period in film history offered a wide variety of classic
motion pictures, which younger generations of film students are redis-
covering today! One of these was the 1933 production of *Cavalcade*, released through the Fox Film Corporation, which, just two years before,
was absorbed by Darryl F. Zanuck's 20th Century Pictures. Based on the
1931 British stage play by Noel Coward, this rather episodic account of
two British families takes us from New Years Eve of 1899 right up to modern times (1933, to be exact). It is through the eyes of the upper crust
Marryots and their servants the Bridges that we experience many of the
trials and tribulations stemming from the Boer War, the death of Queen
Victoria, the sinking of the Titanic, the First World War, and finally cli-
maxing amid the Jazz Age.

Aside from the mostly British cast (Clive Brook, Diana Wynyard,
Una O'Connor and Herbert Mundin), the picture is lavishly mounted
with incredible crowd scenes employing hundreds of extras. In addition,
the interior as well as the exterior set designs by William Darling are so

authentic that one would swear that the production company had shot on location! Also, the background music blends perfectly, with tunes like "Land of Hope and Glory", "Nearer My God to Thee", "Pack Up Your Troubles", "Beside the Sea", and many others that add authenticity to the various vignettes, whether it is lending mood or heightening suspense. The highly acclaimed World War I montage sequence, a harrowing depiction of the horrors of war, is dramatized superbly, utilizing various tunes from the era, while the sound of battle blares in the distance. This incredible excerpt, which runs close to ten minutes, is one of the best scenes in the whole film, credited to William Cameron Menzies, whose deftness in set design and special effects was second to none in Hollywood. Many times it was Menzies who would direct the director, especially when he felt that the project was left in inept hands. Previously, he had received Academy Awards for Best Art Direction for *The Dove* and *The Tempest* (one statuette for both 1928 releases) and later for *Gone with the Wind* (1939). His special flair for art design is also evident in such classics as *The Garden of Eden* (1928), *The Adventures of Tom Sawyer* (1938), *Our Town*, *Foreign Correspondent* (both 1940), and *For Whom the Bell Tolls* (1943).

Originally slated to direct *Cavalcade* as of March of 1932 was Frank Borzage, a highly respected stylist whose romantic silent films were very popular in their day. Playwright Noel Coward, who was paid $100,000.00 for the film rights (the highest ever up to that point), intended to travel to America to work closely with Borzage, but according to Coward's memoirs, he never worked on any portion of the film directly. Unfortunately, for whatever reasons, Borzage's contract with Fox was suspended in order that he could direct *A Farewell to Arms* for Paramount, as well as Mary Pickford's last venture, *Secrets*. Taking his place was Frank Lloyd, a highly respected craftsman, whose reputation far exceeded his talent. It seems that Lloyd's secret to success was that he surrounded himself with some outstanding people whenever he worked on a film. Here, with *Cavalcade*, he had a first-rate play by Noel Coward, an excellent cameraman, Ernst Palmer, and the aforementioned William Darling and William Cameron Menzies, not to mention the brilliant cast. The same can be said two years later when Lloyd was awarded the directorial chore of making *Mutiny on the Bounty*. Again, the casting was letter-perfect, backed by a famous book, adapted into a literate script; with excellent camerawork, editing (by Margaret Booth), and a significant budget.

When circumstances weren't as ideal for Frank Lloyd, the results were pleasing, but nothing more, as was the case in 1936, when he made the 20th Century Fox extravaganza, *Under Two Flags*. What should have been one of the biggest films of 1936 turned out to be just another adventure film, even though the cast included Ronald Colman, Claudette Colbert, and Victor McLaglen! Another case in point was the 1938 release of *If I Were King*, again with Ronald Colman playing the role of French poet Francois Villon. Despite a superb script by Preston Sturges, the whole affair was manhandled by a director whose cinematic juices just weren't flowing properly. As it is, it remains a pleasing bit of fluff, but tends to be rather dull, both in the action scenes and the dramatic ones.

Despite Frank Lloyd's numerous shortcomings, he did manage to make *Cavalcade* a memorable film (with a little help from some friends). It garnered three Academy Awards, including Best Picture, Best Director, and Best Art Direction (William S. Darling). Diana Wynyard's portrayal of Jane Marryot was nominated for Best Actress of 1933, but she lost the award to Katharine Hepburn in *Morning Glory*. Reviews were glowing at the time with critic Pare Lorentz claiming, "If there is anything that moves the ordinary American to tears, it is the plight—the constant plight—of dear old England…a superlative newsreel, forcibly strengthened by factual scenes, good music, and wonderful photography." Louella Parsons was even more congratulatory, saying that *Cavalcade* was "greater even than *Birth of a Nation*."

Modern audiences today might feel that the film, as a whole, is generally slow in its exposition, and if they feel that the whole photoplay feels like déjà vu, it is because of a television series in the 1970s called *Upstairs, Downstairs*, whose theme is very similar. However, there is much to behold in this production, which is probably the most forgotten of all the films that have won the Academy Award for Best Picture.

The Bitter Tea of General Yen (1933)

A Columbia Picture. A Frank Capra Production. Produced by Walter Wanger. Directed by Frank R. Capra. Screenplay by Edward Paramore, based on the novel "The Bitter Tea of General Yen" by Grace Zaring Stone. Photography by Joseph Walker. Edited by Edward Curtis. Musical Score by W. Frank Harling. Sound by E. L. Bernds. Assistant Director: C. C. Coleman. 88 min.

Cast: Barbara Stanwyck (Megan Davis), Nils Asther (General Yen), Toshia Mori (Mah-Li), Walter Connolly (Jones), Gavin Gordon (Doctor Robert Strike), Lucien Littlefield (Mr. Jackson), Richard Loo (Captain Li), Helen Jerome Eddy (Miss Reed), Emmett Corrigan (Bishop Harkness), Clara Blandick (Mrs. Jackson), Moy Ming (Doctor Lin), Robert Wayne (Reverend Bostwick), Knute Erickson (Doctor Hansen), Ella Hall (Mrs. Hansen), Arthur Millette (Mr. Pettis), Martha Mattox (Miss Avery), Jessie Arnold (Mrs. Blake), Ray Young (Engineer), Lillianne Leighton, Harriet Lorraine, Nora Cecil, and Robery Bolder (Missionaries), Miller Newman (Doctor Mott), Arthur Johnson (Doctor Shuler), Adda Gleason (Mrs. Bowman), Daisy Robinson (Mrs. Warden), Doris Louellyn (Mrs. Meigs), Willie Fung, Jessie Perry, and Milton Lee (Extras).

Frank Capra's pre-*It Happened One Night* films have often been overlooked for the more polished, more prestigious late thirties offerings such as *Mr. Deeds Goes to Town* (1936), *Lost Horizon* (1937), *You Can't Take It With You* (1938), and *Mr. Smith Goes to Washington* (1939). But prior to these bona-fide classics, there are underlying traces of the man's genius in such forgotten gems as *The Matinee Idol* (1928), *The Younger Generation*, *Platinum Blonde* (both 1931), *American Madness* (1932), and *The Bitter Tea of General Yen* with Barbara Stanwyck and Nil Asther. An unusually unique film, especially for Capra, this tale of a young American woman who travels to China in order to marry a missionary and aid him in his work for the welfare of its country's inhabitants, is probably one of the director's most curious forays. None of Capra's optimism or idealism is evi-

The Bitter Tea of General Yen (1933) Poster (AB)

dent. The story begins in China, where a local revolution is taking place. During all the excitement, the woman is separated from her future husband, gets knocked unconscious, and awakens in the palace of the Chinese warlord, General Yen, who immediately takes a liking to the young bride. There, Megan Davis (Stanwyck) tries to dissuade his amorous advances and soon learns of his tyrannical nature and the sudden death to anyone who opposes him. At first she is repulsed by his seemingly heartless manner, but eventually learns to accept him when she gets to know

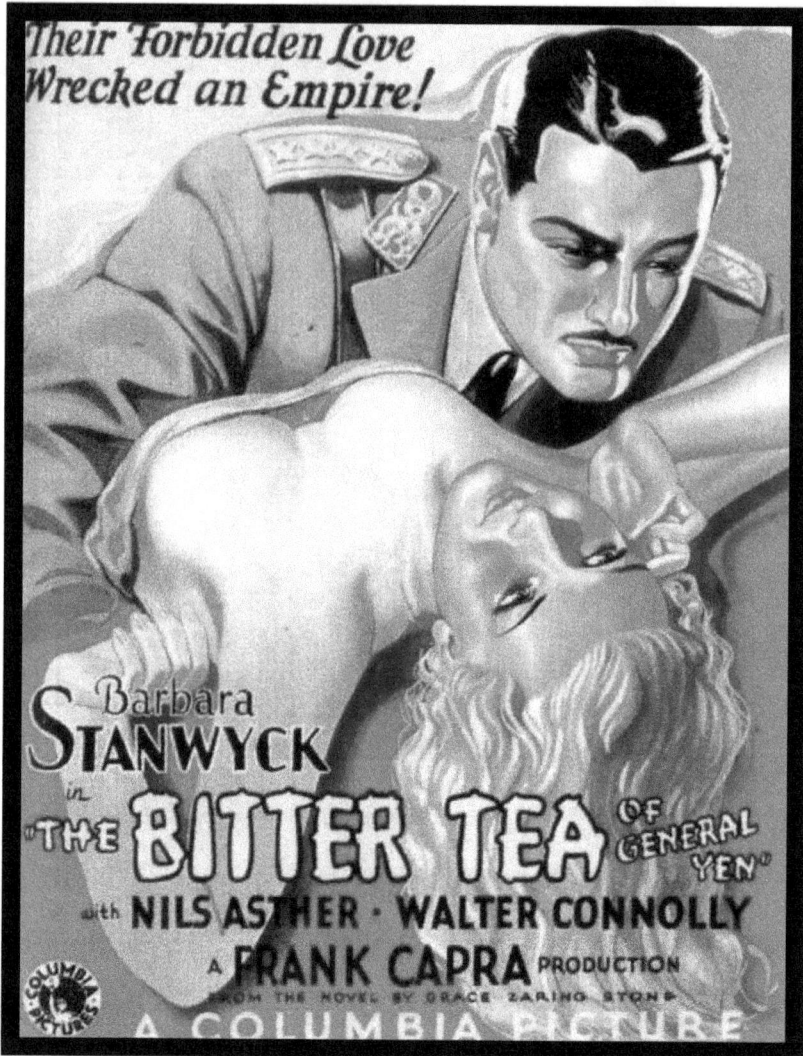

The Bitter Tea of General Yen (1933) Alternate poster (AB)

his more humane side, while also coming to a better understanding of the Asian customs. Contrary to all of Hollywood's taboos, Megan soon finds herself attracted to the general and begins falling in love with him, having totally forgotten about her missionary fiancé.

This love story about an inter-racial relationship fared rather dismally at the box-office; although it helped to boost the career of Stanwyck, while administering a much-needed shot in the arm for Nil Asther's flagging career. Beginning in films in the teens, the Swedish-born actor was a

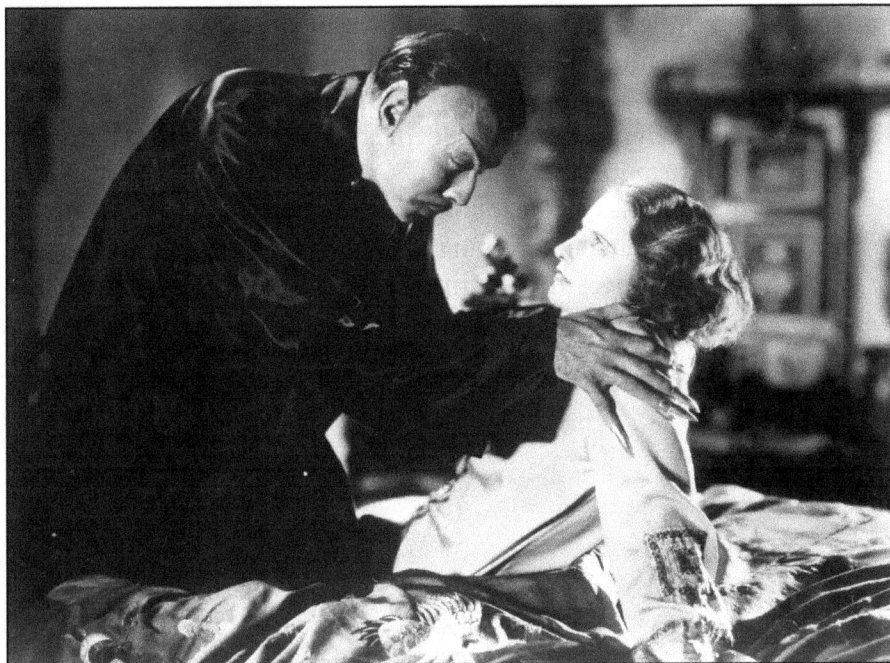

The Bitter Tea of General Yen (1933) Missionary Megan Davis (Barbara Stanwyck) has a dream where she fantasizes that General Yen (Nils Asther) rapes her. (AB)

graduate of the famed Royal Dramatic Theatre when he was approached by director Mauritz Stiller, whose later protégé was Greta Garbo. After appearing in films in Sweden and Germany, he arrived in Hollywood in 1927 where his career really seemed to be going places. However, with the arrival of sound, Asther found, to his dismay, his accent would prove a hindrance rather than an asset, limiting him considerably. Once in a while he would land good parts in films like *Letty Lynton* and *But the Flesh is Weak* (both 1932), but it was Frank Capra who really allowed him to shine in this 1933 minor classic.

Technically, *The Bitter Tea of General Yen* is a lavish picture, considering that it was produced by an unimportant "poverty row" studio like Columbia. The opening sequence involving the Chinese revolution almost seems like a test run for the beginning scenes of Capra's later classic *Lost Horizon* with Ronald Colman. Cameraman Joseph Walker, who Capra used extensively during his tenure at Columbia, cunningly uses matte backgrounds and rear projection to cover up for the production's sometimes shoddy budget. His expertise is heightened during a sensual dream sequence in which Megan dreams that she is being raped by the barbarian Yen, only to be saved in the nick of time by a masked man, who turns out to be none other than the general himself! Of course the audience anticipates the worst as her terror mounts, but it never comes. Instead, recoiling tension turns to an expression of passion as she ends up in his arms in a surrendering embrace!

Today, this film has a cult following which grows with each passing year, due to the continued interest in the films of Frank Capra. At the time of its release, it was selected to be the first film to play at the new Radio City Music Hall on January 11, 1933.

Employees' Entrance (1933)

A First National Pictures Release. Directed by Roy Del Ruth. Screenplay by Robert Presnell. Based on a play by David Boehm. Edited by James Gibbon. Art Direction by Robert M. Haas. Photography by Barney Mc-Gill. Gowns by Orry-Kelly. Vitaphone Orchestra Conducted by Leo F. Forbstein. 75 min.

Cast: Warren William (Kurt Anderson), Loretta Young (Madeline Walters), Wallace Ford (Martin West), Alice White (Polly), Hale Hamilton (Monroe), Albert Gran (Ross), Marjorie Gateson (Mrs. Hickox), Ruth Donnelly (Miss Hall), Frank Reicher (Garfinkle), Charles Sellon (Higgins), Berton Churchill (Bradford), Allen Jenkins (Store Detective), Edward McWade (Employee), George Irving (Advertising Executive), Oscar Apfel (Member of Board of Directors), Elinor Van Der Veer (Head of Department), Charles Levison/Lane (Shoe Salesman), Florence Roberts (Customer), George Miller (Employee), Sam McDaniel (Janitor).

AN INTERESTING CHARACTER STUDY, *Employees' Entrance* contains a vivid portrayal by Warren William cast as the ruthless head of a major department store who stops at nothing in achieving its success. Under-rated and somewhat forgotten, Warren William's niche in film history can be seen in similar roles in which he can be seen as a tough businessman, or lawyer, or even a hard-boiled detective like Philo Vance!

Employees' Entrance, a film about moral dilemmas, shows just how far a man like Kurt Anderson (William) will go, no matter who gets in his way or who he ruins. His decisions are made without a thought given to morals. He relies only on logic, keeping the bottom line in mind at all times. This keeps the audience from warming up to his character until he finally makes one decision with his heart, when he covers up Wallace Ford's attempt to kill him. As a result, one comes feeling a sense of

Employees' Entrance (1933) Kurt Anderson (Warren William) barges in on Polly (Alice White) while she is in a state of undress...but she doesn't seem to mind a bit. (AB)

respect for Anderson in spite of his ruthlessness because there is some justification for what he does. During a conversation with Ross (Albert Gran) during the climax of the film, he talks about the fate of hundreds of Franklin, Monroe, & Co. employees who will be out of jobs if the store fails. As much as he wants success for his own reasons, here he shows that he does have a compassionate side.

Loretta Young as Madeline also faces moral dilemmas, such as when she sleeps with her boss in order to obtain a position with the firm. Eventually when she meets and falls in love with Martin West (Wallace Ford), her past is temporarily forgotten, until after their wedding. Martin has his own choices to make between his marriage and his work. He chooses to keep his marriage a secret from Anderson in order to please him, even though it makes Madeline unhappy. Madeline, on the other hand, has had enough of Anderson's running Martin's life and insists that Martin tell Anderson about his marriage. This causes a spat between the couple and results in Madeline cheating on her husband at a New Years Eve Party with...you guessed it!

Employees' Entrance (1933) Kurt Anderson (Warren William) seduces innocent Madeline (Loretta Young). Does she succumb to his charms? (AB)

As always, despite its short running time of only 75 minutes, *Employees' Entrance* is a fast-paced, enjoyable film, credited not only to its three lead players, but to the multi-talented director, Roy Del Ruth. As always, the Warner Bros. stock company is always a delight, with such stalwarts as Alice White, cast as a social climber who uses sex to achieve her goals, sharp-tongued Ruth Donnelly, the ever put-upon store detective Allen Jenkins, and the pitiable Charles Sellon.

She Done Him Wrong (1933)

A Paramount Picture. Produced by William Le Baron. Directed by Lowell Sherman. Screenplay by Harvey Thew and John Bright. Based on the stage play *Diamond Lil* by Mae West. Photography by Charles Lang. Edited by Alexander Hall. Art Direction by Bob Usher. Music by Ralph Rainger. Songs: "I Wonder Where My Easy Rider's Gone", "A Guy What Takes His Time", and "Frankie and Johnny". Costumes by Edith Head. 64 min.

Cast: Mae West (Lady Lou), Cary Grant (Captain Cummings), Owen Moore (Chick Clark), Gilbert Roland (Serge Stanieff), Noah Beery (Gus Jordan), David Landau (Dan Flynn), Rafaela Ottiano (Russian Rita), Dewey Robinson (Spider Kane), Rochelle Hudson (Sally Glynn), Tammany Young (Chuck Connors), Grace La Rue (Frances), Fuzzy Knight (Ragtime Kelly), Robert E. Homans (Doheney), Louise Beavers (Pearl), Wade Boteler (Pal), Aggie Herring (Mrs. Flaherty), Arthur Housman (Barfly), Tom Kennedy (Big Bill), James C. Eagle (Pete), Tom McGuire (Mike), Frank Moran (Framed Convict), Lee Kohlmar (Jacobson), Harry Wallace (Steak McGarry), Mary Gordon (Cleaning Woman).

MAE WEST HAD OFTEN CREDITED herself as being the person solely responsible for the discovery of Cary Grant by introducing him to movie audiences in her first starring picture, *She Done Him Wrong*. Nothing could be farther from the truth since Grant, who was first seen in a one-reel musical comedy called *Singapore Sue* (1932), was put under a four-year contract with Paramount Pictures a year prior. Commencing with a delightful Lubitsch-like musical comedy entitled *This Is the Night* (1932), Grant was seen in films such as *Sinners in the Sun, Merrily We Go to Hell, The Devil and the Deep, Blonde Venus, Hot Saturday* and *Madame Butterfly* (all 1932), co-starring with such big-name leading ladies as Carole Lombard, Tallulah Bankhead, Nancy Carroll, Marlene Dietrich, and Sylvia Sidney, before he was even cast in *She Done Him Wrong*.

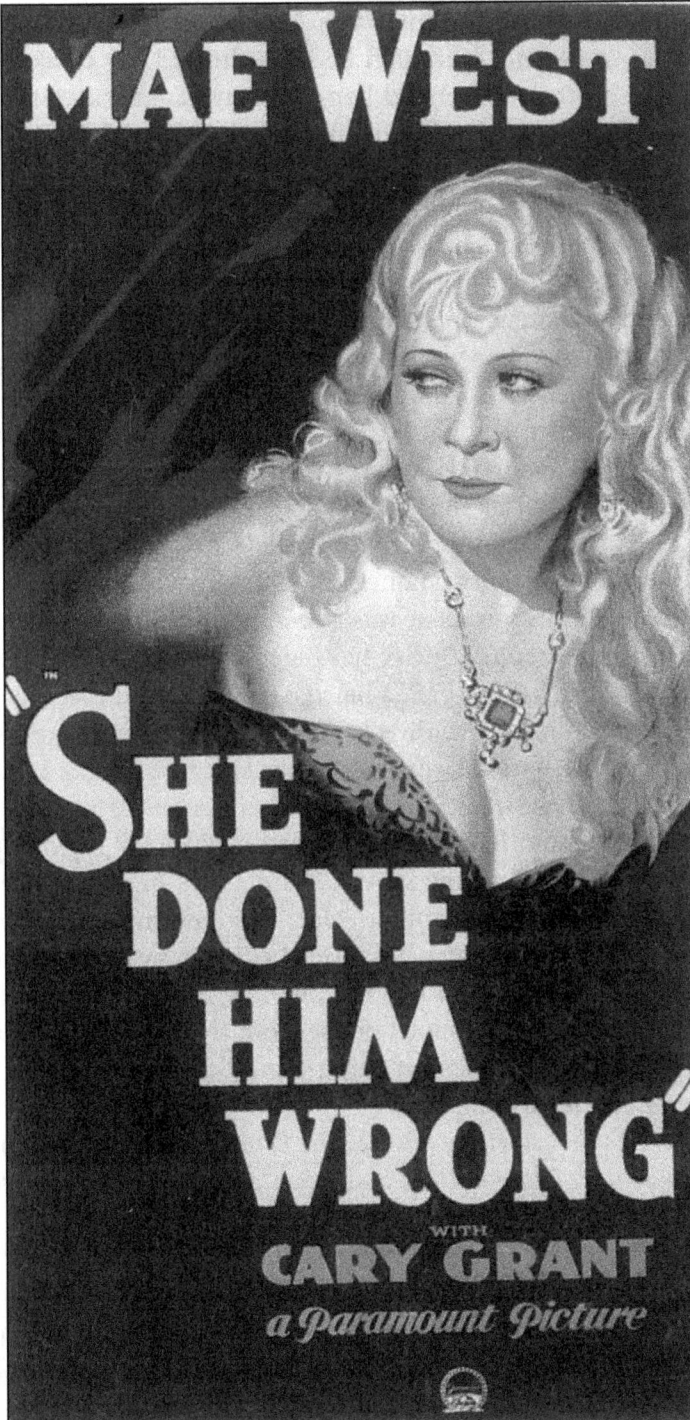

She Done Him Wrong (1933) Poster art from Mae West's first starring vehicle. (RF)

The statement that Cary Grant was a Mae West discovery had always irritated him to no end. Although he had admired her unique persona (both on and off the screen) and her enduring popularity, his bitter remarks about her seemed fully justified. Years later, when asked about Miss West, Grant replied, "She always got a great deal of publicity for herself. She was intent upon what she wanted to do and did it. Everyone else suffered the consequences…I could never understand the woman. I thought she was brilliant with the one character she portrayed, but she was an absolute fake as a person. You would shudder from it. I never knew anyone like her. She wore so much makeup and all that figure and those tall high heels. You couldn't find Mae West in there. I'm not attracted to artificiality. I'm not attracted to makeup. And certainly Mae wore more of it than anyone I've ever seen in my life."

Born in Brooklyn in 1893 (a fact she always attempted to conceal), Mae West was the daughter of prizefighter Jack West, who was, according to the actress, "an abusive father." In 1901 she was already working in amateur shows, and soon after, was a featured performer in an array of revues on various circuits. One of her biggest hits, and one that she personally wrote, was *Diamond Lil*, a bawdy, risqué period piece, which ran on Broadway for ninety-seven weeks, making it one of the most successful plays of its time. In 1932, during the bleakest years of the Depression, Miss West was in Hollywood and made her screen debut in a George Raft/Constance Cummings vehicle entitled *Night After Night*. Upon her first appearance, well into the movie, she delivers one of her best lines, when a hatcheck girl comments to Mae, "My goodness, what beautiful diamonds!" Without missing a beat, Mae begins to sashay into the nightclub and exclaims, "Goodness had nothing to do with it, dearie." Her supporting role received unanimous praise from the critics, and as a result, she was awarded carte blanche at Paramount Pictures, where she was immediately put under contract.

Mae West's first starring vehicle, *She Done Him Wrong*, was based on her Broadway hit, *Diamond Lil*, and upon release, earned the ire of the Catholic Church, who found the story, which centered on white slavery, totally objectionable. Directed with great attention to detail, depicting the 'gay nineties' with unerring accuracy by part-time actor Lowell Sherman, the film certainly proves his mettle here as a filmmaker, and probably rates as his best work. Of course, all of the negative press by churches and women's groups caused a veritable sensation, with theatre-goers anxiously standing in long lines, patiently waiting to see what all the fuss was about. As expected, exhibitors were elated that the movie was such a box-office smash, and it reportedly saved the faltering Paramount Pictures from financial ruin.

The prestigious *National Board of Review* magazine wrote that "*She Done Him Wrong* is something lustier, the overtly and successful predatory female against a colorful Bowery background. It is as frank as an old *Police Gazette*, and much livelier and more picturesque. It is an odd companion to be bracketed with *Little Women* and *State Fair* and *Mama Loves Papa*, but it belongs with them as a faithful bit of Americana. Incidentally, the overpowering Mae West personality shouldn't hide the fact that Lowell Sherman's direction figured pretty largely in the picture's effectiveness." The film did receive an Oscar nomination for Best Picture but lost the award to Fox's overblown super-production, *Cavalcade*.

Hard to Handle (1933)

A Warner Bros. and Vitaphone Picture. Directed by Mervyn LeRoy. Screenplay by Wilson Mizner and Robert Lord. Based on a story by Houston Branch. Photography by Barney "Chick" McGill. Art Direction by Robert Haas. Edited by William Holmes. Music by Leo F. Forbstein. Costumes by Orry-Kelly. Makeup by Perc Westmore. 78 min.

Cast: James Cagney (Lefty Merrill), Mary Brian (Ruth Waters), Ruth Donnelly (Lil Waters), Allen Jenkins (Radio Announcer), Claire Dodd (Marlene Reeves), Gavin Gordon (John Hayden), Emma Dunn (Mrs. Hawks, Landlady), Robert McWade (Charles Reeves), John Sheehan (Ed McGrath), Matt McHugh (Joe Goetz), Louise Mackintosh (Mrs. Weston Parks), William H. Strauss (Antique Dealer), Bess Flowers (Merrill's Secretary), Lew Kelly (Hash-Slinger), Berton Churchill (Colonel Wells), Harry Holman (Colonel's Assistant), Grace Hayle (Fat Lady with Vanishing Cream), George Pat Collins (Dance Judge), Douglass Dumbrille (District Attorney), Sterling Holloway (Andy), Charles Wilson (Jailer), Jack Crawford, Stanley Smith, Walter Walker and Mary Doran (Extras).

PROBABLY CONSIDERED ONE of the funniest James Cagney vehicles, not to mention one of the funniest Pre-Code films, *Hard to Handle* is one of those frenetically paced films with the star virtually never slowing down and delivering his dialogue at breakneck speed. Originally titled *Bad Boy*, which was probably studio head Jack Warner's opinion of the belligerent star, since Cagney had once again staged another "walk-out" in order to get a significant raise in salary from the studio, the title was soon changed to *The Inside*. Apparently, the title *Hard to Handle* was just another dig at Cagney, courtesy of Mr. Warner.

This release, made after the disappointing *Winner Take All* (1932), was a tremendous improvement, driven by an excellent screenplay by Wilson Mizner and Robert Lord. The main character, Lefty Merrill, was

Hard to Handle (1933) Conman Myron "Leftie" Merrill (James Cagney) tries to convince girlfriend, Ruth Waters (Mary Brian) that he's on the level. (RF)

an ideal role for Mr. Cagney and his limitless energy. Also on hand were Allen Jenkins, in a small but very funny role as a radio announcer of a dance marathon, and the lovely Mary Brian (seen here as a blonde), who had been a delight in Warners' earlier comedy *Blessed Event* (1932) opposite Lee Tracy. But the real treat in store for audiences is Ruth Donnelly playing Mary's domineering mother, whose larcenous character will do anything, and I mean anything, to land a rich husband for her daughter, whether she loves him or not! This has to be the one and only time that James Cagney was ever upstaged by anyone else, and she is superb. As a matter of fact, she just about highlights every scene she appears in! In later years, Cagney stated that Miss Donnelly was a lot of fun to work with around the set, but that she could be a "tough dame if you rubbed her the wrong way."

Although *Hard to Handle* was shot without incident, making it seem that things were running smoothly during production, James Cagney didn't find Mervyn LeRoy's direction to his liking. Although he never went into detail, he felt that LeRoy was one of the most overrated filmmakers in Hollywood, even though his filmography includes such classics as *I am a Fugitive From a Chain Gang* (1932), *Gold Diggers of 1933* (1933), *They Won't Forget* (1937), and *Random Harvest* (1942). Even so, *Hard to Handle* received excellent reviews, with *The Hollywood Herald* claiming that it "will be marked by reviewers and public for its presentation of a new picture-stealer who may very well become a leading screen comedienne in her own right. Remember the gal who played the secretary to Lee Tracy in *Blessed Event*? She stood out like a sore thumb in that part, and how she ran away with it! She means every bit as much to the picture as Cagney, and that is saying plenty. In the role of the promoting mother, anxious to get on Easy Street for her daughter's sake, and quite as much for her own, Miss Donnelly is nothing less than riotous…Cagney is back with a bang, and brings a most promising comedienne along with him." After that glorious review, one would think that Miss Donnelly would reach far greater heights. Unfortunately, her roles were generally in the supporting nature, but we should be thankful for her performance in *Hard to Handle*.

The film is also brimming with rapid-fire dialogue with Cagney delivering his lines so fast that at times they seem almost unintelligible. Also, pay close attention to some funny inside gags (like the one about grapefruit) and some amusing references to 1930s bandleader Paul Whiteman and the Simmons Mattress Company!

Mystery of the Wax Museum (1933)

Warner Bros. Produced by Henry Blanke. Directed by Michael Curtiz. Screenplay by Carl Erickson and Don Mullaly. Based on a play by Charles Belden. Photography by Ray Rennahan. Edited by George Amy. Art Direction by Anton Grot. Music by Cliff Hess. Musical Direction by Leo F. Forbstein. Costumes by Orry-Kelly. Makeup by Perc Westmore and Ray Romero. Special Effects by Rex Wimpy. Filmed in Two-Strip Technicolor. 77 min.

Cast: Lionel Atwill (Ivan Igor), Fay Wray (Charlotte Duncan), Glenda Farrell (Florence Dempsey), Frank McHugh (Jim), Allen Vincent (Ralph Burton), Gavin Gordon (George Winton), Edwin Maxwell (Joe Worth), Holmes Herbert (Doctor Rasmussen), Claude King (Mr. Galatalin), Arthur Edmund Carewe (Prof. Darcy/Sparrow), Thomas Jackson (Detective), DeWitt Jennings (Police Captain), Matthew Betz (Hugo), Monica Bannister (Joan Gale), Bull Anderson (Janitor), Frank Darien (Autopsy Surgeon), William B. Davidson (Detective), James Donlan (Morgue Attendant), Robert E. Homans (Desk Sergeant), Perry Ivins (Copy Editor), Edward Keane (Doctor), Robert Emmett O'Connor (Joe the Cop), Pat O'Malley (Plainclothesman), Lon Poff (Thin Man), Guy Usher (Detective).

PRIOR TO THE HORROR CYCLE of movies that swept Hollywood in the early 1930s, beginning with *Dracula*, which was released on Valentine's Day of 1931, there had been an abundant interest in the genre in the silent era as well. As far as historians can surmise, the Germans were probably the first filmmakers who made a grand attempt with their release of *The Cabinet of Dr. Caligari* (1919), combining elements of horror, fantasy, and psychological drama all into one very entertaining film. Other German-made films followed, with *The Golem* (1920), and two legendary classics, *Dr. Mabuse* and *Nosferatu* (both 1922). Eventually, American studios tried their hand at horror, with enough successful entries such as Para-

Mystery of the Wax Museum (1933) Badly deformed Ivan Igor (Lionel Atwill) has some very odd intentions for his next "model," Charlotte Duncan (Fay Wray). (RF)

mount's *Dr. Jekyll and Mr. Hyde* (1920), which starred John Barrymore in the dual role, and others like *The Phantom of the Opera* (1925) with Lon Chaney, both of which spawned numerous remakes of these classic stories. It was in 1927 that Universal Pictures, under the aegis of Carl Laemmele, released the classic "old house" horror film, *The Cat and the Canary*, directed by Paul Leni, which brought the genre into full swing. It wasn't until four years later that the studio began production on Bram Stoker's *Dracula*, intending to borrow horror great Lon Chaney from MGM to play the lead. Unfortunately, Chaney had died from throat cancer when the production was in its early stages, so director Tod Browning, also on loan from MGM, requested a Hungarian actor named Bela Lugosi, whose successful portrayal of the Count was receiving rave notices on Broadway. Bringing his character lovingly to the screen, Bela Lugosi has ultimately become a household name, the same way that Boris Karloff did following his successful role in *Frankenstein* as the dreaded monster. Viewing these Universal releases and their subsequent sequels today, one cannot overlook their Germanic influences, with their European locales, Gothic ruins, and period costumes.

Keeping up with the horror trend that had caught hold of audiences of the 1930s, rival studio MGM hopped on the bandwagon and made its own rather handsomely-mounted gothic horror films as well. Films like *Mark of the Vampire* (1935), a remake of the now-lost Chaney silent *London After Midnight*, as well as *Mad Love* (1935), starring Peter Lorre in his American film debut, were so good that major contract players at MGM were now cast in the genre as well!

Not to be outdone, Warner Bros. began production on their own series of horror films, but with a different twist. Their productions would take place not only in modern times, but in New York City as well, a favorite locale for almost all of the Warners Pre-Code output. Not only that, their first two entries were filmed in the early two-strip Technicolor process! The first, *Dr. X* (1932), was a rather tired "whodunit", although enlivened considerably by the brash performance of newcomer Lee Tracy. The second on the agenda was the far superior *Mystery of the Wax Museum*, directed by Michael Curtiz, before his days as Warners' premier director on the lot! It's hard to imagine that this once lost film had not seen the light of day in America following its initial release until the late 1960s, when a lone 35mm nitrate print was found in the vaults of studio head Jack Warner's personal collection. Of course, prior to its rediscovery, there was much anticipation and plenty of hoopla that finally a long lost classic was to be screened after over thirty years! Unfortunately, the many archives, including the American Film Institute, who were bidding for the rights to finance the film's restoration, were highly disappointed after seeing the film and backed out of this financial burden. Warner Bros., the distributor, did make a negative as quickly and as cheaply as possible. The prints that resulted were poorly made, with the vivid early Technicolor process looking like a mere faded Eastman color print.

Nevertheless, seen today, the print still delights audiences, with villain Lionel Atwill's bravura performance as the crazed sculptor Igor sending chills up one's spine in the film's exciting (and rather campy) climax!

42nd Street (1933)

A Warner Brothers Picture. Produced by Darryl F. Zanuck. Directed by Lloyd Bacon. Dances by Busby Berkeley. From the novel of the same name by Bradford Ropes. Adaptation and Dialogue by James Seymour and Rian James. Art Direction by Jack Okey. Assistant Direction by Gordon Hollingshead. Costumes by Orry-Kelly. Photography by Sol Polito. Edited by Thomas Pratt. Songs by Al Dubin and Harry Warren: "42nd Street", "Shuffle Off to Buffalo", "You're Getting to Be a Habit With Me", "Young and Healthy", "It Must Be June". 89 min.

Cast: Warner Baxter (Julian Marsh), Bebe Daniels (Dorothy Brock), George Brent (Pat Denning), Una Merkel (Lorraine Fleming), Ruby Keeler (Peggy Sawyer), Guy Kibbee (Abner Dillon), Dick Powell (Billy Lawler), Ginger Rogers (Ann Lowell/"Anytime Annie"), George E. Stone (Andy Lee), Robert McWade (Al Jones), Ned Sparks (Thomas Barry), Edward Nugent (Terry Neil), Allen Jenkins (MacElory), Harry Akst (Jerry), Clarence Nordstrom (Groom, "Shuffle Off to Buffalo"), Henry B. Walthall (The Actor), Al Dubin and Harry Warren (Songwriters), Toby Wing ("Young and Healthy" Girl), Pat Wing (Chorus Girl), Tom Kennedy (Slim Murphy), Wallis Clark (Dr. Chadwick), Jack La Rue (A Mug), Louise Beavers (Pansy); Dave O'Brien (Chorus Boy), Patricia Ellis (Secretary), George Irving (House Doctor), Charles Lane (An Author), Milton Kibbee (News Spreader), Rolfe Sedan (Stage Aide), Lyle Talbot (Geoffrey Waring), Gertrude Keeler, Helen Keeler, Geraine Grear/Joan Barclay, Ann Hovey, Renee Whitney, Dorothy Coonan, Barbara Rogers, June Glory, Jayne Shadduk, Adele Lacy, Loretta Andrews, Margaret LaMarr, Mary Jane Halsey, Ruth Eddings, Edna Callahan, Patsy Farnum, Maxine Cantway, Lynn Browning, Donna Mae Roberts, Lorena Layson, Alice Jans (Chorus Girls).

AFTER THE RELEASE OF the first commercially successful sound film *The Jazz Singer* in 1927, Hollywood coined the phrase "All Talking-All Singing-All Dancing" to publicize the new sound medium. Almost overnight, theaters across the country were heralding a new film genre—the musical. Unfortunately, these films were quite static, unimaginative, and lacking the overall quality of the later efforts. Films like *The Hollywood Revue of 1929* (1929), *Paramount on Parade* (1930), and countless others were merely musical reviews with stars telling jokes, singing, or dancing on stage as if it were a variety show. The immobile camera was placed on a tripod held in longshot with the actors simply playing without any imaginative cut-away shots or close-ups.

Finally in 1930, producer Samuel Goldwyn brought vaudeville comic Eddie Cantor to Hollywood to star in the motion picture adaptation of his

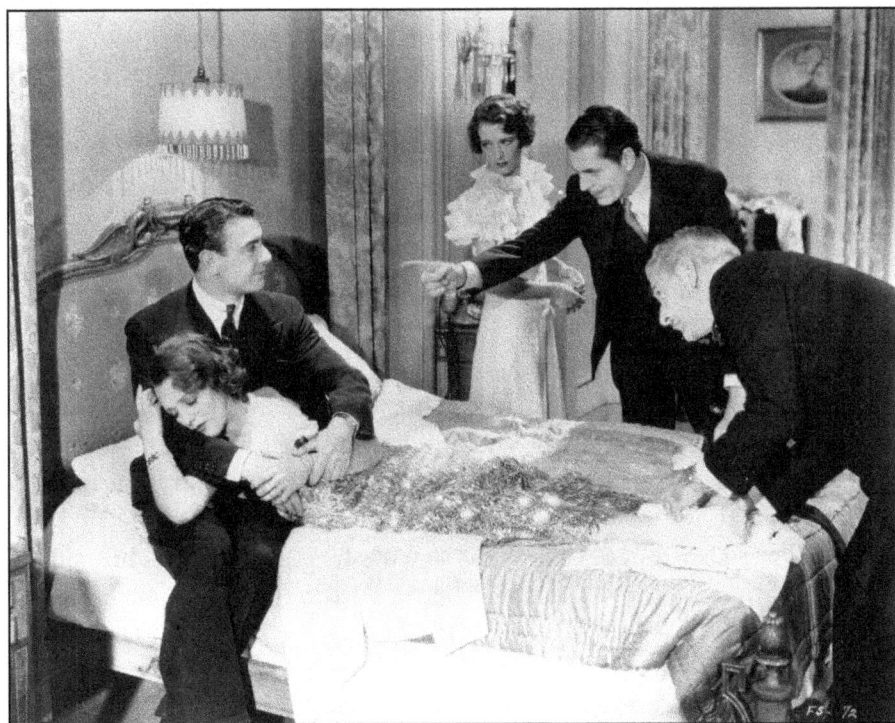

42nd Street (1933) Star of "Pretty Lady," Dorothy Brock (Bebe Daniels) has just broken her leg while boyfriend, Pat Denning (George Brent) comforts her (watch that left hand, George). Understudy, Peggy Sawyer (Ruby Keeler) stands by with producer, Julian Marsh (Warner Baxter), who seems to need a sedative, while the house doctor (George Irving) tends to Miss Brock's ankle. (RF)

stage hit *Whoopee*. Along with Cantor, he enlisted the services of ex-army drill instructor turned choreographer Busby Berkeley, and the result was pure gold. After a few additional efforts with the bug-eyed comedian, producer Darryl F. Zanuck lured the new dance director to Warner Bros. to film *42nd Street*. His style differed greatly from that of other musicals of the day with his employing of hundreds of beautiful women, dancing uniformly and creating kaleidoscopic formations when photographed from above. This remarkable innovation resulted in Berkeley being solely credited for bringing respectability back to the movie musical. He would also take responsibility for further molding the careers of Judy Garland and Mickey Rooney in their later musicals at MGM.

While *42nd Street* has arguably been referred to as the yardstick by which all other movie musicals are measured, it was not a project that studio head Jack Warner had much faith in. Unlike Zanuck, he believed that audiences were tiring of musicals, but Warner decided to give Zanuck the 'go-ahead' to make the picture. While the musical numbers were choreographed by Busby Berkeley, the bulk of the film was directed by Lloyd Bacon. The two men collaborated again on two other occasions: *Footlight Parade* (1933) and *Wonder Bar* (1934).

Filming went smoothly enough; however, there were some problems with the Hays Office (the censorship board) resulting in a few changes from the original story. Some details such as Dorothy Brock's untiring thirst for sex had to be eliminated. Also, there had originally been a love affair between producer Julian Marsh and boy singer Billy Lawler that would just not fly in the movie version. When the film was finally released, more cuts had to be made, in particular the total elimination of Ginger Rogers' character "Anytime Annie" when screened in Australia. In Ohio, certain lines were cut, like Rogers' sarcastic statement about the girl who "makes $45 a week and sends her mother a hundred of it." Una Merkel's risqué retort to a male cast member during a musical number rehearsal was also edited. Curious as to why she is squirming while sitting on his lap, the chorus boy asks, "Where ya' sittin'?" Her response: "On a flagpole, dearie!"

The casting of the film is first rate. As the beleaguered producer Julian Marsh, who is attempting to make one final musical success before his health gives out, Warner Bros. borrowed from Fox Studios matinee idol Warner Baxter. Never before had Baxter given such a forceful performance, injecting his character with a most serious case of broken-down nerves combined with unending adrenaline. Bebe Daniels as Dorothy

42nd Street (1933) Producer Julian Marsh (Warner Baxter) admonishes Peggy Sawyer (Ruby Keeler, left center) as "Anytime Annie" (Ginger Rogers, right, center) takes instructions. (RF)

Brock plays a character unlike the usual "nice girl" types that she played so well in the silent era opposite Harold Lloyd.

Another "first" in *42nd Street* was the initial teaming of Dick Powell and Ruby Keeler. Ruby, who had been Al Jolson's wife at the time, just recently joined her husband in California after appearing on the Broadway stage. For a while she seemed content just being the wife of Al Jolson, but soon boredom began setting in. She would find herself idly socializing on the sets of her husband's films, until one day someone suggested that she audition for *42nd Street*. Although Keeler's dancing prowess was not all that great (she would later be dubbed "Old Leadfoot"), Warner Bros. felt that they had found a star, a product of the Depression, and ample proof that a "nobody" can gain stardom. Dick Powell was brought over to Warner Bros. to play the obnoxious crooner Bunny Harmon in his first film *Blessed Event* (1932) opposite Lee Tracy, who was cast as a Walter Winchell clone. What followed were many first-rate musicals in which Powell and Keeler starred together.

Zoo in Budapest (1933)

Fox Film Corporation. Produced by Jesse Lasky. Directed by Rowland V. Lee. Screenplay by Dan Totheroh, Louise Long and Rowland V. Lee from a story by Milville Barker and John Kirkland. Photography by Lee Garmes. Edited by Harold Schuster. Music by Louis De Francesco. Art Direction by William Darling. 85 min.

Cast: Loretta Young (Eve), Gene Raymond (Zani), O. P. Heggie (Dr. Grunbaum), Wally Albright (Paul Vandor), Paul Fix (Heinie), Murray Kinnell (Garbosh), Ruth Warren (Katrina), Roy Stewart (Karl), Frances Rich (Elsie), Niles Welch (Mr. Vandor), Lucille Ward (Miss Murst), Russell Powell (Toski), Dorothy Libaire (Rosita).

A **DEFINITE CANDIDATE WORTHY** of rediscovery, *Zoo in Budapest* was once considered a lost film until a 35mm nitrate print was found in the 20th Century Fox film vaults by filmmaker Alex Gordon and film historian William K. Everson. This long lost treasure, directed by Rowland V. Lee, never seems to make its way to revival houses due to the scarcity of prints. However, for those who are fortunate enough to screen this cherished gem, it certainly isn't a movie one can easily forget. Beautifully filmed at the old Fox Studios before it merged with 20th Century Pictures, the superb camera work by Lee Garmes is definitely one of the high marks of cinematic technique.

Basically a love story, *Zoo in Budapest* has all the earmarks of a fairy tale, set in a Hungarian zoo, complete with hazy mists emerging from placid pools of water in this most innocent locale. The young lovers, played by Loretta Young and Gene Raymond, are indeed the perfect couple, caught in the midst of good and evil. Raymond is a zoo employee who was literally brought up in this most idyllic utopia, where he has grown to understand all of the animals, including the most savage of beasts. His "Garden of Eden" is one day visited by Eve (Young), with

Zoo in Budapest (1933) Zani (Gene Raymond) and Eve (Loretta Young) finally have a moment's peace after escaping from the zoo officials. (RF)

whom he is immediately smitten after seeing her on a weekly visit with other inmates from the local orphanage. Eve is an orphan who is about to be sold on her eighteenth birthday, sentenced to three years of hard labor until she reaches legal age and attains eventual "freedom." Urged by Zani (Raymond) whom she has met previously, she makes a desperate escape into the arms of her beloved paramour. With orphanage officials and zoo attendants hot on their heels, the young lovers manage to elude them, temporarily at least, until a disastrous chain of events almost costs the life of Zani when all of the animals in the zoo are mistakenly set free. Do the young lovers eventually find happiness as in all fairy tales? This is the question that is answered as the story unfolds.

Technically dazzling, this production's greatest asset is the huge sound stage depicting the Budapest Zoo, complete with foliage, animal cages, and pools of water. Apparently, Fox spared no expense in erecting this lavish set, which reminds one of the even more elaborate city that was built six years earlier for the Fox release, *Sunrise*, directed by F.

W. Murnau. If any complaint is to be lodged against *Zoo in Budapest*, it would have to be the unnecessary climax, in which all of the animals in the zoo are released from their cages with the hero trying to restore order. This sequence seemed to be standard fodder for thirties audiences who would insist on a lively climax, almost obliterating the beauty and poetic magic of the first two thirds of the film. The narrative is also hampered by an imposing musical score, which just about drowns out parts of the dialogue. But, to its credit, the score does succeed in establishing a surreal environment, substantiating the fact that this is, after all, a fairy tale!

The characters' names also bear some significance, with the mean zoo official, played by Murray Kinnell, called Garbosh (Garbage), and the wicked Paul Fix, complete with hunchback and exaggerated horror-like make-up christened 'Heinie'. The good doctor is played by the "saintly looking" O. P. Heggie, who two years later, gained immortality when he was cast as the blind hermit who befriends Frankenstein's monster in James Whale's *The Bride of Frankenstein*. Impressive casting indeed! Loretta Young's Eve is innocently alluring with her baby-doll face totally unblemished. One cannot blame the hero for this sudden infatuation. Gene Raymond's depiction of Zani is considered to be one of his best portrayals, along with his role in the Joan Crawford vehicle *Sadie McKee* the following year, in which he played against type as a ne'er do well. Usually Raymond played rather weak characters opposite the likes of Clark Gable or Robert Montgomery, or was wasted in grade B productions when he eventually moved to RKO.

The Devil's Brother (1933)

MGM/Roach. Produced and Directed by Hal Roach. Assistant Director: Charles Rogers. Photographed by Art Lloyd and Hap Depew. Edited by Bert Jordan and William Terhune. Based on the 1830 comic opera "Fra Diavolo" by Daniel Francois Auber. Screenplay by Jeanie MacPherson. Sound by James Greene. Music by Auber. Musical Direction by LeRoy Shield. British Title: *Fra Diavolo*. Reissued as *Bogus Bandits* and *The Virtuous Tramps*. 90 min.

Cast: Stan Laurel (Stanlio), Oliver Hardy (Ollio), Dennis King (Fra Diavolo), Thelma Todd (Lady Pamela Rocberg), James Finlayson (Lord Rocberg), Henry Armetta (Matteo), Lane Chandler (Lieutenant), Arthur Pierson (Lorenzo), Lucille Browne (Zerlina), Wilfred Lucas (Alessandro), James C. Morton (Old Woodchopper), Matt McHugh (Francesco), Nina Quartaro (Rita), George Miller (Village Minister), Stanley J. Sandford (Tremulous Woodchopper), Jack Hill, Dick Gilbert, Arthur Stone (Brigands), John Qualen (Man Who Owns Bull), Edith Fellows and Jackie Taylor (Village Children), Rolfe Sedan, Kay Deslys, Leo White, Lillian Moore, Walter Shumway, Louise Carver (Tavern Patrons), Harry Bernard (Bandit), Frank Terry (Waiter).

BY 1929, IT WAS APPARENT to producer Hal Roach that his new comedy team of Laurel and Hardy had become an instant hit. Making their way from silent short subjects through the transition of talking pictures with ease, their popularity knew no bounds. As a matter of fact, theatre owners were now heralding their two-reelers on the marquee over the featured picture! With audiences wanting more of the simple antics of the fat one and the thin one, Roach's distributor MGM decided to cash in on their names by giving them an eight minute sequence in their all-star, all talking, all singing, all dancing extravaganza, *The Hollywood Revue of 1929*.

215

The Devil's Brother (1933) Inept bandits Ollio (Oliver Hardy) and Stanlio (Stan Laurel) encounter Fra Diavolo (Dennis King), who thinks he can use them in his next heist. (RF)

The following year, MGM decided to "borrow" the boys again for comic support in the all Technicolor production of *The Rogue Song*. Metropolitan Opera star, Lawrence Tibbett was cast in the lead as the roguishly charming bandit, Yegor, whose two inept accomplices, Ali-Bek (Hardy) and Murza-Bek (Laurel), provide the laughs for this lavish operetta. With its assured success, it became evident to Hal Roach that his winning comedy team was destined to star in feature-length productions. So, in 1931, the first starring Laurel and Hardy feature, entitled *Pardon Us*, was released in August, followed by *Pack Up Your Troubles* the following year.

For their third feature length production, Roach decided to cash in on the success of their former hit *The Rogue Song* by casting them in yet another operetta. This time, Hal Roach himself was slated to direct, with gagman Charley Rogers, also one of Stan Laurel's best friends and confidantes, to co-direct the Laurel and Hardy related scenes. *Fra Diavolo*, based on the 1830 comic opera by Daniel Francois Auber, was re-christened *The Devil's Brother*, at the behest of MGM studio head Louis B.

The Devil's Brother (1933) Much of Nina Quartaro's role as Rita wound up on the cutting room floor. She only appears briefly in the first scene. (RF)

The Devil's Brother (1933) A scene with Dennis King and Nina Quartaro, which was cut prior to the film's release. (RF)

Mayer. According to Hal Roach, Mayer asked him, "What the hell kind of title is *Fra Diavolo*? What does it mean?" to which Roach replied, "The Devil's Brother." With that, Mayer retorted, "Then, that's what we'll call it! Nobody has ever even heard of the operetta, anyway!" Having no choice, Roach acquiesced begrudgingly, but slyly placed the notation "from the comic opera, *Fra Diavolo*" immediately under the title.

When the film was released on May 5th, 1933, it generally received good to excellent reviews, breaking all previous box office records for the little studio in Culver City. The cast featured Laurel and Hardy's regular nemesis, walrus-mustached James Finlayson as the pompous Lord Rocberg, and beautiful Thelma Todd as his wife Lady Pamela. But the icing on the cake was Shakespearean actor Dennis King, marvelously portraying Diavolo, who masquerades as the Marquis de San Marco, "in order to mingle with the rich nobility and locate their wealth." Also cast in the proceedings is Italian comedian Henry Armetta, playing a perplexed innkeeper, who keeps witnessing two childish hand games that Stan is showing his partner. These two examples of physical dexterity called "finger wiggle" and "kneesie, earsie, nosie" provide two of the funniest sequences in the film, especially when Armetta attempts to master them himself!

There are many other excellent moments to behold in *The Devil's Brother*, which is why this ranks as one of the team's best pictures, as well as being one of Stan Laurel's personal favorites.

The Story of Temple Drake (1933)

A Paramount Picture. Produced by Benjamin Glazer. Directed by Stephen Roberts. Screenplay by Oliver H. P. Garrett. Based on the novel *Sanctuary* by William Faulkner. Photography by Karl Struss. 72 min.

Cast: Miriam Hopkins (Temple Drake), Jack LaRue (Trigger), William Gargan (Stephen Benbow), William Collier, Jr. (Toddy Gowan), Irving Pichel (Lee Goodwin), Sir Guy Standing (Judge Drake), Elizabeth Patterson (Aunt Jennie), Florence Eldridge (Ruby Lemar), James Eagles (Tommy), Harlan E. Knight (Pap), James Mason (Van), Jobyna Howland (Miss Reba), Henry Hall (Judge), John Carradine (Courtroom Extra), Frank Darien (Gas Station Proprietor), Clarence Sherwood (Lunch Wagon Proprietor), Oscar Apfel (District Attorney), Kent Taylor and Clem Beauchamp (Jellybeans), Arthur Belasco (Wharton), Grady Sutton (Bob), George Pearce (Doctor), Hattie McDaniel (Minnie).

WILLIAM FAULKNER'S SEXY NOVEL, *Sanctuary*, which dealt with Southern decadence, rape, and murder, had been a property of Paramount Pictures for a few years before they attempted to adapt it for the screen. Their main concern was not box-office response, but the Hays Office. The censors had seemingly become rather lax in their restrictions of late, as was evident with the release of such outrageous potboilers as *Call Her Savage*, *Red-Headed Woman*, and *She Done Him Wrong* (all 1932). But more recently, they were beginning to come down hard on Hollywood, due to public outcries from the Catholic Church. In order to get this project off the ground, Paramount decided that the book's title would have to be changed to *The Shame of Temple Drake*, with William Faulkner getting screen credit without acknowledging the original title of the book. Studio publicity dreamed up the absurd tagline for the picture "a love story understandable to every woman...pulsing with all the emotional power of *A Farwell to Arms*. Despite this rather feeble attempt at placat-

The Story of Temple Drake (1933) Van (James Mason) bursts in on overnight "guest" Temple Drake (Miriam Hopkins) with various "things" on his mind. (AB)

The Story of Temple Drake (1933) "Trigger" (Jack La Rue) tells Temple Drake's (Miriam Hopkins, right) former boyfriend, Stephen Benbow (William Gargan) to leave, now that she has taken on a new "occupation." (AB)

ing the censorship board, Faulkner's lurid tale had nothing whatsoever in common with Hemingway's sensitive love story. *The New York Times*, in an editorial, demanded, "What is the function of the Hays Office if it doesn't keep projects like this off the screen?"

Nevertheless, the project began production, in spite of *The New York Times*' article, women's leagues, and the Catholic Church. In order to placate the Legion of Decency, the screenwriter, Oliver H. P. Garrett, had the almost impossible task of watering down most of the objectionable scenes. Because of the notoriety the novel *Sanctuary* had gained, the studio decided to disassociate itself from the book as much as possible by changing the title to *The Story of Temple Drake*.

Miriam Hopkins, a relative newcomer to the screen, had gained studio recognition in pictures like the breezy Ernst Lubitsch vehicles *The Smiling Lieutenant* (1931) and *Trouble in Paradise* (1932), and Mamoulian's *Dr. Jekyll and Mr. Hyde* (1931). She was the perfect choice for the spoiled Southern belle who is kidnapped by a two-bit hoodlum and bootlegger named Trigger, continuously raped by him, and ultimately becoming his personal plaything and prostitute, before she eventually kills him in self defense. George Raft, who had made a career out of playing denizens of the underworld, was given first choice as the repulsive Trigger. However, Raft felt that the role had no redeemable qualities and would result in "screen suicide." Instead, the studio screen-tested Jack LaRue, a bit player, sometimes in support, who worked in Warner Bros. films mainly as a gangster. In his role as Trigger, LaRue excelled beyond anybody's dreams, and this was probably the film for which he was best remembered.

The degradation felt by Temple Drake is heightened by the dimly lit, soft-focus photography of Karl Struss, who was one of Hollywood's best cinematographers. The director, Stephen Roberts, also does an outstanding job of capturing the sordidness of an imprisoned life of immorality. Roberts, by the way, never achieved the fame he deserved. For some reason, he was never awarded another ambitious project like *The Story of Temple Drake*, probably due to the fact that his name would be forever linked to one of Hollywood's most controversial films of all time. Although he did direct some mildly diverting projects later, such as two romantic comedies, *One Sunday Afternoon* (1933) and *Romance in Manhattan* (1934), as well as a pair of excellent "whodunits" with William Powell entitled *Star of Midnight* (1935) and *The Ex-Mrs. Bradford* (1936), his career was halted suddenly by his untimely death in 1936. *The Story*

The Story of Temple Drake (1933) "Trigger" (Jack La Rue) offers Temple Drake (Miriam Hopkins) a cup of coffee after brutally raping her. (AB)

of Temple Drake remains Stephen Roberts' best picture and it eventually became one of the biggest moneymakers of 1933, despite the controversy that surrounded it. Unfortunately, it was never reissued (surprise!) nor was it ever broadcast on American television. The reason it was never televised is because the property was bought lock, stock, and barrel by 20th Century Fox in 1960, when that studio decided to remake the film and shelve the original. Co-starring Lee Remick and Yves Montand, the remake, which was titled *Sanctuary*, was a far cry from the original 1933 version!

The Little Giant (1933)

A First National & Vitaphone Picture. Supervised by Ray Griffith. Directed by Roy Del Ruth. Screenplay by Robert Lord and Wilson Mizner. Based on an original story by Robert Lord. Photography by Sid Hickox. Art Direction by Robert Haas. Music by Leo Forbstein. Edited by George Marks. 74 min.

Cast: Edward G. Robinson (James Francis "Bugs" Ahearn), Helen Vinson (Polly Cass), Mary Astor (Ruth Wayburn), Kenneth Thompson (John Stanley), Russell Hopton (Al Daniels), Shirley Grey (Edith Merriam), Donald Dillaway (Gordon Cass), Louise Mackintosh (Mrs. Cass), Berton Churchill (Donald Hadley Cass), Helen Mann (Frankie), Selmer Jackson (Voice of Radio Announcer), Dewey Robinson (Butch Zanwutoski), John Kelly (Tim), Sidney Bracy (Butler), Bob Perry, Adrian Morris (Joe Milano's Hoods), Rolfe Sedan (Waiter), Charles Coleman (Charteris), Bill Elliott (Guest), Leonard Carey (Ingleby), Nora Cecil (Maid), Lester Dorr, Lorin Raker (Investment Clerks), Tammany Young (Hymie), Guy Usher (Detective), John Marston (D.A.), Harry Tenbrook (Pulido).

WITH THE ADVENT of talking pictures in 1927, a new genre called the gangster film was introduced and soon became the rage among the movie-going public. Gangsters like Al Capone, Bonnie and Clyde, and John Dillinger were lauded as heroes by the tabloids, resulting in Hollywood's interest in these ruthless personalities. Studios like Warner Bros. decided to romanticize their exploits by gaining audience sympathy for the villain and blaming the Depression for his road to crime. *Lights of New York*, released in 1928, was the first "all-talking" feature, and incidentally a gangster film. Although when seen today it seems very primitive, it nevertheless succeeded in convincing Americans that these menaces of society fought the Depression head-on (albeit illegally) and won! As a result of this current popular art form, many new faces were showing up

The Little Giant (1933) Shirley Grey as gun moll Edith Merriam with Edward G. Robinson as "Bugs" Ahearn. (RF)

with increasing regularity. Up-and-coming stars like Paul Muni, Edward G. Robinson, James Cagney, George Raft, and Humphrey Bogart were picked up from the New York stage and found their niche in this new art form. Films like *Little Caesar* and *The Public Enemy* (both 1931) and *Scarface* (1932) were among the biggest box-office draws of the early thirties, with more gangster films to follow.

By 1932, the Catholic Church and other civic groups began objecting to these movies and stated that Hollywood was glorifying these "enemies of society." Violence, sex, drugs, booze, and wholesale killing were reaching a high crescendo, and moviemakers had to abide by the increasing pressure of these righteous groups. Of course, Hollywood would not give up without a battle. They decided to put Robinson and Cagney on the right side of the law and have them combat the criminal much in the same under-handed manner as when they weren't working for Uncle Sam! The resulting films like *G-Men* (1935) and *Bullets or Ballots* (1936) were just as violent as *The Public Enemy*; however now Cagney and Robinson were the pursuers rather than the pursued.

The Little Giant (1933) Former bootlegger "Bugs" Ahearn wants to break into high society after the repeal of Prohibition by purchasing some "abstract" paintings for starters. When he points to one of his "works of art" on the wall, he asks his partner-in-crime, Al Daniels, "Did you ever see anything like that before?" "Not since I've been off cocaine," is his answer. Edith Merriam (Shirley Grey) looks on in amazement. (RF)

Another way Hollywood could go on with the gangster film without abolishing it entirely would be to spoof the genre, having the same stars satirizing their former screen personalities. By 1933 this was the new channel of thinking, and films like *The Little Giant* and *Lady Killer* were filmdom's way of "cleaning up their act."

Watching *The Little Giant* today is an utter delight. Edward G.'s performance is wonderful. He tackles comedy superbly without losing any of his Little Caesar characteristics. Also, the screenplay by Robert Lord and Wilson Mizner is executed in a breathtakingly fast pace, leaving no time for the audience to catch every risqué line of dialogue (with some inside gags and references to former Cagney and Robinson movies that go over present-day audiences' heads). The supporting cast is also first-rate, with young Mary Astor looking every bit the ingenue and appearing extremely delicate and lady-like, quite the contrast to her Bridgit O'Shaunnessey in

John Huston's *The Maltese Falcon* eight years later. Character actor Russell Hopton is also effective in his role as Bugs Ahearn's cohort in crime, and has his best moments in this film.

Wrote Mordaunt Hall of *The New York Times*: "Edward G. Robinson, as the prime player, reveals himself as no mean comedian, and yesterday afternoon, the audience roared when the gangster, who is known here as Bugs Ahearn, tackles a French menu and when he turns up at an informal afternoon party in full regalia...(He) is alert and forceful even in this light affair."

So successful was *The Little Giant* that Warners subsequently cast Mr. Robinson in two more humorous spoofs, *A Slight Case of Murder* in 1938 and *Larceny Inc.* in 1942, which delighted audiences then and continue to do so now!

I Cover the Waterfront (1933)

A United Artists Release. Executive Producer: Joseph Schenck. Produced by Edward Small. Directed by James Cruze. Screenplay by Wells Root. Based on the book *I Cover the Waterfront* by Max Miller (the unique and personal experiences of a newspaper reporter covering a pacific waterfront). Photography by Ray June. Additional Dialogue by Jack Jevne. Art Direction by Albert D'Agostino. Assistant Director: Vernon Keays. Sound by Oscar Lagerstrom. Edited by Grant Whytock. 70 min.

Cast: Claudette Colbert (Julie Kirk), Ben Lyon (H. Joseph Miller), Ernest Torrence (Eli Kirk), Hobart Cavanaugh (McCoy), Maurice Black (Ortegas), Wilfred Lucas (Randall), Harry Beresford (Old Chris), Purnell Pratt (John Phelps), Lee Phelps (Reporter), Lillian Harmer (Gossip), Kay Deslys (Speakeasy Extra), Al Hill (Sailor).

TYPICAL OF THE PRE-CODE ERA was the gutsy, sometimes shocking newspaper film of the 1930s. Complete with hard-hearted editors, ruthless owners, and fast-talking, browbeaten reporters, this genre proved extremely successful with cynical, depression-worn audiences. Whether played for laughs or straight drama, films like *The Front Page* (1931), *Five Star Final* (1931), *Blessed Event* (1932), and *Hi Nellie!* (1933) provided tough, hard-hitting depictions of the newspaper game, with fast-talking stars like Pat O'Brien and Lee Tracy chewing up the scenery to the hilt!

An unjustly overlooked film, *I Cover the Waterfront* contains one of Claudette Colbert's best performances of her long career, despite such classic roles as *The Sign of the Cross* (1932), *It Happened One Night* (1934), *Cleopatra* (1934), *Imitation of Life* (1934), *Private Worlds* (1935), *Midnight* (1939), *It's a Wonderful World* (1939), *Drums Along the Mohawk* (1939), *The Palm Beach Story* (1942), *Since You Went Away* (1944), *Three Came Home* (1950), and scores of others. A thorough professional and an extremely versatile actress, Colbert made the transition from drama

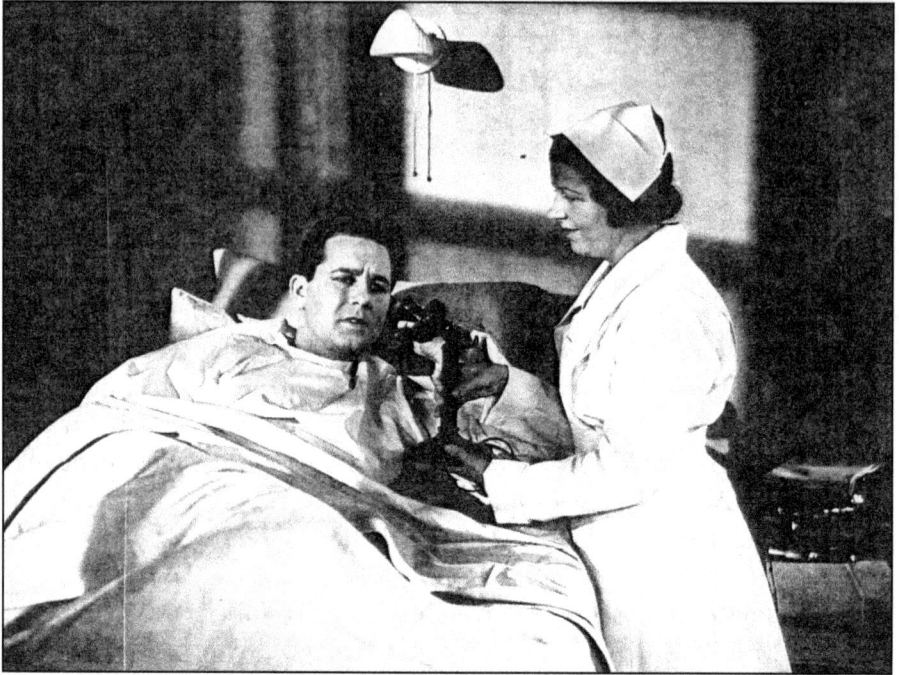

I Cover the Waterfront (1933) Reporter H. Joseph Miller (Ben Lyon) is about to be released from the hospital after being shot by his girlfriend's father. (RF)

to comedy with such ease and grace that sometimes the viewer has to remind himself (or herself) that the woman who played Cleopatra is the same actress who romped through the Preston Sturges classic *The Palm Beach Story* as the flighty Geraldine Jeffers!

James Cruze, the director of *I Cover the Waterfront*, started out as an actor on Broadway in 1906, eventually moving over to film, resulting in him directing numerous comedies with Wallace Reid and Fatty Arbuckle. The movie which catapulted Cruze to the higher echelon of distinguished directors was the large-scale *The Covered Wagon* of 1923. Throughout the twenties, he brought delighted audiences and critics a wide array of box office hits, such as the surrealistic *Beggar on Horseback* (1925), *The Pony Express* (1925), and *Old Ironsides* (1926). With the advent of talkies Cruze was able to adjust to the new medium with the greatest of ease, turning out good films as long as the scripts he accepted were better than mediocre.

Such was the case with *I Cover the Waterfront*, another film utilizing the 'moral dilemma' theme so prevalent in early thirties cinema. The three leads (Colbert, Lyon, and Torrence) are all so convincing in their

I Cover the Waterfront (1933) Joe Miller (Ben Lyon) tries to get some information from Julie Kirk (Claudette Colbert) about her father's alleged smuggling activities by "romancing" her.

roles that it leads one to believe that they were enthusiastic about this particular project.

Many scenes are standouts and should be mentioned, such as the one where Julie Kirk (Colbert) tracks down her errant father (Torrence) at a house of ill repute. Inquiring of the madam where her drunken parent might be, Julie is told that he'll be out in a few minutes. Realizing that her father is occupied with a prostitute, she waits at the bar among the drifters and low-lifes that would frequent such an establishment! Religious symbolism is used very effectively, especially during the death scene of Captain Eli, who commits murder to escape the Feds but ultimately turns to God at the last minute. As was always the case with a film of this nature, it is filled with ethnic as well as racist remarks, aimed mainly toward the yellow race (apparently the reason for its lack of exposure on television). A film which delves into the seedy lives of newspaper reporters, it never glorifies their existences but rather paints a very dark picture.

Professional Sweetheart (1933)

An RKO-Radio Picture. Produced by H. N. Swanson. Directed by William A. Seiter. Executive Producer: Merian C. Cooper. Screenplay by Maurine Watkins. Based on a story by Maurine Watkins. Photography by Edward Cronjager. Art Direction by Van Nest Polglase and Carroll Clark. Edited by James Morley. Sound by Clem Portman. Musical Direction by Max Steiner. Makeup by Mel Berns. Song: "My Imaginary Sweetheart" by Edward Eliscu and Harry Akst. 67 min.

Cast: Ginger Rogers (Glory Eden), Norman Foster (Jim Davey), ZaSu Pitts (Esmeralda de Leon), Frank McHugh (Speed), Allen Jenkins (O'Connor), Gregory Ratoff (Ipswich), Edgar Kennedy (Kelsey), Lucien Littlefield (Announcer), Franklin Pangborn (Childress), Frank Darien (Appleby), Betty Furness (Reporter), Sterling Holloway (Scribe), Theresa Harris (Maid), Grace Hayle (Reporter).

ALTHOUGH CONSIDERED MERELY an unimportant "programmer" at the time, *Professional Sweetheart* holds up extremely well today. This was made at a time when Ginger Rogers' career needed a slight jolt for studio heads to sit up and take notice. Sadly, this was not to be the case with this release. However, it was a useful springboard in which director William Seiter was to utilize her comedic talents.

Seiter, an expert at frothy romantic comedies and light drama, is almost totally forgotten today. This is regrettable, for although not many of his films were ever considered "bona-fide" classics, he was a filmmaker who could extract the most from his performers and technicians, in spite of a weak script. An easygoing craftsman, whose beginnings in film ranged from screenwriter to assistant director, he eventually learned the fundamentals of filmmaking the hard way, through the knockabout, pie-in-the-face school of Mack Sennett. His warm sense of fun is evident in many of his 1930s releases, such as *The Richest Girl in the World* (1934), *In*

Person (1935), *If You Could Only Cook* (1935), and *The Moon's Our Home* (1936). Even the era's comedians would put him in great demand, with the comedy team of Bert Wheeler and Robert Woolsey using him constantly throughout the early thirties in *Peach O'Reno* (1931) and *Caught Plastered* (1931), while Laurel and Hardy found him to be their ideal director in their classic *Sons of the Desert* (1933).

While it was only a matter of months before Ginger Rogers would be cast opposite Fred Astaire in their first outing together, *Flying Down to Rio* (1933), she did, however, have a few good roles already under her belt. *Professional Sweetheart* happened to be a leading role in which she receives excellent backing from some of Hollywood's best character actors. If there was ever an example of superb ensemble acting, then it can be found in this entry. Even leading man Norman Foster is seen to good advantage as a naïve country bumpkin, whose infatuation with the "Purity Girl" leads him into a publicity stunt with hysterical results. Allen Jenkins and Frank McHugh (both borrowed from Warner Bros.) are up

Professional Sweetheart (1933) A great array of classic character actors lend support in Professional Sweetheart including Franklin Pangborn (Herbert Childress), Frank McHugh (Speed Dennis), Gregory Ratoff (Samuel Ipswich) and Frank Darien (Appleby). (RF)

Professional Sweetheart (1933) Radio's "Purity Girl" Glory Eden (Ginger Rogers) tells her maid, Vera (Theresa Harris) that she wants to go to Harlem to smoke, drink and "sin." (RF)

to their usual shenanigans as opposing publicists. But the real icing on the cake is Edgar (slow-burn) Kennedy, who plays a dishrag magnate, Zasu Pitts as a gossip columnist, Gregory Ratoff as the president of Ipsy-Wipsy, an opposing dishrag company, and the dithery Franklin Pangborn as an effeminate interior decorator. Other standouts include Sterling Holloway,

Betty Furness, and Theresa Harris, a black actress whose depiction of the "snow white purity girl" continues to arouse controversy in these "politically-correct" times.

Since this was a 1933 release, the censorship board (the Hays Office) found the character of Glory Eden to be a girl with "questionable morals." True, there are some wonderful double entendres and racy dialogue, which is why the film holds up so well today. Even in Great Britain the title of the film was changed to *Imaginary Sweetheart* because the British censors felt that the original title had a suggestive meaning.

One curious bit of trivia which I find most baffling about *Professional Sweetheart* is why the director felt that he had to dub Ginger's voice when she sings the title song. Perhaps he hadn't seen her yet in *Gold Diggers of 1933*? Whatever the reason, the individual who sings "Imaginary Sweetheart" for Miss Rogers and Theresa Harris is "blues vocalist" Etta Moten who made a career (or so it seemed) out of dubbing for actresses whose singing abilities were less than adequate. She can, however, be seen warbling "The Carioca" in *Flying Down to Rio*.

The critics did enjoy this slight offering, with Frank Nugent of *The New York Times* stating, "Radio's sacred cows, the sponsors of commercial broadcasts and the entertainers featured therein, are taken for a midsummer's sleigh ride in *Professional Sweetheart*...A competent cast, headed by Ginger Rogers and Norman Foster, has found much that is amusing in the industry to which Radio City was dedicated...Miss Rogers has rarely been more entertaining."

International House (1933)

Paramount Pictures. Directed by Edward Sutherland. Screenplay by Francis Martin and Walter DeLeon. Photographed by Ernest Haller. Based on a story by Louis E. Heifetz and Neil Brant. Music and Lyrics by Ralph Rainger and Leo Robin. Song: "Reefer Man". 70 min.

Cast: Peggy Hopkins Joyce (Herself), W. C. Fields (Professor Quail), Stuart Erwin (Tommy Nash), Sari Maritza (Carol Fortescue), George Burns (Dr. Burns), Gracie Allen (Nurse Allen), Bela Lugosi (General Petronovich), Edmund Breese (Doctor Wong), Lumsden Hare (Sir Mortimer Fortescue), Franklin Pangborn (Hotel Manager), Harrison Greene (Herr Von Baden), Henry Sedley (Serge Borsky), James Wong (Inspector Sun), Sterling Holloway (Entertainer: Sailor), Rudy Vallee (Himself), Colonel Stoopnagle and Budd (Themselves), Cab Calloway and His Orchestra (Themselves), Baby Rose Marie (Herself), Ernest Wood (Newsreel Reporter), Edwin Stanley (Mr. Rollins), Clem Beauchamp/Jerry Drew (Cameraman), Norman Ainslee (Ticket Manager), Louis Vincenot (Hotel Clerk), Bo-Ling (Chinese Girl at Cigar Counter), Etta Lee (Peggy's Maid), Bo-Ching (Bellhop), Lona Andre (Chorus Queen), Andre Cheron (Guest).

AFTER THE SUCCESS OF PARAMOUNT'S all-star *The Big Broadcast* the previous year, studio executives thought up another conglomeration of unabashed insanity, naming it *International House*. Similar to the previous film, *House* featured big name stage and radio stars, including W. C. Fields, Burns and Allen, Stuart Erwin, Bela Lugosi (cast against type in a rare comedic role), and Cab Calloway singing the censorable "Reefer Man".

Although Fields is the real star, he receives second billing to Peggy Hopkins Joyce, one of the former starlets of *The Ziegfeld Follies* whom Fields had worked with in 1917. Their scenes together in this film are

International House (1933) The Cellophane "Chorus" from the "She Was a China Tea-cup and He Was Just a Mug" number (Music by Ralph Rainger and lyrics by Leo Robin). For the record, the scantily-clad girls are (left to right) Mary Jane Sloan, Lona Andre and Gwen Zetter. (RF)

remarkably racy, replete with some outrageous double-entendres, so delightful that it won Fields a three-year contract with Paramount.

Others in the cast include fluttery Franklin Pangborn, splendid as always in his perennial role as the hotel manager, Baby Rose Marie who later achieved fame as a regular on *The Dick Van Dyke Show*, and Sterling Holloway, who later provided the voice of Winnie the Pooh.

The director of *International House* was A. Edward Sutherland, who eventually graduated from stuntman to assistant director in 1923, having previously worked with Fields on *Tillie's Punctured Romance* (1914) and *The Old Army Game* (1926). A director known for an easy-going style which made him a particular favorite among the Hollywood comedians, he later directed such near-classics as *Palmy Days* (1931) with Eddie Cantor and Charlotte Greenwood, *Mississippi* (1935) and *Poppy* (1936) both again with Fields, *The Flying Deuces* (1939) with Laurel and Hardy, and *One Night in the Tropics* (1940) with Abbott and Costello in their first film.

Reviews from the *Motion Picture Herald* read thusly: "Primarily it is a gag-inspired ribald comedy. Action and dialogue are fast and furious. But much of the double-meaning dialogue is of the ultra-risqué type that is apt to start censors on the warpath. Constructed along the lines of a mammoth vaudeville show, the motivating story often is sidetracked entirely to permit a lot of unrelated hokum comedy. The radio personalities are rung in by means of a television gag, with the exception of Burns and Allen, who run a close second to, if they do not top, W. C. Fields in fun creation."

The Life of Jimmy Dolan (1933)

Warner Bros. Produced by Hal B. Wallis. Directed by Archie Mayo. Screenplay by David Boehm and Erwin S. Gelsey. Based on the play *Sucker* by Bertram Millhauser and Beulah Marie Dix. Photography by Arthur Edeson. Edited by Bert Levy (Herbert I. Leeds), Art Direction by Robert M. Haas. Costumes by Orry-Kelly. Music by Bernhard Kaun and Leo F. Forbstein. 88 min.

Cast: Douglas Fairbanks, Jr. (Jimmy Dolan), Loretta Young (Peggy), Aline MacMahon (Mrs. Moore), Guy Kibbee (Phlaxer), Lyle Talbot (Doc Woods), Fifi D'Orsay (Budgie), Harold Huber (Reggie Newman), Shirley Grey (Goldie West), George Meeker (Charles Magee), John Wayne (Smith), Arthur Hohl (Herman Malvin), Edward Arnold (Inspector Ennis), Joan Barclay (Well-Wisher), Robert Barrat (Sheriff), Joseph Belmont (Bit), Don Brodie (Man on Stairway), George Chandler (Boxing Handler), Billy Coe (Fight Timekeeper), Arthur Dekuh (Louie Primaro), James Donlan (Man Offering Drink), David Durand (George Lewis), Adolph Faylauer (Fight Spectator), Sam Godfrey (Reporter), Alan 'Farina' Hoskins (Sam), John Kerns (Fight Opponent), Mike Lally (Reporter in Ring), Larry McGrath (First Referee), Clarence Muse (Masseur), Bradley Page (Dolan's Backer), Lee Phelps (Ring Announcer), Mickey Rooney (Freckles), John Sheehan (Fight Manager), Charles Sherlock (Reporter in Ring), Dawn O'Day/Anne Shirley (Mary Lou), Sammy Stein (King Cobra), Arthur Vinton (Matt Lenihan), Huey White (Handler).

A **FILM WHICH DOESN'T** get much exposure these days, *The Life of Jimmy Dolan* is a title that tends to be overlooked, with television stations favoring the remake, *They Made Me a Criminal* (1947) instead. This doesn't mean that the earlier version is poor…it's just that the remake, with its powerhouse performances by John Garfield and Claude Rains, virtually captivates the viewer's attention. The 1933 version, on the other hand, though flawed, has much to recommend it, with the snappy dialogue—a sure-fire audience grabber in many Warner Bros. pictures—keeping the film moving at a brisk pace. However, the 1939 version has John Garfield and Claude Rains reciting the exact same dialogue as Doug Fairbanks and Guy Kibbee in an even more intense manner and at break-neck speed.

The Life of Jimmy Dolan (1933) Prizefighter Jimmy Dolan (Douglas Fairbanks, Jr.) tries to keep his real identity a secret after he accidentally killed a reporter back east. He winds up on a health farm for sick children and tries to help the owners out of some financial difficulties by returning to the ring. That's Aline MacMahon as Mrs. Moore, the owner of the establishment.

Comparing both versions can't be helped, since they are so similar that it almost seems that with the earlier version, you are watching understudies playing the parts in some instances. The always delightful Aline MacMahon is far better than the boisterous bravado of May Robson in the remake and although Guy Kibbee can't compete with the likes of Claude Rains, he does manage to turn in a restrained, sympathetic performance as Phlaxer, the detective who once arrested the wrong party on a murder charge and the real killer wasn't found until the innocent man had been executed! Another point of interest is the casting of unbilled youngsters Mickey Rooney, Alan "Farina" Hoskins, and Dawn O'Day (who later changed her name to Anne Shirley), who are a far cry from the rough-hewn antics of the 'Dead End' Kids, and would seem rather out of place on a farm! One highlight of the film has a young John Wayne, woefully miscast here playing the role of a scared prizefighter who must face his opponent in order to get money for his pregnant wife. Wayne seems so out of sorts in a role, which was tailor-made for the likes of Louis Jean Heydt, who is perfect in the remake.

The movie was released in Britain as *The Kid's Last Flight*, based on an off-Broadway play entitled *Sucker*, which opened on April 4, 1933. It didn't take Warner Bros. long to purchase the rights to the play, which was written by Beulah Marie Dix. Shot in twenty-eight days at a budget of $202,000, *The Life of Jimmy Dolan* does indeed keep the viewer guessing, considering the fact that the lead character is guilty of accidental manslaughter (a plot device which was changed in the remake for the sake of the Hays Office).

Loretta Young, a beautiful leading lady, whose career had begun in the silent era when she was a mere child playing opposite the likes of Lon Chaney and other silent greats, is delightfully enchanting. Later, managing to make the transition into adult roles successfully at the age of sixteen, she appeared with Douglas Fairbanks, Jr. in some other Warner Bros. entries, such as *Fast Life* (1929), *Loose Ankles* (1930), *I Like Your Nerve* (1931), and others. Their "on-screen" chemistry seemed perfect for Depression-era audiences, who wanted to see more of this handsome young couple.

Born in 1909 into Hollywood Royalty, Douglas Fairbanks, Jr. began his career at the age of seven in silent movies, and like Loretta Young, was able to succeed in adult roles at an early age. In 1929, he landed a contract with Warners and was seen to great effect in some 'Pre-Code' potboilers such as *Little Caesar* (1931), *Union Depot, Love is a Racket* (both 1932) and others. Unfortunately, he never gained the reputation and stature of his superstar father, due to his lack of enthusiasm for picture making. It was later in the decade that he made two excellent films where he received rave reviews, *The Prisoner of Zenda* (1937) with Ronald Colman and *Gunga Din* (1939) with Cary Grant and Victor McLaglen.

While *The Life of Jimmy Dolan* is brimming with sentimentality, it still holds up on its own quite well today. Reviews at the time were quite assuring, with hard-nosed *Variety* stating that the film was "a neat, sure-footed picture that's easy on the eye and ear."

Gold Diggers of 1933 (1933)

Warner Bros. Directed by Mervyn LeRoy. Based on the play "Gold Diggers" by Avery Hopwood. Adaptation by Erwin Gelsey and James Seymour. Dialogue by David Boehm and Ben Markson. Photography by Sol Polito. Edited by George Amy. Dances staged by Busby Berkeley. Songs: "The Gold Diggers Song (We're in the Money)", "I've Got to Sing a Torch Song", "Pettin' in the Park", "The Shadow Waltz", "Remember My Forgotten Man" by Harry Warren and Al Dubin. Remake of *Gold Diggers of Broadway* (1929). 96 min.

Cast: Warren William (J. Lawrence Bradford), Joan Blondell (Carol), Aline MacMahon (Trixie Lorraine), Ruby Keeler (Polly Parker), Dick Powell (Brad Roberts/Robert Treat Bradford), Guy Kibbee (Thaniel H. Peabody), Ned Sparks (Barney Hopkins), Ginger Rogers (Fay Fortune), Clarence Nordstrom (Gordon), Robert Agnew (Dance Director), Tammany Young (Gigolo Eddie), Sterling Holloway (Messenger Boy), Ferdinand Gottschalk (Clubman), Lynne Browning (Gold Digger Girl), Charles C. Wilson (Deputy), Billy Barty ("Pettin' in the Park" Baby), Fred "Snowflake" Toones and Theresa Harris (Negro Couple), Joan Barclay (Chorus Girl), Wallace MacDonald (Stage Manager), Wilbur Mack, Grace Hayle, Charles Lane (Society Reporters), Hobart Cavanaugh (Dog Salesman), Bill Elliott (Dance Extra), Dennis O'Keefe (Extra during Intermission), Busby Berkeley (Call Boy), Fred Kelsey ("Detective Jones"), Frank Mills (First Forgotten Man).

FILM DIRECTOR AND CHOREOGRAPHER Busby Berkeley (1895–1976) gained his reputation after working on the Broadway stage in musicals following service in the First World War. Landing a contract with renowned film producer Sam Goldwyn, he was awarded the task of directing the musical numbers in Eddie Cantor's first talkie, *Whoopee!* in 1930. By this time, audiences had begun to tire of the many musicals that

Gold Diggers of 1933 (1933) It looks like everyone wants to dance with torch singer, Carol King (Joan Blondell) including Brad Roberts (Dick Powell) and his brother, Lawrence (Warren William)...and who could blame them? (RF)

Hollywood was churning out, and Berkeley realized that he had to invent a new style to recapture the public. His ingenious innovation of arranging his chorus girls in a rhythmic kaleidoscope set in motion brought rave reviews from critics, who praised this new form of choreography. After a few more Eddie Cantor vehicles for Goldwyn, Berkeley was lured over to Warner Bros. to handle the musical numbers for *42nd Street*, which also boasted the first teaming of crooner Dick Powell and hoofer Ruby Keeler. Realizing that he had an unprecedented success on his hands, studio head Jack Warner hurriedly made plans for a follow-up film entitled *Gold Diggers of 1933*.

Brimming with outstanding musical numbers by Harry Warren and Al Dubin, the film not only cashed in on the success of Berkeley, but the teaming of Powell and Keeler as well. First billed was Warren William (although he makes his initial appearance half-way through the film), an actor who had made an art of playing political cads and assorted other reprobates. This time he is cast against type in a rare likeable role. Second billed is the delightful Joan Blondell, forever wisecracking her way through this and many other comedies of the 1930's. In addition, she gets a chance to warble the downbeat "Remember My Forgotten Man" number to an army of the unemployed. During rehearsals, Berkeley found, to his dismay, that Blondell couldn't carry a tune, so it is blues singer Etta Moten's voice that is heard on the soundtrack.

Gold Diggers of 1933 (1933) Ginger Rogers as Fay Fortune sings the hit Depression-era number "We're in the Money" in pig-Latin. (RF)

The prophetic tune "We're in the Money", sung by a pre-Astaire Ginger Rogers, was a result of on the set inspiration when Busby Berkeley heard her clowning around singing the song in pig-Latin! This tickled every member of the cast and crew so much that Berkeley insisted that Ginger sing it that way in the film.

One of the most creative numbers, "The Shadow Waltz" was delayed during filming by an earthquake, which collapsed the stairway set and left the crew without lights until all was repaired by evening and filming resumed. To attain the proper effect of dancing chorus girls carrying illuminated neon violins, each girl was wired to bulky battery packs! The racy number "Pettin' in the Park" was another one of Berkeley's "dirty jokes," in which a bevy of beautiful girls tire of their beaus mauling them in public, so they each don clothing made of armor to dissuade them, just in time for a baby (played by midget Billy Barty) to accommodate the overzealous male population with can-openers!

Almost equaling the success of *42nd Street*, *Gold Diggers of 1933* proved to be another overwhelming hit for Warner Bros. And although Busby Berkeley only directed the dance numbers in the picture (Mervyn LeRoy directed the non-musical scenes), he would go on to be the sole director in future musicals at Warners and MGM. In later years, when asked which his favorite movie was, Berkeley curiously selected 1939's *They Made Me a Criminal* with John Garfield and the Dead End Kids, a non-musical. However, there is one delightful "inside gag" in that particular film with Dead-Ender Huntz Hall singing "By a Waterfall" (off key, of course), as he pours a bucket of water on John Garfield to simulate a shower.

Picture Snatcher (1933)

A Warner Bros. & Vitaphone Picture. Directed by Lloyd Bacon. Screenplay by Allen Rivkin and P.J. Wolfson. Based on a story by Danny Ahern. Dialogue Director: William Keighley. Photography by Sol Polito. Art Direction by Robert Haas. Edited by William Holmes. Musical Conductor: Leo F. Forbstein. Costumes by Orry-Kelly. Make-up by Perc Westmore. 77 min.

Cast: James Cagney (Danny Kean), Ralph Bellamy (McLean), Patricia Ellis (Patricia Nolan), Alice White (Allison), Ralf Harolde (Jerry the Mug), Robert Emmett O'Connor (Casey Nolan), Robert Barrat (Grover), George Pat Collins (The Fireman), Tom Wilson (Leo), Barbara Rogers (Olive), Renee Whitney (Connie), Alice Jans (Colleen), Jill Dennett (Speakeasy Girl), Billy West (Reporter), George Daly (Machine Gunner), Arthur Vinton (Head Keeper), Stanley Blystone (Prison Guard), Don Brodie (Hood), George Chandler (Reporter), Sterling Holloway (Journalism Student), Donald Kerr (Mike, Colleen's Boyfriend), Hobart Cavanaugh (Pete), Phil Tead (Reporter Strange), Charles King (Sick Reporter), Milton Kibbee (Reporter Outside Prison), Dick Elliott, Vaughn Taylor (Reporters), Bob Perry (Bartender), Gino Corrado (Barber), Maurice Black (Speakeasy Proprietor), Selmer Jackson (Record Editor), Jack Grey (Police Officer), John Ince (Captain), Cora Sue Collins (Jerry's Little Girl).

BY 1933, it was becoming obvious to James Cagney that his movie career was going places! After a succession of screen hits including *Blonde Crazy* (1931), *Taxi!* (1932), and *Hard to Handle* (1933), Warner Bros. was confident about casting Jim (he hated being called Jimmy) in films which called for plenty of action, wisecracks, and snappy dialogue. Obviously, these were tagged "men" pictures, but the cagey Warners would throw in a dash of romance to keep the women happy as well.

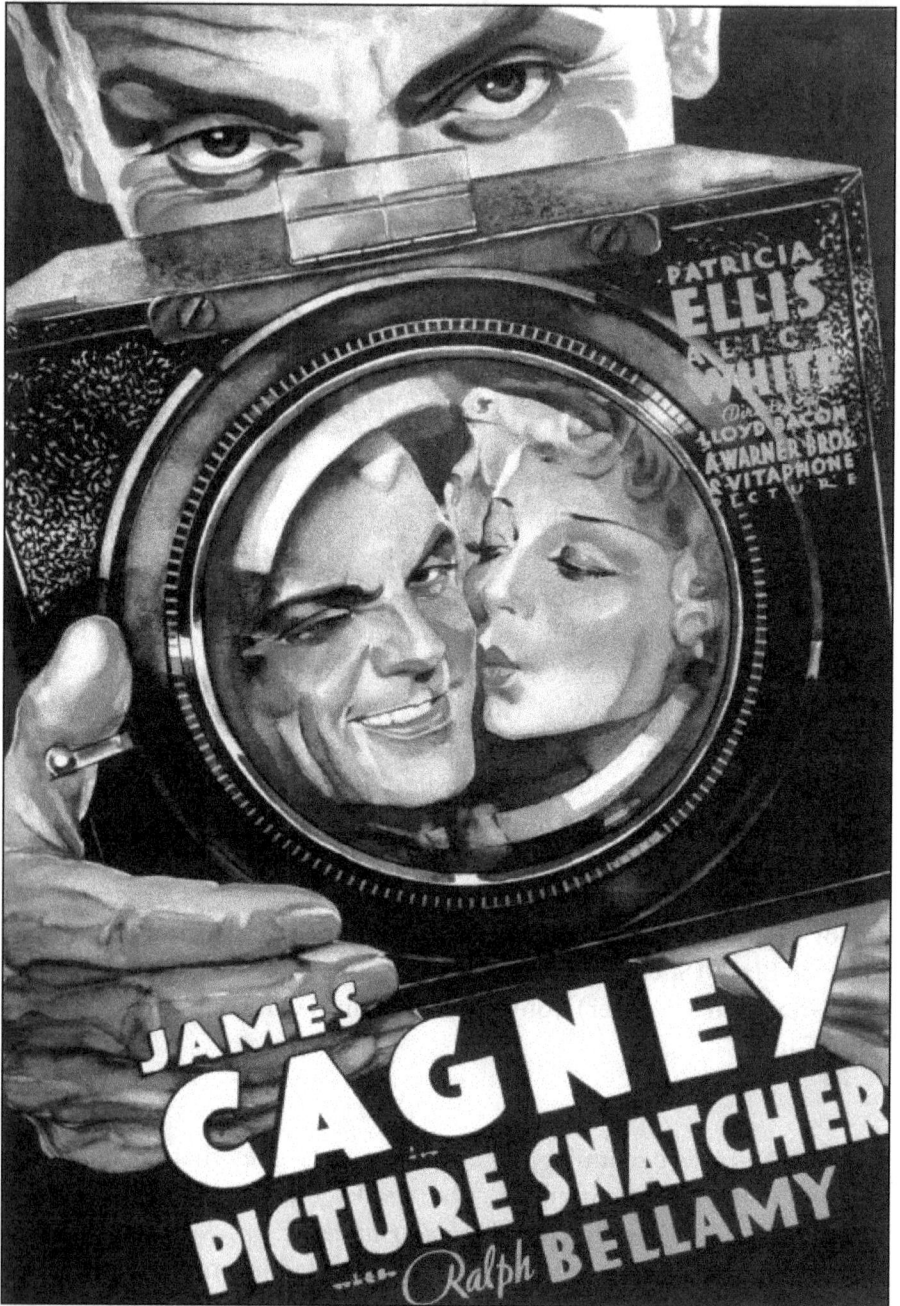

Picture Snatcher (1933) Original poster art. (AB)

One of his best Pre-Code actioners was the fast-paced *Picture Snatcher*, in which ex-con Cagney lands a job with a disreputable newspaper as a photographer. After a string of successes obtaining scandalous photographs and incriminating stories through his most unorthodox methods, he finagles his biggest assignment—the execution of a woman. Cagney smuggles his camera, which is strapped to his ankle, past the "green door" of Sing-Sing, to give a full account of capital punishment via the electric chair a la Ruth Snyder. Of course, he lands a front-page story, but gets the police inspector, who happens to be his girlfriend's father, demoted for negligence in the process. Soon after, he redeems himself by snapping a picture of a notorious gangster just as he's meeting his violent end and throwing all the credit for his capture to that same police inspector!

Director Lloyd Bacon keeps this lively action yarn moving at a good pace, with great support by Ralph Bellamy, who plays Jim's newspaper associate (Cagney and Bellamy met on the set of this picture and remained

Picture Snatcher (1933) Danny Keane (James Cagney) is caught fooling around with Allison (Alice White), the girlfriend of his boss, J. R. "Al" McLean (Ralph Bellamy), who's just barged in. (AB)

lifelong friends). The love interest (for what it's worth) is provided by pretty Patricia Ellis, a Warners contract player whose career never rose above appearing in programmers and "B" pictures. One of her last films was in Laurel and Hardy's excellent 1938 feature, *Block-Heads*. But the icing on the cake is the performance by pert Alice White, nearly stealing the show as the girlfriend of Ralph Bellamy, who wouldn't mind a bit of double-dealing with Cagney. Of course Jim gets on to her, and in the film's very funny finale, knocks her out cold! According to Cagney, he had a problem filming this scene because Alice White's head suddenly nodded slightly forward just as Jim was supposed to fake the punch. What resulted was a hysterical Alice White with a bruised jaw and a very apologetic Mr. Cagney. Incidentally, sexy blonde comedienne Thelma Todd was originally slated to play Alice's role but was unavailable since she was busy making her series of short subjects over at the Hal Roach Studio.

Critics unanimously praised the picture, citing, "*Picture Snatcher* is a vulgar but generally funny collection of blackouts…This is the third successive Warner Brothers picture to be distinguished by lavatory scenes (the other two were *Baby Face* and *Union Depot*). A happy thought was the teaming of the tough, noisy Alice White with tough, noisy Cagney. Without plot restriction, it is doubtful who would have won the bout." The film was even earning the plaudits of *The London Times*, who wrote, "Artistically, the best thing in the film is the consistency which Mr. Cagney delivers between the superficial cleverness and the extreme thoughtlessness of the snatcher. Mr. Cagney makes this character credible and interesting."

Baby Face (1933)

A Warner Bros. Picture. Directed by Alfred E. Green. Produced by Ray Griffith. Screenplay by Gene Markey and Kathryn Scola. Story by Mark Canfield (Darryl F. Zanuck). Photography by James Van Trees. Edited by Howard Bretherton. Art Direction by Anton Grot. Costumes by Orry-Kelly. 70 min.

Cast: Barbara Stanwyck (Lily Powers), George Brent (Mr. Trenholm), Donald Cook (Mr. Stevens), Arthur Hohl (Ed Sipple), John Wayne (Jimmy McCoy, Jr.), Henry Kolker (Mr. Carter), James Murray (Brakeman), Robert Barrat (Nick Powers), Margaret Lindsay (Ann Carter), Douglass Dumbrille (Mr. Brody), Theresa Harris (Chico), Renee Whitney (The Girl), Nat Pendleton (Stolvich), Alphonse Ethier (Cragg), Harry Gribbon (Doorman), Arthur De Kuh (Lutza), Toby Wing (Secretary).

"I HAVE NEVER WORKED with an actress who was more cooperative, less temperamental, and a better workman," said director Cecil B. DeMille in his autobiography regarding Barbara Stanwyck. Although she only worked with him once in 1939's *Union Pacific*, other directors like Frank Capra and William Wellman shared DeMille's sentiments as well.

Born Ruby Stevens on July 16, 1907, in Brooklyn, New York, she was orphaned in early childhood. At thirteen, she quit school to work in a low-paying job as a parcel wrapper, while at night she studied dancing, and would later appear for Florenz Ziegfeld of Follies fame. Through ambition and solid perseverance, she landed the lead in the Broadway play *The Noose* in 1926. Two years later she found herself under contract with Warner Bros., but on loan-out to Columbia, she starred in three films directed by Frank Capra entitled *Ladies of Leisure* (1930), *The Miracle Woman* (1931), and *The Bitter Tea of General Yen* (1933). Back at Warners she starred in other notable vehicles such as *Night Nurse* (1931), *Ladies They Talk About* (1933, a prison comedy-drama complete with homosexual overtones), *Gambling Lady* (1934), and the controversial *Baby Face*.

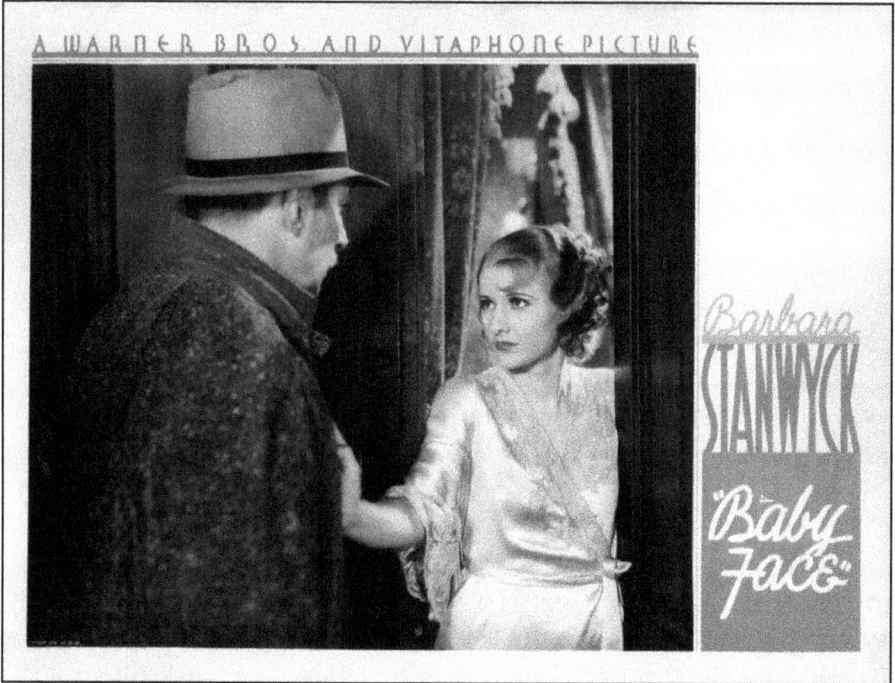

Baby Face (1933) Looks like Lily Powers (Barbara Stanwyck) won't let former conquest Brody (Douglass Dumbrille) into her apartment because she's busy "entertaining" her next conquest. (AB)

Made at a time when Hollywood's film output was at its raunchiest, *Baby Face* proved to be so risqué that ads for the film warned, "Parents: Please do not bring your children!" Aside from the film's questionable subject matter, this title happens to be the genesis for Stanwyck's later performance in the 1944 classic, *Double Indemnity*.

The director for *Baby Face* was Alfred E. Green, who started directing silent two-reel comedies in 1913 before graduating to features in 1917. By 1929, he was an accomplished filmmaker, having directed the great George Arliss in *Disraeli*, which incidentally was nominated for the best picture award, losing to Lewis Milestone's *All Quiet on the Western Front* (1930). Other notable releases to Green's credit include *Smart Money* (1931, the only teaming of Edward G. Robinson and James Cagney), *Union Depot* (1932) with Douglas Fairbanks, Jr., *Gentlemen Are Born* (1934, a tough, but forgotten social drama, depicting the fates of three college chums who find nothing but tragedy after futile attempts finding employment during the depression), *Dangerous* (1935) with Bette Davis,

Baby Face (1933) Lily (Barbara Stanwyck) is giving another one of her beaus, Jimmy McCoy (John Wayne) the "brush off."

Baby Face (1933) Lily (Barbara Stanwyck) working in her father's brothel along with her friend, Chico (Theresa Harris). (AB)

East of the River (1940) with John Garfield, and *The Jolson Story* (1946) with Larry Parks in the title role.

The photographer of *Baby Face* was James Van Trees, who utilizes his talents by effectively encompassing the screen with dominant grays, heightening a depression-era atmosphere to the proceedings.

Due to the stir created by the release of this film, *Variety*, in its review, dubbed the movie "blue and nothing else," continuing with "This is reputed to be a remake of the first print, which was considered too hot!"

Lastly, let's give an affectionate nod of approval to George Brent, who was one of Bette Davis' favorite leading men. Here he gives a convincing performance as the one man Lily Powers (Stanwyck) learns to love. Oh, and yes, that IS the Duke, John Wayne, playing office employee Jimmy McCoy, six years before achieving major stardom in John Ford's *Stagecoach* (1939), in which he portrayed the Ringo Kid!

The Mayor of Hell (1933)

A Warner Bros. and Vitaphone Picture. Directed by Archie Mayo. Screenplay by Edward Chodorov. Based on a story by Islin Auster. Photography by Barney "Chick" McGill. Art Direction by Esdras Hartley. Edited by Jack Killifer. Music by Leo F. Forbstein. Costumes by Orry-Kelly. Makeup by Perc Westmore. Assistant Director: Frank Shaw. 91 min.

Cast: James Cagney (Patsy Gargan), Madge Evans (Dorothy Griffith), Allen Jenkins (Mike), Dudley Digges (Mr. Thompson), Frankie Darro (Jimmy Smith), Allen "Farina" Hoskins (Smoke), Dorothy Peterson (Mrs. Smith), John Marston (Hopkins), Charles Wilson (Guard), Hobart Cavanaugh (Tommy's Father), Raymond Borzage (Johnny Stone), Robert Barrat (Mr. Smith), George Pat Collins (Brandon), Mickey Bennett (Butch Kilgore), Arthur Byron (Judge Gilbert), Sheila Terry (The Girl), Harold Huber (Joe), Edwin Maxwell (Louis Johnston), William V. Mong (Walters), Sidney Miller (Izzy Horowitz), George Humbert (Tony's Father), George Offerman, Jr. (Charlie Burns), Charles Cane (Tommy Gordon), Wallace MacDonald (Johnson's Assistant), Adrian Morris (Car Owner), Fred "Snowflake" Toones (Hemingway), Wilfred Lucas (Guard), Bob Perry, Charles Sullivan (Collectors), Ben Taggart (Sheriff).

USUALLY MISTAKEN FOR A JAMES CAGNEY vehicle even though he receives top billing, *The Mayor of Hell* is actually a showcase for young Frankie Darro, whose portrayal later that year in the classic social drama *Wild Boys of the Road* gave him a far greater opportunity to display his versatility. The son of circus performers, young Frank made his movie debut at age six and was generally cast in unimportant, small-child roles until his opportunity in *The Public Enemy*, where he played James Cagney's sidekick Matt Doyle as a boy. His small frame and tough looks made him a natural at portraying young hoodlums victimized by the Depression. In William Wellman's *Wild Boys of the Road* (1933), he plays a likeable teenager whose father has lost his job and can't seem to keep up with the mortgage payments. Feeling that his parents would be better off with one less mouth to feed, Frankie, along with another friend, packs a duffel and hops a freight, hoping to find a job in another area so that he will wire some money home. To his dismay, he finds that the grass isn't greener anywhere else and the law enforcement officials are all but immune to the many hundreds of homeless waifs and their hopeless plights. The film, like most social dramas of the 1930s, ends on a hopeful note, with Frank finding a job, through the courtesy of a helpful juvenile authority, and with every intention of going back to his parents.

Like *Wild Boys of the Road*, *The Mayor of Hell* was meant as a social drama, focusing on a reform school, the corrupt officials who run it, and the violent physical abuse inflicted on the boys. Unfortunately, *Mayor* fails to be as compelling as some of the other socially-significant films of the 1930s like *I Am a Fugitive From a Chain Gang* (1932) and *They Won't*

The Mayor of Hell (1933) Tough hoodlum, Patsy Gargan (James Cagney, center), tells reform school superintendent, Thompson (Dudley Digges), that young Jimmy Smith (Frankie Darro) has endured enough of a beating, while nurse Dorothy Griffin (Madge Evans) prepares to take the boy to the infirmary. The guard on the left is Wilfred Lucas. (RF)

Forget (1937). However, it does work on a different level as an entertaining melodrama that doesn't take itself too seriously. One of the film's deficits is that Frankie Darro's character, as well as his buddies, are all unlikable hoodlums, who would be better off in reform school. But once James Cagney takes over the reformatory from the abusive school superintendent the boys quickly (and unconvincingly) conform to Cagney's way of thinking and become ideal inmates, for the time being anyway. Before long, through a series of odd circumstances, the old superintendent is back running the school while Cagney is on the lam from the law for an attempted murder rap.

When one of the young boys dies at the hands of the school official after being put into a freezer as punishment, the young inmates decide to take the law into their own hands and perform their own execution. The superintendent hastily escapes the wrath of the youngsters, but is eventually cornered atop a barn rooftop. In a chilling sequence reminiscent of the last few minutes of James Whale's *Frankenstein* (1931), the kids rapidly transform into an angry lynch mob with torches blazing, setting the barn afire. The real shocker comes when, in a panic, the superintendent falls off of the rooftop and ultimately breaks his neck, leaving the school's inhabitants responsible—or so the viewer thinks! In true "Pre-Code" fashion, Cagney is back as superintendent and the kids are not held responsible for the death of his predecessor.

Critically, *The Mayor of Hell* failed to generate much excitement, with the *New York Herald Tribune* complaining that it is "purportedly a social document, a sort of case study in reformatory methods, it is actually a wild hodgepodge of melodrama and sentiment. Even the splendid performances of James Cagney and Dudley Digges and a score of excellent boy actors are powerless to shape the work to distinctive or artistic form." Regardless, the film scored heavily at the box-office, probably on behalf of the assured appeal of Cagney alone.

When *The Mayor of Hell* was to go into production, Cagney's original choice for his leading lady was the appealing Joan Blondell, but sadly, Miss Blondell was unavailable. The studio's second choice happened to be Glenda Farrell, who was busy elsewhere on the lot as well. Finally, Warners cast beautiful Madge Evans after borrowing her from MGM. Although she does do an admissible job, one wonders how much better Blondell or Farrell would have fared.

Five years later Warner Bros. would take the original story *Reform School* by Islin Austin out of mothballs and recycle it not once, but twice, as vehicles for the "Dead End Kids". These films, *Crime School* (1938) and *Hell's Kitchen* (1939), were perfect for the six hooligans, and although they were shot on tight budgets, they did make enough money for the studio. Before long, however, the Hays Office decided it was high time to soften their unruly images in films like *The Angels Wash Their Faces* and *On Dress Parade* (both 1939).

Hold Your Man (1933)

A Metro Goldwyn Mayer Release. Produced and Directed by Sam Wood. Story by Anita Loos. Screenplay by Anita Loos and Howard Emmett Rogers. Title Song, *Hold Your Man* by Arthur Freed and Nacio Herb Brown. Art Direction by Cedric Gibbons and Merrill Pye. Wardrobe by Adrian. Set Decorations by Edwin B. Willis. Photography by Harold G. Rosson. Edited by Frank Sullivan. Sound by Douglas Shearer. 86 min.

Cast: Jean Harlow (Ruby Adams), Clark Gable (Eddie Hall), Stuart Erwin (Al Simpson), Dorothy Burgess (Gypsy), Gary Owen (Slim), Muriel Kirkland (Bertha Dillon), Barbara Barondess (Sadie Kline), Paul Hurst (Aubrey Mitchell), Elizabeth Patterson (Miss Tuttle), Theresa Harris (Lily Mae Crippen), Inez Courtney (Maizie), Blanche Frederici (Mrs. Wagner), Helen Freeman (Miss Davis), George Reed (Reverend Crippen), Louise Beavers (Washroom Attendant), Jack Cheatham and Frank Hagney (Cops), Jack Randall (Dancer), G. Pat Collins (Phil Dunn), Harry Semels (Neighbor), Nora Cecil (Sewing Teacher), Eva McKenzie (Cooking Teacher).

AFTER THE RELEASE OF MGM'S classic *Red Dust*, it was only a matter of coming up with another screenplay for their newest screen team of Gable and Harlow. Ultimately it was *Red Dust* that elevated both luminaries to superstar status, although they had appeared together previously in 1931's *The Secret Six*, a vehicle for tough-macho men Wallace Beery and Johnny Mack Brown. *Hold Your Man* was their third film together, an entertaining yet not wholly satisfying release due to the complete mood change from comedy to maudlin (and I don't use that word loosely) drama! Metro's top scenarist Anita Loos was slated to write a frothy screenplay for the studio's newest stars. What resulted was a racy, no-holds barred first half followed by an unsatisfactory ending that included an embarrassingly bad crying scene with Gable pleading to a black minis-

Hold Your Man (1933) Con man Eddie Hall (Clark Gable) bursts into Ruby Adams'
(Jean Harlow) bathroom while trying to elude the police. (RF)

ter to perform a wedding ceremony for Harlow and himself before the
police come to arrest him. Undoubtedly, this sappy ending was inserted
by studio-head Louis B. Mayer, who reveled in the corniest of situations.

Sam Wood, the director of *Hold Your Man*, was probably the most
over-rated director in Hollywood, miraculously securing some of the

most prestigious assignments of the 30s and 40s. Some of his credits include *Christopher Bean* (1933), *A Night at the Opera* (1935), *A Day at the Races* (1937), scenes from *Gone with the Wind* (1939; only when Victor Fleming took ill), *Goodbye Mr. Chips* (1939), *Kitty Foyle* (1940), *The Devil and Miss Jones* (1941), *Kings Row* (1942), and *The Pride of the Yankees* (1942). All impressive titles indeed. Considering the mega-star power and good scripts, how could these films have missed? To elaborate, another over-rated director named Frank Lloyd was given the task of directing such classics as *Cavalcade* (1933) and *Mutiny on the Bounty* (1935). Both films won Best Picture Oscars, merely because sluggish direction was compensated for by fine performances, first rate camera work, and scripts that were surefire!

As for Gable and Harlow, they quickly became hot commodities and worked splendidly together. Had *Hold Your Man* and *Red Dust* been the only films they made as a team, they would have still gone down in film history as one of the most popular. Luckily, however, they were cast opposite one another in *China Seas* (1935), the under-rated *Wife vs. Secretary* (1936), and *Saratoga* (1937).

Kate Cameron of the *New York Daily News* wrote, "Jean Harlow gives a pretty good imitation of a tough baby as Ruby Adams, and she surprises us by showing that she packs a powerful wallop in her delicate-looking left arm. When Dorothy Burgess, as Gypsy, slaps Miss Harlow across the face, the latter returns a short jab with her left hand to Dorothy's chin that looks like a stunner." Despite its shortcomings in the latter half, *Hold Your Man* still warrants attention as one of the better examples of Pre-Code Hollywood.

Moonlight and Pretzels (1933)

Universal Pictures. Presented by Carl Laemmle. Produced by Monte Brice and William Rowland. Directed by Karl Freund. Original Story by Sig Herzig. Screenplay by Jay Gorney, Monte Brice, Arthur L. Jarrett. Photography by William Miller. Edited by Robert R. Snody. Music Supervision by Jay Gorney. Dance Direction by Bobby Connolly. Costumes by Brooks, Brymer and Eaves. 83 min.

Cast: Leo Carrillo (Nick Pappacroplis), Mary Brian (Sally Upton), Roger Pryor (George Dwight), Herbert Rawlinson (Sport Powell), Lillian Miles (Elsie Warren), Bobby Watson (Bertie), William Frawley (Mack), Jack Denny and His Waldorf Astoria Orchestra, Frank and Milt Britton and Band, Alexander Gray (Singer), Bernice Claire (Singer), The Eton Boys, The Girlfriend Trio, John Hundley (Man in Bed), Doris Carson (Woman in Bed), Helen Bennett (Showgirl), James B. Carson (Beer Drinker), Geraldine Dvorak (Party Guest), Richard Keene, Mary Lange, Alexander Campbell, Max Stamm (Bit Parts), Donald MacBride (Business Associate), Doro Merande (Hymn-singing Lady), Phil Regan (End Man), Louis Sorin (Hobart), Jean Stuart, Anya Taranda, Sonny Walters, Mildred Webb (Showgirls).

BEST DESCRIBED AS AN ODDITY, *Moonlight and Pretzels* is one of those musicals that followed closely (almost too closely) in the Busby Berkeley/Warner Bros. style of filmmaking. Using the same plot device of putting on a Broadway musical with a young, inexperienced ingénue quickly replacing the star, as in the previously released *42ⁿᵈ Street* (March 3, 1933) and *Gold Diggers of 1933* (May 27, 1933), it makes one wonder how Universal got away with plagiarizing these Warners' outings without being slapped with a lawsuit! Not only are some of the stage numbers choreographed in much the same manner, but the show's finale consists of a number called *Dusty Shoes*, which is a complete rip-off of the *Remember My Forgotten Man* finale in *Gold Diggers of 1933*.

Moonlight and Pretzels (1933) Songwriter George Dwight (Roger Pryor, in his screen debut) does a quick "two-step" with Sally Upton (Mary Brian). (RF)

Filmed on a shoestring budget of $100,000, this was Universal's attempt to cash in on the renewed interest in the movie musical following the Warner Bros. releases. With the working title *Shoot the Works*, producers William Rowland and Monte Brice hired newcomer Roger Pryor, a stage star who had acquired a name for himself on Broadway after appearing in *Saturday's Children* (1927) opposite Ruth Gordon, and *The Front Page* (1931), where he replaced Lee Tracy, who had been recently brought to Hollywood. It was his performance in the play *Blessed Event* that made New York movie executives really take notice of Pryor. As a result, he was signed to star in *Moonlight and Pretzels* after both Dick Powell and Lew Ayres proved unavailable. Shot at the Astoria studio and the Casino Theatre in Manhattan in a mere eighteen days, the film seems to have been put into distribution in a hurry, most likely to cash in on the musical craze that had profited Warner Bros. recently. Despite having Karl Freund as director, whose credits would include horror classics such as *The Mummy* (1932) and *Mad Love* (1935), there doesn't seem to have been time for revisions or retakes, and it certainly shows.

Moonlight and Pretzels (1933) Roger Pryor and Mary Brian. (RF)

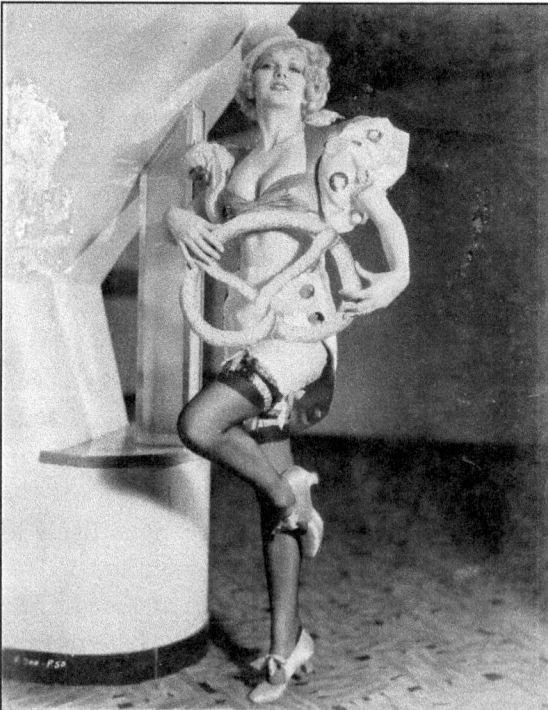

Moonlight and Pretzels (1933) A provocative pose by one of the dancers in the "Moonlight and Pretzels" number. (RF)

Even though some of the numbers are relatively good, there remain some poorly executed scenes that could have used some tightening. It's obvious that Roger Pryor (whose best film was *Belle of the Nineties* a year later with Mae West) and the usually winsomely charming Mary Brian aren't as appealing as Dick Powell and Ruby Keeler here, and the dance numbers can be at times heavy-handed and downright embarrassing, making this effort a curio at best. The *Dusty Shoes* finale number is probably the most impressive portion of the film. It utilizes actual newsreel footage in a well-edited montage, interspersed with the impressive vocalizing of Lillian Miles, who belts out the lyrics. Why Miss Miles was soon relegated to short subjects and bit parts at Hal Roach (*Apples to You!* and *Roamin' Vandals*) and other studios is indeed puzzling because she does possess an exuberant personality and charm.

Although well-received in its day both critically and financially, *Moonlight and Pretzels* has lost much of its appeal, apparently due to the manner in which it was hastily put together. Today, it is all but forgotten. However, this "abandoned orphan", as William K. Everson called it, should be reassessed and appreciated for its lack of pretense.

Tugboat Annie (1935)

MGM. Directed by Mervyn LeRoy. From the Saturday Evening Post stories by Norman Reilly Raine. Screenplay by Zelda Sears and Eve Greene. Photography by Gregg Toland. Edited by Blanche Sewell. Art Direction by Cedric Gibbons. Sound by Douglas Shearer. 87 min.

Cast: Marie Dressler (Annie Brennan), Wallace Beery (Terry Brennan), Robert Young (Alec Brennan), Maureen O'Sullivan (Pat Severn), Willard Robertson (Red Severn), Tammany Young (Shif'less), Frankie Darro (Alec as a Boy), Jack Pennick (Pete), Paul Hurst (Sam), Oscar Apfel (Reynolds), Robert McWade (Mayor of Secoma), Robert Barrat (First Mate), Vince Barnett (Cabby), Robert E. Homans (Old Salt), Guy Usher (Auctioneer), Willie Fung (Chow, the Cook), William Burress (Meyer), Hal Price (Sailor), Christian Rub (Sailor), Major Sam Harris and Joe Young (Onlookers).

DURING HOLLYWOOD'S GOLDEN AGE, many screen teams emerged, usually by accident. What made these pairings so unique was the superb chemistry between two participants, who displayed an unusual knack for excellent repartee and could work in perfect unison with one another. Teams like Gable and Harlow, Tracy and Hepburn, Powell and Loy, MacDonald and Eddy, and Rooney and Garland became recognizable through their last names only. They became so popular, as a matter of fact, that audiences clamored for more and more pictures featuring their favorite teams.

One of the most unlikely teamings, however, was Marie Dressler and Wallace Beery, a homely couple, to say the least. Dressler, with her rubbery, withered, bulldog features, became one of the most popular staples at MGM, after years of character roles in countless shorts and silent features. The same could be said for Beery, who with his gravel-voice and barreled physique tried untiringly in the silent era to achieve star status as a comedic actor. Beginning with Mack Sennett and co-starring with his then wife, Gloria Swanson, Beery excelled in comic villain roles, always getting his comeuppance from much smaller (in frame) leading men, thereby making his downfall even funnier.

In early 1930, Beery and Dressler were teamed for the first time in *Min and Bill*, an overly sentimental comedy drama, exploiting the un-tapped talents of these two stars. To the studio's amazement, it was an unprecedented hit with the public and made both of these actors the top box-office attractions of the early 1930s. Of course, another re-teaming was inevitable, with the MGM story department going to great lengths to find a worthy vehicle for its two stars. The result was *Tugboat Annie*, a rather episodic venture, concentrated on the roller-coaster relationship between husband and wife tugboat owners Annie Brennan and her ne'er do-well alcoholic spouse, Terry. The film, although not as good as *Min and Bill*, was successful enough to warrant more movies with its famous stars. However, during production of *Tugboat Annie*, it was learned that Marie Dressler was dying of cancer. Studio head, Louis B. Mayer, tried keeping this information from his popular star, telling her that she was

Tugboat Annie (1933) Annie Brennan (Marie Dressler) and her troublesome husband Terry (Wallace Beery). (RF)

overworking and that she needed a rest. Undaunted, Dressler persevered and worked in short shifts, resting between takes. Amazingly, Miss Dressler would go on to do two more films for MGM before succumbing the following year.

Beautifully photographed by Gregg Toland, eight years before his masterful job on *Citizen Kane*, and directed by MGM's new resident director turned producer, Mervyn LeRoy, *Tugboat Annie* is one those films which is enhanced by a strong supporting cast (Robert Young and Maureen O'Sullivan as the young lovers) and location shooting (a rarity during those depression years). LeRoy, a veteran director who had just finished a successful stint at Warner Bros., was lured to the home of Leo the lion to fill a void as producer, left vacant by Irving Thalberg, then on sick leave. In between producing chores, LeRoy did direct some of Metro's top stars, in popular vehicles such as *Waterloo Bridge* (1940) with Vivien Leigh and Robert Taylor, and *Random Harvest* (1942) with Ronald Colman and Greer Garson.

Three Cornered Moon (1933)

Paramount Pictures. Produced by B. P. Schulberg. Directed by Elliott Nugent. Screenplay by Ray Harris and S.K. Lauren. Based on a play by Gertrude Tonkonogy. Photography by Leon Shamroy. Edited by Jane Loring. Music by John Leipold. Costumes by Travis Banton. Sound by Earl S. Hayman. Special Photographic Effects by Gordon Jennings. 77 min.

Cast: Claudette Colbert (Elizabeth Rimplegar), Richard Arlen (Dr. Alan Stevens), Mary Boland (Mrs. Nellie Rimplegar), Wallace Ford (Kenneth Rimplegar), Lyda Roberti (Jenny), Tom Brown (Eddie Rimplegar), Joan Marsh (Kitty), Hardie Albright (Ronald), William Bakewell (Douglas

Three Cornered Moon (1933) Dr. Alan Stevens (Richard Arlen) is in love with his landlady's daughter, Elizabeth Rimplegar (Claudette Colbert). (AB)

Three Cornered Moon (1933) However, Elizabeth (Claudette Colbert) is in love with lazy no-account "artist" Ronald (Hardie Albright). (AB)

Rimplegar), Sam Hardy (Hawkins), Joan Clark (Stage Lady), Margaret Armstrong (Mrs. Johnson), Clara Blandick (Ronald's Landlady), Edward Gargan (Mike the Landlord), Sam Godfrey (Albert-Laundry Man), John Kelly (Truck Driver), George LeGuere (Call Boy), Charlotte Merriam (Gracie), Elliott Nugent (Stock Broker), Fred Stanley (Margin Clerk), Joe Sauers/Sawyer (Swimming Pool Instructor), John M. Sullivan (Griggs), Nick Thompson (Apple Peddler).

DIRECTOR FRANK CAPRA HAD ALWAYS CLAIMED that he made the very first screwball comedy with *It Happened One Night* in 1934. This is far from the truth, since romantic comedies about wacky families and the idle rich had been around for quite some time before that. True, Capra's film did solidify the appeal of the genre, but during the twenties, there were many forerunners, which were quite popular both commercially and critically, such as *The Marriage Circle* (1924), *Are Parents People?* (1925), *The Garden of Eden*, and *The Patsy* (both 1928). A year before *It Happened*

One Night was released, MGM came out with a wonderfully written comedy called *Bombshell*, a scathingly funny film about the life of a Hollywood sex symbol, played to perfection by Jean Harlow. Loud-mouthed Lee Tracy played her publicist, whose made up outrageous yarns about her "private life" became so scandalous that she attempts to abandon her career. Of course, her studio can't afford to lose her and it's up to Lee Tracy to bring her back, but not before a series of hilarious mishaps occur.

Also, in 1933, Paramount Pictures brought forth a delightful little film called *Three Cornered Moon*, a rather unimportant, tight-budgeted film with no aspirations artistically, but nevertheless fondly remembered by those who have seen it. It's another one of those Great Depression comedies of the thirties that Hollywood made an abundance of (*If You Could Only Cook*, *My Man Godfrey*, *You Can't Take It with You*) and although it's not as funny as the many superior comedies that followed, it still was a welcome attraction during those lean years when America was suffering financial ruin.

The film centers on a rather wacky Brooklyn family named the Rimplegars (the name is funny in itself), consisting of three brothers (Wallace Ford, William Bakewell, and Tom Brown) a sister (Claudette Colbert) and the head of the household, their totally ditzy mother (played to perfection by the delightful Mary Boland). One of the brothers is in love with a girl who is constantly cheating on him, while another fancies himself as a great stage actor, prancing about in full costume, reciting lines for a play that he hasn't even been cast in. The third son is just home from college and lies around the house. The sister, also out of work, is smitten with a struggling artist who doesn't believe in hard work. After he gets evicted from his rooming house for failure to pay the rent, he moves in with the Rimplegars! Then, there's the family physician, played by Richard Arlen (who is not only a paying tenant—the sole viable means of support for the family—but is also in love with the daughter), the only sane one who attempts to keep this family of ne'er do wells focused on getting jobs in the midst of the worst year of the Depression, after the bank tries to foreclose on their home.

For some, the film might hit too closely to home to really find it amusing. One wonders how audiences reacted to it in 1933. Directed by Elliott Nugent, who also appears briefly as a stockbroker, it's interesting to think how Gregory La Cava or William A. Seiter might have fared, had one of them directed it. Nevertheless, *Three Cornered Moon* did brisk enough business during the height of the Great Depression, and was a welcome remedy for those who were feeling its woeful effects.

Dinner at Eight (1933)

A Metro-Goldwyn-Mayer Picture. Produced by David O. Selznick. Directed by George Cukor. Based on the 1932 play by George S. Kaufman and Edna Ferber. Screenplay by Frances Marion and Herman J. Mankiewicz. Photography by William Daniels. Edited by Ben Lewis. Additional Dialogue by Donald Ogden Stewart. Original Music by Dr. William Axt. Art Direction by Hobe Erwin and Fredric Hope. Costume Designs by Adrian. Sound by Douglas Shearer. 113 min.

Cast: Marie Dressler (Carlotta Vance), John Barrymore (Larry Renault), Wallace Beery (Dan Packard), Jean Harlow (Kitty Packard), Lionel Barrymore (Oliver Jordan), Lee Tracy (Max Kane), Edmund Lowe (Dr. Wayne Talbot), Billie Burke (Millicent Jordan), Madge Evans (Paula Jordan), Jean Hersholt (Jo Stengel), Karen Morley (Lucy Talbot), Louise Closser Hale (Hattie Loomis), Phillips Holmes (Ernest DeGraff), May Robson (Mrs. Wendel, the Cook), Grant Mitchell (Ed Loomis), Phoebe Foster (Miss Alden), Elizabeth Patterson (Miss Copeland), Hilda Vaughn (Tina, Kitty's Maid), Harry Beresford (Fosdick), Edwin Maxwell (Mr. Fitch, Hotel Manager), John Davidson (Assistant Manager), Edward Woods (Eddie), George Baxter (Gustave, the Butler), Herman Bing (The Waiter), Anna Duncan (Dora, the Maid), Edward Arnold (Hotel Manager).

MOST FILM HISTORIANS CLAIM that 1939 was the greatest year in motion picture history. That assessment certainly rings true, considering the wealth of wonderful classics that were produced during that time. Recently, many have been taking notice that 1933 (although there are far fewer classics that year) had an outstanding output of vastly entertaining films as well. True, *Cavalcade* won the Best Picture Academy Award that year and has not retained a great reputation. One of the movies, which was not nominated (and should have won) was *Dinner at Eight* directed by George Cukor, whose career would flourish with films like *Little Wom-*

en (1933), *David Copperfield* (1935), *Holiday* (1938), *The Women* (1939), *Gaslight* (1944), and many more.

After the success of MGM's all-star extravaganza *Grand Hotel* the previous year, the studio thought that they would attempt to repeat that film's success with another follow-up film. When production head Irving Thalberg took a leave of absence from the studio for health reasons, Louis B. Mayer brought in his son-in-law David O. Selznick to take over his duties temporarily. The first project he selected was *Dinner at Eight*, based on a 1932 hit play written by George Kaufman and Edna Ferber. Selznick had seen a performance of the play and liked the idea of multiple plots being intertwined in one narrative, so he brought in screenwriters Herman J. Mankiewicz and Frances Marion to work on a script. Casting proved somewhat easy since MGM had boasted that they had "more stars than there are in the heavens", with Selznick envisioning this production to include Wallace Beery, Marie Dressler, Clark Gable, and John Barrymore. George Cukor had suggested that Jean Harlow be added to the cast as

Dinner at Eight (1933) Much younger Paula Jordan (Madge Evans) is having an illicit affair with washed up movie actor, Larry Renault (John Barrymore). (RF)

Dinner at Eight (1933) Carlotta Vance (Marie Dressler) has some news for Paula Jordan (Madge Evans) about Larry Renault while her boyfriend, Ernest DeGraff (Phillips Holmes), waits patiently. (RF)

Kitty Packard, the neglected wife of Wallace Beery, after he had seen her in *Red-Headed Woman* and *Red Dust*. Now, with this excellent cast of ensemble players (except Clark Gable, who was replaced by Edmund Lowe), George Cukor began filming what was to be his biggest undertaking to date. Fortunately, everything ran rather smoothly among the actors, who all proved to be very professional during the twenty-four day shoot. John Barrymore based his character of has-been, drunken actor Larry Renault on his own past experiences with the bottle, and threw in some aspects of his father-in-law, Maurice Costello, whose career had fallen from grace, and silent star-turned-director, Lowell Sherman. Barrymore's performance was probably his crowning achievement, along with *Counsellor at Law*, which he had just finished making at Universal.

There are so many terrific performances in *Dinner at Eight*, one doesn't know where to begin to sing all of their praises. Wallace Beery and Jean Harlow were perfectly matched as the bickering Packards. According to studio publicity, neither of them got along at all during the entire shoot, with Beery, who considered Harlow a tramp, and Jean later stating that "when he dies, I'll piss on his grave!" Perhaps this mutual hate for one another is the reason why both of them are so great in every scene they appear in.

Also, during production, Billie Burke's husband, legendary show-man Florenz Ziegfeld, who had been critically ill, died before the film was completed. When *Dinner at Eight* premiered on August 23rd, 1933, it won the applause of critics as well as audiences throughout the entire country. Its production cost of $387,000 netted a tidy profit of over a million, and was one of the biggest box-office draws of the 1933-34 season. Many crit-ics claimed that the movie was an improvement over the original play, and writer Donald Odgen Smith's last exchange between Marie Dressler and Jean Harlow has become Hollywood folklore, with Jean's Kitty Pack-ard saying to Marie Dressler's Carlotta Vance that she's just read a "book the other day. It's all about civilization or something…a nutty kind of a book. Do you know that the guy said that machinery is going to take the place of every profession?" Marie, examining Jean up and down and side to side, quickly responds, "Oh, my dear, that's something you need never worry about!"

Note: Just before *Dinner at Eight* was released, the writers changed the name of Marie Dressler's dog from Mussolini to Tarzan to promote MGM's upcoming feature, *Tarzan and His Mate* (1934).

The Masquerader (1933)

A Samuel Goldwyn Production released thru United Artists. Produced by Samuel Goldwyn. Directed by Richard Wallace. Screenplay by Howard Estabrook and Moss Hart from the play by John Hunter Booth and the novel by Katherine Cecil Thurston. Photgraphy by Gregg Toland. Musical Score by Alfred Newman. Art Direction by Richard Day. Edited by Stuart Heisler. Sound by Vernon Vinton. 75 min.

Cast: Ronald Colman (John Chilcote and John Loder), Elissa Landi (Eve Chilcote), Juliette Compton (Lady Diana Joyce), David Torrence (Fraser), Claude King (Lakely), Halliwell Hobbes (Brock), Helen Jerome Eddy (Robbins), Eric Wilton (Alston), Montagu Shaw (Speaker of the House), Charlie Hall (Man in Park).

WHEN WRITING ABOUT A PRODUCER as prolific as Samuel Goldwyn, one recalls the many classic motion pictures he released through United Artists. Titles like *Bulldog Drummond* (1929), *Whoopee!* (1930), *The Greeks Had a Word For Them* (1932), *The Dark Angel* (1935), *Dodsworth* (1936), *These Three* (1936), *Dead End* (1937), *Stella Dallas* (1937), *The Hurricane* (1937), *Wuthering Heights* (1939), and *The Westerner* (1940) were not only big box-office hits but secured Goldwyn's reputation within the film community and earned him respect from most of his colleagues. Of course there were disappointments too, with releases of such flops as *The Wedding Night* (1935, Goldwyn's second attempt to make a big-named star of Anna Sten), *The Adventures of Marco Polo* (1938, with Gary Cooper hilariously miscast in the title role), and the all-time cure for insomnia, *The Goldwyn Follies* (1938). The 1940s brought audiences a wide array of worthwhile entertainment also, like *The Little Foxes* (1941), *Pride of the Yankees* (1942), and *The Best Years of Our Lives* (1946) to name a few. Goldwyn's secret for these successes was the many talented writers (Sinclair Lewis, Ben Hecht, Lillian Hellman, and Sidney Kingsley) he employed, not to mention first-rate directors like William Wyler, John Ford, and Lowell Sherman.

The Masquerader utilizes a variety of talent behind the camera, with Gregg Toland responsible for the glistening camerawork, before eventually shooting Orson Welles' *Citizen Kane* in 1941. Directing honors go to Richard Wallace, an underrated artist, whose films were popular with audiences at the time but are all but forgotten today. After a brief tenure as comedy director at the Hal Roach Studio, he is best remembered for films like *The Little Minister* (1934), *Wedding Present* (1936), and *The Young In Heart* (1938, a delightful screwball comedy featuring a family of con artists named the Carletons, played by Janet Gaynor, Douglas Fairbanks, Jr., Billie Burke, and Roland Young), and *A Night to Remember* (1942, a fast-paced detective comedy/murder mystery with Loretta Young and Brian Aherne as husband and wife sleuths a la *Thin Man*). The art director for *The Masquerader* was Canadian-born Richard Day, who later won Academy Awards for his work on *The Dark Angel* (1935), *Dod-*

The Masquerader (1933) Drug-addicted member of Parliament, Sir John Chilcote (Ronald Colman) lies helplessly unconscious, while his faithful manservant, Brock (Halliwell Hobbes) has plans for John Loder (Ronald Colman in a dual role). (RF)

sworth (1936), *How Green Was My Valley* (1941), *This Above All* (1942), *My Gal Sal* (1942), *A Streetcar Named Desire* (1951), and *On the Water-front* (1954).

The Masquerader gives Ronald Colman the difficult task of portraying a morphine-addicted Member of Parliament, as well as the man who is to assume that same role when the former is unable to appear. Having the same basic premise as the Colman/Selznick collaboration *The Prisoner of Zenda* (1937), it would be most interesting to screen both titles on a double bill for comparison. Like Colman's much later *Random Harvest* (1942), the two leads carry off the unlikely plot with no wasted time for the audience to question logic.

Moral groups weren't pleased with the depiction of a drug-addicted politician, nor were they elated with the fact that two unmarried people were living together! To make matters worse, once the real husband dies from an overdose, the look-alike and the former's wife go on with their marital bliss, carrying even further their masquerade.

The female lead was originally intended for beautiful Elissa Landi, who fell ill prior to production. In ironic haste, Goldwyn cast the future Mrs. Ronald Colman, Benita Hume, but luckily Landi recuperated sooner than expected and resumed the role. The part of John Chilcote's faithful manservant is played by scene-stealing Halliwell Hobbes, whose scene with the imposter, where he describes his master's peculiar habits, is a hoot, especially where he imitates his master ("Don't bother me! Don't bother me!" and "Why are you always whispering behind my back?").

After a contractual dispute, Colman left Sam Goldwyn's employ after nine years. He then freelanced and eventually became one of Hollywood's leading matinee idols. He died of pneumonia in 1958 after completing the abysmal *The Story of Mankind*.

Bureau of Missing Persons (1933)

Warner Bros./First National. Produced by Henry Blanke. Directed by Roy Del Ruth. Based on a story *Missing Men* by John H. Ayres and Carol Bird. Screenplay by Robert Presnell. Photography by Barney McGill. Edited by James Gibbon. Art Direction by Robert M. Haas. Original Music by Bernhard Kaun. Musical Direction by Leo F. Forbstein. Director Assistance by Chuck Hansen. 75 min.

Cast: Bette Davis (Norma Roberts), Lewis S. Stone (Captain Webb), Pat O'Brien (Detective Butch Saunders), Glenda Farrell (Belle Howard Saunders), Allen Jenkins (Detective Joe Musik), Ruth Donnelly (Gwendolyn 'Pete' Harris), Hugh Herbert (Detective Hank Slade), Alan Dinehart (Therme Roberts), Marjorie Gateson (Mrs. Paul), Tad Alexander (Caesar Paul), Noel Francis (Alice Crane), Wallis Clark (Mr. Paul), Adrian Morris (Detective Irish Conlin), Clay Clement (Burton C. Kingman), Henry Kolker (Mr. Theodore Arno), George Chandler (Homer Howard), Jack Baxley (Homicide Detective), Harry C. Bradley (Mr. Newberry), Hobart Cavanaugh (Mr. Harris), G. Pat Collins (Rejected Husband), Dorothy Christy (Actress), Frank Darien (Father), Sol Gorss (Dock Worker), Grace Hayle (Rich Lady), John Hyams (Apartment House Owner), Edward Keane (Hotel Manager), Edward McWade (Tom, the Dock Watchman), Jean Muir (Louise Kane), Edward Pawley (Waterfront Diner Patron), Dewey Robinson (Waterfront Diner Patron), Christian Rub (Apartment House Manager), Charles Sellon (Funeral Director), John Sheehan (Tom, the Morgue Attendant), Tom Wilson (Tony, Investigator), Jack Wise (Mr. Engel).

ONE OF THE MORE UNIQUE 'programmers' coming from the Warner Bros. library, *Bureau of Missing Persons* succeeds on all levels, making it one of the fastest paced films of the 'Pre-Code' era. Directed vigorously by the talented Roy Del Ruth, whose other films during this period included *Taxi!*, *Blessed Event* (both 1932), *Employees' Entrance*, *Lady Killer*

Bureau of Missing Persons (1933) Detective "Butch" Saunders (Pat O'Brien) asks Norma Roberts (Bette Davis) if he can stay and have breakfast in the morning. (AB)

and *The Little Giant* (all 1933), the film offers stark melodrama sprinkled with some sick morbid humor, typical of the Warners tradition.

Although he gets third billing, the film belongs entirely to Pat O'Brien, appearing in his first film for the studio after making a name for himself in pictures like *The Front Page* (1931), *American Madness* (1932), and *Bombshell* (1933). His early characterizations differed greatly from the ones he later portrayed when he was typecast as a priest, a cop, or a prison warden. His "Pre-Code" characterizations would usually have him playing a wizened reporter or a loud-mouthed detective, delivering his lines in rapid-fire succession, something that his later films lacked. To add more to his frustrations, he was always cast against a much more colorful character like Cagney, Bogart, or Garfield, given the uneasy task of reforming them. It's not that his later characterizations are bad in any way, they are just less interesting and his early roles are so much more rewarding, especially when he gets the chance to play the antagonist. In films like *I've Got Your Number* (1934) and *Back in Circulation* (1938), both in which he played opposite perky Joan Blondell, it's a delight to hear the machine-gun dialogue between the two stars, proving once and for all that nobody could deliver lines faster than Pat O'Brien!

Lewis Stone, appearing in a rare non-MGM picture (he was on loan-out), plays the type of role that Pat O'Brien would be cast in a few years later. Here, Mr. Stone seems to be playing his part as if it were a 'dry run' for his later recurring role as Judge Hardy in the 'Andy Hardy' series a few years later. Bette Davis, billed first in *Bureau of Missing Persons*, doesn't make her initial entrance until the fourth reel. Looking particularly attractive (she was only twenty-five at the time), Miss Davis isn't really given an opportunity to do anything but move the second half of the proceedings forward. In later years, she would always discredit these early films that she did while under contract to her home studio. It wasn't until a year later when she was loaned out to RKO that she would undertake her best role in the early thirties, *Of Human Bondage*, where she was cast as the heartless waitress who befriends crippled Leslie Howard. It's a wonderful characterization, with Bette pulling no punches. Watching her self-inflicted degradation is one of the most memorable moments in those waning days of "Pre-Code" Hollywood. Subsequently, she would become the reigning queen of the Warner Bros. lot throughout the next ten years in films like *Jezebel* (1938), *Dark Victory* (1939), *The Letter* (1940), and *Now, Voyager* (1942).

When *Bureau of Missing Persons* was released in September of 1933, it was received in a positive manner. Mordant Hall of *The New York Times* said of it: "Saviors of the slapstick genre of comedy…Bette Davis does well and Pat O'Brien acts with necessary vigor and humor…The film, for the most part, is set forth in jesting style." Another review by *Motion Picture Herald* reads "the picture moves fast. The dialogue is peppy and there is plenty of exciting action that leads to two surprising climaxes…a novel and colorful comedy." Not seen much today, *Bureau of Missing Persons* remains a fun way to spend 75 minutes, and continues to prove how fast-paced movies were back then, with not a wasted moment and totally devoid of unnecessary padding.

The Bowery (1933)

A 20th Century Pictures Release for United Artists. Produced by Darryl F. Zanuck. Associate Producers: William Goetz and Raymond Griffith. Directed by Raoul Walsh. Based on the novel "Chuck Connors" by Michael L. Simmons and Bessie Roth Solomon. Screenplay by Howard Estabrook and James Gleason. Music by Alfred Newman. Art Direction by Richard Day. Photography by Barney McGill. Edited by Allen McNeil. 90 min.

Cast: Wallace Beery (Chuck Connors), George Raft (Steve Brodie), Jackie Cooper (Swipes McGurk), Fay Wray (Lucy Calhoun), Pert Kelton (Trixie Odbray), George Walsh (John L. Sullivan), Oscar Apfel (Mr. Herman), Harold Huber (Slick), Fletcher Norton (Googie Cochran), John Kelly (Lumpy Hogan), Lillian Harmer (Carrie Nation), Ferdinand Munier (Honest Mike, the Bartender), Herman Bing (Mr. Rummel), Tammany Young (Himself), Esther Muir (The Tart), John Bleifer (Mumbo the Mute), Pueblo Jim Flynn, Al McCoy, Joe Glick, Phil Bloom, Joe Herrick, Jack Herrick, Sailor Vincent, Kid Broad, Dick Gilbert (Pugs), Heinie Conklin (Drunk/Fight Spectator), Andrew Tombes (Shill), Irving Bacon (Hick with Tailors), Harry Semels (Artist), Phil Tead (Tout), Charles Lane (Doctor), Charles Middleton (Detective), Fred Kelsey (Detective), Harvey Perry (Stunt Double for George Raft), Bobby Dunn (Violinist), Lucille Ball (Bit Part).

DIRECTOR RAOUL WALSH BEGAN his career in pictures as assistant director and actor under the tutelage of D. W. Griffith at his Biograph Studio in 1912. One of his first directorial efforts was *The Life of General Villa* (1914), which mixed real documentary footage and staged sequences of bandit Pancho Villa's military campaign. The following year, he made movie history as John Wilkes Booth in Griffith's *The Birth of a Nation*. Eventually, he became a master of fast-paced action dramas, utilizing the he-man talents of James Cagney, Humphrey Bogart, Errol

The Bowery (1933) "Stop dat! People'll tink I'm yer mudder!" complains Chuck Connors (Wallace Beery) to "Swipsey" McGurk (Jackie Cooper). (RF)

Flynn, Clark Gable, and Gary Cooper. Among his classics are *In Old Arizona* (1929; the first talkie filmed outdoors), *The Big Trail* (1930; filmed in primitive wide-screen and John Wayne's first starring role), the underrated *Big Brown Eyes* (1936; one of Cary Grant's most impressive early works), *High Sierra* (1941; a film that boosted Bogart's reputation), *The Strawberry Blonde* (1941; like *The Bowery* takes place at the turn of the century), and *They Died with Their Boots On* (1941; with Errol Flynn's excellent portrayal of George Custer). Always a stickler for authenticity, Walsh's depiction of turn of the century "Bowery" hits the bulls-eye with unerring accuracy.

Not seen on television or theatrical revivals until recently due to apparent racist views, the scriptwriters were cunning enough not to come down on merely one nationality or race. Instead, in the first ten minutes of *The Bowery* everyone is stereotyped, so nobody should feel really offended! As the film progresses, it delves into the seedier side of life with the likes of real-life characters such as Steve Brodie (who actually jumped off the Brooklyn Bridge on a dare), Chuck Connors, John L. Sullivan (played by the director's brother, George Walsh), and a person who I'm sure would have been a prime candidate to head the Hays office, Carrie

Nation. All in all a truly colorful cast of players with Wallace Beery out-mugging and overacting to the hilt!

The producer of *The Bowery* was none other than Darryl F. Zanuck, who had just started his own company, 20th Century Pictures, which later merged with the faltering William Fox Productions to form 20th Century Fox in 1935. *The Bowery* was the first release of the new 20th Century Pictures and luckily proved to be a winner due to the box-office attraction of Wallace Beery and Jackie Cooper, who two years prior caused a sensation with the release of *The Champ*. Critics and the public were so enthused that two more Beery/Cooper releases followed: *Treasure Island* (1934) and *O'Shaughnessy's Boy* (1935), but none could match the sheer charm or capture the overall mood of *The Bowery*.

I'm No Angel (1933)

Paramount Pictures. Directed by Wesley Ruggles. Story by Mae West and Lowell Brentano. Adaptation by Harlan Thompson. Dialogue by Mae West. Photography by Leo Tover. Edited by Otho Lovering. Sound by Phil S. Wisdom and F. E. Dine. Songs by Harvey Brooks, Gladys du Bois, Ben Ellison: "They Call Me Sister Honky Tonk", "No One Loves Me Like that Dallas Man", "I Found a New Way to Go to Town", "I Want You, I Need You", "I'm No Angel". 87 min.

Cast: Mae West (Tira), Cary Grant (Jack Clayton), Edward Arnold (Bill Barton), Ralf Harolde (Slick Wiley), Russell Hopton (Flea Madigan), Gertrude Michael (Alicia Hatton), Kent Taylor (Kirk Lawrence), Dorothy Peterson (Thelma), Gregory Ratoff (Benny Pinkowitz), Gertrude Howard (Beulah Thorndike), William Davidson (Ernest Brown, the Chump), Nigel de Brulier (Rajah), Irving Pichel (Bob, the Attorney), George Bruggeman (Omnes), Nat Pendleton (Harry), Harry Schultz (Strongman), Morrie Cohen (Chauffeur), Walter Walker (Judge), Monte Collins (Sailor), Ray Cooke (Sailor), Hattie McDaniel (Maid), Libby Taylor (Libby), Dennis O'Keefe (Reporter), Jack Pennick (Lighting Technician).

IN 1932, at the height of the Great Depression, one of the major Hollywood studios was facing near bankruptcy, namely Paramount Pictures. Then, Paramount released probably one of the most famous sleepers of the year, *She Done Him Wrong* with Mae West, putting that studio back on its feet! Mae was born in Brooklyn, New York on August (one of the hot months) 17, 1892, the daughter of a heavyweight boxer. By the time she reached the tender age of five, she was already entertaining audiences singing and dancing, billed as "The Baby Vamp" in burlesque houses. As she progressed through her early teenage years, Mae was soon writing her own material, eventually causing some raised eyebrows when she penned her first play entitled *Sex* in 1926, which she also produced and directed

I'm No Angel (1933) Sideshow barker "Flea" Madigan (Russell Hopton) introduces
Tira (Mae West) to an all-male audience. (AB)

on Broadway. Arrested on charges of obscenity, Mae was jailed for ten days
before causing another sensation, directing a play called *Drag*, a shocking comedy about homosexuality. Her big break came in 1928, landing
the title role in *Diamond Lil* on Broadway, which eventually became her
ticket to Hollywood to film the movie version. Full of double entendres,
Paramount rechristened it *She Done Him Wrong* (1932), resulting in one
of the biggest box-office hits of that year! However, all was not well with
the Hays office, which warned Paramount to tone down the sex angle in
all subsequent West vehicles.

The result was *I'm No Angel* (1933), an even more outrageous comedy, which bears the distinction of Miss West's enticing a wooden Cary
Grant to "come up and see me." Directed by the ever-reliable Wesley Ruggles (brother of character-actor Charles Ruggles), one wonders just how
much input he was able to inject in Mae West's performance, if any.

Incidentally, contrary to Hollywood legend Mae West did not discover Cary Grant, nor was *She Done Him Wrong* his first film. By the time
Mae requested Grant's services, he had already completed seven films,

I'm No Angel (1933) Mae West as Tira. (AB)

having been cast opposite such leading ladies as Thelma Todd (in his delightful first role in *This is the Night*), Carole Lombard, Sylvia Sidney, Tallulah Bankhead, and Marlene Dietrich. By the time he did *I'm No Angel* in 1933, he had four more features (and one short subject) under his belt. Although major stardom was hard to come by (one only has to look at his dismal early performances), Grant finally was able to find his niche in comedy, with the release of two of his most important early films, *Big Brown Eyes* (1936; a long overlooked gem) and Hal Roach's *Topper* (1937).

Jon Tuska of *Views and Reviews* wrote of *I'm No Angel*, "No scene in *I'm No Angel* is extraneous. It is interesting, compelling, and enjoyable throughout. One scene played with rare distinction is that of Cary Grant's initial visit to Tira's apartment, when she decides to let Kent Taylor go, but wants Cary instead. The camera takes a three-quarters shot as the conversation straggles to its conclusion, with both their minds on something other than what's being said."

As for the Hays office, they certainly were not amused with this sort of low-class comedy, and when the following year Hollywood decided to impose their own set of strict rules to avoid further problems from the Catholic Church, Mae West found herself in whitewashed vehicles displaying only a hint of her genius.

Bombshell (1933)

A Metro Goldwyn-Mayer Release. Produced by Hunt Stromberg. Directed by Victor Fleming. Screenplay by John Lee Mahin and Jules Furthman from a play by Mark Crane and Caroline Francke. Photography by Harold Rossen and Chester A. Lyons. Edited by Margaret Booth. Art Direction by Merrill Pye. Costumes by Adrian. Sound by Douglas Shearer. Interior Designs by Edwin B. Willis. Re-released as "Blonde Bombshell". Scene from "Hold Your Man" (1933), starring Clark Gable and Jean Harlow used in montage. 95 min.

Cast: Jean Harlow (Lola Burns), Lee Tracy (Space Hanlon), Frank Morgan (Pop Burns), Franchot Tone (Gifford Middleton), Pat O'Brien (Jim Brogan), Una Merkel (Miss Mac), Ted Healy (Junior Burns), Ivan Lebedeff (Marquis DiBinelli), Isabel Jewell (Junior's Girlfriend), Louise Beavers (Loretta), Leonard Carey (Winters), Mary Forbes (Mrs. Middleton), C. Aubrey Smith (Mr. Middleton), June Brewster (Alice Cole), Gus Armhein (Himself/Bandleader), Dorothy DeBorba (Little Girl).

WHEN THE NAME VICTOR FLEMING comes up, people usually are reminded of the two timeless classics he directed in 1939: *The Wizard of Oz* and *Gone with the Wind*. Even if these were the only films this no-nonsense director ever made, his name would still be placed among the leading filmmakers in the annals of film history. Known primarily as an action filmmaker, Fleming seemed more comfortable with leading macho men like Clark Gable, Spencer Tracy, and Wallace Beery, than with the temperamental female stars on the MGM lot. His rather impressive credits include the first teaming (they both appeared in a film the previous year, but not as a team) of Gable and Harlow in *Red Dust*, as well as the third film starring Wallace Beery and Jackie Cooper: *Treasure Island* (1934). Other blockbusters were *Captains Courageous* (1937), *Test Pilot* (1938), *A Guy Named Joe* (1943), and *Joan of Arc* (1948).

Starting his career as a noted pilot and motorcyclist, he eventually worked his way up the Hollywood ladder, from crewmember to cinematographer to assistant director. Actor Douglas Fairbanks, Sr. took a liking to the young man and saw to it that he received director credit on the silent classic starring Fairbanks, *Till the Clouds Roll By* (1920). Later, Fleming found himself working with the likes of Clara Bow in *Mantrap* (1926), Emil Jannings in *The Way of All Flesh* (1927), and Gary Cooper in his first talkie *The Virginian* (1929). His tough guy attitude helped him gain the respect of actors and technicians alike, although some were rather taken aback by his salty language and uncouth behavior.

One of his best thirties films was a satire on Hollywood and its sex sirens entitled *Bombshell*, which insured the success of superstar Jean Harlow and gave Lee Tracy another chance at playing a totally repulsive although rather roguishly appealing publicity agent. By this time, Tracy had signed a most lucrative contract at Metro, following a steady ascension to stardom under his previous Warner Bros. contract. The film also gave newcomer Franchot Tone a chance to spoof the type of roles he was

Bombshell (1933) Movie sex-siren Lola Burns (Jean Harlow) has a new boyfriend, director Jim Brogan (Pat O'Brien), for the time being. (RF)

becoming accustomed to at this time, the rather boring but good-natured leading man (a role that he would later claim to have hated). Pat O'Brien, who two years before had scored a hit in Lewis Milestone's *The Front Page* as Hildy Johnson, plays a Hollywood director patterned after Victor Fleming himself! This extremely witty photoplay was written by John Lee Mahin and, although it seems like it paralleled Jean Harlow's life very closely, it was actually based on the life of silent star, Clara Bow, whom Fleming had had a torrid affair with a few years earlier! (I guess it would be fairly safe to assume that Fleming had a bit of a hand in the actual writing of the photoplay as well.)

Raucous, wild, extremely fast-paced, with excellent, sharp-tongued dialogue, this is one of those films that must be seen more than once or twice to catch all of the brilliantly sharp wit. Mordaunt Hall of *The New York Times* wrote, "This farce comedy, which is based on an unproduced play by Caroline Francke and Mack Crane, enjoys itself at Hollywood's expense, and as it spins its slangy but mirthful yarn, it has some unexpected and adroitly conceived turns...Miss Harlow is thoroughly in her element as Lola. For the greater part of the time she is a firey platinum blonde, but when she hopes to be entrusted with an infant, she, as Lola, assumes a strangely quiet and sympathetic mood."

Broadway Thru a Keyhole (1933)

A 20th Century Picture released through United Artists. Executive Producer: Darryl F. Zanuck. Produced by William Goetz and Raymond Griffith. Directed by Lowell Sherman. Screenplay by C. Graham Baker and Gene Towne from a story by Walter Winchell. Photography by Barney McGill. Edited by Maurice Wright. Music by Alfred Newman. Songs and Lyrics by Mack Gordon and Harry Revel. Choreography by Jack Haskell. Art Direction by Richard Day and Joseph C. Wright. Costumes by Gwenn Wakeling. 90 min.

Cast: Constance Cummings (Joan Whalen), Russ Columbo (Clark Brian), Paul Kelly (Frank Rocci), Blossom Seeley (Sybil Smith), Gregory Ratoff (Max Mafoofski), Texas Guinan (Tex Kaley), Abe Lyman (Orchestra Leader), Hugh O'Connell (Chuck Haskins), Hobart Cavanaugh (Peanuts Dinwiddie), Frances Williams (Herself), Eddie Foy, Jr. (Joan's Dance Partner), George Mann (Himself/Columnist), C. Henry Gordon (Tim Crowley), William Burress (Thomas Barnum), Helen Jerome Eddy (Esther), Edith Allen (Girl with Louie), Franklyn Ardell (Columnist #1), Lucille Ball (Girl with Louie), Ronnie Cosby (Little Boy), Susan Fleming (Chorine), Arthur Franklin (Pianist), Mary Gordon (Cleaning Woman), Theresa Harris (Joan's Maid), Rodney Hildebrand (Member of Rocci's Mob), John Kelly (Louie), Ethan Laidlaw (Member of Rocci's Mob), Charles Lane (Columnist #2), Tom London, George Magrill (Mobsters), Sam McDaniel (Gus), Marceline Medcalf (Little Girl), Edmund Mortimer, Bud Flanagan/Dennis O'Keefe (Nightclub Extras), Wheeler Oakman (Sam), Donna Mae Roberts, Ann Sothern (Chorines), Fred Santley (Decorator), Billy Sullivan (Mobster), Andrew Tombes (Sidney/Columnist), Bradley Ward (Willie Stacko), Walter Winchell (Himself).

THERE SEEMED TO BE far more drama "behind the scenes" of *Broadway Thru a Keyhole* than in front of the cameras. The film is based on a real life incident chronicled by columnist Walter Winchell concerning the love affair between Ruby Keeler (who was once a "featured" dancer in Texas Guinan's Nightclub) and racketeer Larry Fay. There was much speculation about how their relationship would end, especially since Miss Keeler was also seeing entertainer Al Jolson simultaneously. Apparently, Fay was initially "fired" with jealous rage when he found out that the "toast of Broadway" was having an affair with his girlfriend. But ultimately, Fay

Broadway Thru a Keyhole (1933) A bit of "cross-dressing" with Constance Cummings as nightclub entertainer, Joan Whelan.

Broadway Thru a Keyhole (1933) Constance Cummings.

came to his senses and, realizing that he didn't stand a chance, later told Jolson that it was alright to go on seeing Ruby and he would step out of the picture. He also warned Jolson that if he ever mistreated her, he would be back to make life very difficult for him.

When *Broadway Thru a Keyhole* was in production, there was much gossip about the screenplay being based on the Keeler/Fay/Jolson triangle, which infuriated Al Jolson. On the night of July 21st, 1933 (three months before the film's release), Walter Winchell happened to pass Jolson at the American Legion Stadium and the temperamental songster confronted

Winchell and "decked" him. Later, when asked if his story was based on the Keeler/Fay love affair, Winchell denied all allegations, merely stating that it was about Larry Fay's relationship with "a woman who is now happily married."

Darryl F. Zanuck's new production company (this was their 2nd release), 20th Century Pictures, paid Walter Winchell $25,000 for the rights to his story and hired actor/director Lowell Sherman to direct the picture. Originally for the role of Joan Whelan, Ginger Rogers was their first choice, but Miss Rogers was in the middle of another big production over at RKO, *Flying Down to Rio*, where she was teamed for the first time with Fred Astaire. Zanuck then borrowed actress Constance Cummings from Columbia to fill the bill. The role of Joan's best friend, Sybil Smith, went to the much-married socialite, Peggy Hopkins Joyce, but following her collapse during filming, Lilyan Tashman was cast in her place. After shooting began, the role changed hands again with Blossom Seeley replacing Lilyan Tashman, who had to undergo emergency surgery.

Paul Kelly, who played gangster Frank Rocci, had a rather colorful past. Beginning in movies as a child actor at the age of twelve in 1911, he was soon to graduate to larger roles both on the stage and in the movies. In late 1926, he was introduced to the dance team of Dorothy MacKaye and her husband, Ray Raymond, who were both appearing in the Ziegfeld Follies. The three became friends, but a mutual attraction between Paul Kelly and Mrs. Raymond soon developed into a torrid love affair. Apparently MacKaye and Raymond's marriage had been "on the rocks" due to his excessive drinking and spousal abuse. Eventually, Raymond learned of the illicit affair and confronted the two of them, resulting in a fight with Kelly beating Raymond to a pulp, eventually leading to his death a few days later of a brain hemorrhage on April 16th, 1927. Kelly served twenty-five months in jail for manslaughter, and Dorothy MacKaye was convicted as an accessory and served ten months. After Kelly was released, the two began dating again and ended up getting married in 1931. Their marriage lasted until MacKaye's untimely death in an automobile accident in 1940. *Broadway Thru a Keyhole* was Paul Kelly's first film after his release from prison and he went on to become a familiar fixture in many films and stage plays until his death in 1956.

Another member of the cast was popular crooner and rival to Bing Crosby, Russ Columbo, whose popularity as a major recording artist was already established before he achieved stardom. He was romantically involved with actress Carole Lombard at the time of his tragic death a year after *Broadway Thru a Keyhole* was made. The circumstances surrounding his death are very bizarre indeed. The most common account given was that Columbo was visiting a photographer friend at his studio. The friend struck a match on the wooden butt end of a French pistol and the flame apparently penetrated into the shooting chamber, causing the gun to go off. The bullet ricocheted off the wall and hit Columbo in the head and killed him. Sounds logical, doesn't it? Carole Lombard was naturally grief-stricken, but was very concerned about Columbo's mother, who had been in ill health recently. Both Lombard and Columbo's father planned an elaborate subterfuge telling Mrs. C. that her son had been called away and his career was in full swing. For eight years, until her death in 1942, they were able to convince her that her son was alive and well with her husband forging letters and sending them to her to continue the ruse.

The famed nightclub owner of a string of speakeasies during Prohibition, Texas Guinan, landed the role of Tex Kaley, a role that seemed autobiographical, even down to her signature "Hello Suckers," as her opener to her patrons. Looking far older than publicity accounts testify (forty-nine years), Miss Guinan looks like she was in ill health and might have had some plastic surgery done to conceal her real age. Sadly, she died on November 5th, 1933, three days after *Broadway Thru a Keyhole* was released.

While the film may not be the classic one would hope, it still is a fascinating movie with a great cast supplemented by some great dialogue. Russ Columbo's velvet voice is wonderful, however the production numbers, which were clearly inspired by the Busby Berkeley craze, are pretty poor. One wonders if this was done purposely, since the dance director in the film, Max Maffofski (Gregory Ratoff) is a self-important blowhard. Director Lowell Thomas keeps his audience's attention throughout and the 'Pre-Code' ending is quite good. Sherman's career as a director was certainly going places at this time and a year later he began working on the first Technicolor feature, *Becky Sharpe*, starring Miriam Hopkins. During production, he died of pneumonia on December 28th, 1934. He had been engaged to actress Geneva Mitchell at the time.

Chance at Heaven (1933)

An RKO-Radio Picture. Produced by Merian C. Cooper. Directed by William A. Seiter. Screenplay by Julian Josephson and Sarah Y. Mason. Based on a story by Vina Delmar. Photography by Nick Musuraca. Art Direction by Van Nest Polglase and Perry Ferguson. Edited by James B. Morley. Sound by Forrest Perley. Music by Max Steiner. Makeup by Mel Burns. 70 min.

Cast: Joel McCrea (Blacky Gorman), Ginger Rogers (Marje Harris), Marian Nixon (Glory Franklyn), Andy Devine (Al), Virginia Hammond (Mrs. Franklyn), Lucien Littlefield (Mr. Harris), Ann Shoemaker (Mrs. Harris), George Meeker (Sid Larrick), Herman Bing (Chauffeur), Betty Furness (Betty), Harry Bowen (First Reporter).

BY 1933, ACTRESS GINGER ROGERS' career was steadily surging onward. It was apparent to studio executives that she could sing and dance (*Sitting Pretty* and *Gold Diggers of 1933*) and could handle comedy deftly (*42nd Street* and *Professional Sweetheart*). Now, the question was, "Could she act?" RKO decided to cast Ginger in a film based on a story by Vina Delmar (*The Awful Truth*) entitled *Chance at Heaven*, which would give the actress a "chance at drama." Given an excellent director in William Seiter, who was a specialist at light comedies and romantic dramas, this overlooked little programmer excels due to Miss Rogers' sensitive performance as the jilted girl-next-door. In the film, Marje Harris (Rogers) is in love with grease monkey Blackie Gorman (Joel McCrea). But fate intervenes when Blackie meets rich socialite Glory Franklyn (Marian Nixon), a spoiled, flighty individual, who acts more like a thirteen-year-old than a woman in her early twenties. Of course, blinded by wealth and a "chance at heaven," Blackie, forgetting that Marje would make a perfect wife, marries Glory. All is everything but blissful...Glory's snooty mother feels that her wonderful daughter has married a man beneath her dignity,

Chance at Heaven (1933) "Blackie" Gorman (Joel McCrea) has two girls after him...
wealthy socialite Glory Franklyn (Marian Nixon) and hard working "Marje" Harris
(Ginger Rogers). (AB)

so she bides her time until the right moment to break them up presents itself. In the meantime, Marje has decided to let bygones be bygones and tries to teach the inexperienced Glory how to cook and run a household, to no avail.

Then the showstopper occurs when Glory announces that she is pregnant. Of course, Blackie is elated, Mother is distraught, and Glory just can't handle the added responsibility. To ease her pressure, Mother suggests taking her daughter to the city for "proper" medical care and to think things over. Months pass, and Glory doesn't return, leaving a worried Blackie, who decides to fetch his errant bride back home. He finds, to his dismay, that his child-wife has refused to return and that the baby... well, the doctors were mistaken about the pregnancy. Of course, all ends happily with Blackie coming home to Marje's open arms!

Very few films of the Pre-Code era have dealt with abortion. Never is the word mentioned, but the audience knows full well what has occurred. A year later, MGM released the hospital drama *Men in White* with Clark

Gable and Myrna Loy, which explored the dangers of a botched-up abortion and its tragic aftermath.

Reviews for *Chance at Heaven* were quite good, many citing the excellent performance of Ginger Rogers. The Hollywood Spectator wrote, "If this picture gets by with the average audience, it will be on Ginger Rogers' account. I understand some expert told her she'd been given bad 'camera angles' in the film. If that's so, I suggest she stick to bad ones in the future, because they resulted in the most convincing job she's done to date."

During filming of the movie, Ginger's previous RKO release *Flying Down to Rio* (1933) was in the process of being edited and scored. Although not the stars of the picture, this was the first time Miss Rogers was teamed with the elegant Fred Astaire. Together, they danced exquisitely to the Carioca, and their way into audience's hearts as well! Like Katharine Hepburn once said, "Ginger gave Fred sex appeal, while Fred gave Ginger class."

The Kennel Murder Case (1933)

Warner Bros. Produced by Robert Presnell. Directed by Michael Curtiz. Based on the book *The Return of Philo Vance* by S. S. Van Dine. Screenplay by Robert N. Lee and Peter Milne. Photography by William Rees. Edited by Harold McLernon. Art Direction by Jack Okey. Music by Bernard Kaun. Costumes by Orry-Kelly. Musical Direction by Leo F. Forbstein. 73 min.

Cast: William Powell (Philo Vance), Mary Astor (Hilda Lake), Eugene Pallette (Sergeant Ernest Heath), Ralph Morgan (Raymond Wrede), Robert McWade (District Attorney John F. X. Markham), Robert Barrat (Archer Coe), Frank Conroy (Brisbane Coe), Etienne Girardot (Dr. Doremus), James Lee (Liang), Paul Cavanagh (Sir Thomas MacDonald), Arthur Hohl (Gamble the Butler), Helen Vinson (Doris Delafield), Jack La Rue (Eduardo Grassi), Wade Boteler (Police Desk Sergeant), James Burke (Policeman), George Chandler (Cub Reporter), Spencer Charters (Sergeant Snitkin), Milton Kibbee (Reporter), Henry O'Neill (Dubois, Fingerprint Expert), Cliff Saum (Night Patrolman), Leo White (Chicago Hotel Clerk), Charles C. Wilson (Hennessey).

HOLLYWOOD'S SEEMINGLY ENDLESS fascination with super-sleuth crime fighters like Ellery Queen, Sam Spade, Miss Marple, Sherlock Holmes, Charlie Chan, Mr. Moto, and others can be attributed to the public's considerable appetite for solving complex murder mysteries. When Paramount Pictures purchased the rights to S. S. Van Dine's (pen name for Willard Wright) Philo Vance novels, they cast a supporting actor who had been working in pictures for years, primarily as slimy villains: William Powell. The first of these ventures, *The Canary Murder Case* (1929), began filming as a silent, but when sound proved to be such a tremendous success, they went back and re-filmed it as a talkie. Seen today, the film suffers from static camerawork, unsure direction, and some rather awkward dialogue enhanced by stiff acting, which was quite common in early sound pictures from 1928 through 1931. It did, however, make William Powell an overnight star, and the studio did cast him in two more Philo Vance murder mysteries entitled *The Greene Murder Case* (1929), which also featured a young Jean Arthur, and *The Bensen Murder Case* (1930). Also cast in these was comic actor Eugene Pallette, as the much harried, over anxious Sergeant Heath, who proved an excellent foil for the debonair Vance.

A year later, Powell found himself at Warner Bros. in some snappy Pre-Code films such as *High Pressure, Lawyer Man, Jewel Robbery*, and *One Way Passage* (all 1932). The following year, Warners cast him with Eugene Pallette in tow once again as Sergeant Heath in what was to be his last, and perhaps best, outing as Philo Vance in *The Kennel Murder Case*. By this time talking films had matured considerably, and this fast-paced "whodunit" about a ruthless art collector who is found murdered hasn't a wasted frame in its seventy-three minutes' running time.

The Kennel Murder Case (1933) Philo Vance (William Powell) has found the murderer while Hennessey (Charles C. Wilson) and another unnamed detective (Monte Vandergrift) and District Attorney Markham (Robert McWade) stand by. (RF)

The Kennel Murder Case (1933) Philo Vance (William Powell), Inspector Heath (Eugene Pallette) and District Attorney Markham (Robert McWade) discuss the murder of Archer Coe. (RF)

Warner Bros. future ace director, Michael Curtiz would eventually go on to direct such classics as *Captain Blood* (1935), *Angels With Dirty Faces*, *The Adventures of Robin Hood* (both 1938), *Dive Bomber* (1941), *Yankee Doodle Dandy* (1942), *Casablanca*, *This Is the Army* (both 1943), and *Mildred Pierce* (1945), but his earlier "lesser" films, such as *The Kennel Murder Case*, are certainly not without merit. Two of his earlier films for Warners, *Dr. X* (1932) and *The Mystery of the Wax Museum* (1933) were filmed in the innovative two-strip Technicolor process. Curtiz also was responsible for giving Spencer Tracy a needed boost in his career by casting him as a tough, young gangster who was sent up the river in *20,000 Years In Sing-Sing* (1932).

As for William Powell, the most prestigious of studios, Metro-Gold-wyn-Mayer, would sign him to a long-term contract in 1934, where he would enjoy the biggest successes of his career. That year he would be cast as Nick Charles and teamed with his perfect "on-screen" wife, Myrna Loy, in six "Thin Man" movies, which would run through 1947. The original theatrical trailer to the first of these films has Philo Vance, played by

Powell, strolling past a bookstore displayed with an oversized book of *The Thin Man* with Powell's picture on the cover as Nick Charles. Vance and Charles proceed to carry on a conversation heralding the arrival of MGM's newest picture, informing audiences that it will be just as good (if not better) than *The Kennel Murder Case.*

An unmitigated success, *The Kennel Murder Case* did indeed warrant further adventures with the suave sleuth, albeit without Powell, who went on to bigger and better things. Others who would portray S. S. Van Dine's charming detective were Basil Rathbone, Warren William, Paul Lucas, Wilfrid Hyde-White, Grant Richards, James Stephenson, Alan Curtis, and many more. But none would capture the unadulterated charm, sophistication, and overall brilliance of this 1933 effort starring William Powell!

Man's Castle (1933)

Columbia Pictures. Produced and Directed by Frank Borzage. Screenplay by Jo Swerling from a play by Lawrence Hazard. Photography by Joseph H. August. Edited by Viola Lawrence. Art Direction by Stephen Goosson. Assistant Director: Lew Borzage. Original Music by W. Franke Harling. Musical Direction by Constantine Bakaleinikoff. Sound Engineer: Wilbur Brown. Original Running Time: 75 min. Reissued at 66 min.

Cast: Spencer Tracy (Bill), Loretta Young (Trina), Marjorie Rambeau (Flossie), Glenda Farrell (Fay La Rue), Walter Connolly (Ira), Arthur Hohl (Bragg), Dickie Moore (Joey), Harvey Clarke (Café Manager), Helen Jerome Eddy (Mother), R. Henry Grey (Head Waiter), Kendall McComas (Slades), Tony Merlo (Waiter), Henry Roquemore (Roue), Hector Sarno (Grocer), Harry Watson (Baseball Team Captain).

LONG FORGOTTEN AND NOT SEEN on television in decades or on video until recently, *Man's Castle* is one of those curious films which seems better every time it is revisited. Directed by Frank Borzage, who is never remembered as prominently as his contemporaries like Ford, Hitchcock, Lubitsch, or Capra, this Depression-era romantic drama was just the sort of film fodder that he was famous for. If his films seem overly sentimental today, one should overlook that aspect by examining his artistic style, which was coupled with a fluid, almost melodic camera in soft focus, thus heightening passion on the screen. His early years were spent working in a silver mine, until he was sidetracked by a touring stage troupe. Realizing that his ambitions as an actor might bring him to Hollywood, he found that his dreams would soon become true. Borzage landed bit parts in westerns and comedies, and eventually found work behind the camera as well. The behind-the-scenes work became of more importance, and soon he would go on to direct such romantic classics as *Seventh Heaven* (1927) with Janet Gaynor and Charles Farrell, *A Farewell to Arms* (1932)

Man's Castle (1933) Glenda Farrell as Fay La Rue sings "Surprise," and is she in for one here! (RF)

with Helen Hayes and Gary Cooper, *Desire* (1936) with Marlene Dietrich, *History is Made at Night* (1937) with Jean Arthur and Charles Boyer, and two excellent Margaret Sullavan vehicles, *Three Comrades* (1938) and *The Mortal Storm* (1940).

By the time *Man's Castle* was made, actor Spencer Tracy was working at the William Fox Studio, where he was shoehorned into making some entertaining, though forgettable films like *Six Cylinder Love*, *Goldie* (both 1931), *Young America* (1932), and *Shanghai Madness* (1933). Although he did make some very good movies at Fox, like *Quick Millions* (1931) and *The Power and the Glory* (1933), which was a forerunner to Orson Welles' *Citizen Kane*, with a near-perfect script by Preston Sturges, Tracy fared much better when he was on loan to other studios like Warner Bros. or Columbia. *Man's Castle* was made when he was loaned out to Columbia under the domain of Harry Cohn. He was set to co-star with the already established Loretta Young, who'd been borrowed (from Warner Bros.). Young, who had a barrage of hits behind her already, was enjoying considerable success, even though she had not yet reached her twentieth birthday! Her succession of box-office hits included such Pre-Code vehicles as *Big Business Girl* (1931), *They Call it Sin* (1932), and *Employees' Entrance* (1933).

Of course, *Man's Castle* proved to be a big gamble for both stars, since this film would be produced at a second-rate studio (Columbia) and produced on a minimal budget. Among the factors that made the film so successful were the sincere performances of both stars (who were engaged in an off-screen love affair at the time) and the perfect direction of Frank Borzage, aided by the excellent screenplay by Jo Swerling. Also, supporting cast members such as Walter Conolly and Marjorie Rambeau add much to the film. Rambeau's fine portrayal of a sympathetic, boozy prostitute named Flossie is memorable. Seven years later, she would be nominated for a similar role in the Ginger Rogers-Joel McCrea melodrama *The Primrose Path*. As fate would have it, Marjorie inherited the role of Flossie in *Man's Castle* from Helen MacKellar, who for some unknown reason dropped out of the film mid-way into the production.

If modern day audiences feel that *Man's Castle* seems rather choppy in parts, it is because the film was code-cut on its reissue in the early thirties, where it was whittled down to a 66 minute running time. Gone is the actual murder/suicide ending that audiences observed in 1933, along with the opening scene where Spencer Tracy meets up with down-on-her-luck Loretta Young for the first time. Feeling sorry for her, he treats her to a sumptuous meal at a posh Park Avenue restaurant, where he matter-of-factly suggests that "no female should starve in a town like this", and implies that she walk the streets! It seems a shame that these scenes and other little snippets are lost forever since these so-called "code-cuts" were made on the actual camera negative!

Dancing Lady (1933)

Metro-Goldwyn-Mayer. Produced by David O. Selznick. Directed by Robert Z. Leonard. Screenplay by Allen Rivkin and P.J. Wolfson. Based on the novel by James Warner Bellah. Photography by Oliver T. Marsh. Music by Burton Lane, Harold Adamson, Richard Rodgers, Lorenz Hart, Jimmy McHugh and Dorothy Fields. Costumes by Adrian. Edited by Margaret Booth. Art Direction by Merrill Pye. Sound by Douglas Shearer. Special Effects by Slavko Vorkapich. 92 min.

Cast: Joan Crawford (Janie Barlow), Clark Gable (Patch Gallagher), Franchot Tone (Tod Newton), May Robson (Dolly Todhunter), Winnie Lightner (Rosette LaRue), Fred Astaire (Himself), Robert Benchley (Ward King), Ted Healy (Steve), Arthur Jarrett (Himself), Grant Mitchell (Jasper Bradley, Sr.), Nelson Eddy (Himself), Maynard Holmes (Jasper Bradley, Jr.), Sterling Holloway (Pinky), Gloria Foy (Vivian Warner), Moe Howard (Moe), Curly Howard (Curly), Larry Fine (Harry), Jean Alden, Gail Arnold, Lee Bailey, Lynn Bari, Bonita Barker, Kathryn Barnes, Esther Brodelet, Edna Callahan, Lorena Carr, Shirley Chambers, Dalie Dean, Shirley Deane, Dorothy Dearing, Dale Dee, Nadine Dore, Veleda Duncan, Eleanor Edwards, Fay Estelle, Muriel Evans, Kay Gordon, Mary Halsey, Edith Haskins, Peaches Jackson, Patsy Lee, Chicquita Marcia, Miriam Marlin, Margaret O'Connell, Lucille Miller, Ruth Moody, Iris Nicholson, Patsy O'Dea, May Packer, Jackie Page, Linda Parker, Frances Sawyer, Geneva Sawyer, Anita Thompson, Irene Thompson, Marjorie Timm, Ardelle Unger, Zelda Webber, Marion Welden, Mary Wilbur (Chorus Girls), Eve Arden (Marcia), Jack Baxley (Burlesque Barker), Stanley Blystone (Traffic Cop), Harry C. Bradley (Pinky's Pal), Bill Elliott (Café Extra), Ferdinand Gottschalk (Judge), Frank Hagney (Policeman), Jean Howard (Girl with Tod), Isabelle Keith (Miss Allen), Robert Lees (Dancer), Harry LeRoy, Leo Willis (Burlesque Patrons), Matt McHugh (Marcia's Agent), Florine McKinney (Grace Newton), Edmund Mortimer (Man in Bradley's Office), Lee Phelps (Bailiff), Vic Potel (Worker), C. Montague Shaw (First

Nighter), John Sheehan (Pinky's Pal), Pat Somerset (Tod's Friend), Larry Steers (First Nighter), Charles Sullivan (Taxi Driver), Charles Williams (Man Arrested), Charles C. Wilson (Club Manager).

WHAT WAS FRED ASTAIRE'S first movie? In what movie did Eve Arden have her first speaking role? What was the name of the film that had a cast that included Clark Gable, Joan Crawford, Fred Astaire, Nelson Eddy, and the Three Stooges? In what film did the classic tune "Everything I Have is Yours" debut? The answer to all of these questions is *Dancing Lady*.

By 1933, after Warner Bros. had produced a rash of extremely successful backstage musicals, starting with *42nd Street*, MGM decided to jump on the bandwagon with their version of a big-budgeted musical with some of their biggest named stars. Studio production head, Irving Thalberg, had just suffered a heart attack and was on an extended "leave of absence," so company boss Louis B. Mayer decided to bring in his son-in-law David O. Selznick to resume Thalberg's duties until he was able to return. Selznick had done quite well for himself at RKO, where he produced some of that studio's biggest moneymakers, including *Little Women* and *King Kong* (both 1933). Realizing that musicals were being revitalized by people like Ernst Lubitsch and Rouben Mamoulian at Paramount, and Busby Berkeley at Warners, Selznick got the "go ahead" to produce a bigger, more lavish production under the aegis of the MGM banner. Of course, bigger does not necessarily guarantee that a film will be better, and although *Dancing Lady* had much going for it with its lavish production numbers and stellar cast, it just didn't have the originality or the chemistry that the earlier ventures had at Warner Bros. or Paramount. Selznick had brought in a team of great songwriters, including Rodgers and Hart, Jimmy McHugh, and Dorothy Fields; and, with the exception of the aforementioned "Everything I Have is Yours", most of the other numbers were rather forgettable.

When production for *Dancing Lady* commenced in June of 1933, leading man Clark Gable fell ill with a toxic leg condition (!) and was ordered by his physician to rest a few weeks. Filming around his absence, Gable was then hospitalized for an appendectomy, further delaying the production considerably. Impatient with their ailing star, MGM considered casting William Gargan, and later Lee Tracy in Gable's role of Patch Gallagher, but fortunately decided to wait until Gable was fit to return,

Dancing Lady (1933) Ted Healy (center) directs Janie Barlow (Joan Crawford) to stage producer, Patch Gallagher (off screen) as his "Stooges," Moe Howard, Curly Howard and Larry Fine look on. (RF)

which he did on August 29th. Studio executives were quite upset with the errant star, feeling that he had taken far too long to recuperate, and after the production wrapped, "punished" Gable by sending him to Columbia Pictures (which was considered "poverty row") to appear in a low-budget film based on a short story called *Night Bus*. Re-titled *It Happened One Night*, that film would go on to win all five major Academy Awards, including Best Picture, Best Director (Frank Capra), Best Actress (Claudette Colbert), Best Screenplay (Robert Riskin), and Best Actor (Clark Gable), which I'm sure had Gable amused at having the last laugh on his studio bosses.

Joan Crawford, whose last two MGM films (*Letty Lynton* and *Today We Live*) were box-office flops, really needed a surefire vehicle to keep her name in the upper echelon of film stars. Although she had danced in films before—*Our Dancing Daughters* (1928) and *The Hollywood Revue of 1929* (1929)—she had never been singled out for her terpsichorean skills in the past, and her style of dance was similar to that of fellow "hoofer" Ruby Keeler, whose nickname "old lead-foot" became a source of humor throughout the industry. As a result, David Selznick brought in newcom-

Dancing Lady (1933) Ted Healy clowning with Curly Howard, Moe Howard and Larry Fine. (RF)

er Fred Astaire from RKO to coach Miss Crawford, doing his best to have her attain a more graceful manner in their dance number together.

Nelson Eddy, in one of his earliest screen appearances, is on hand doing quite nicely, along with Ted Healy and his Stooges (they later became the Three Stooges) to provide some rather low comedy. Healy and his Stooges (Larry Fine, Moe Howard, and his younger brother, Jerome "Curly" Howard) came directly from the burlesque and vaudeville houses and were signed by MGM to do a series of unremarkable musical short subjects. After about a year of being slapped around and abused by Ted Healy, Moe, Larry, and Curly left the act (and MGM) and signed a contract with Columbia Pictures and remained with their shorts department from 1934 to 1959, grinding out an incredible 190 comedies as well as appearing in feature length films until 1965. To this day, the Three Stooges have come into their own and are still revered as one of the best comedy acts ever. Perhaps their wild brand of violent humor isn't everyone's cup of tea, but it must be said that they had the longest run of any comedy team ever!

Dancing Lady (1933) Between scenes: Joan Crawford doing some needlepoint while Ted Healy picks up another "Stooge" in the person of director Robert Z. Leonard (standing between Curly and Moe). (RF)

While *Dancing Lady* did brisk box-office business, it was also greeted with some positive reviews with Richard Watts of the *New York Herald Tribune* claiming that "the story…is almost furiously conventional in the manner in which it eludes none of the familiar clichés of its familiar school, but it is pleasantly enough played and effectively enough produced to make for pleasant if far from exciting cinema entertainment… Miss Crawford, I think, is decidedly charming as the hopeful show girl, playing the role with humor, enough feeling, and with a sort of good-natured gayety which makes the heroine a rather gallant young woman. Miss Crawford's tap dance is excellent and the music is fair."

Sitting Pretty (1933)

Paramount Pictures. Produced by Charles R. Rogers. Directed by Harry Joe Brown. Screenplay by Jack McGowan, S. J. Perelman and Lou Breslow. Based on an original story by Nina Wilcox Putnam. Photography by Milton Krasner. Art Direction by David Garber. Dances by Larry Ceballos. Costumes by Travis Banton. Orchestrations by Howard Jackson. 74 min.

Cast: Jack Oakie (Chick Parker), Jack Haley (Pete Pendleton), Ginger Rogers (Dorothy), Thelma Todd (Gloria Duval), Gregory Ratoff (Tannenbaum), Lew Cody (Jules Clark), Harry Revel (Pianist), Jerry Tucker (Buzz), Mack Gordon (Song Publisher), Hale Hamilton (Vinton), Walter Walker (George Wilson), Kenneth Thomson (Norman Lubin), William B. Davidson (Director), Lee Moran (Assistant Director), Art Jarrett (Singer), Anne Nagel (Girl at Window), Joyce Matthews (Blonde Chorus Girl), Irving Bacon, Stuart Holmes (Dice Players), Fuzzy Knight (Stock Clerk), Harvey Clark (Motorist), Wade Boteler (Jackson), Frank La Rue (Studio Gateman), Sidney Bracey (Manager), Jack Mower (Clark's Aide), Frank Hagney (Bar Manager), Larry Steers, Henry Hall (Party Guests), Russ Powell (Counterman), Charles Williams, George Brasno, Olive Brasno (Neighbors), Rollo Lloyd (Director), Lee Phelps (Studio Aide), Harry C. Bradley (Set Designer), Phil Tead (Aide), Dave O'Brien (Assistant Cameraman), Charles Coleman (Butler), James Burtis (Mover Foreman).

A MUSICAL COMEDY which has been out of circulation for a number of years because of the uncooperative practices of its copyright owners, *Sitting Pretty* is one of those films that seems to engender enthusiasm from audiences seeing it for the first time. The songs by Harry Revel and Mack Gordon, who briefly appear in the picture, are extremely pleasing, with "Good Morning Glory" being a distinct standout, where, in the film, its contagious melody spreads throughout the neighborhood. Another Revel/Gordon number, "Did You Ever See a Dream Walking", became so popular that it was used by Paramount as incidental music in countless other films, not to mention being featured in a Popeye cartoon called *A Dream Walking* the following year.

First-billed Jack Oakie, who is always a welcome addition to any movie, gets many chances to out-mug his co-stars and generally to insert his special brand of energetic charm into the proceedings. Making his stage debut in George M. Cohan's *Little Nellie Kelly* in 1922, Oakie became a popular attraction on the Broadway circuit until he was lured to Hollywood in 1928. Usually cast as a carefree, happy-go-lucky buffoon, he enlivened many films of the 1930s with his easy-going attitude and excellent comedic timing. In the 1932 political satire *Million Dollar Legs*, Oakie holds his own against an array of co-stars who were well-known scene-stealers, such as W. C. Fields, Lyda Roberti, and Hugh Herbert. His ultimate role came in 1940, when he portrayed Benzino Napaloni, dictator of Bacteria, a takeoff on Mussolini opposite Chaplin's interpretation of Hitler in *The Great Dictator*. Again, Oakie chewed up the scenery and gave the most memorable performance opposite such stalwart character

Sitting Pretty (1933) Songwriting team Chick Parker (Jack Oakie) and Pete Pendleton (Jack Haley) are both trying to get into the "big time." (RF)

actors as Henry Daniell, Reginald Gardiner, and Billy Gilbert, not to mention the temperamental Chaplin himself!

By the time *Sitting Pretty* was made, Ginger Rogers was on the brink of becoming RKO's biggest female star, when she was teamed with Fred Astaire for the first time in *Flying Down to Rio* a few months later. Miss Rogers, up to this point, had been cast in some excellent roles, most notably as "Anytime" Annie in Warners' *42ⁿᵈ Street*, and later in *Gold Diggers of 1933*, where she sings "We're in the Money" in Pig-Latin! Always a minor star attraction, Ginger nevertheless found approval from both the public and film critics, with Richard Watts of the *New York Herald Tribune* commenting that "Miss Rogers is always one of the pleasures of the cinema; a girl who combines looks, grace and an unaffected wit."

Boston born Jack Haley, on the other hand, was never more than a mediocre comedian at best, on stage and screen, whose performances relied totally on how the character was depicted as written and whether or not Mr. Haley could pull it off. Too many times, his characterizations would border on a hapless dolt or misfit who would miraculously win the girl at the end of the picture! In films like *Mr. Cinderella*, he comes off neither funny nor sympathetic, which makes the viewer wonder how this idiot could ever overcome his adversities. Of course, in 1939, Mr. Haley won his best-remembered role (by default) as the Tin Man in Victor Fleming's *The Wizard of Oz*, which has become a timeless classic as well as an American Treasure.

Producer/director Harry Joe Brown's direction is right on target, probably due to the fact that he was a veteran of vaudeville houses and Broadway revues, making him the perfect choice for *Sitting Pretty*. Curiously, he found his niche producing and directing "B" westerns with Reed Howes, Ken Maynard, and later with Randolph Scott throughout the late twenties on up to the early fifties. He retired from filmmaking in 1967 and lived another five years. His son, Harry Joe Brown, Jr., was also a film producer.

Counsellor at Law (1933)

A Universal Picture. Produced by Carl Laemmle, Jr. Directed by William Wyler. Screenplay by Elmer Rice. Based on the stage play by Elmer Rice. Photography by Norbert Brodine. Edited by Daniel Mandell. Art direction by Charles D. Hall. Sound by Gilbert Kurland. 80 min.

Cast: John Barrymore (George Simon), Bebe Daniels (Regina Gordon), Doris Kenyon (Cora Simon), Onslow Stevens (John P. Tedesco), Isabel Jewel (Bessie Green), Melvyn Douglas (Roy Darwin), Thelma Todd (Lillian LaRue), Marvin Kline (Herbert Weinberg), Conway Washburn (Arthur Sandler), John Qualen (Johann Breitstein), J. Hammond Dailey (Charlie McFadden), Clara Langsner (Lena Simon), Malka Kornstein (Sarah Becker), Angela Jacobs (Goldie Rindskopf), T. H. Manning (Peter J. Malone), Elmer Brown (F. C. Baird), Vincent Sherman (Harry Becker), Bobby Gordon (Henry Susskind), Barbara Perry (Dorothy Dwight), Richard Quine (Richard Dwight, Jr.), Victor Adams (David Simon), Mayo Methot (Zedora Chapman), Frederick Burton (Crayfield), Ed Mortimer (Man in waiting room), George Humbert (Italian Client).

AN UNJUSTLY FORGOTTEN CLASSIC, which until fairly recently never seemed to turn up, *Counsellor at Law* is an excellent example of a stage play superbly adapted to the screen. Based on the Elmer Rice drama, which ultimately became the Broadway hit of the 1931-32 season, the film version was one of the biggest money-makers of 1933 and was an unprecedented success for Universal Pictures. Originally cast in the stage play was Paul Muni, who Universal tried to sign for the film version after the film rights were purchased for a then hefty $175,000. Muni, however, was skeptical, fearing that he would be forever typecast in Jewish roles (having already been a member of the Yiddish Theatre).

John Barrymore, now freed from his contract at Metro-Goldwyn-Mayer, was the eventual replacement, and although devoid of Jewish ste-

313

reotypes, he turns in one of his finest performances ever, despite his deteriorating health. Also cast as Barrymore's love interest was Bebe Daniels, a most versatile actress who started her career at the Hal Roach Studios in the Harold Lloyd comedies.

The director of *Counsellor at Law* was the up and coming William Wyler, who until that time was busy directing minor westerns and melodramas. Wyler succeeds incredibly in working his actors at break-neck speed to accentuate the rapid dialogue, which heightens the proceedings. Barrymore, who had a reputation of being very difficult on a movie set, must have admired Wyler's style, for he would listen to every suggestion and even obeyed orders when Wyler recommended that Barrymore "tone down" a bit on the Jewish gestures and intonations. This does not mean that the film is devoid of any stereotypes. Many of the characters, who pop in and out of the office, especially Barrymore's mother, fall into this category.

Counsellor at Law (1933) Accused murderess, Zadorah Chapman (Mayo Methot) tells receptionist Bessie Green (Isabel Jewel) that she would like to see George Simon (John Barrymore). (RF)

The supporting cast is also excellent, with Doris Kenyon as the loathsome wife of the leading character, George Simon. Together with her two spoiled brat children, they seem so convincing in their parts that one wonders if they could ever play more amiable roles. Onslow Stevens, who plays Simon's Italian associate John Tedesco, is always reassuring and understanding, while Isabel Jewell, as the switchboard operator, is put there as comedy relief.

The commercial and critical success of *Counsellor at Law* proved to be a shot in the arm for director William Wyler, for in only two years he was to be producer Samuel Goldwyn's premier director. Together they would churn out some of the greatest classics imaginable, such as *Dodsworth* (1936), *Dead End* (1937), *Wuthering Heights* (1939), *The Westerner* (1940), *The Little Foxes* (1941), *The Best Years of Our Lives* (1946), and many others. As for John Barrymore, he was relegated to second leads in movies, and as a result of his failing health due to alcoholism, was soon consigned to "B" movies supporting personalities like Kay Kyser, Patsy Kelly, and Lupe Velez. Alas, a sad end to one of the greats of stage and screen.

By Candlelight (1933)

By Candlelight (1933) A Universal Picture. Presented by Carl Laemmle. Produced by Carl Laemmle, Jr. Directed by James Whale. Screenplay by Hans Kraly, Ruth Cummings, F. Hugh Herbert and Karen DeWolf. Based on the play *Kleine Komedie* by Siegfried Geyer and its English adaptation *By Candlelight* by Harry Graham. Photography by John J. Mescall. Edited by Ted Kent. Original Music by W. Franke Harling. Art Direction by Charles D. Hall. Makeup by Jack Pierce. Sound by William Hedgcock. Song: "Love Me Some More" by Sam Donaldson. 70 min.

Cast: Elissa Landi (Marie), Paul Lukas (Joseph), Nils Asther (Prince Alfred von Rommer), Dorothy Revier (Countess von Rischenheim), Lawrence Grant (Count von Rischenheim), Esther Ralston (Baroness von Ballin), Warburton Gamble (Baron von Ballin), Lois January (Ann the Maid), Luis Alberni (Train Porter), Andre Cheron (Croupier), Paul Porcasi (Train Conductor).

To CONTEMPORARY AUDIENCES, director James Whale is associated most closely with the horror film genre. One can readily see why, since his *Frankenstein* (1931), *The Old Dark House* (1932), *The Invisible Man* (1933), and *The Bride of Frankenstein* (1935) are all bona-fide classics and have been in constant circulation since their initial releases. Sadly, Whale's non-horror efforts have all been swept under the carpet, for the most part, and films like the first version of *Waterloo Bridge* (1931), *The Kiss Before the Mirror* (1933), *One More River* (1933), *Remember Last Night?* (1935), and *Show Boat* (1936) have all been kept out of circulation for years, until recent re-evaluations have proven what a great filmmaker he really was.

One of these, *By Candlelight*, is another unheralded, forgotten gem, which was originally intended as a vehicle for Robert Wyler (older brother of director William Wyler), who was to make his directorial debut with this light-hearted, frothy romantic comedy. Wyler had convinced studio head Carl Laemmle, Jr. to purchase the rights to the play, which MGM had already owned. Now, MGM had interest in producing a filmed version of H. Rider Haggard's *She* in exchange for *By Candlelight*. So, the trade was made, and with numerous screenwriters working intermittently on the script, it was announced in mid-August that Paul Lukas would star in the role of the amorous manservant of Prince Alfred von Rommer, Josef. Soon after, beautiful Elissa Landi, who had caused quite a stir in films like *The Yellow Ticket* (1931) and DeMille's *The Sign of the Cross* (1932) was added to the cast as Marie. As things seemed to be progressing, it was discovered that Universal had never really owned the rights to *She*, so the trade was now void. Universal decided to scrap the whole project, but Robert Wyler decided to make one final plea to Carl Laemmle, Sr. to purchase the rights to *By Candlelight* outright. Closing the deal for just under $15,000, Universal immediately resumed casting for their upcoming picture. The role of Prince Alfred was originally intended for Laurence Olivier and then John Boles, who both refused, and when filming began in September of 1933, it was announced that Swed-

By Candlelight (1933) A "chance meeting" between Marie (Elissa Landi) and Josef (Paul Lukas) turns into mutual attraction and "double deception." (RF)

By Candlelight (1933) Both Maria (Elissa Landi) and Josef (Paul Lukas) have secrets about themselves they do not wish to divulge. (RF)

ish star, Nils Asther (*Our Modern Maidens, The Bitter Tea of General Yen*) would assume the role.

Before long, it became apparent that Robert Wyler wasn't making any progress with the filming, so as a result, Wyler was taken off the production and was replaced by James Whale. What resulted was a delightful bedroom farce, loaded with innuendo about bored married women who are seduced by a Prince, and of his devoted butler, Josef, who tries to emulate him in every way he can. On board a train, Josef meets a stunningly beautiful woman and, thinking that she is of royal blood, attempts to romance her by assuming his employer's identity. What follows is a series of memorable vignettes, with numerous mistaken identities (a device used frequently in many romantic comedies) keeping the plotline flowing perfectly.

Filming ended on October 21st, with the exception of some retakes. Whale obviously enjoyed himself, making what most critics called "a delightful comedy in the Ernst Lubitsch tradition." Even Carl Laemmle, Jr. had to admit that *By Candlelight* was "one of the most ingenious and amusing pictures" of 1933. *Variety* noted that the film was "a nice little class picture that should make money all around."

Flying Down to Rio (1933)

RKO. Directed by Thornton Freeland. From a play by Anne Caldwell. Screenplay by Louis Brock. Dances by David Gould. Photography by J. J. Faulner. Edited by Jack Kitchin. Songs: "Flying Down to Rio", "The Carioca", "Orchids in the Moonlight" and "Music Makes Me" by Vincent Youmans, Edward Eliscu and Gus Kahn. 89 min.

Cast: Dolores Del Rio (Belinha de Rezende), Gene Raymond (Roger Bond), Raul Roulien (Julio Rubeiro), Ginger Rogers (Honey Hale), Fred Astaire (Fred Ayres), Blanche Frederici (Dona Elena), Walter Walker (Senor de Rezende), Etta Moten (Negro Singer), Roy D'Arcy, Maurice Black and Armand Kaliz (Greeks), Paul Porcasi (Mayor), Reginald Barlow (Banker, Alfredo), Alice Gentle (Concert Singer), Franklin Pangborn (Hammerstein, Hotel Manager), Eric Blore (Assistant Manager), Luis Alberni (Casino Manager), Ray Cooke (Banjo Player), Wallace MacDonald (Pilot), Gino Corrado (Messenger), Mary Kornman (Blonde Friend), Clarence Muse (Caddy), Harry Semels (Sign Poster), Jack Rice (Musician), Eddie Borden (Musician), Betty Furness and Lucile Browne (Ladies at Table), Julian Rivero, Pedro Regas and Movita Castenada (Bit Parts), Martha La Venture (Dancer), Sidney Bracey (Rodriguez, Chauffeur) The Brazilian Turunas and American Clipper Bands.

A FILM THAT IS REMEMBERED MAINLY for introducing the team of Fred Astaire and Ginger Rogers, *Flying Down to Rio* is one of those fun-filled exercises into the surreal world of bizarre Hollywood musicals. A typical Pre-Code entry, replete with outrageous costumes, a chorus of girls strapped to the wings of an airplane in flight clad in sheer see-through outfits, and Miss Rogers appearing in the most provocative outfit in any of her movies, the film is also graced with some smart double-entendres. As a matter of fact, RKO features what is probably the most risqué line ever uttered in a Pre-Code picture. When referring to star Dolores Del

319

Flying Down to Rio (1933) starred Dolores Del Rio and Gene Raymond, but it was supporting players, Ginger Rogers as Honey Hale and Fred Astaire as Fred Ayres, who received all of the attention. (AB)

Rio's sexual allure, a young lady (former Our Gang star, Mary Kornman) asks her female friends, "What is it these South Americans have below the Equator that we haven't?"

Flying Down to Rio was originally intended as a vehicle for Dolores Del Rio and Joel McCrea, who made the screen sizzle in *Bird of Paradise* the previous year with a nude swimming sequence. However, McCrea was already busy filming elsewhere at the studio when they signed Gene Raymond to fill his shoes. Singer Raul Roulien was also hired as a secondary lead, a role in which he would sing "Orchids in the Moonlight" to Miss Del Rio, who was more interested in Gene Raymond's advances. Fred Astaire, who had just finished making a film at MGM opposite Joan Crawford and Clark Gable entitled *Dancing Lady*, hadn't made much of an impression on audiences or the studio, and was quickly let go to freelance. He was signed along with Arline Judge in support of the two stars. Miss Judge found, to her disappointment, that she didn't meet the requirements opposite the high expectations of Mr. Astaire. Ginger Rogers, whose career was steadily gaining momentum, had just finished a musical on loan-out to Paramount Pictures called *Sitting Pretty*. Since she was already a contract player for RKO, she was quickly recruited to play opposite Astaire, little realizing that within a year, they would be that studio's and the industry's top box-office draws!

The Carioca, which was the film's biggest dance number, became a favorite for audiences of 1933 and 1934, with Fred and Ginger working gamely for hours to perfect the dance. The number, which was one of the

Flying Down to Rio (1933) Lobby card features Fred and Ginger doing the "Carioca" (music by Vincent Youmans with lyrics by Gus Kahn and Edward Eliscu). (RF)

longest musical interludes up to that time, features expert camera work as well as lightning-paced editing and superb dancing from the whole ensemble. As an added attraction, noted blues singer Etta Moten gets to belt out a chorus or two of *The Carioca* as well, while a team of black entertainers dance vigorously, almost giving the illusion that their feet are barely touching the dance floor! Unfortunately, due to the bluesy manner in which the music is played with blacks dancing the number in jive, this portion has been missing from most prints of the film until recently.

Since he was the director of Pan American Airways, producer Merian C. Cooper wanted to promote air travel in *Flying Down to Rio* by depicting many scenes with airplanes. Although not one member of the cast ever takes off in a plane, he made sure that dozens of PAA Sikorsky clippers were used throughout the production. For the final number, they had motorless planes hanging from the ceiling of the soundstage by wires with huge wind machines giving the illusion that they were in flight!

The musical score by Max Steiner is another highlight, as are the songs by Vincent Youmans, whose last film this was. The reviewer for the *New York American* noted, "The inspired music of Vincent Youmans, the grace of Fred Astaire, the dark beauty of Dolores Del Rio, Raul Roulien's singing, the comedy of Ginger Rogers, and the love-making of Gene Raymond combine to make a glorious Hollywood holiday."

Queen Christina (1933)

A Metro-Goldwyn-Mayer Picture. Produced by Walter Wanger. Directed by Rouben Mamoulian. Screenplay by Salka Viertel, H. M. Harwood, S. N. Behrman and (uncredited) Ben Hecht. From an original story by Salka Viertel and Margaret P. Levine. Photography by William Daniels. Edited by Blanche Sewell. Art Direction by Alexander Toluboff and Edwin B. Willis. Sound by Douglas Shearer. Music by Herbert Stohart. Costumes by Adrian. 100 min.

Cast: Greta Garbo (Queen Christina), John Gilbert (Don Antonio), Ian Keith (Magnus), Lewis Stone (Oxenstierna), Elizabeth Young (Ebba), C. Aubrey Smith (Aage), Reginald Owen (Prince Charles), Georges Renavent (French Ambassador), Gustav von Seyffertitz (General), David Torrence (Archbishop), Ferdinand Munier (Innkeeper), Akim Tamiroff (Pedro), Cora Sue Collins (Christina as a child), Edward Norris (Count Jacob), Barbara Barondess (Servant Girl), Paul Hurst (Swedish Soldier), Edward Gargan, Wade Boteler (Rabble-rouser), Fred Kohler (Member of the Court), Stanley J. Sandford (Waiter).

THROUGHOUT THE YEARS, there have been a number of romantic screen teams who have left an indelible mark in the minds of the public. Humphrey Bogart and Lauren Bacall, Katharine Hepburn and Spencer Tracy, Elizabeth Taylor and Richard Burton, Charles Farrell and Janet Gaynor, William Powell and Myrna Loy are just a few of the great movie duos who come to mind. But in the twenties, John Gilbert and Greta Garbo were the premier couple whose films captivated audiences in those waning days of the silents. Gilbert, born into a theatrical family, was already a seasoned veteran of the stage when he was cast at the age of seventeen in the William S. Hart classic *Hell's Hinges* in 1916. Shortly after working opposite Mary Pickford and Colleen Moore, he wound up at the newly formed Metro-Goldwyn-Mayer Studio, where he found himself in

Queen Christina (1933) Christina, Queen of Sweden (Greta Garbo) spends the night in a tavern with Spanish envoy, Antonio (John Gilbert). This scene certainly earned the ire of the censors at the time. (RF)

such commercial hits as *The Man Who Gets Slapped* (1924) and *The Merry Widow* (1925). But his biggest success was yet to come in the outstanding World War I drama *The Big Parade* (1925), which was directed by King Vidor. It was Gilbert's performance that won accolades nationally, and his brilliant portrayal remains one of the best of all time. As a matter of fact, the movie was one of the biggest box-office successes of the silent era.

To capitalize on his enormous popularity, MGM matched him opposite their newest Swedish discovery, Greta Garbo, who was rapidly becoming the studio's number one female star. After three highly successful pictures together, *Flesh and the Devil* (1926), *Love* (1927), and *A Woman of Affairs* (1928), both of their careers were to remain on solid ground… for a while anyway. An off-screen romance eventually ensued, and marriage was planned but never materialized. According to eyewitnesses, the heartbroken John Gilbert ended up punching his boss Louis B. Mayer after Mayer had made a crude remark about Miss Garbo.

It has been said for many years that the sad fate of John Gilbert's career was the result of having a high-pitched voice that didn't record well during the early talkie era. Nothing could be further from the truth. Reportedly, after the altercation, Mayer deliberately sabotaged Gilbert's career by putting him in inferior quality films, which were poorly written and hampered by incredibly bad dialogue. In the sound era, only two of Gilbert's films are worth noting, *Downstairs* (1932), which he wrote himself and where he proves what a versatile actor he really was by playing a totally despicable cad, and the superb *Queen Christina* (1933).

After an absence from the screen of over a year, having walked out on her studio and returning to her native Sweden, Greta Garbo was lured back to Hollywood with a more lucrative contract and a two-picture a year deal. One project that intrigued her was based on the life of the Swedish monarch Queen Christina (1626-1689), whose renowned liaisons with both sexes became legendary. Commissioned to write the screenplay was Garbo's good friend, Salka Viertel. The finished project proved to be vintage Garbo, superbly produced with all of the visual gloss so prominent in many MGM super productions, and directed by Rouben Mamoulian, whose screen credits included such classics as *Applause* (1929), *Dr. Jekyll and Mr. Hyde* (1931), and *Love Me Tonight* (1932). By the time *Queen Christina* was about to go into production, John Gilbert's career had sadly faded drastically and, according to various film historians, it was Garbo who took pity on her former lover and requested that he be cast opposite her rather than twenty-six year old Laurence Olivier, who was the studio's original choice for the role of Don Antonio.

Unfortunately, the movie didn't turn out to be a huge "comeback" film for John Gilbert, although he turned in a solid, hugely-satisfying performance. No longer was his name above the title alongside Garbo's in the film's credits, but below the title in small letters, obviously another fatal stab by the heartless Mr. Mayer! What's even sadder was that John Gilbert was dead a short three years later, a victim of alcohol abuse, spurned by severe depression at the age of thirty-eight.

When viewed today, *Queen Christina* loses none of its elegant beauty. The love scene in the tavern remains one of the most beautiful in film history, and the exquisite lighting by Garbo's favorite cameraman, William Daniels, is breathtaking. Although not the box-office attraction MGM had hoped for, *Queen Christina* received unanimous glowing reviews. Walter Ramsey of *Modern Screen* wrote, "Triumph for Garbo! One of the great pictures of the past few years, this historical epic makes a sustained drive for artistry. Besides, we have Garbo and Gilbert, very good indeed. One of the best scenes discloses Garbo, traveling as a man, and stopping at a wayside inn, there to be placed in the same room with a nobleman from Spain (Gilbert) because all other rooms are occupied. (No reason to censor and even reason to try.) One does not resent the situation because it is so beautifully handled. The picture is an unending series of exceptional scenes, packed with fine characterizations and good direction. A triumph for Garbo, a comeback for Gilbert, with an orchid for Messrs. Stone and Keith. The production is in a class by itself, so you cannot afford to miss it." Amazingly, *Queen Christina* didn't receive one single Academy Award nomination in any category. Today, it is regarded as Garbo's best film, even though there were to be many other high points to come for the remainder of the decade, such as *Anna Karenina* (1935), *Camille* (1937), and the delightful Ernst Lubitsch film *Ninotchka* (1939), where Miss Garbo successfully appeared in her first comedy. After one more film, however, the rather tepid *Two-Faced Woman* (1941), she quietly walked away from her career, never looking back, never granting interviews, and never appearing in public. She died quietly in Manhattan on April 15, 1990.

Lady Killer (1933)

A Warner Bros. & Vitaphone Picture. Directed by Roy Del Ruth. Production Supervisor: Henry Blanke. Screenplay by Ben Markson. Based on "The Finger Man" by Rosalind Keating Shaffer. Adaptation by Ben Markson and Lillie Hayward. Photography by Tony Gaudio. Art Direction by Robert Haas. Edited by George Amy. Musical Director: Leo F. Forbstein. Costumes by Orry-Kelly. Makeup by Perc Westmore. Assistant Director: Chuck Hansen. 74 min.

Cast: James Cagney (Dan Quigley), Mae Clarke (Myra Gale), Leslie Fenton (Duke), Margaret Lindsay (Lois Underwood), Henry O'Neill (Ramick), Willard Robertson (Conroy), Douglas Cosgrove (Jones), Raymond Hatton (Pete), Russell Hopton (Smiley), William Davidson (Williams), Marjorie Gateson (Mrs. Wilbur Marley), Robert Elliott (Brannigan), John Marston (Kendall), Douglass Dumbrille (Spade Maddock), George Chandler (Thompson), George Blackwood (The Escort), Jack Don Wong (Oriental), Frank Sheridan (Los Angeles Police Chief), Edwin Maxwell (Theatre Manager), Phil Tead (Usher Sargeant Seymour), Dewey Robinson (Movie Fan), Tammany Young (Movie Fan), H. C. Bradley (Man with Purse), Harry Beresford (Dr. Crane), Olaf Hytten (Butler), Harry Strong (Ambulance Attendant), Al Hill (Casino Cashier), Bud Flanagan/Dennis O'Keefe (Man in Casino), James Burke (Hand-Out), Robert Emmett Homans (Jailer), Clarence Wilson (Lawyer), Sam McDaniel (Porter), Spencer Charters (Los Angeles Cop), Herman Bing (Western Director), Harold Waldridge (Letter-Handler), Luis Alberni (Director), Ray Cooke (Property Man), Sam Ash (Hood).

FOR YEARS HOLLYWOOD has had a field day spoofing the movie industry. Films like *Show People* (1928), *Movie Crazy* (1932), *Bombshell* (1933), *Stand-In* (1937), *Pick a Star* (1937), *Something to Sing About* (1937), and *Sullivan's Travels* (1941) all depicted an extremely eccentric

Hollywood, to say the least, with their temperamental stars, egocentric German directors (complete with riding breeches and megaphone), and up and coming starlets who sacrifice their all to attain stardom. While some of these films offered pure escapism with their Cinderella-like themes, others like *Bombshell* and *The Bad and the Beautiful* (1952) took a more cynical view, elaborating more on studio politics and back-stabbing publicists.

Lady Killer fits into the first category, bringing movie tough guy James Cagney to Hollywood, where he ultimately breaks into moving pictures while on the lam from the police. Of course, since this is a Pre-

Lady Killer (1933) The unjustly forgotten Mae Clarke as gun moll Myra Gale. (RF)

Lady Killer (1933) Despite the braids, that's not Pocahontas on the left, but James Cagney as gangster-turned-movie extra, Dan Quigley, along with publicist, George Thompson (George Chandler) and picture star, Lois Underwood (Margaret Lindsay). (RF)

Code production, Cagney's involvement in a murder is overlooked, and all ends happily.

Incidentally, during this period, Warner Bros. was receiving negative feedback from the Hays Office, who charged that the studio was glorifying the gangster with such movies as *Little Caesar* (1930) and *The Public Enemy* (1931). To appease the critics, Warners decided to cast their two biggest stars in spoofs of their former gangster films. Edward G. Robinson made three excellent comedies entitled *The Little Giant* (1933), *A Slight Case of Murder* (1938), and *Larceny, Inc.* (1942), all dealing with Robinson's depiction of a gangland boss who decides to go 'legit' after making his fortunes illegally (although still emphasizing that "CRIME DOES PAY!" much to the chagrin of the production code). In *Lady Killer* there is also a direct reference to Cagney's classic *The Public Enemy*, wherein Mae Clarke, who is also on the lam, suggests to Cagney that they should hide out in California. While reading aloud a travel folder, she comes upon a passage saying "California! The land of sunshine, oranges, grapefruit..." at which point she stops reading, with a moment's apprehension. It's a wonderful "throw-away" gag, since it was Mae Clarke who was at the receiving end of James Cagney's grapefruit in *The Public Enemy*. As an added bonus, the two stars stage a slugfest with Cagney dragging Clarke across the room by her hair!

Short and snappy, and without one wasted moment (always an asset of 'Pre-Code' Warners movies), *Lady Killer* was directed by Roy Del Ruth, a veteran of fast-paced, hard-hitting comedies. He always proved to be the perfect choice in that genre.

The *New York Evening Post* wrote, "The reason for the picture's existence seems to have been due to a desire to give the versatile and gifted Mr. Cagney a chance to show himself in an all-around way, and *Lady Killer* is therefore a kind of resume of everything he has done to date in the movies. His method is straight from the shoulder and decisive, and though the grapefruit trick is omitted, his activities leave no doubt in the end that his attitude toward women is of the rough-and-tumble variety." More than just a curio piece on Hollywood, this film still delights despite its age!

Sons of the Desert (1933)

A Metro-Goldwyn-Mayer Picture. Produced by Hal Roach. Directed by William A. Seiter. Associate Direction by Lloyd French. Photography by Kenneth Peach. Story by Frank Craven. Edited by Bert Jordan. Continuity by Byron Morgan. Sound by Harry Baker. Music by Marvin Hatley and LeRoy Shield. Dance Direction by Dave Bennett. 65 min.

Cast: Stan Laurel (Himself), Oliver Hardy (Himself), Charley Chase (Himself), Mae Busch (Mrs. Lottie Hardy), Dorothy Christy (Mrs. Betty Laurel), Lucien Littlefield (Dr. Horace Meddick), John Elliott (Exalted Ruler), Charita (Lead Hula Dancer), Ty Parvis (Singer), Charley Young, John Merton, William Gillespie, Charles McAvoy, Bobby Burns, Al Thompson, Eddie Baker, Jimmy Aubrey, Chet Brandenberg, Don Brodie (Sons of the Desert Coterie), Philo McCullough (Assistant Exalted Ruler), Harry Bernard (Police Officer), Sam Lufkin, Ernie Alexander, Charlie Hall (Waiters), Baldwin Cooke (Steamship Official), Stanley Blystone, Max Wagner (Speakeasy Managers), Pat Harmon (Doorman), Blade Stanhope Conway/Bob Cummings (Crowd Extra).

SONS OF THE DESERT IS CONSIDERED by many to be Laurel and Hardy's feature-length masterpiece, regarded much the same as Chaplin's *City Lights* (1931), Harold Lloyd's *The Kid Brother* (1927), the Marx Brothers' *Duck Soup* (1933), and W. C. Fields' *It's a Gift* (1934). By 1933, L&H were the most popular comedy team in the world. Their faces were the most recognizable, with the possible exception of Chaplin's. Now they were to embark on their fourth starring feature-length comedy. The first three, *Pardon Us* (1931), *Pack Up Your Troubles* (1932), and especially *The Devil's Brother/Fra Diavolo* (1933) were enormous hits and made huge sums of money, not only for Hal Roach Studios, but for Roach's releasing company, Metro-Goldwyn-Mayer as well.

Sons of the Desert (1933) "Hear no evil, see no evil, speak no evil." Stan Laurel, Oliver Hardy and Charley Chase attend the Sons of the Desert convention in Chicago. The lead hula dancer standing between Hardy and Chase is billed as Charita. (RF)

A remake of one the boys' last silent two-reelers, *We Faw Down* (1928) and an early Mack Sennett comedy called *Ambrose's First Falsehood* (1914), which starred Mack Swain and Charley Chase, the boys' co-star in *Sons of the Desert*, this film remains a favorite for audiences, even those who never really warmed to the team. Shot in October of 1933 by veteran director William A. Seiter, who turned out to be Laurel and Hardy's best director, it's one of those pictures that keeps building throughout until the hilarious finale, all told in a compact, no time wasted 65 minutes! Seiter, a specialist in romantic comedies and light dramas, proved extremely adept at making a mediocre script look much better than it really was. Films like *Hot Saturday* (1932), *Professional Sweetheart* (1933), *Rafter Romance* (1934), *In Person*, and *If You Could Only Cook* (both 1935) were prime examples of Seiter's expertise at bringing life to an ordinary story. He was a favorite to many stars, most notably Ginger Rogers, who always credited him as one of her favorite directors! He was a good pal to Hal Roach and Stan Laurel. Here, in *Sons*, he was able to take a short subject plot or incident and expand it to feature-length, making it one of the top ten money-makers of 1934.

Portraying Ollie's wife in *Sons of the Desert* was silent film star Mae Busch, whose career had sadly come to an almost grinding halt, only to be resuscitated by Hal Roach, who cast her in on one of Laurel and Hardy's

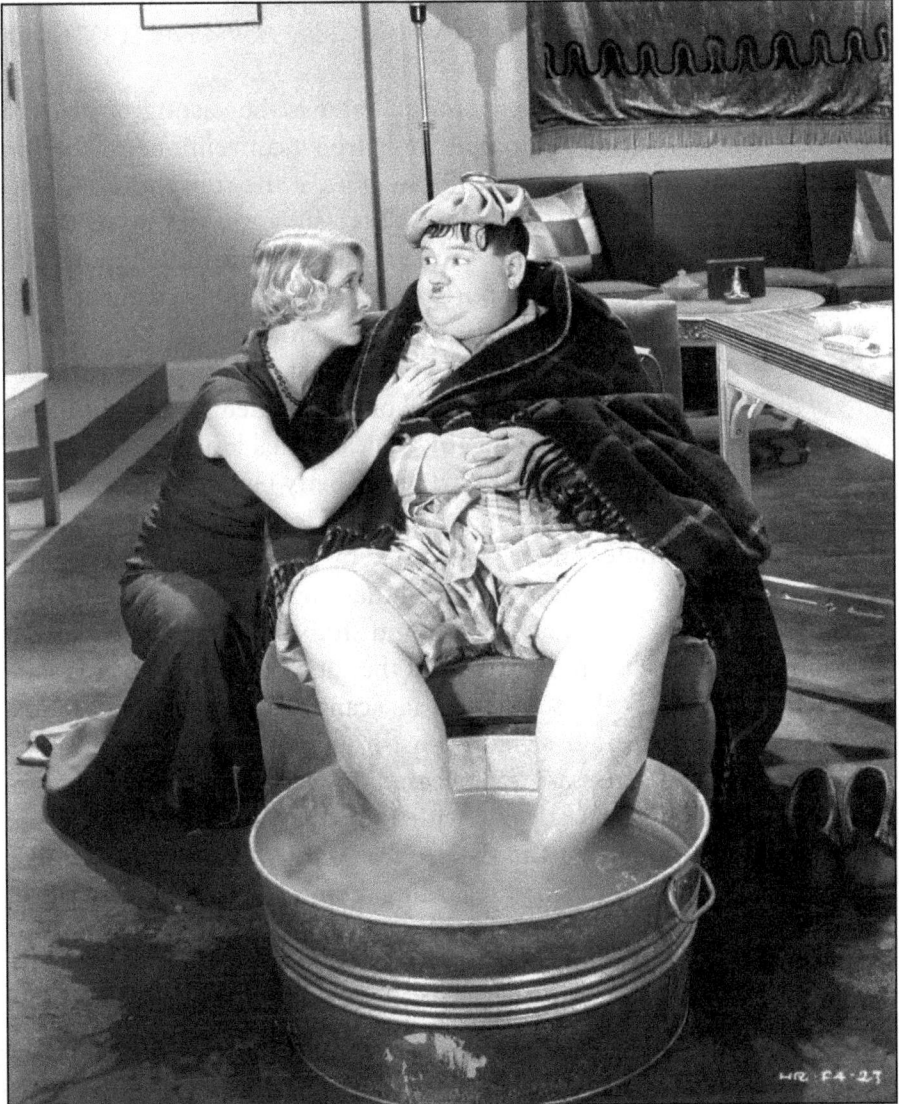

Sons of the Desert (1933) Mrs. Lottie Hardy (Mae Busch) tends to her "sick" husband, who's suffering from a "nervous shakedown." (Oliver Hardy). (RF)

earliest endeavors, entitled *Love 'em and Weep* (1927), a film where both Stan and Ollie were featured but not as yet working as a team. Two years later, in L&H's first 'all-talking' short subject, *Unaccustomed As We Are*, Mae was cast for the first time as Hardy's wife, a role that she would repeat in other of their comedies. According to Stan Laurel, Mae Busch was one of the most talented of all of their leading ladies, and he utilized her talents to the fullest as much as possible. Stan's wife is played by beautiful, statuesque Dorothy Christy, a happy replacement for Patsy Kelly, who was working on another picture for Metro, *Going Hollywood* (1933) with Bing Crosby.

The 'coup de grace' of *Sons of the Desert* is the casting of beloved comedian Charley Chase as an obnoxious fellow conventioneer who has an uproariously funny sequence with the boys at the convention. Chase, a comedy veteran of silent and sound short subjects, was a favorite at the Hal Roach Studios. From 1924 to 1936, he was one of the mainstays, churning out countless quality shorts, as well as directing many of them himself. Tragically, he died in 1940 at the age of forty-six.

One 'Pre-Code' element, which was eliminated from many prints of *Sons of the Desert*, is a delightful musical number called "Honolulu Baby", written by Marvin Hatley and sung by a Dick Powell lookalike named Ty Paris, who was a former dancing partner of Betty Grable's when the two appeared in vaudeville. According to Hatley, "Honolulu Baby" was composed in twenty minutes and was recorded by an eight-piece band. Publicity by the *Hollywood Reporter* claimed that the "song will accompany a line of hula dancers in a cabaret scene and studio feels it will be a hit." It probably would have been more of a hit than it was had the various state censor boards not cut the scene with its scantily clad hula girls, almost topless, gyrating their bodies vigorously throughout the number.

When *Sons of the Desert* was released on December 29, 1933, it was generally greeted enthusiastically, with Richard Watts of the *New York Herald-Tribune* noting that the theatre was "crowded with ecstatic delegates who showed every sign of regarding themselves as being in an ideal world where there were two Chaplins working in one film." Andre Sennwald of *The New York Times* wrote that the film "has achieved feature length without benefit of the usual distressing formulae of padding and stretching. It is funny all the way through."

Even contemporary film historians and critics hold *Sons of the Desert* in high esteem. In William K. Everson's excellent study of the team, *The Films of Laurel and Hardy*, he states that the picture "has fewer virtuoso comedy episodes than such other major features as *Block-heads* and *Way Out West,* but thanks largely to Seiter's handling, it has that indefinable quality of charm which broadens its appeal quite beyond the legions of Laurel and Hardy devotees. Just as many of Seiter's films of the twenties, never considered either major works of art or important box office contenders, prove to be amazingly durable today and of more value than many of their more highly regarded contemporaries, so I suspect in years to come will *Sons of the Desert* come to be regarded as one of the most accomplished comedies of the early '30s."

Hi Nellie! (1934)

Warner Bros./First National. Produced by Robert Presnell. Directed by Mervyn LeRoy. Original Story by Roy Chanslor. Screenplay by Abem Finkel and Sidney Sutherland. Photography by Sol Polito. Edited by Bill Holmes. Art Direction by Robert Haas. Costumes by Orry-Kelly. Original Music by Bernhard Kaun. 75 min.

Cast: Paul Muni (Brad Bradshaw), Glenda Farrell (Gerry Krale), Ned Sparks (Shammy McClure), Robert Barrat (Beau Brownell), Berton Churchill (John L. Graham), Kathryn Sergava (Grace), Hobart Cavanaugh ('Fully' Fullerton), Douglass Dumbrille (Harvey Dawes), Edward Ellis (Mr. O'Connell), Paul Kaye (Helwig), Donald Meek ('Durky' Durkin), Dorothy Le Baire (Rosa Marinello), Marjorie Gateson (Mrs. Frank J. Canfield), George Meeker (Jimmy Sheldon), Harold Huber (Leo), Allen Vincent (Nick Grassi), Pat Wing (Susie), Frank Reicher (Nate Nathan), George Chandler (Danny Sullivan), George Humbert (Mike Marinello), Nina Campana (Italian Woman), James Dolan (Evans), Antonio Filauri ("Merry-Go-Round" Headwaiter), Howard C. Hickman (Dr. John W. Wilson), Milton Kibbee (Charlie Dwyer), Frank Marlowe (Henchman), Ralph McCullough (Poker Player), Harold Miller (Graham's Secretary), Sidney Miller (Louie), Bob Montgomery (Henchman), Bert Moorhouse (Extra at Nightclub), John Qualen (Steve), Gus Reed (Mac), Harry Seymour (Drunk at Bar), Sidney Skolsky (Skolsky), Renee Whitney (Telephone Operator), Jack Wise (Vital Statistics Clerk).

A MOVIE WHICH WAS a veritable flop upon its initial release, *Hi Nellie!* is one of the few Paul Muni films that people never seem to recollect. Perhaps it's because of the uninspired title, which means nothing to the average moviegoer, or maybe it's because it is considered such a minor film in Mr. Muni's filmography. *Variety* even panned the picture by stating that it "barely gets by as fair entertainment." Whatever the reason for

Hi Nellie! (1934) Managing editor Brad Bradshaw (Paul Muni) has been demoted by his newspaper to write a "lonely hearts" column, while his sympathetic colleague, Gerry (Glenda Farrell), tries to get him to stop drinking. (AB)

this unjust oversight, *Hi Nellie!* was and is a good way to spend seventy-five minutes and it seems rather refreshing to see Mr. Muni in something other than a big-budgeted historical drama, where we often can't even recognize this talented actor. According to Bette Davis, Muni once approached her and curiously asked why he wasn't as popular as James Cagney or Edward G. Robinson or Humphrey Bogart. Davis' reply simply was "Because nobody knows what you really look like underneath all that makeup!" This assumption might be the partial truth, because in all of his most famous roles—*Story of Louis Pasteur* (1936), *The Life of Emile Zola*, *The Good Earth* (both 1937), and *Juarez* (1939)—he was hidden underneath false beards, wigs, fake noses, and gobs of greasepaint!

Born Muni Wisenfreund in Poland in 1895, Muni started on the stage as a youngster. His parents were professional actors who taught their young son to love the theatre as well and eventually the family immigrated to the United States and worked on the Yiddish stage. Young Paul (as he was now called) later joined the once famed Yiddish Art Theatre Company and made quite a name for himself here and abroad. When

Hollywood beckoned the young actor he ventured out to the west coast, making two films for Fox in 1929. Not quite pleased with Hollywood, he returned to Broadway where he later landed the lead in the Elmer Rice hit play *Counsellor-at-Law*, which was a big success. Again, he was asked to reenact his stage role in the movie adaptation, but declined because he was afraid that he would be typecast in Jewish roles. Instead he signed a long-term contract at Warner Bros., where he would eventually be treated like Hollywood royalty and given the privilege of full script and director approval on all his pictures. In 1932 he made two of his most famous films: *Scarface* (on loan to Howard Hughes), and what was to become the greatest of all social dramas of the thirties, *I am a Fugitive From a Chain Gang*, for which he received his first Academy Award nomination. He later won the Oscar for his portrayal of Louis Pasteur and the New York Film Critics Award for *The Life of Emile Zola*. As the thirties progressed, Mr. Muni again became tired of Hollywood and resented the way Warner Bros. was using him, so he alternated between the stage and the screen for the rest of his career.

Mervyn LeRoy, whose outstanding directorial achievements helped make *I am a Fugitive From a Chain Gang* the classic that it is, was also responsible for *Hi Nellie!* A most versatile director, whose picture titles read like a list of "must see" classics, LeRoy's filmography includes such notables as *Little Caesar* (1931), *Three on a Match* (1932), *Gold Diggers of 1933* (1933), *Anthony Adverse* (1936), *They Won't Forget* (1937), *Waterloo Bridge* (1940), *Random Harvest* (1942), and many more.

While audience reactions to *Hi Nellie!* proved tepid, apparently Warner Bros. felt that the story might still have value, so they remade it in 1937 under the title *Love is on the Air*, with Ronald Reagan (his first film role) and June Travis, which fared no better. Undaunted, the studio attempted another go at it in 1942 under the title *You Can't Escape Forever*. This time, with leads George Brent and Brenda Marshall, the film did manage to bring in more revenue at the box-office, although critics still weren't thoroughly impressed. In 1949, they tried yet again, under the title *House Across the Street* with Wayne Morris and Janis Paige. *The New York Times*' downhearted review called it "A woefully frail and feeble thing." Although *Hi Nellie!* is considered at best a "forgotten curio," seen today it is a fast-paced, enjoyable romp with Paul Muni and the always delightful Glenda Farrell in top form!

Palooka (1934)

United Artists Release. Produced by Edward Small. Directed by Benjamin Stoloff. Based on the comic strip *Joe Palooka* by Ham Fisher. Screenplay by Jack Jevne, Arthur Kober and Gertrude Purcell. Additional Dialogue by Murray Roth and Ben Ryan. Photography by Arthur Edeson. Edited by Grant Whytock. Art Direction by Albert S. D'Agostino. Original Music by Joseph Burke and Burton Lane. Sound by Karl Zint. Musical Direction by Constantine Bakaleinikoff. 86 min.

Cast: Jimmy Durante (Knobby Walsh), Lupe Velez (Nina Madero), Stuart Erwin (Joe Palooka), Marjorie Rambeau (Mayme Palooka), Robert Armstrong (Pete "Goodtime" Palooka), Mary Carlisle (Anne), William Cagney (Al "Mac" McSwatt), Thelma Todd (Trixie), Gus Arnheim (Orchestra Bandleader), Franklyn Ardell (Doc Wise), Tom Dugan (Whitey), Louise Beavers (Crystal), Fred "Snowflake" Toones (Smokey), Brooks Benedict (Slugs), Stanley Blystone (Second House Detective), Andre Cheron (First Headwaiter), Gordon De Main (Photographer's Official), Stanley Fields (Blacky Wolfe), Kit Guard (McSwatt's Handler), Otis Harlan (Riley the Doorman), Al Hill (Dynamite Wilson), Donald Kerr (Bellboy), Ivan Linow (Fourth Fixed Fighter), Alphone Martell (Nightclub Headwaiter), Tom McGuire (House Detective), Frank Mills (Congratulator), Bert Moorhouse (Desk Clerk), Jack Mower (Reporter), Wheeler Oakman (Rafferty), Frank O'Connor (Ringsider), Bob Perry (Referee), Rolfe Sedan (Alphonse), Larry Steers (Photographer), Carl Stockdale (Mailman), Harry Tenbrook (McSwatt's Handler), Guinn "Big Boy" Williams (Slats), Norman Willis (Second Fixed Fighter).

ONE OF THE LAST PRE-CODE FILMS released before the institution of the production code, *Palooka* (retitled in Great Britain as *The Great Schnozzle*) was one of those happy affairs which pulled Depression-era audiences out of the doldrums. Based on Ham Fisher's comic strip *Joe*

Palooka, this movie version, which boasted five screenwriters, utilized every one of their writing skills to the fullest! For those who are old enough to remember characters Joe Palooka and "Knobby" Walsh, it seems that the casting for the film version was done very haphazardly, because none of the cast even remotely resemble the comic strip characters. Had the film been done a few years later by Warner Bros., a perfect choice for the title role would have been a young Wayne Morris, who essayed a similar role in *Kid Galahad* three years later. Stuart Erwin, cast here in the role of the younger Palooka, is totally acceptable as the wide-eyed hayseed, until he dons his boxing trunks. Looking as if he should have consulted with Richard Simmons or Jack LaLanne before accepting this role, he nevertheless comes off as a pleasing lead, underplaying his part, nicely counterbalancing the brashness of the "Knobby" Walsh character, played with overwhelming gusto by the inimitable Jimmy Durante.

The female lead is the "Mexican Spitfire" Lupe Velez, whose vivacious screen persona made her a formidable foil to Jimmy Durante. Audiences enjoyed their constant badgering at one another so much that they were cast two more times that year in MGM's extravaganza *Hollywood Party* and RKO's *Strictly Dynamite*. Velez, whose real name was Maria Guadalupe Velez de Villalobos, began her career dancing in Mexican cantinas and Hollywood nightclubs before breaking into films in 1926 at the Hal Roach Studio, playing in support of Laurel and Hardy and others. Her fiery personality got her work as Douglas Fairbanks' leading lady in *The Gaucho* (1927), and later in Cecil B. DeMille's *The Squaw Man* (1931). It was during *Palooka* that film executives found to their delight that she was perfectly cast in comedy roles as excitable, often hot-tempered tamales, whose short-fused dispositions would be doused before the final reel unwound.

Jimmy Durante, on the other hand, was a product of New York's Hell's Kitchen, where his career as a ragtime pianist brought him accolades at the young age of sixteen. Known for his rather large proboscis, he was nicknamed "Schnozzola," before being cast in the Florenz Ziegfeld production *Show Girl* in 1930, along with his partner Lou Clayton. His film debut came a year later when he signed a five-year contract with MGM, primarily to co-star with silent film legend Buster Keaton, whose career was in need of a boost. Unfortunately, for the most part, these films, although big money makers, are considered unfunny today, and before long, due to Keaton's love for the bottle, his career was relegated to the scrap heap! On loan from MGM, Mr. Durante's untiring vivacity

Palooka (1934) Thelma Todd in her brief, but memorable role as Trixie. (RF)

keeps *Palooka* moving at a good pace, with his rendition of *Inka-Dinka-Doo*, which he wrote, being a highlight!

Also on hand in the production is the lovely Thelma Todd, in an all-too-brief role, as a cheap dancehall girl who gets clobbered by Joe's mother Mayme (Marjorie Rambeau) after she finds that her husband (Robert Armstrong) has been unfaithful. Also of interest is the casting of James Cagney's lookalike younger brother Bill, who would later become his brother's producer and manager. The resemblance and mannerisms are uncannily similar, and one wonders why Bill hadn't been more successful as an actor.

Ben Stoloff, *Palooka*'s director, had a career that began mainly with short comedies and continued with "B" pictures of varying degrees of quality. What success *Palooka* possesses might rely on the appeal of its three leads. There are some that find the overwrought antics of Jimmy Durante and Lupe Velez unappealing. Nevertheless, the film garnered good reviews, with *Variety* declaring that the picture was "a laugh riot, the nearest approach to a Marx picture that's been around."

Two Alone (1934)

RKO Pictures. Produced by Merian C. Cooper. Associate Producer: David Lewis. Directed by Elliott Nugent. Based on the play *Wild Birds* by Dan Totheroh. Screenplay by Josephine Lovett and Joseph Moncure March. Photography by Lucien Andriot. Edited by Arthur Roberts. Art Direction by Charles Kirk and Van Nest Polglase. Music by Max Steiner. Sound by John L. Cass. Special Effects by Harry Redmond Sr. 72 min.

Cast: Jean Parker (Mazie), Tom Brown (Adam), Zasu Pitts (Esthey Roberts), Arthur Byron (Slag), Beulah Bondi (Mrs. Slag), Nydia Westman (Corie), Willard Robertson (George Marshall), Charley Grapewin (Sandy Roberts), Emerson Treacy (Milt Pollard), Paul Nicholson (Sheriff), Wade Boteler and Jim Farley (Bit Parts), Zeffie Tilbury (Old Lady).

BASED ON THE PLAY *WILD BIRDS* by Dan Totheroh (brother of cameraman Roland Totheroh), whose screenplay credits include both versions of *The Dawn Patrol* (1930 and 1938), *The Count of Monte Cristo* (1934), the deliciously black-comedy murder mystery *Remember Last Night?* (1935), and the surreal *The Devil and Daniel Webster* (1941), *Two Alone* is one of his lesser-known efforts. Remembered chiefly for its brief nude swimming scene at the beginning of the picture, which was trimmed in several states due to censorship restrictions, the film does feature some fine performances from its two young stars, Jean Parker and Tom Brown. Parker, borrowed from MGM, was rather new to the film industry, making an impression on audiences and critics in movies like *Gabriel Over the White House* and *Lady for a Day* (both 1933), combining her demure natural beauty with her sincere acting. Her best performance to date was as the ill-fated Beth in David Selznick's *Little Women* (1933), where she keeps up with some pretty stiff competition opposite Katharine Hepburn, Joan Bennett, and beautiful Frances Dee, cast as her siblings. After a successful turn at MGM, her roles became rather typical, and she eventually wound up doing "B" pictures for studios like Monogram, until her retirement in 1944.

Tom Brown, on the other hand, began his career in show business before he could barely walk. His father, Harry Brown, a famous vaudevillian, and mother, Marie, a musical comedy star, would use the toddler in both of their acts. Enrolled in the Professional Children's School at age nine, he soon found employment doing radio and stage work by the following year, along with some film acting as well. By the early 1930s, he was usually cast as "boy-next-door" types, clean-cut college kids, or the younger brother of the leading star, because of his all-American looks. His more important thirties appearances were in films like *Tom Brown of Culver*, *Hell's Highway* (both 1932), *Three Cornered Moon* (1933), *Anne of Green Gables* (1934), *In Old Chicago*, and *Merrily We Live* (both 1938). After serving in World War II as a paratrooper, he returned to films, trying to shake the clean-cut image from his resume by playing heavies and various other characters. Later, after being recalled into the service during the Korean War, where he reached the rank of lieutenant colonel, he returned to work mainly in television, on shows such as *Gunsmoke* and *General Hospital*.

Two Alone (1934) Adam (Tom Brown) and Maizie (Jean Parker) in a brief tender moment. (RF)

Directed by Elliott Nugent, whose career began in much the same manner as Tom Brown's, *Two Alone* never had much exposure on television until the 1980s, due to its subject matter. The idea of attempted rape by a psychotic guardian, the love affair of two unwed teenagers, and the resulting violence that ensues when the guardian finds out that his ward is pregnant, was considered far too offensive in 1934. Reviews were generally negative and the film received a rather limited release schedule.

Dividing his time between writing books and plays and directing pictures, Elliott Nugent's film career was generally successful. He worked mainly at Paramount Pictures with many comedians of the day, such as Harold Lloyd, Bob Hope, and others. By the 1950s, his film career had all but diminished, due to a complete mental breakdown brought on by acute alcoholism. He returned to the Broadway stage, producing and directing shows before his retirement in 1957. His autobiography, entitled *The Events Leading Up to the Comedy*, was published in 1965. After a long and varied career in show business, working in virtually every aspect of the medium, Mr. Nugent passed away in 1980 at the age of eighty-one.

Hips, Hips, Hooray! (1934)

An RKO Release. Produced by Merian C. Cooper. Directed by Mark Sandrich. Associate Producer: H. N. Swanson. Screenplay by Bert Kalmar, Harry Ruby, and Edward Kaufman. Story, Music, and Lyrics by Bert Kalmar and Harry Ruby. Art Direction by Van Nest Polglase and Carroll Clark. Costumes by Walter Plunkett. Photography by David Abel. Photographic Effects by Vernon Walker. Musical Direction by Roy Webb. Sound Recording by Phillip J. Faulkner, Jr. Dances by Dave Gould. Sound Cutter: George Marsh. Edited by Basil Wrangell. 67 min.

Cast: Bert Wheeler (Andy Williams), Robert Woolsey (Dr. Bob Dudley), Ruth Etting (Herself), Thelma Todd (Amelia Frisby), Dorothy Lee (Daisy Maxwell), George Meeker (Armand Beauchamp), James Burtis (Detective Sweeney), Matt Briggs (Detective Epstein), Spencer Charters (Mr. Clark), Phyllis Barry (Madame Irene), Carlyle Moore, Jr. (Clark's Assistant), Marion "Peanuts" Byron, Jean Carmen, Patricia Parker (Lipstick Girls), Dorothy Granger (Miss Cole, Stenographer), Bobby Watson (Choreographer), Elise Cavanna (Miss Pilot, Radio Announcer), Otto Fries and Walter James (Mountaineers), True Boardman (Himself), Alfred P. James (Mule Driver), Stanley Blystone (Racing Car Driver), Nat Carr (Gas Station Proprietor), Joe Marba (Poolroom Proprietor), Lee Shumway (Policeman), Doris McMahon (Maid), June Brewster (Receptionist).

YOU MIGHT SAY THAT the comedy team of Bert Wheeler and Robert Woolsey is an acquired taste. Their output of feature-length films from 1929 to 1938 ranges from sublime to dreadful. Why Wheeler and Woolsey's popularity has not sustained throughout the years is somewhat of a mystery, for in the thirties, they were ranked above the Marx Brothers and second only to Laurel and Hardy in the public's eyes. Their initial Hollywood venture, the Technicolor *Rio Rita* (1929), cast them as mere

Hips, Hips, Hooray! (1934) Robert Woolsey as Doctor Bob Dudley along with sexy Thelma Todd as Amelia Frisby. (RF)

Hips, Hips, Hooray! (1934) Looks like Robert Woolsey and Thelma Todd have changed identities in this "gag" photo. (RF)

Hips, Hips, Hooray! (1934) Daisy Maxwell (Dorothy Lee), looking very sexy as Bert Wheeler's leading lady. (RF)

comic relief to the so-called stars Bebe Daniels and John Boles, who were overshadowed by the antics of this new team.

After a few shaky starts in primitive early talkies, Bert and Bob eventually hit their stride, churning out entertaining musical comedy vehicles, with Wheeler playing the dimwitted but likable love interest usually opposite adorable Dorothy Lee, while Robert Woolsey supplied a generous amount of wisecracks (a la Groucho Marx). Some of their better earlier entries included *Caught Plastered* (1931), *Hold 'em Jail* and *Girl Crazy* (both 1932), and the hilarious political spoof *Diplomaniacs* (1933), which is usually compared to the Marx Brothers classic *Duck Soup* of the same year.

But, for sheer uninterrupted pure Wheeler and Woolsey fare, none stands up better than their 1934 feature *Hips, Hips, Hooray!* This Pre-Code farce was able to sneak into release just prior to the revamping of the production code. Director Mark Sandrich proved to be a perfect choice in handling the antics of W&W, for after another entry entitled *Cockeyed Cavaliers* (1934), he graduated to the new Fred Astaire-Ginger Rogers unit. There, he turned out such musical classics as *Top Hat* (1935) and *Follow the Fleet* (1936).

Along with the aforementioned Dorothy Lee, the supporting cast is excellent, with the wonderful Thelma Todd delightfully keeping up with the boys. Thelma was currently under contract to Hal Roach, turning out short comedies in which she was teamed with Zasu Pitts and later with Patsy Kelly. A superb comedienne with brilliant timing and beauty to match, Miss Todd was always on loan to different studios and was quite active up until her untimely death in 1935 at the age of twenty-nine. Billed directly under Wheeler and Woolsey is singer Ruth Etting, who was later immortalized in the Doris Day/James Cagney vehicle *Love Me or Leave Me* (1955). However, she appears only in the first scene, in which she warbles "Keep Romance Alive" in the midst of a bevy of naked beauties taking baths, while her other numbers apparently ended up on the cutting room floor. Nevertheless, Miss Etting received a whopping sum of $10,000 with which she purchased a new house and fur coat!

Critic Andre Sennwald of *The New York Times* proclaimed that "there are three reasonably hilarious gags and perhaps fifty more that depend on whether you are for or against the ex-vaudeville clowns to begin with." Today there is a renewed interest in the films of Wheeler and Woolsey. True, they don't have the soul of a Laurel and Hardy, or the comic genius of the Marx Brothers. But what these films do possess is a record of two expert funnymen who crafted their style seamlessly with the sole purpose of making us laugh.

Midnight (1934)

An All-Star Production released by Universal Pictures. Produced by Carl Laemmle, Jr. Directed by Chester Erskine. Screenplay by Chester Erskine. Based on a play by Claire and Paul Sifton. Photography by William O. Steiner and George Webber. Edited by Leo Zoching. Set Decorations by Sam Corso. Makeup by Eddie Senz. Sound by C. A. Tuthill. Music by Victor Alix. 75 min.

Cast: Sidney Fox (Stella Weldon), O. P. Heggie (Edward Weldon), Henry Hull (Nolan), Margaret Wycherly (Mrs. Weldon), Lynne Overman (Joe Biggers), Katherine Wilson (Ada Biggers), Humphrey Bogart (Gar Boni), Richard Whorf (Arthur Weldon), Granville Bates (Henry McGrath), Cora Witherspoon (Elizabeth McGrath), Helen Flint (Ethel Saxon), Moffat Johnston (District Attorney Plunkett), Henry O'Neill (Ingersoll).

NOT TO BE CONFUSED WITH the superb screwball comedy of 1939, *Midnight* is one of those unfortunate films that never seems to be awarded the praise it deserves. A taut social melodrama, dramatizing the influence of a jury foreman responsible for the unjust execution of a woman, and the negative press he receives thereafter. Unfortunately, as the film unfolds, he finds his daughter has killed her gangster boyfriend after he has jilted her, similar to the events surrounding the convicted woman. What transpires makes for an unexpected surprise ending that might raise a few eyebrows in this totally forgotten 'Pre-Code' entry.

Filmed in 1933 at the Thomas Edison Studio in New York, at an incredibly meager budget of $50,000 (some short subjects had cost more to produce), this Universal release employed different members of the Broadway stage, utilizing their talents on a low budget. Humphrey Bogart, for instance, was appearing in a short-lived comedy called *The Mask and the Face* with Shirley Booth, Leo G. Carroll, and Judith Anderson, when his old drinking buddy, Lynne Overman, who'd already been cast

Midnight (1934) Convicted murderer Ethel Saxton (Helen Flint) prepares to "walk the last mile" to the electric chair. (RF)

Midnight (1934) Stella Weldon (Sidney Fox) flirts with newspaperman, Nolan (Henry Hull) as they await the execution. (RF)

in *Midnight*, informed Bogie that they were recasting for the part of Gar Boni, the small-time hood, after the original actor had fallen ill. Needing money desperately, Bogart accepted the small role reluctantly, since his last movie tenure in Hollywood had been a veritable disaster.

The star of *Midnight* was twenty-three-year-old Sidney Fox, today a forgotten actress, who unfortunately never achieved stardom. After only fifteen movies, she retired from movies later that year, following the release of the dreadful *Down to Their Last Yacht* (1934). By the late 1930s she was considered a has-been, and in 1942, died from an overdose of sleeping pills. She was only thirty-one.

Henry Hull, who plays the reporter Nolan, went on to become a favorite character actor in films like *Great Expectations* (1934), *Jesse James* (1939), and *High Sierra* (1941). In *Midnight*, we are fortunate to be able to see him in a leading role, playing a part similar to the ones he played on the New York stage. Another cast member, O. P. Heggie, who portrays the much put-upon jury foreman, is best remembered as the blind hermit in the classic Universal horror film *The Bride of Frankenstein*

Midnight (1934) Humphrey Bogart (in an early role) as Gar Boni, who is later shot and killed by Stella Weldon (Sidney Fox) whom he has spurned. (RF)

(1935). Also on hand, playing the mother, is the versatile actress Margaret Wycherly, whose screen career was capped years later when she landed her best screen role as James Cagney's Ma Barker-like mother in *White Heat* (1949).

Commercially, the film was a box-office failure because of lack of star power. But critically, the movie was praised, except for the performance by O. P. Heggie, who, as one critic noted, "repeatedly suffers at the top of his lungs." *The New York Times* called it "a story of unusual interest...a nervous and somewhat hysterical tale, blurred occasionally in the telling."

Years later, when Humphrey Bogart had reached the heights of a superstar, Universal reissued *Midnight*, re-christening it *Call It Murder*, with all publicity materials giving Bogart top billing!

Jimmy the Gent (1934)

A Warner Bros. Picture. Produced by Jack L. Warner. Directed by Michael Curtiz. Screenplay by Bertram Milhauser. Based on an original story by Laird Doyle and Ray Nazarro. Dialogue Director: Daniel Reed. Photography by Ira Morgan. Art Direction by Edras Hartley. Edited by Thomas Richards. Music by Leo F. Forbstein. Costumes by Orry-Kelly. Makeup by Perc Westmore. 67 min.

Cast: James Cagney (Jimmy Corrigan), Bette Davis (Joan Martin), Alice White (Mabel), Allen Jenkins (Louie), Arthur Hohl (Joe Rector/ Monty Barton), Alan Dinehart (James J. Wallingham), Philip Reed (Ronnie Gatston), Hobart Cavanaugh (The Imposter), Mayo Methot (Gladys Farrell), Ralf Harolde (Hendrickson), Joseph Sawyer (Mike), Philip Faversham (Blair), Nora Lane (Posy Barton), Joseph Crehan (Judge), Robert Warwick (Civil Judge), Merna Kennedy (Jitters), Renee Whitney (Bessie), Monica Bannister (Tea Assistant), Don Douglas (Man Drinking Tea), Bud Flanagan/Dennis O'Keefe (Chester Coote), Leonard Mudie (Man in Flower Shop), Harry Holman (Justice of the Peace), Camille Rovelle (File Clerk), Stanley Mack (Pete), Tom Costello (Grant), Ben Hendricks (Ferris), Billy West (Hally), Eddie Schubert (Tim), Lee Moran (Stew), Harry Wallace (Eddie), Robert Homans (Irish Cop), Milton Kibbee (Ambulance Driver), Howard Hickman (Doctor), Eula Guy (Nurse), Juliet Ware (Viola), Rickey Newell (Blonde), Lorena Layson (Brunette), Dick French (Second Young Man), Jay Eaton (Third Young Man), Harold Entwhistle (Reverend Amiel Bottsford), Charles Hickman (Bailiff), Olaf Hytten (Steward), Vesey O'Davoren (Second Steward), Lester Dorr (Chalmers), Pat Wing (Secretary).

Jimmy the Gent (1934) Jimmy Corrigan (James Cagney) is about to "lay it on the chin" of Charles Wallingham (Alan Dinehart) while Joan Martin (Bette Davis) and Lou (Allen Jenkins) approvingly look on. (RF)

BY 1934, IT WAS RATHER APPARENT that James Cagney's meteoric rise to stardom in only three short years was nothing short of incredible. After his huge success in the 1931 Warner Bros. gangster era saga *The Public Enemy*, Jim had become everybody's favorite tough guy. However, his clashes on the movie screen with the law were nothing compared to his off-screen battles with studio head Jack L. Warner for better wages and script approval. Now, Cagney, who was tiring of "tough guy" roles, wanted to do something entirely different, but Warner was adamant, stating that the public wanted Jim shooting it out with the police or slapping dames around!

When Cagney was handed the script for *Jimmy the Gent*, he threatened to walk out on his contract because his character was yet another hoodlum, and to make matters worse, a totally illiterate thug! Losing his battle with Warner, he appeared on the set on the first day of shooting and shocked the entire cast and crew with his new "look." Sporting an Erich von Stroheim haircut, and looking like a stereotyped Prussian general, he highlighted this appearance by adding fake bottle scars on the back of his clean-shaved head, to make it look as if he had been in numerous scuffles with various adversaries. The rebellious actor was taken aside by the film's director Michael Curtiz, who looked at Jim and pleaded in his thick Hungarian accent, "Why, Jeemy, why?" "You wanted hoodlum, well, you got hoodlum," was his quick reply, hoping that this would get back to "the Shvontz", Cagney's nickname for Jack Warner.

Based on a story entitled *The Heir Chaser* by Laird Doyle and Ray Nazzaro, the movie went into production with the working title *Always a Gent* and later changed to *Blondes and Bonds* before its eventual release under the title of *Jimmy the Gent*. A unique gangster-comedy much in the tradition of Edward G. Robinson's two excellent gangster spoofs *The Little Giant* (1938) and *A Slight Case of Murder* (1938), this film follows Jimmy Corrigan (Cagney), a two-bit hood who sets up his own racket of hunting down missing heirs to unclaimed estates, and then hiring a phony to pose as the rightful heir. Of course, Jimmy has a girlfriend, who works for a competitor who is in the same racket. His rival (Alan Dinehart) is deemed reputable, but we all know better! How this is all resolved, with Jimmy's girl finally seeing the light, is the highlight of this fast-paced, hysterical comedy, sprinkled with saucy dialogue and a magnificent supporting cast of excellent players from the Warner Bros. stock company.

Mordaunt Hall of *The New York Times* wrote, "Jimmy Cagney's latest pictorial feature, *Jimmy the Gent*, is a swift-paced comedy in which he gives another of his vigorous, incisive portrayals." And Richard Watts of the *New York Herald Tribune* added, "Mr. Cagney, his hair cropped short and his manner as incisive as ever, plays the head of the heir-chasing industry with all of his engaging and forthright candor…Best of the women is Alice White, as a punch-drunk tool of the heir-chasing racketeer. Miss Bette Davis is satisfactory as the heroine."

Men in White (1934)

A Metro Goldwyn-Mayer Release. Produced by Monta Bell. Directed by Richard Boleslawski. Screenplay by Waldemar Young. Based on the play by Sidney Kingsley. Photography by George Folsey. Music by William Axt. Edited by Frank Sullivan. Art Direction by Cedric Gibbons. Sound by Douglas Shearer. 74 min.

Cast: Clark Gable (Dr. Ferguson), Myrna Loy (Laura), Jean Hersholt (Dr. Hochberg), Elizabeth Allan (Barbara), Otto Kruger (Dr. Levine), C. Henry Gordon (Dr. Cunningham), Russell Hardie (Dr. Michaelson), Henry B. Walthall (Dr. McCabe), Wallace Ford (Shorty), Russell Hopton (Pete), Samuel S. Hinds (Dr. Gordon), Frank Puglia (Dr. Vitale), Leo Chalzel (Dr. Wren), Donald Douglas (Mac).

THROUGHOUT THE 1930S, movie audiences were drawn to the unselfish men and women nobly saving lives in the hospital melodramas that Hollywood was churning out. Following the release of such hits as *Night Nurse* (1931), *Life Begins* (1932), and *Private Worlds* (1935), studio heads began to take notice of the profitable receipts these films were chalking up. Eager to step on the bandwagon, MGM decided to buy the rights of the famous Dr. Kildare stories from their creator Max Brand. Unfortunately, the studio found, to its dismay, that Paramount Pictures had bought the rights from Brand a year earlier and had starred Joel McCrea in the first Kildare vehicle, *Internes Can't Take Money* (1937). Not exactly pleased with audience response from this initial venture, Paramount obligingly sold the rights to MGM, after which the studio produced nine of these hospital dramas with usually good results.

During this period, MGM was also trying to soften Clark Gable's screen image considerably. After numerous tough guy roles the time had come for producers to cast Gable as a young intern in the film *Men in White*, based on the Sidney Kingsley play. Hired to direct was Polish-born director Richard Boleslavsky. A master in undertaking difficult assignments, he would achieve the near impossible task of successfully guiding his actors through unfamiliar territory. He was the individual responsible for Irene Dunne's first successful venture into screwball comedy in *Theodora Goes Wild* (1936), and successfully cast tough guy Chester Morris in

Men in White (1934) Dr. George Ferguson (Clark Gable) tends to a patient, while adoring nurse, Barbara Denham (Elizabeth Allen) assists. Dr. Cunningham (C. Henry Gordon) has his doubts, though. (AB)

a western entitled *Three Godfathers* (1936). But his two biggest productions were *Rasputin and the Empress* (1933), which starred the three Barrymores, and the 1935 version of *Les Miserables* with Fredric March and Charles Laughton.

Men in White, which deals with the everyday life of doctors, interns, and nurses in a Manhattan hospital, reveals the long working hours and stressful existence common to this profession. It also depicts an emotionless view of death by some of the other interns, which in its day would have shocked most audiences. The abortion issue, which is more than hinted at in the film, raised many eyebrows in the 1930s. Made at the end of Hollywood's Pre-Code era, this scene would have definitely been eliminated if it were released only months later!

Even so, *Men in White* doesn't work on all levels as well as earlier hospital ventures. There are certain scenes that come off as laughable to today's audiences, like the typical MGM crying scene by Mr. Gable (undoubtedly at Louis B. Mayer's behest). Also, Myrna Loy, looking extremely emotionless throughout, is totally wasted in a most unsympathetic role and probably would have fared much better in the part played by Elizabeth Allan (although the latter is perfect in the part and practically steals the whole picture as it is).

The movie did well both financially and critically, with most of the plaudits aimed at Gable. As an example, the *Motion Picture Herald* commented, "It is a film long to be remembered—fine and honest. In the scene with the little sick girl, Gable does a remarkable acting job. And he has your sympathy all through the episode with the nurse who dies as a result of an operation that should not have been performed. (Jean) Hersholt tops all previous performances. And what a trooper Elizabeth Allan is! Otto Kruger, C. Henry Gordon, too."

Death Takes a Holiday (1934)

Paramount Pictures. Produced by E. Lloyd Sheldon. Directed by Mitchell Leisen. Screenplay by Maxwell Anderson and Gladys Lehman from the play by Alberto Casella as adapted by Walter Ferris. Photography by Charles Lang. Sound by Harold Lewis. 78 min.

Cast: Fredric March (Prince Sirki), Evelyn Venable (Grazia), Sir Guy Standing (Duke Lambert), Katherine Alexander (Alda), Gail Patrick (Rhoda), Helen Westley (Stephanie), Kathleen Howard (Princess Maria), Kent Taylor (Corrado), Henry Travers (Baron Cesaria), G. P. Huntley, Jr. (Eric), Otto Hoffman (Fedele), Edward Van Sloan (Dr. Valle), Hector Sarno (Pietro), Frank Yaconelli (Vendor), Anna De Linsky (Maid).

DEATH TAKES A HOLIDAY WAS BASED ON a play by a young Italian writer named Alberto Casella, who'd been inspired to write a story while he was fighting in the trenches in World War I. As he watched his comrades falling in battle around him, he pondered what it would be like if Death decided to stop claiming the lives of men and go on a vacation? This idea intrigued him, and after the Armistice, he decided to write a play based on this premise. He called his rather black comedy *Death Takes a Holiday*. It opens with Death, tiring of his loneliness, deciding to find out why mortals are so desperate to cling onto life and why they fear his presence. To accomplish this ruse, he poses as a recently deceased Prince and announces that he will spend a three-day visit with a duke in his posh Italian villa. As it turns out, he begins to experience what life is all about, learning about its ups and downs, and, more importantly, the meaning of love with a young Italian beauty named Grazia.

A big hit in Italy and in Europe, the play was written as a black comedy, but when it eventually toured the United States, it took on darker, more brooding characteristics. The reason for this was that producer Lee Shubert hired playwright Walter Ferris, and his interpretation of Death

Death Takes a Holiday (1934) Grazia (Evelyn Venable) is charmed by Prince Sirki (Fredric March). (RF)

gave it a more serious outlook, presenting death as a grim reaper imposed on a frightened society. It was in this capacity that the play opened on Broadway in 1929 with character actor Philip Merivale taking on the title role with lovely Rose Hobart as Grazia. Critics received the play rather coolly, but public reaction grew steadily until the play became one of the season's hottest properties!

In 1933, Paramount Pictures bought the screen rights and cast their biggest star, Fredric March in the lead with the beautiful but forgotten young actress Evelyn Venable opposite him. Virginia-born Venable was a twenty-one year old farm girl from an old-fashioned American family, who only had one movie under her belt at the time, entitled *Cradle Song* (1933). By the time she made *Death Takes a Holiday* (released on March 30th, 1934), she had gained some positive press while touring with producer Walter Hampden's company of touring artists. Here, she gives a sensitively warm performance as the doomed lover Grazia, who accompanies Death into the darkness of the eternity's unknown. Remarkably, Miss Venable's contract stated that she could not and would not

Death Takes a Holiday (1934) Fredric March and Evelyn Venable. (RF)

indulge in any on-screen kissing scenes, a clause that was enforced by her strict college professor father, skeptical about his daughter's profession. Despite the positive reviews she received for *Death Takes a Holiday*, this ridiculous stipulation made good roles difficult to come by for the young actress, who would later appear in movies like *Alice Adams* (1935) opposite Katharine Hepburn and Fred MacMurray, and *Vagabond Lady* (also 1935) with Robert Young. Her best remembered role was as the Blue Fairy in Walt Disney's 1940 animated classic *Pinocchio*, in which the character was modeled after her, with Venable supplying the voice as well.

As for Fredric March, he previously won an Oscar as best actor for his performance in *Dr. Jekyll and Mr. Hyde* (1931), and later for the outstanding *The Best Years of Our Lives* (1946). Other notable entries in his long career included *The Sign of the Cross* (1932), *Design for Living* (1933), *The Barretts of Wimpole Street* (1934) as Robert Browning, *Anna Karenina* (1935) as Count Vronsky, *Anthony Adverse* (1936), the original *A Star is Born* and *Nothing Sacred* (both 1937), *Death of a Salesman* (1951) as Willy Loman, *Inherit the Wind* (1960), and many more!

Director Mitchell Leisen, whose film credits consisted mainly of romantic comedies and dramas, was known as a "woman's director" because of his fine handling of some of the most difficult actresses in Hollywood. His thorough professionalism was highly praised throughout the film industry and he enjoyed a rather prolific (but brief) period in the late 1930s when he was awarded some excellent screenplays by some of the best writers in the industry, like Billy Wilder and Preston Sturges, before they became first-rate directors in their own right!

You're Telling Me! (1934)

Paramount Pictures. Produced by William Le Baron. Directed by Erle C. Kenton. Screenplay by Walter De Leon and Paul M. Jones. Adapted from "Mr. Bisbee's Princess," a 1925 Redbook Magazine short story by Julian Leonard Street. Dialogue by J. P. McEvoy. Photographed by Alfred Gilks. Art Direction by Hans Dreier and Robert Odell. Edited by Otho Hovering. Sound by Earl S. Hayman. 67 min.

Cast: W. C. Fields (Sam Bisbee), Joan Marsh (Pauline Bisbee), Larry "Buster" Crabbe (Bob Murchinson), Adrienne Ames (Princess Lescaboura), Louise Carter (Mrs. Bessie Bisbee), Kathleen Howard (Mrs. Murchinson), James B. "Pop" Kenton (Doc Beebe), Robert McKenzie (Charlie Bogle), George Irving (President of the Tire Company), Jerry Stewart (Frobisher), Del Henderson (Mayer Brown), Nora Cecil (Mrs. Price), George MacQuarrie (Crabbe), John M. Sullivan (Gray), Vernon Dent (Fat man in train), Tammany Young (Caddy), Lee Phelps (First Cop), Dorothy Vernon Bay (Mrs. Kendall), Edward Le Saint (Conductor), Elise Cavanna (Mrs. Smith), Eddie Baker (Motorcycle cop escort), James C. Morton (George Smith), Billy Engle (First lounger), George Ovey (Second lounger), Al Hart (Third lounger), Alfred Del Cambre (Phil Cummings), Frederic Sullivan (Mr. Murchinson), William Robyns (Postman), Harold Berquist (Doorman), Frank O'Connor (Second cop), Florence Enright (Mrs. Kelly), Isabelle La Mal (Rosita), Hal Craig (Motor cop), Josephine Whittell (Bit Part).

BY 1934, COMEDIAN W. C. FIELDS was able to reflect on his moderately successful film career with a certain degree of pride. His silent period, which began in 1915 with a one-reel comedy entitled *Pool Sharks*, is a curio at best, featuring his famous pool routine, which he used repeatedly when he was with the *Ziegfeld Follies*. After a few other rather weak outings, Fields was later cast in some feature-length comedies, most no-

You're Telling Me! (1934) Sam Bisbee (W. C. Fields) is greeted by his servants. (RF)

tably *Sally of the Sawdust* (1925) and *It's the Old Army Game* (1926). The comedian liked these two plot lines so much that he later remade them both after talkies arrived, naming them *Poppy* (1936) and his timeless classic *It's a Gift* (1934).

When talkies were in full swing, Fields was able to sign a contract with Paramount Pictures after appearing in one film for Warners entitled *Her Majesty Love* (1931). The problem was that Paramount knew that the veteran comedian had talent, but felt that he couldn't sustain a feature film alone and that he should be teamed with somebody else. After all, the Marx Brothers and Laurel and Hardy were packing them in at the box-office, so why not experiment with another "new" team? So, Fields went to work sharing the spotlight with other comics on the Paramount lot. It seemed for a while that the studio executives were content with Allison Skipworth as his partner, who appeared in three movies with him, *If I Had a Million* (1932), *Tillie and Gus* (1933), and *Six of a Kind* (1934). However, Fields was not satisfied with the results and convinced the studio to cast him as a single in yet another remake of one of his earlier successes entitled *So's Your Old Man* (1926). The powers that be finally agreed and gave W. C. the "go-ahead" to begin his first solo outing since his moderately successful four short subjects with Mack Sennett in 1933.

Based on a 1925 *Redbook* magazine short story by Julien Leonard Street entitled "Mr. Bisbee's Princess," the picture took on the rather absurd title of *You're Telling Me!* Directed by Mack Sennett graduate Erle C. Kenton, and shot in a small town near Los Angeles called Sierra Madre, the movie company was met with much trouble during the shooting. According to the Hollywood trade papers: *The cast of* You're Telling Me! *shot some scenes in the town of Sierra Madre, but now Paramount and the cast have declared an embargo on the town. They were there this week (February 3, 1934) to shoot scenes. They rented a frame cottage. When time came to record with camera and sound, the lady of the house next to the studio cottage turned on her radio. Gnashing of teeth prevailed. They approached the lady and she said she had the right to play her own radio in her own sitting room. The assistant director paid her ten dollars to shut it off. More scenes had to be shot the next day, and when Fields and his troop got to Sierra Madre bright and early, a little boy ran indoors, told his mother the movie people were there, and in a jiffy the radio was going again. Then the little boy and his brother were out in the yard not ten feet from the scene of action playing hockey with cans and broomsticks, yelling their heads off. An ambassador from the movie outing went to see the woman, but she wanted one hundred dollars to turn off her radio and get the kids inside. At that point, the movie people did an automobile trip in a Paul Revere style to the office of the Sierra Madre Chamber of Commerce and the chief of police. The chief and the chamber secretary hurried up to talk things over with the lady and asked her in the name of civic pride to lay off—which she did for payment of one hundred and fifty dollars. But as the shooting was starting, the lady two doors away and her family moved a bunch of card tables into the front yard and this ambitious woman began selling sandwiches and lemonade to all the curious who had been attracted to the scene. In between clinks of glasses and the hum of chatter, Fields went through the scenes of his script, but all you have to do now is say Sierra Madre to Bill (Fields) and he will fall into a swoon...*

So, there we have a perfect idea for a forthcoming Fields film...

When the picture wrapped, it received generally good notices, with critics citing that W. C. Fields could "hold his own in a feature-length picture." The film mixes comedy and pathos successfully, the latter being a rarity in any Fields film. Also, audiences are treated to his classic golf routine, which he did in vaudeville and again in his 1930 two-reeler, *The Golf Specialist.*

As an added note, the catchy music heard on the radio at the beginning of the film is from the currently released Paramount musical *Sitting Pretty* entitled "Good Morning Glory," which starred Jack Oakie, Jack Haley, and Ginger Rogers.

Viva Villa! (1934)

A Metro-Goldwyn-Mayer Picture. Produced by David O. Selznick. Directed by Jack Conway. Suggested by the book by Edgcumb Pinchon and O. B. Stade. Screenplay by Ben Hecht. Edited by Robert J. Kern. Photography by James Wong Howe and Charles G. Clarke. Assistant Directors: Art Rosson and Johnny Walters. Musical Consulting by Juan Aguilar. Interior Decorations by Edwin B. Willis. Technical Advisor: Carlos Novarro. Technical Associate: Matias Santoyo. Sound by Douglas Shearer. Art Direction by Harry Oliver. Costumes by Dolly Tree. Music by Herbert Stothart. Original Running Time: 115 min.

Cast: Wallace Beery (Pancho Villa), Fay Wray (Teresa), Leo Carrillo (Sierra), Donald Cook (Don Felipe), Stuart Erwin (Johnny Sykes), George E. Stone (Chavito), Joseph Schildkraut (Pascal), Henry B. Walthall (Madero), Katherine DeMille (Rosita), David Durand (Bugle Boy), Phillip Coover (Villa as a Boy), Frank Puglia (Father), John Merkel (Pascal's Aide), Charles Stevens, Steve Clemento, Pedro Regas and George Regas (Staff), Carlos De Valdez (Old Man), Harry Cording (Majordomo), Sam Godfrey (Prosecuting Attorney), Nigel de Brulier (Political Judge), Charles Requa, Tom Ricketts (Grandees), Clarence Hummel Wilson (Jail Official), James Martin (Mexican Officer), Anita Gordiana (Dancer), Francis McDonald (Villa's Man), Harry Semels (Soldier), Julien Rivero (Telegraph Operator), Bob McKenzie (Bartender), Dan Dix (Drunkard), Paul Stanton (Newspaper Man), Mischa Auer (Military Attache), Belle Mitchell (Spanish Wife), John Davidson, Brandon Hurst, Leonard Mudie (Statesmen), Herbert Prior, Emil Chautard (Generals), Adrian Rosley, Hector Sarno, Henry Armetta (Mendoza Brothers), Ralph Bushman/Francis X. Bushman, Jr. (Calloway), Arthur Treacher (English Reporter), William Von Brincken (German Reporter), Andre Cheron (French Reporter), Michael Visaroff (Russian Reporter), Shirley Chambers (Wrong Girl), Arthur Thalasso (Butcher), Chris-Pin Martin, Nick de Ruiz (Peons).

DAVID O. SELZNICK'S NAME has become synonymous with quality motion pictures. He gained his reputation when he was under contract to RKO (Radio-Keith-Orpheum) Studios, producing some of their biggest blockbusters from 1932-33. *Morning Glory, Little Women*, and *King Kong* were just a few of his hits, which convinced his father-in-law, MGM mogul Louis B. Mayer, to sign on the talented production chief at his Culver City studio to fill in for the ailing Irving Thalberg. Once there, the erstwhile producer delivered solid box-office hits, which were usually based on plays (*Dinner at Eight*) or literary works (*David Copperfield, A Tale of Two Cities* and *Anna Karenina*). One of his brightest accomplishments was the sprawling action-drama *Viva Villa!*, based on the life of Francisco "Pancho" Villa, but with total disregard for fact.

Due to Selznick's winning record, the studio provided him with Howard Hawks, a top-flight director, who had an incredible reputation for tackling difficult projects, along with one of Hollywood's best screenwriters, Ben Hecht. As if this wasn't enough, MGM granted Hawks permission to shoot *Viva Villa!* in Mexico (a rarity, particularly in those days when travel, especially in rural areas, was almost unheard of). The casting of Pancho Villa was another surprise, since the studio executives decided on serio-comic star Wallace Beery. This decision was not met with popular approval by the Mexican population, whose concerns were eventually eliminated after they saw the first few "rushes". A perfect bit of casting saw Lee Tracy in the role of Johnny Sykes, the American reporter who befriends Villa, and eventually becomes his conscience as well as his guiding light. At this time, Tracy's career was growing in leaps and bounds, having just ended a successful stay with Warner Bros. Rather than remaining at that studio, where he was playing second fiddle to James Cagney, he signed on with MGM to advance his career further.

Unfortunately, filming of the movie did not go smoothly right from the beginning. When the film company arrived in Mexico, they were invited by the local politicians to a dinner in their honor. With many dignitaries present that evening, they were immediately taken aback by the absence of their star. Insulted, they insisted on the dismissal of Beery, who actually had a good reason for not being present. After each shooting day would end, the actor would personally fly his private plane back to Los Angeles religiously so that he could be with his wife, who was recuperating from an operation. However, when Beery returned, he was ordered to "settle the rough waters" by accepting luncheon invitations with the Mexican authorities.

Viva Villa! (1934) Pancho Villa (Wallace Beery) is attacked by Don Felipe de Castillo (Donald Cook) after he witnesses Pancho beating his sister, Teresa (Fay Wray) with a bullwhip. (AB)

As if that weren't enough, when the picture just about "wrapped," the Mexican military decided to send the film company off with a farewell parade in their honor. Reportedly, Lee Tracy, a notorious drinker, had been out the night before celebrating. In the middle of the festivities, he came out onto the balcony of his hotel room, exposed himself, and urinated on the passing soldiers, infuriating the Mexican officials, who ordered his immediate arrest. Worried about a Mexican embargo on their product, Louis B. Mayer instructed director Hawks to testify against the penitent actor, whose future was not looking too promising at present. The director, being a friend (and drinking buddy) of Tracy's, refused, which prompted his immediate dismissal, leaving the studio executives the unpleasant task of "calming things down." After his incarceration, Lee Tracy was released from his contract and would thereafter be relegated to "B" movies forever.

Just when Louis B. Mayer thought that he could breathe a sigh of relief, another tragic incident occurred. En route back to Hollywood, the plane, which carried thousands of feet of exposed film ready for editing, crashed and was never recovered. After months of work, all the studio had was some location footage and establishing shots taken by a second unit director, and a few reels of actual footage, which had been sent on ahead, prior to the tragedy. Rather than scrapping the whole project, director Jack Conway was summoned to salvage what little footage remained and reshoot the rest in Culver City.

With Lee Tracy now contracted to RKO, producer David O. Selznick signed light comedian Stuart Erwin to play the role of Johnny Sykes. Evidently, there was much rewriting involved due to this change in casting, because both actors' styles contrasted enormously. The final result is pleasing, with Erwin definitely making the grade. However, it would have been fascinating to see what kind of an edge Lee Tracy would have given to the role!

Although Wallace Beery missed out on being nominated for his portrayal of the controversial Mexican hero, the film was nominated for Best Picture, Best Screenplay, and Best Sound Recording, but lost on all three counts. The film did, however, win the obscure category of Best Assistant Director (John Waters).

The Black Cat (1934)

A Universal Picture. Produced by Carl Laemmle, Jr. Directed by Edgar G. Ulmer. Supervised by E. M. Asher. Screenplay by Peter Ruric (based on a story by Edgar Ulmer and Peter Ruric, suggested by *The Black Cat* by Edgar Allan Poe). Photography by John J. Mescall. Art Direction by Charles D. Hall. Musical Direction by Heinz Roemheld. Edited by Ray Curtiss. Continuity by Tom Kilpatrick. Makeup by Jack Pearce. Special Effects by John P. Fulton. Assistant Directors: W. J. Reiter and Sam Weisenthal. Camera Operator: King Gray. 65 min.

Cast: Boris Karloff (Hjalmar Poelzig), Bela Lugosi (Dr. Vitus Werdegast), David Manners (Peter Alison), Jacqueline Wells/Julie Bishop (Joan Alison), Lucille Lund (Karen), Egon Brecher (The Majordomo), Harry Cording (Thamal), Albert Conti (The Lieutenant), Henry Armetta (The Sergeant), Anna Duncan (The Maid), Herman Bing (Car Steward), George Davis (Bus Driver), Andre Cheron (Conductor), Luis Alberni (Train Steward), Alphonse Martell (Porter), Tony Marlow (Patrolman), Paul Weigel (Station Master), Albert Polet (Waiter), Rodney Hildebrand (Brakeman), Virginia Ainsworth, Michael Mark, Symona Boniface, Paul Panzer, Lois January, King Baggot, Peggy Terry (Satanists), John Carradine (Organist).

AFTER THE CRITICAL AND FINANCIAL successes of Universal's *Dracula* and *Frankenstein* in 1931, it was only a matter of time before the studio would dream up the idea of teaming its two leading horror stars, Bela Lugosi and Boris Karloff. No more based on Edgar Allan Poe's *The Black Cat* than *The Raven* was in 1935, this was the first of many teamings of the duo. Since the studio was still in the earlier stages of establishing the Lugosi and Karloff characters, this initial venture seems rather odd, since it appears that the two stars were cast in each other's roles. In this, Lugosi is cast more or less as the hero, while Karloff's character is without any redeemable qualities. In their next film together, this casting problem

371

The Black Cat (1934) Peter Alison (David Manners) carries his new bride, Joan (Jacqueline Wells/Julie Bishop) to their bedroom. It seems that Miss Wells is carried by someone throughout the entire picture. (RF)

would be remedied with Lugosi playing the embodiment of evil, and Karloff more sympathetic.

Shot in nineteen days on a meager budget of $95,745 and running a mere 65 minutes, there is not a wasted frame in *The Black Cat*. Director Edgar G. Ulmer, a former set designer in Germany, began his career with Max Reinhardt's stage productions. Immigrating to America, he eventually came to Hollywood where he worked with F. W. Murnau, assisting him on two of his most famous classics: *Sunrise* (1927) and *Tabu* (1931). Before this, his magnificent set designs for the 1925 Lon Chaney chiller *The Phantom of the Opera* caught the eye of Universal studio head, Carl Laemmle, whose son, Carl Laemmle, Jr. would later give Ulmer his first chance to direct. According to some sources, it was Edgar Ulmer who dreamed up the idea of teaming the two horror stars, in what he hoped would be a German style horror picture.

The outstanding photography by John Mescall was done in a grand scale fashion, utilizing every facet of the art deco set designs and mov-

The Black Cat (1934) Dr. Vitus Werdegast (Bela Lugosi) is shocked to find the corpse of his deceased wife preserved in the home of Hjalmar Poetzig (Boris Karloff). (RF)

The Black Cat (1934) Devil worshipper Hjalmar Poetzig (Boris Karloff) has now married the daughter of Dr. Werdegast, Karen (Lucille Lund). (RF)

ing the camera freely throughout the various rooms. Apparently Mescall must have also made a good impression on the studio's leading director, James Whale, because Whale would go on to use him exclusively in films like *The Bride of Frankenstein* (1935), *Showboat* (1936), and *The Road Back* (1937). Sadly, Mescall's career was curtailed by his acute alcoholism.

While *The Black Cat* was being edited for preview, the Hays Office was only months away from setting their censorship standards into motion. By this time, many civic groups were fed up with the amount of sex and violence, which permeated the screen, and *The Black Cat* was considered far worse. By 1934 standards, this was considered pretty potent stuff, with its daring subject matter taking on Satanism, perversity, sadism, and even a hint of necrophilia thrown in for good measure! With all of this negative publicity, the film did rather spectacularly at the box-office. Chalking up a profit of $140,000, it was one of Universal's highest grossing pictures that year. Also, it was one of the few 'Pre-Code' releases that was never reissued in the 1940s (wonder why?). In Great Britain, it was retitled *The House of Doom* and received an "H" (Horrific) rating, which is equivalent to todays "X" rating in America.

Born to Be Bad (1934)

A 20ᵗʰ Century Pictures/United Artists Presentation. Produced by Darryl F. Zanuck. Directed by Lowell Sherman. Story, dialogue and adaptation by Ralph Graves. Continuity by Harrison Jacobs. Photography by Barney McGill. Edited by Maurice Wright. Musical Direction by Alfred Newman. Art Direction by Richard Day and Joseph Wright. 61 min.

Cast: Loretta Young (Letty Strong), Cary Grant (Malcolm Trevor), Jackie Kelk (Mickey), Henry Travers (Fuzzy), Russell Hopton (Steve Karns), Andrew Tombes (Max Lieber), Howard Lang (Doctor Dropsy), Harry Green (Adolph), Marion Burns (Alice Trevor), Paul Harvey (Lawyer), Charles Coleman (Butler), Matthew Briggs (Truant Officer), Geneva Mitchell (Miss Crawford).

A FILM WHICH NEVER SEEMS to turn up anywhere, except in revival houses and more recently on DVD, *Born to Be Bad* is one of those pictures which is handicapped by a trashy script and unnecessary tampering by the Hays Office (which is evident through its extremely short running time). Written by ex-silent screen star Ralph Graves, it was apparent that some additional footage involving Letty Strong's affairs with her manager and his clients, plus the incestuous relationship with her little son, which is only hinted at, were deemed objectionable by the production code.

Also, when viewed today in these "politically correct" times, audiences tend to wince at the character of Adolph (portrayed by character actor Harry Green), who makes his interpretation of the stereotyped shyster Jewish lawyer totally offensive. Not to defend filmmakers in the early days, but rather to put their actions into perspective, it should be pointed out that in the twenties and thirties directors were on tight budgets and had to rely on stereotypes to get their points across rather than wasting complete character studies on secondary characters. This was a much easier way to get to the point, and these "fixed notions" were used

Born to Be Bad (1934) Letty Strong (Loretta Young) is giving "Fuzzy" (Henry Travers) some cheap thrills as he fastens her dress for her. (AB)

extensively throughout the era. Blacks, Jews, Italians, Irish, Polish, and especially Asians were fair game for being poked fun of, and today it seems pretty hard to digest.

Actor/director Lowell Sherman does his best with his cast and is given the challenging task of directing Loretta Young in a most atypical role. Usually cast as the "victimized heroine," (during this period anyway), or a product of the Depression, she would always overcome difficult odds and marry the rich young millionaire or the local boy who was assured of prosperity at the conclusion of the final reel. On the other hand, in *Born to Be Bad* she's already a victim who uses sex and deceit to climb the lad-

Born to Be Bad (1934) Loretta Young as Letty Strong is about to blackmail her son's guardian with an incriminating recording. (AB)

Born to Be Bad (1934) Carrying "mother love" a bit too far. Mickey Strong (Jackie Kelk) and his mother, Letty (Loretta Young), in a scene that must have raised the ire of the censors considerably. (AB)

der of success. If this all sounds familiar, MGM tried it already with Jean Harlow in *Red-Headed Woman* in 1932, and Warners followed suit with Barbara Stanwyck in the excellent "Pre-Code" title *Baby Face* the following year. Along with *I'm No Angel* (1933) starring Mae West and *The Story of Temple Drake* (1933) starring Miriam Hopkins, these four films were

Born to Be Bad (1934) Poster art. (RF)

the main reasons for the censorship code which clamped down on Hollywood's rather "matter-of-fact" views on sex, violence, drugs, and other assorted vices. By the time *Born to Be Bad* was about to be released, it was too late, for already stringent restrictions had to be enforced prior to its initial run. This is too bad, in a way, for it would be interesting to see if additional footage would have saved the film. As it is, Cary Grant is extremely ill at ease, giving one of his worst performances. Luckily, he was to find his screen persona as the suave, debonair lothario when he learned to relax and withdraw all self-consciousness shortly after. Child star Jackie Kelk is probably the main reason why the film just doesn't work. After getting his start in radio, this was to be his first film. As it is, he comes across as the most obnoxious brat ever cast in a movie, and luckily was never heard from again, except in bit parts in the 1950s. Loretta Young's performance is probably the only saving grace that the film has, even though her character is so unlikable. As a matter of fact, none of the cast is very likeable, which gives the viewer absolutely no one to root for!

If I'm being unkind to *Born to Be Bad*, the reason is, it deserves it! One of the film's few positive aspects is its short running time (61 minutes). The film does move indeed, and one does not feel short changed as one might if it were a two-hour movie! Some critics at the time felt totally ripped off, with Mordant Hall of *The New York Times* whining, "Ralph Graves, who has given several interesting performances, is responsible for the narrative of *Born to Be Bad*. If this opus is any criterion of Mr. Graves' literary skill, he is scarcely to be congratulated on having temporarily abandoned his acting. It is a hopelessly unintelligent hodgepodge, wherein Loretta Young and Cary Grant have the misfortune to be cast in the leading roles."

Murder on the Blackboard (1934)

RKO Radio Picture. Produced by Pandro S. Berman. Associate Producer: Kenneth MacGowan. Directed by George Archainbaud. Screenplay by Willis Goldbeck from a novel by Stuart Palmer. Photography by Nicholas Musuraca. Original Music by Max Steiner and Bernhard Kaun. Edited by Archie Marshek. Art Direction by Albert S. D'Agostino and Van Nest Polglase. Costumes by Walter Plunkett. Assistant Director: Thomas Atkins. Sound by John L. Cass. Assistant Cameraman: Willard Booth. Camera Operator: Frank Redman. 72 min.

Cast: Edna May Oliver (Hildegarde Withers), James Gleason (Inspector Oscar Piper), Bruce Cabot (Addison "Ad" Stevens), Gertrude Michael (Jane Davis), Regis Toomey (Detective "Smiley" North), Tully Marshall (Mr. MacFarland), Frederick Vogeding (Otto Schweitzer), Edgar Kennedy (Detective Donahue), Jackie Searl (Leland Stanford Jones), Barbara Fritchie (Louise Halloran), Gustav von Seyffertitz (Dr. Max Von Immen), Tom Herbert (Detective McTeague), Jed Prouty (Dr. Levine), Wade Boteler (Bearded Diner), Tommy Bupp (School Boy), Frank Mills (Diner Counterman), Monte Vandergift (Policeman).

THE DETECTIVE OR GUMSHOE in film has been a popular staple since the time movies began. Super-sleuths like Sherlock Holmes, Nick Charles, Charlie Chan, Ellery Queen, Bulldog Drummond, Miss Marple, and Philip Marlowe have been dazzling audiences for decades, solving near impossible murders and various other assorted crimes. As a matter of fact, many of these popular detectives would eventually be featured in their own series, with varying degrees of success. One of these, the Hildegarde Withers and Inspector Piper series, one of the most forgotten (until recently), still holds up rather well. Based on a series of stories written by Stuart Palmer, RKO Radio Pictures purchased the rights from the author for a song, casting the wonderfully eccentric Edna May Oliver as the fud-

Murder on the Blackboard (1934) Edna May Oliver is back again as schoolmarm, Hildegarde Martha Withers with James Gleason as Inspector Oscar Piper. (RF)

dy-duddy schoolmarm Hildegarde Martha Withers, who has a penchant for solving crimes on the side. Also cast as the gruff Inspector Oscar Piper was character actor James Gleason, whose personality contrasts strikingly and delightfully with that of spinsterish Oliver.

In 1932, RKO released the first of six of these Hildegarde Withers murder mysteries entitled *The Penguin Pool Murder*, which convinced exhibitors and the studio that more of this series would soon follow. The second was *Murder on the Blackboard*, reuniting the two stars with excellent results, and bringing back two of the supporting cast members from the first outing: Edgar Kennedy as a bumbling cop and Gustav von Seyffertitz as Doctor Von Immen. This and the third offering in the series, *Murder on a Honeymoon* (1935), were the best of the six, and kept the series moving at full steam. Sadly, Edna May Oliver left RKO at the end of 1934 and signed a more lucrative contract with MGM. There, she was cast in some of her finest character roles, as Aunt Betsey Trotwood in *David Copperfield* (1935), Miss Pross in *A Tale of Two Cities* (1935), and as haughty Lady Catherine de Bourgh in *Pride and Prejudice* (1940).

Murder on the Blackboard (1934) There's still some "gas" left in the tank between these two middle-aged sleuths…Edna May Oliver and James Gleason getting rather familiar. (RF)

Back at RKO, studio executives, anxious to continue with the Hildegarde Withers/Inspector Piper series, cast character comedienne Helen Broderick (mother of Broderick Crawford) to star in the next outing, which was entitled *Murder on a Bridle Path* (1936). Unfortunately, this entry proved a disaster due to a poor script and lack of chemistry that had previously existed between Miss Oliver and James Gleason. After reading the reviews in the trades, Miss Broderick wisely bowed out of the role, resulting in the studio hiring the delightfully dithery comedienne Zasu Pitts as the third Miss Withers. This adventure, *The Plot Thickens* (1936), was a big improvement over the previous film, and it seemed that the series was once again back on track. Unfortunately, the next release proved to be the worst of all. *Forty Naughty Girls* (1937), which relied more on low knock-about comedy than on the murder mystery, was so bad that RKO finally gave up the ghost and decided to end the production of these moderately successful programmers.

In reevaluating the series as a whole, one thing is certain: the first three entries remain an excellent example of a perfect teaming working in total harmony. It's just a shame that Edna May Oliver left RKO for greener pastures. On the other hand, we should be grateful that *The Penguin Pool Murder*, *Murder on the Blackboard*, and *Murder on a Honeymoon* are all first rate!

Cockeyed Cavaliers (1934)

RKO Radio Pictures. Produced by Pandro S. Berman. Directed by Mark Sandrich. Screenplay by Edward Kaufman and Ben Holmes. Additional Dialogue by Grant Garrett and Ralph Spence. Art Direction by Van Nest Polglase and Carroll Clark. Costumes by Walter Plunkett. Photography by David Abel. Photographic Effects by Vernon Walker. Musical Direction by Roy Webb. Music and Lyrics by Will Jason and Val Burton. Edited by Jack Kitchin. 72 min.

Cast: Bert Wheeler (Bert), Robert Woolsey (Bob), Thelma Todd (Lady Genevieve), Dorothy Lee (Mary Ann Dale), Noah Beery (the Baron), Robert Greig (The Duke of Weskit), Henry Sedley (The Baron's Friend), Franklin Pangborn (Town Crier), Alfred P. James (Squire Dale), Jack Norton (The King's Physician), Snub Pollard (The Physician's Assistant), Kate Price (Maid), Frank Mills (Brawler), Kewpie Morgan (Andrew), Billy Gilbert (Landlord), Charlie Hall (Coachman), Kit Guard (Peasant).

AFTER THE RELEASE OF Bert Wheeler and Robert Woolsey's previous hit, *Hips, Hips, Hooray!* (1934), RKO proposed that their next project was to be a college comedy entitled *Frat Heads*. The Marx Brothers, Buster Keaton, and Harold Lloyd had already explored this area thoroughly in their films *Horse Feathers* (1932), *College* (1927), and *The Freshman* (1925), respectively. However, over at the Hal Roach Studio, Laurel and Hardy had been raking in the profits with their recent film, *The Devil's Brother*, which was based on the 1830 opera, *Fra Diavolo* by Daniel Francois Auber, and Eddie Cantor had just made another successful venture for Samuel Goldwyn entitled *Roman Scandals*. As a result, RKO decided to scrap the college film and cast their profitable comics in a period picture entitled *Cockeyed Cavaliers*.

Bringing back director Mark Sandrich, who guided the boys so successfully in their previous effort, was a good move because he apparently

Cockeyed Cavaliers (1934) Five young singing barmaids showing some "girlish laughter." They are Jean Castle, Charlotte Stevens, Josephine Smith, Kay McCoy and June Earl, all unbilled, of course. (RF)

understood comedy and soon was to be graduated to the Fred Astaire/ Ginger Rogers unit in musical classics like *Top Hat* (1935) and *Follow the Fleet* (1936). Bert and Bob have never been better than in this very funny and quite racy laugh fest filled with great "one-liners" and catchy tunes including "And the Big Bad Wolf Was Dead" and "Dilly Dally", both written by Will Jason and Val Burton. Adorable Dorothy Lee was once again delightfully teamed with Bert Wheeler, while beautiful Thelma Todd (looking quite fetching here in period garb as she did in *The Devil's Brother*) was once again teamed with Bob Woolsey for some very spicy gags.

What also makes this comedy so much fun is its cast…Noah Beery is excellent as Thelma's jealous husband, and even gets a chance to sing bass quite effortlessly. Also, there are so many stock players who had graced the Hal Roach lot through the years, including Franklin Pangborn, Billy Gilbert, Charlie Hall, Kewpie Morgan, and Snub Pollard, all getting their chances to shine. For me, I can never decide which one of the W&W pictures I consider their best…*Hips, Hips, Hooray!* or *Cockeyed Cavaliers* are the two films that you should show to people who are unfamiliar with this great comedy team. I guarantee they will become converts.

The Thin Man (1934)

A Metro-Goldwyn-Mayer Picture. Produced by Hunt Stromberg. Directed by W. S. Van Dyke. From the novel by Dashiell Hammett. Screenplay by Albert Hacket and Frances Goodrich. Edited by Robert J. Kern. Photography by James Wong Howe. Sound by Douglas Shearer. Art Direction by Cedric Gibbons. Costumes by Dolly Tree. Music by Dr. William Axt. 93 min.

Cast: William Powell (Nick Charles), Myrna Loy (Nora Charles), Maureen O'Sullivan (Dorothy Wynant), Lieutenant John Guild (Nat Pendleton), Minna Gombell (Mimi), Porter Hall (Herbert MacCauley), Henry Wadsworth (Tommy), William Henry (Gilbert), Harold Huber (Numheim), Cesar Romero (Chris), Natalie Moorhead (Julia Wolf), Edward Brophy (Morelli), Thomas Jackson (First Reporter), Edward Ellis (Wynant), Ruth Channing (Mrs. Jorgenson), Gertrude Short (Marion), Clay Clement (Quinn), Cyril Thornton (Tanner), Robert Emmett Homans (Bill), Raymond Brown (Dr. Walton), Douglas Fowley (Taxi Driver), Sherry Hall (Taxi Driver), Fred Malatesta (Headwaiter), Rolfe Sedan and Leo White (Waiters), Walter Long (Stutsy), Kenneth Gibson (Apartment Clerk), Tui Lorraine (Stenographer), Bert Roach (Foster), Huey White (Tefler), Creighton Hale (Second Reporter), Ben Taggart (Police Captain), Charles Williams (Fight Manager), Garry Owen (Detective).

MURDER MYSTERIES HAVE ALWAYS been a source for prime entertainment, not only in the literary world, but also in the movies. When author Dashiell Hammett (1894-1961) first penned *The Maltese Falcon*, it wasn't long before Warner Bros. bought the property and cast Ricardo Cortez and Bebe Daniels in a first-rate murder crime drama in 1931. Ten years later, screenwriter-turned-director, John Huston, filmed a superior remake, in what was his first directorial effort. Casting former gangster star, Humphrey Bogart, as "tough-as-nails" Sam Spade and Mary Astor as

The Thin Man (1934) Dorothy Wynant (Maureen O'Sullivan) seeks the help of private detective, Nick Charles (William Powell) to find her missing father. (RF)

the conniving "femme-fatale" Bridgit O'Shaugnessey, Huston hit pay dirt, producing a timeless classic.

In 1932, Hammett came out with another "best-seller" entitled *The Thin Man*, which MGM producer Hunt Stromberg had read and eventually convinced studio head Louis B. Mayer to purchase for the price of $21,000. Both Mayer and Stromberg enjoyed considerably the amiable bickering between the husband and wife team of Nick and Nora Charles. According to playwright Lillian Hellman, mistress to the famed author, much of the book's dialogue was based on actual verbal arguments that she and Hammett would have on occasion. In one chapter of the book, detective Charles is wrestling with a female murder suspect in the presence of his wife, Nora. After the scuffle has subsided, Nora walks over to Nick and asks, "Did you have an erection?" Of course, this sort of dialogue had to be eliminated when the screenplay was being written, to appease the Hollywood censors, who were becoming more intolerant of any sexual innuendo.

While the screenplay was being drawn up, Mayer's first concern was who would play the Charles couple. Producer Stromberg had in mind teaming William Powell and Myrna Loy, who had collaborated earlier that year in the MGM gangster saga hit, *Manhattan Melodrama*, which co-starred Clark Gable. Mayer balked that the two stars were not comedy artists and felt unsure whether they could pull it off or not. Little did any of them realize that the team of Powell and Loy would become one of the most famous in film history. Audiences loved them so much that they just assumed that they were really married, resulting in much fan mail being sent to MGM addressed to "Mr. and Mrs." William Powell.

With filming all set to go, the studio decided on W. S. "One-Take Woody" Van Dyke, whose reputation for filming movies within their budget became legendary throughout Hollywood (he would shoot *The Thin Man* in a mere 16 days). What Van Dyke had experienced throughout the shoot was the way Powell and Loy played off one another, and he usually encouraged them to ad-lib little bits of business, of which there were quite a few. Such as Miss Loy's initial entrance where she comes running into a night club, laden with packages, with their dog Asta leading the way, pulling excitedly on his leash, resulting in her falling. Another gem, which wasn't in the script, had Nick laying on a sofa in their apartment, playing with his new Christmas gift from Nora, an air rifle, carefully shooting ornaments off of their Christmas tree. A sequence, which was shot but not scripted, had Nick and Nora walking their dog, with the camera following them along the street and shooting them from the waist up. All of a sudden, Skippy (Asta's real name), stops at a tree and all the audience can see is that the dog leash has changed direction and Nick and Nora stop until Asta has finished his business. It's a wonderful bit with the two stars just going along with the proceedings while Asta steals the scene without even being photographed!

During production, Skippy's trainer told the cast and crew that no one would be allowed to pet nor play with the dog and that he only would obey his master. Once Miss Loy heard this, she went over to pet Skippy and he bit her, after which everybody stayed clear of the temperamental canine star, who would only perform tricks for various treats and a toy mouse, which his master kept in his pocket.

When *The Thin Man* was released in June of 1934, it became not only one of the biggest money-makers of 1934, but it also copped four major Academy Award nominations for Best Picture, Best Actor, Best Director, and Best Screenplay. Unfortunately, it lost on all counts to *It Happened One Night* (for Best Picture), Clark Gable (Best Actor), Frank Capra (Best Director), and Robert Riskin (Best Screenplay). The film received rapturous applause from critics, with *Variety* calling it "a laughing hit that will mean important coin." So popular was *The Thin Man* that MGM produced another five sequels over the next thirteen years along with seven other Powell/Loy non-*Thin Man* movies. For the record, the sequels were *After the Thin Man* (1936), *Another Thin Man* (1939), *Shadow of the Thin Man* (1941), *The Thin Man Goes Home* (1944), and *Song of the Thin Man* (1947). Out of all of these, only the first three hold up considerably well today.

Incidentally, the title of the picture does not refer to Nick Charles as most people have assumed, but to a murder victim, who is mentioned later in the film.

www.ingramcontent.com/pod-product-compliance
Lightning Source LLC
Chambersburg PA
CBHW060323100426
42812CB00003B/870